AF599345

# David Hockney: INSIGHTS
Reflecting the Tate Collection

# David Hockney Insights

## Reflecting the Tate Collection

Herausgegeben von | Edited by
Ingried Brugger, Bettina M. Busse, Veronika Rudorfer

Diese Ausstellung entstand in Zusammenarbeit mit der Tate.
This exhibition was realized in cooperation with Tate.



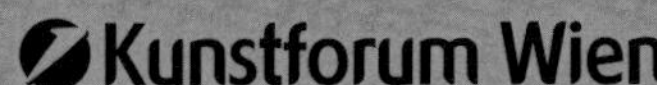

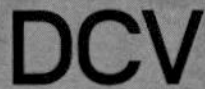

# Inhalt
# Contents

# Vorwort



David Hockney prolongiert mit seinem enormen Werk die Kunstgeschichte über seine eigene Zeitgenossenschaft hinaus. Der Referenzrahmen der Moderne und ihrer Avantgarden – die Errungenschaften autonomer Bildwirklichkeiten jenseits der gesehenen Wirklichkeit – verschleißt sich in dem Maße, wie David Hockney ein neues Bild der Wirklichkeit zeichnet, ja die Wirklichkeit neu erfindet. Dafür korrigiert er unter anderem unsere Sehgewohnheiten ebenso wie die Strategien zum Sehen entlang der Kunstgeschichte.

Oder einfacher: Ein Bild von Picasso kann sich jeder vorstellen. Picasso verzerrt eine Realität, die als solche stets einfach bleibt. Dagegen Bilder von Hockney: Aktives und Passives, skeptisches Zerschneiden der Wirklichkeit, Visionäres neben Konkretem – Erfundenes, Referenzielles und Abbildhaftes wechseln in ihnen ständig. Ein Oszillieren, das aber diskret bleibt, sich ganz langsam in das Bewusstsein des Betrachters zu schleichen vermag. Es existiert in Hockneys konsequent figurativer (gegenständlicher) Malerei ein Gesetz der unbedingten Realität. Einerseits! Auch dann, wenn er den Gegenstand mit höchster formaler Freiheit behandelt, hält er immer an den registrierbaren Elementen fest. Die Menschen, die den Künstler umgeben, seine Familie, seine Freundinnen und Freunde, seine Liebhaber und Partner, manifestieren sich in Bilderzählungen, die umso schärfer werden, je mehr der Pinsel des Künstlers die Quintessenz der Charaktere der Protagonisten pointiert herausarbeitet.

Daneben aber begegnet uns in den Bildern David Hockneys der Esprit, für den auch die geringfügigste Beobachtung den Ausgangspunkt für Veränderungen bildet, der entscheidet, welche Erkenntniskritik und Seinsfrage jeweils in den Vordergrund rückt. Dafür versucht er sich an einem umfangreichen Repertoire an stilistischen und inhaltlichen Definitionen. Hockney hat nicht nur unterschiedlichste Möglichkeiten, ein Bild zu generieren, bedient – von der klassischen, detailverspielten Zeichnung über figurative und reine Malerei, von der „historischen" Druckgrafik bis zu Telefax- und iPad-Bildern. Er spielt auch mit der Semantik seiner künstlerischen Sprache, spielt verschiedene Realitätsebenen gegeneinander aus: Ein Farbstrich da ist nichts weiter als ein Farbstrich, um gleichermaßen oder in einem anderen Bildzusammenhang etwas zu illusionieren, das er de facto nicht ist.

Hockney in seiner Substanz ist elegant – in ästhetischer Hinsicht ebenso wie im inhaltlichen Ausdruck (und auch im vermittelten Leben). Dazu gehört auch sein zwanglos scheinender Umgang mit Homosexualität in einem – wie er sagt – bohèmehaften Leben. Jene Bilder, die dieses Leben widerspiegeln, seine Szenen am Pool oder in der Dusche, seine Verbildlichung dessen, was er als Mensch begehrte, verraten nichts über die finsteren, von gesellschaftlichen Zwängen determinierten Abgründe gelebten Schwulseins.

In dieser Offenheit und Selbstverständlichkeit hat David Hockney schon in den 1960er- und 1970er-Jahren vieles von dem vorweggenommen, was zumindest in den aufgeklärten Gesellschaften unserer Zeit „Normalität" ist. Als Künstler hat er immer schon an einer Kunstgeschichte der Zukunft geschrieben und profiliert sich als einer ihrer Hauptdarsteller.

Der programmatische Titel *David Hockney: INSIGHTS. Reflecting the Tate Collection* verweist auf die schlaglichtartigen Einblicke in das Werk seit den 1950er-Jahren, die diese Ausstellung gibt. Das starke Fundament und immer wieder auch die inhaltliche Klammer bietet die Sammlung der Tate, die Meisterwerke Hockneys ihr Eigen nennt. Die Schau spiegelt und reflektiert die Tate Collection anhand zahlreicher Leihgaben aus internationalen Museen und privaten Sammlungen. „Hockney" im Kunstforum ist die erste umfassende Schau des genialen Künstlers in Österreich.

Mein herzlicher Dank gilt vor allem David Hockney für seine Hilfe und für sein vielfältiges, sich seit sieben Dekaden ständig erneuerndes Werk.

Mein besonderer Dank geht an Edith Devaney und ihre Mitarbeiterinnen Shannan Kelly und Julie Green von David Hockney Inc. für ihre umfangreiche Unterstützung des Projekts. Außerdem danke ich Jonathan Wilkinson.

Ich bedanke mich bei der Tate für die gelungene Kooperation, insbesondere bei Neil McConnon und Lauren Buckley sowie bei Helen Little, die das Projekt als freie Kuratorin begleitet hat.

Mein herzlicher Dank geht an Bettina M. Busse und Veronika Rudorfer vom Bank Austria Kunstforum Wien für ihre kuratorische Arbeit.

Danke allen Leihgebern für ihre großartige Unterstützung. Zahlreiche Kolleginnen und Kollegen, Freundinnen und Freunde haben uns geholfen, diese anspruchsvolle Schau zu realisieren. Mein spezieller Dank geht dabei an Ulrich Luckhardt.

Mein Dank geht weiter an das gesamte Team des Bank Austria Kunstforum Wien, an die Katalogautorinnen und -autoren, an den Verlag DCV in Berlin sowie an Josef Perndl und Aleksandra Gustin für die innovative Buchgestaltung. Ich danke auch Christine Schwaiger und Harald Trapp für die Ausstellungsarchitektur.

Mein großer Dank geht wie immer an die Partner des Bank Austria Kunstforum Wien – Signa, ERGO und Amundi – sowie an die Medienpartner Kurier, Falter und Ö1. Ich danke der UniCredit Bank Austria für ihr großes Engagement.

Ingried Brugger
Direktorin Bank Austria Kunstforum Wien

# Foreword



David Hockney's vast oeuvre extends art history beyond his own contemporariness. The referential framework of modernism and its avant-garde movements – the achievements of autonomous pictorial realities beyond seen reality – is eroded as David Hockney draws a new picture of reality, indeed reinvents reality itself. He corrects our viewing habits as well as the strategies of seeing developed throughout art history.

Or to put it more simply: everyone can picture a painting by Picasso. Picasso distorts reality, while reality per se remains just as it is. Hockney's works, by contrast, are an active and passive, sceptical dissection of reality, at once visionary and concrete – in which the invented, the referential and the naturalistic are forever in flux. This oscillation, however, remains discreet, creeping only slowly into the viewer's consciousness. In Hockney's consistently figurative (representational) painting, a law of unconditional reality exists. On the one hand! Even when handling his subject matter with the highest degree of formal freedom, he always keeps a hold of the graspable elements. The people in the artist's life, his family, his friends, his lovers and partners, manifest themselves in pictorial narratives that are all the sharper for having the essence of their characters teased out so pointedly with the artist's brush.

Yet on the other hand, in David Hockey's images we also encounter a spirit that makes even the most insignificant observation the starting point for change; that selects in each instance an epistemological critique or ontological question to come to the fore. To this end he experiments with a wide repertoire of styles and subject matter. Not only has Hockney made use of a broad selection of means to create an image – from classical drawing with playful details to figurative and pure painting, and from "historical" print techniques to fax and iPad drawings; but he also plays with the semantics of his own artistic language, playing various levels of reality against one another: a paint stroke, which in one pictorial context is nothing more than a paint stroke, may just as easily be deployed to create an illusion of something that it de facto is not.

Everything about Hockney is elegant – from his aesthetics to his subject matter (and of course his public persona). This includes his seemingly casual approach to homosexuality, in a life he himself describes as bohemian. The images that reflect this life are the scenes by the pool or in the shower, depictions of human desires that never hint at the sinister constraints imposed by society on homosexual life.

In this openness and matter-of-factness David Hockney was already anticipating as early as the 1960s and 1970s much of what is now considered "normal", at least in today's more enlightened societies. As an artist he was always writing his own art history (of the future), with himself as the main protagonist.

As its title suggests, *David Hockney: INSIGHTS. Reflecting the Tate Collection* provides insights into his oeuvre, dating back to the 1950s. The strong basis and focus of the exhibition are Hockney's works from the Tate Collection. The exhibition brings together numerous additional loans from international museums and private collections to shed light and reflect on the masterpieces in the Tate Collection. It is the first comprehensive show of this ingenious artist in Austria.

First and foremost, I must express my heartfelt gratitude to David Hockney for his help and support, and for his multifaceted oeuvre, which has been in a constant state of renewal for seven decades.

I am extremely grateful to Edith Devaney and her colleagues Shannan Kelly and Julie Green of David Hockney Inc. for their generous support of the project. I would also like to thank Jonathan Wilkinson.

Thanks also to the Tate for a very successful collaboration, and in particular to Neil McConnon and Lauren Buckley as well as Helen Little, who accompanied the project as a freelance curator.

My heartfelt thanks also extend to Bettina M. Busse and Veronika Rudorfer from Bank Austria Kunstforum Wien for their curatorial work.

I am very grateful for the support of all those who have loaned works. This ambitious exhibition would have been impossible without the help of so many friends and colleagues. Here I would particularly like to thank Ulrich Luckhardt.

My thanks also extend to the entire team of Bank Austria Kunstforum Wien, the catalogue's authors, DCV publishers in Berlin, as well as Josef Perndl and Aleksandra Gustin for the innovative book design. Thanks, too, to Christine Schwaiger and Harald Trapp for the exhibition architecture.

As ever, my gratitude goes out to all the partners of the Bank Austria Kunstforum Wien – Signa, ERGO and Amundi – as well as our media partners Kurier, Falter and Ö1. And a huge thank you to UniCredit Bank Austria for its unwavering commitment.

Ingried Brugger
Director Bank Austria Kunstforum Wien

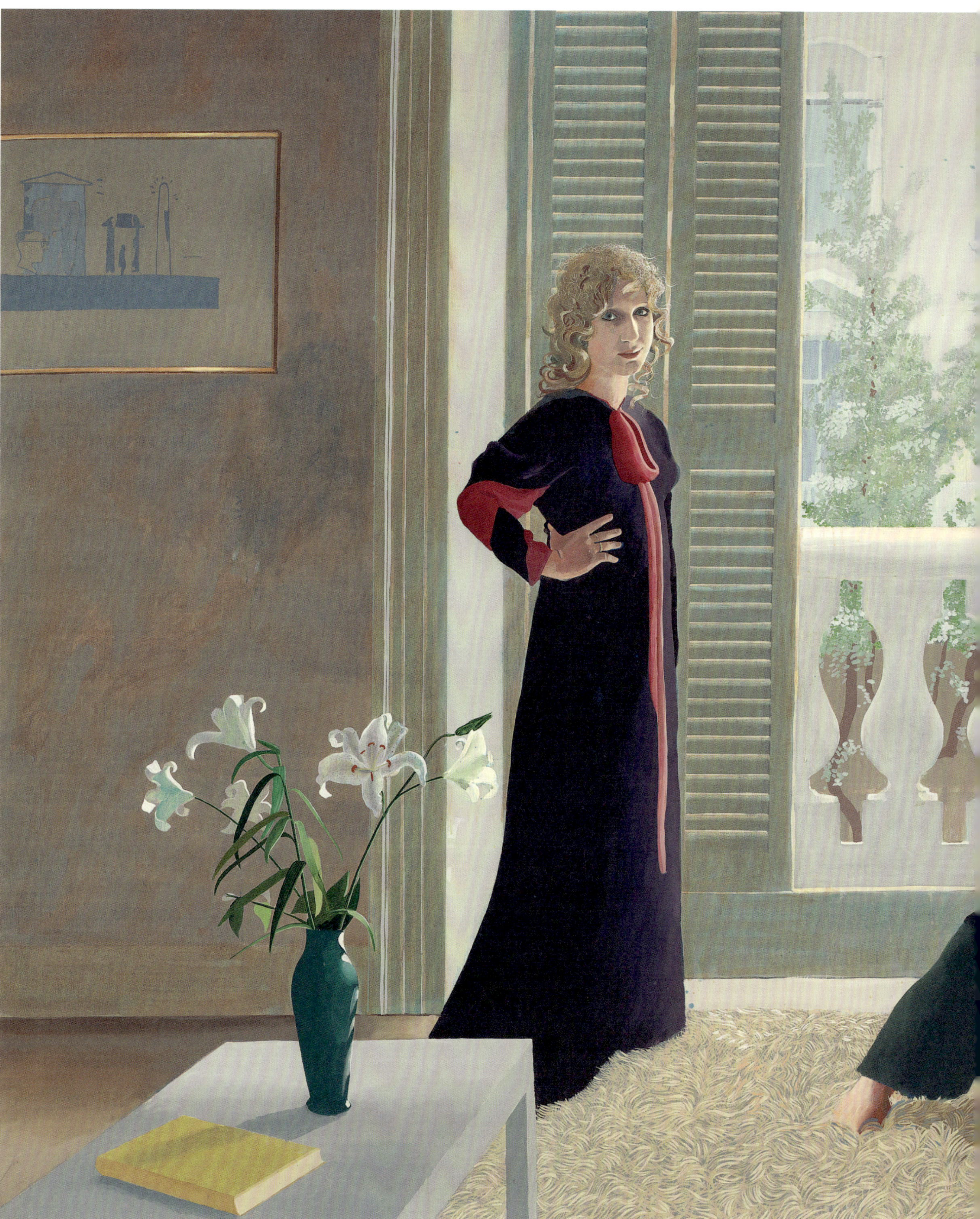

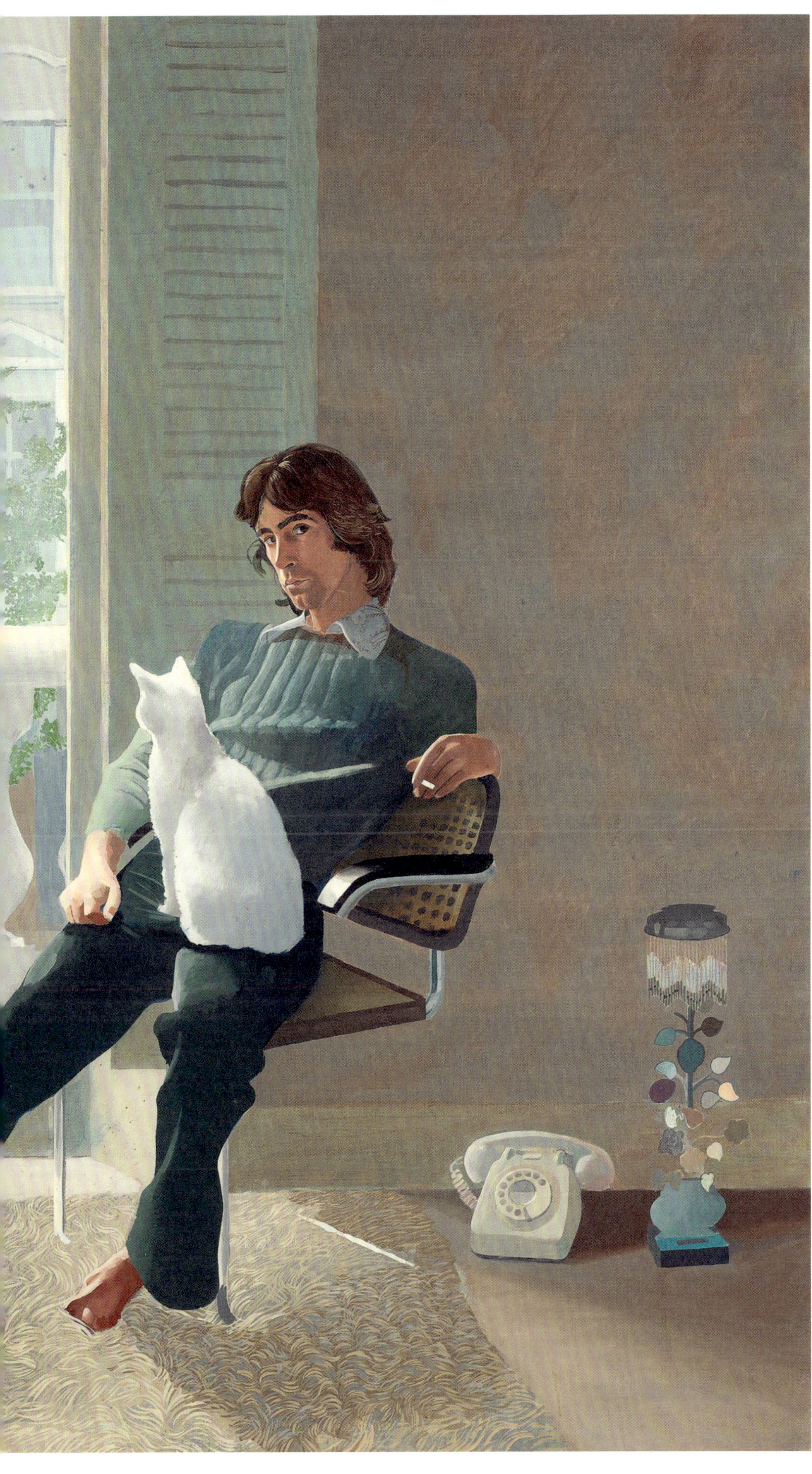

**Mr and Mrs Clark and Percy,** 1970–1971
Acryl auf Leinwand | Acrylic on canvas,
213,4 x 304,8 cm
Tate: Presented by the Friends
of the Tate Gallery 1971
Inv. Nº T01269

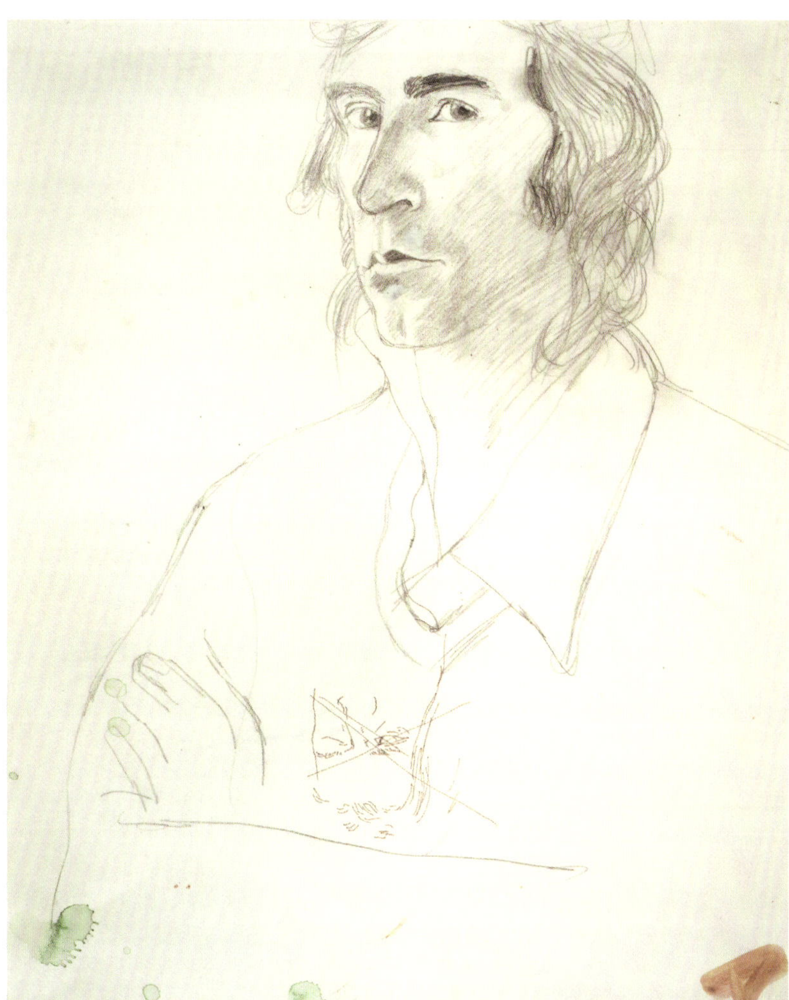

**Study for Mr and Mrs Clark and Percy,** 1970
Bleistift auf Papier | Pencil on paper,
42,9 × 35,6 cm
Tate: Presented by the artist 1972
Inv. N° T01515

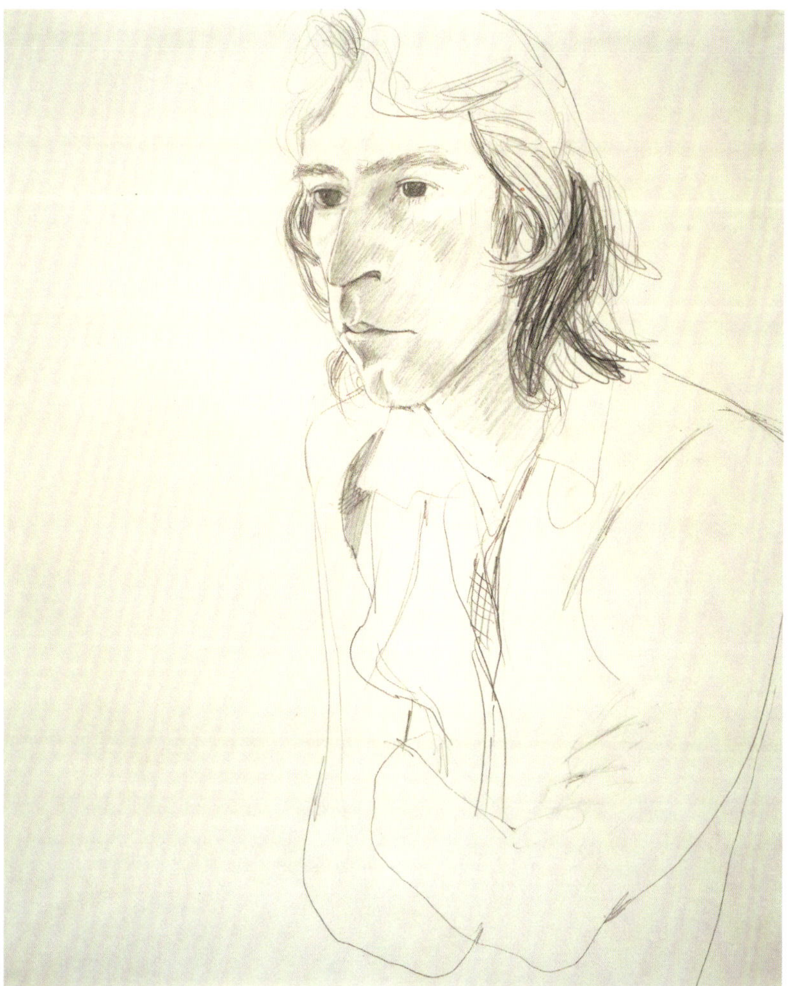

**Study for Mr and Mrs Clark and Percy,** 1970
Bleistift auf Papier | Pencil on paper,
43,2 × 35,2 cm
Tate: Presented by the artist 1972
Inv. N° T01516

13

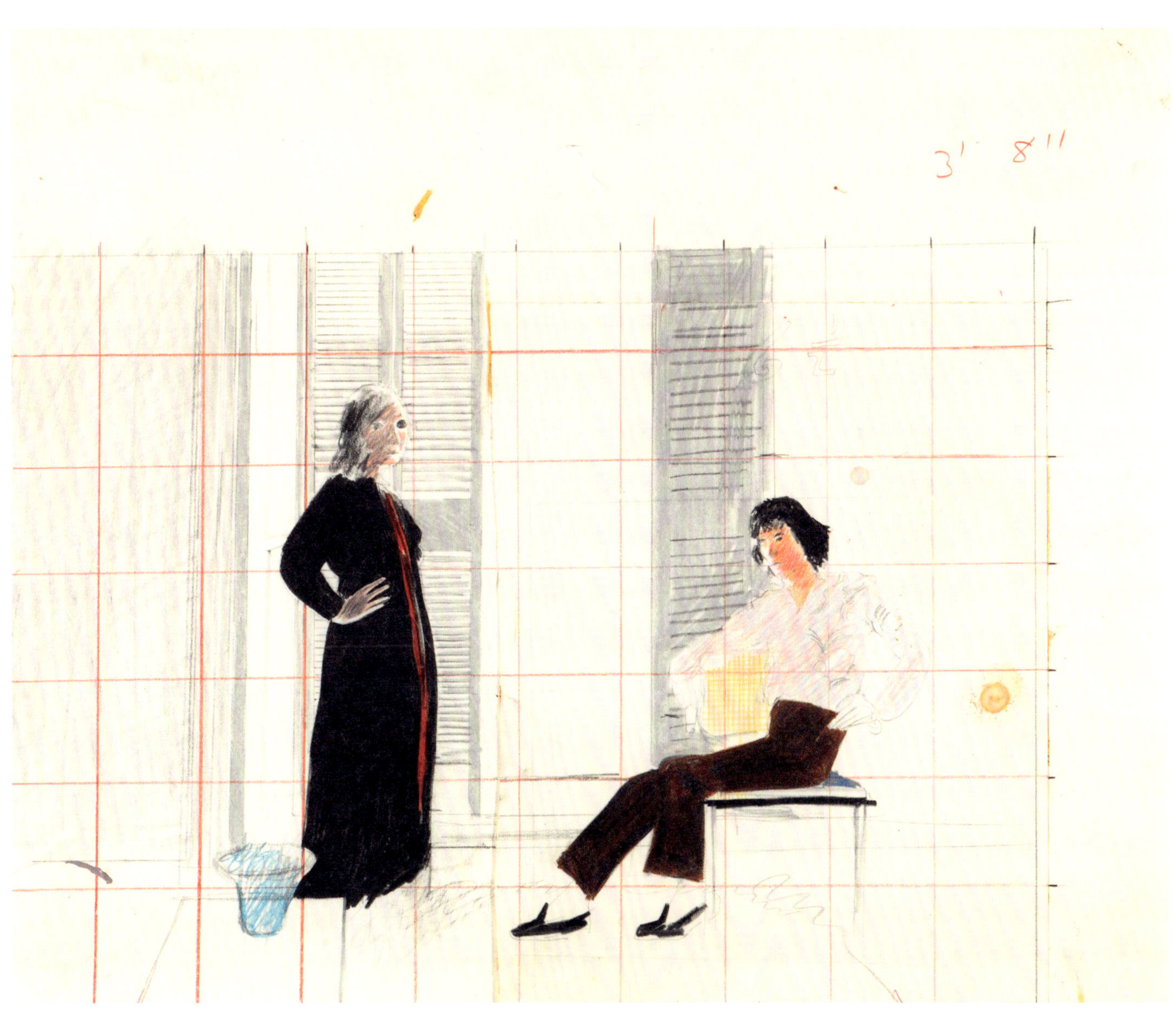


**Study for Mr and Mrs Clark and Percy,** 1970
Bleistift und Buntstift auf Papier |
Pencil and coloured pencil on paper,
35,5 × 43 cm
Tate: Presented by the artist 1972
Inv. N° T01517

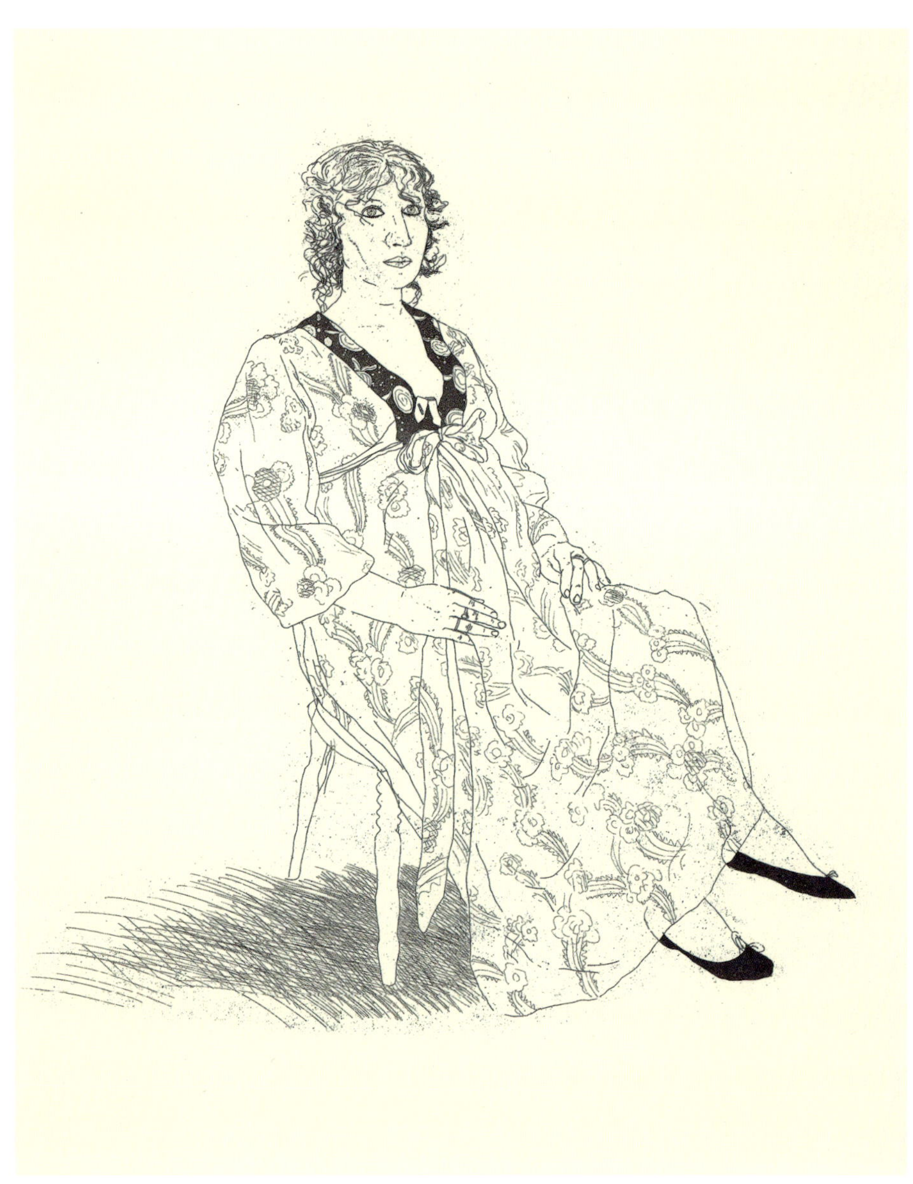

**Celia,** 1969
Radierung und Aquatinta auf Papier (Auflage von 75) | Etching and aquatint on paper (Edition of 75), 68,5 × 54,5 cm
Tate: Presented by Klaus Anschel in memory of his wife Gerty 1997
Inv. N° P11497

15

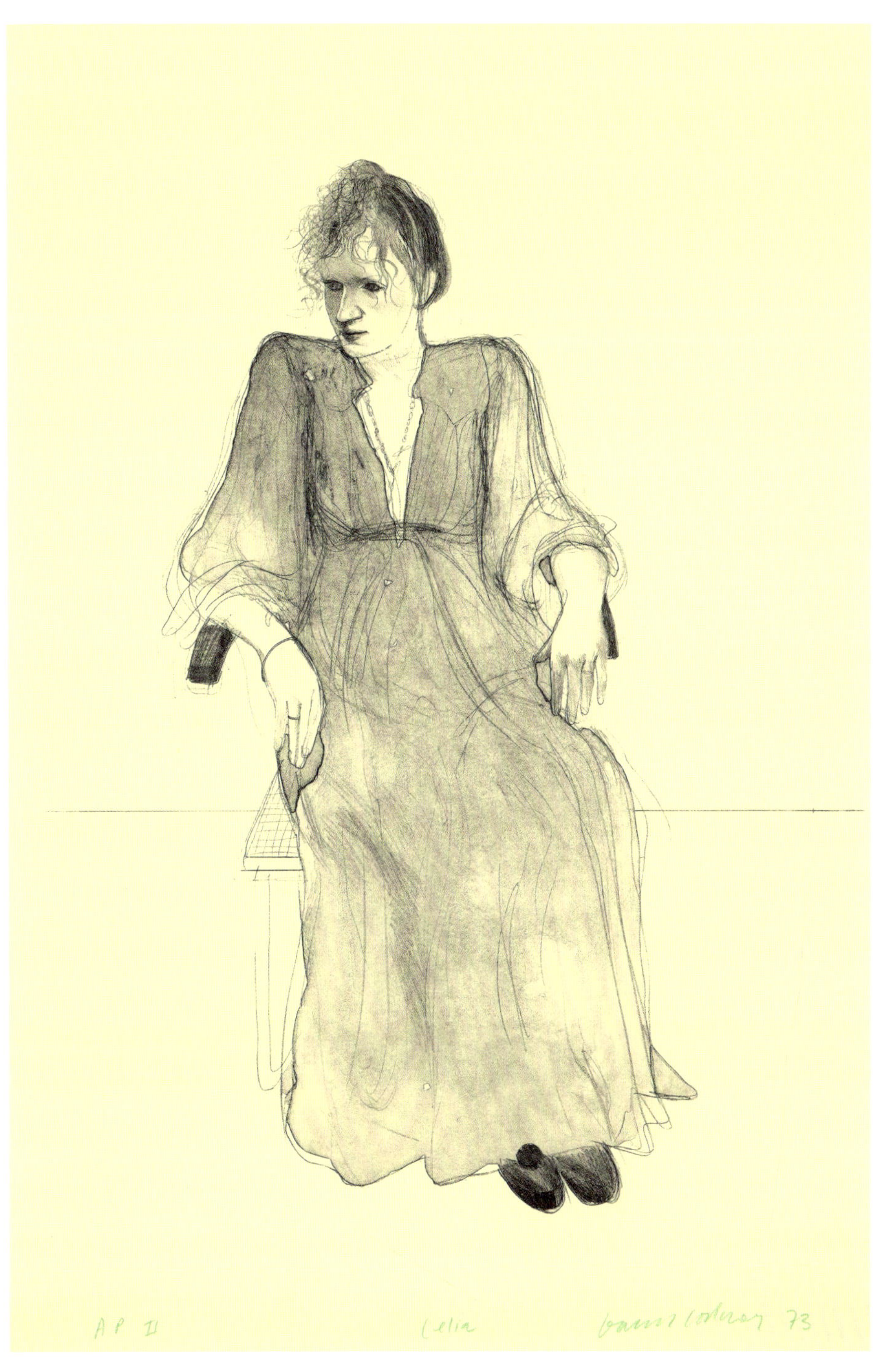


**Celia,** 1973
Lithografie auf Papier (Auflage von 52) |
Lithograph on paper (Edition of 52),
108,5 × 72,5 cm
Tate: Presented by Klaus Anschel
in memory of his wife Gerty 1997
Inv. N° P11498

17

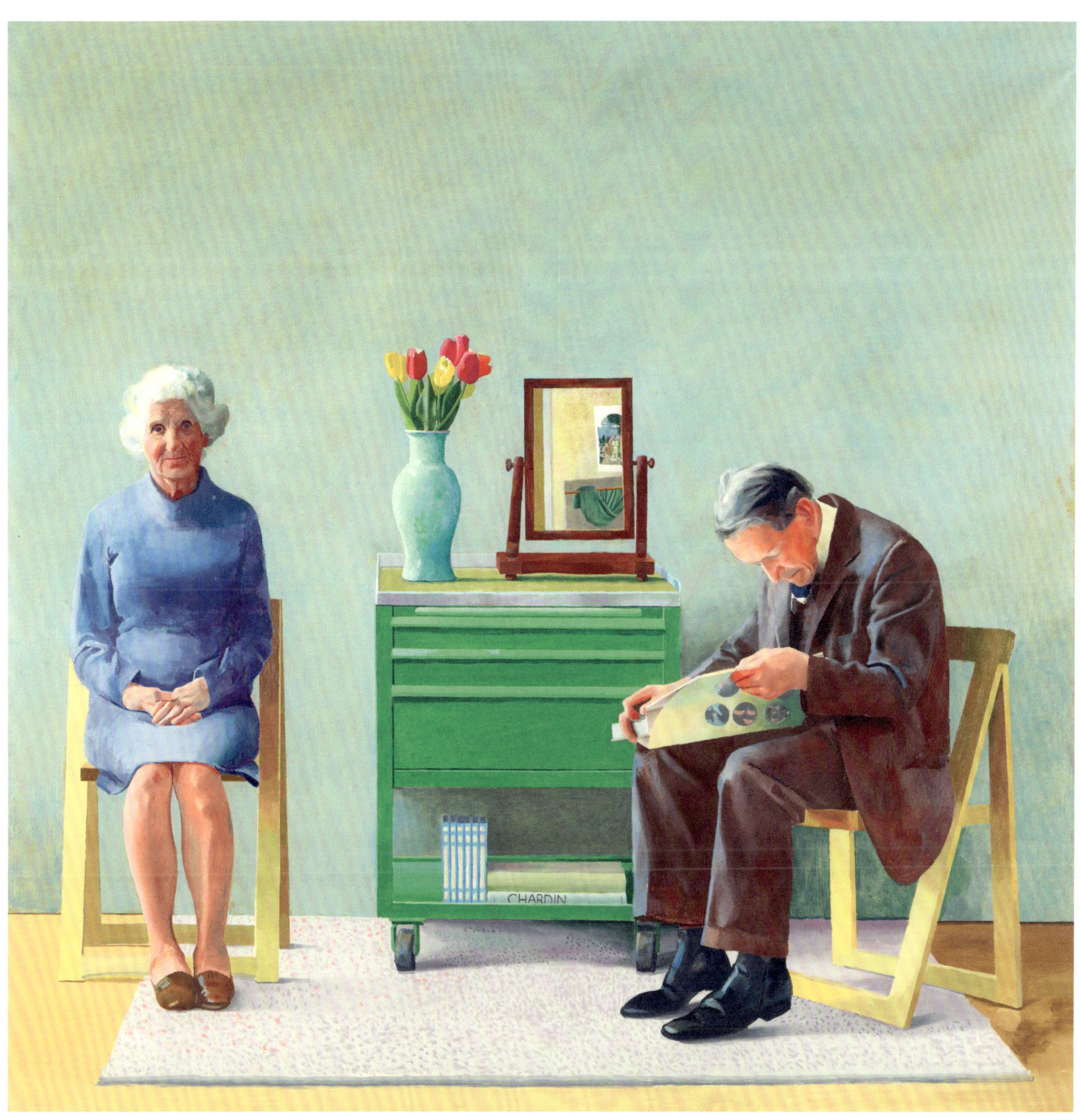


**My Parents,** 1977
Öl auf Leinwand | Oil on canvas,
182,9 × 182,9 cm
Tate: Purchased 1981
Inv. N° T03255

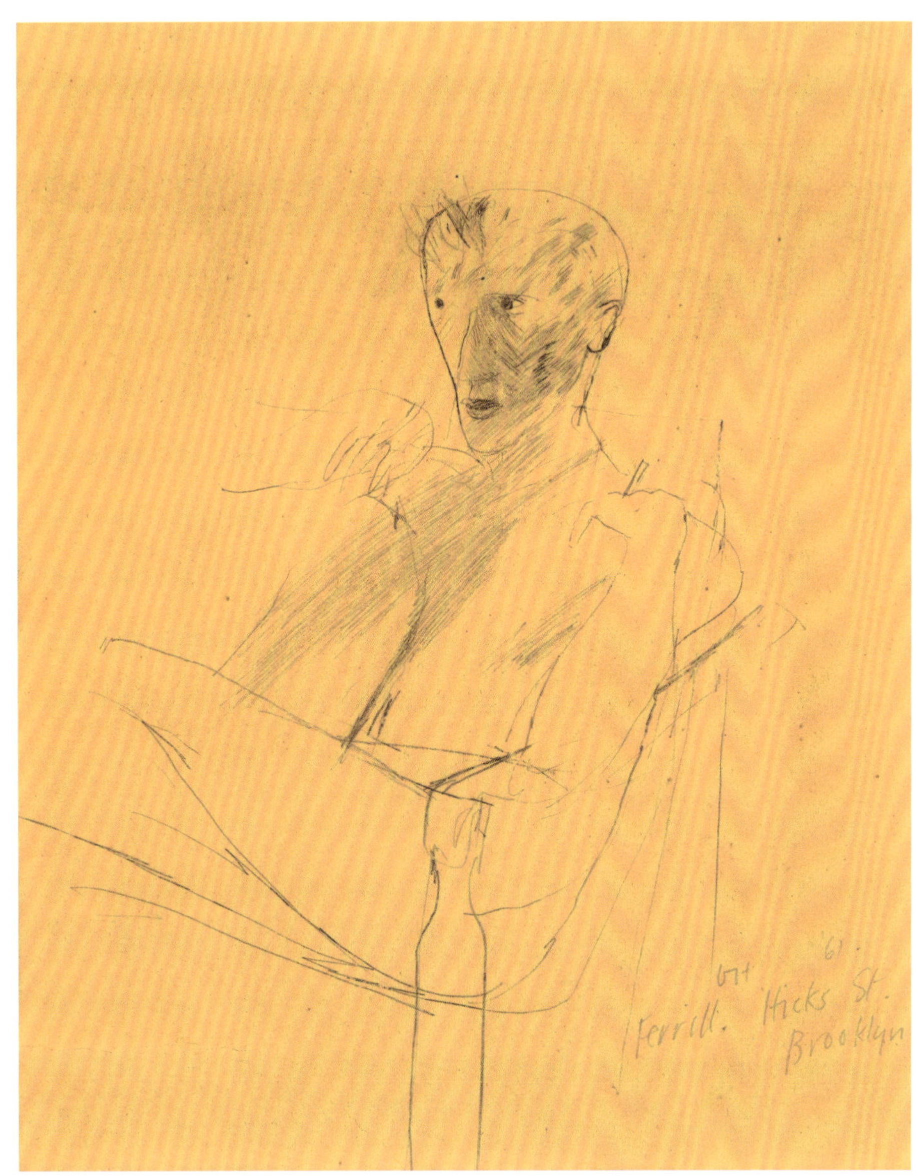


**Ferrill Amacker,** 1961
Bleistift auf Papier | Pencil on paper,
61 × 25,6 cm
Privatsammlung | Private Collection

19

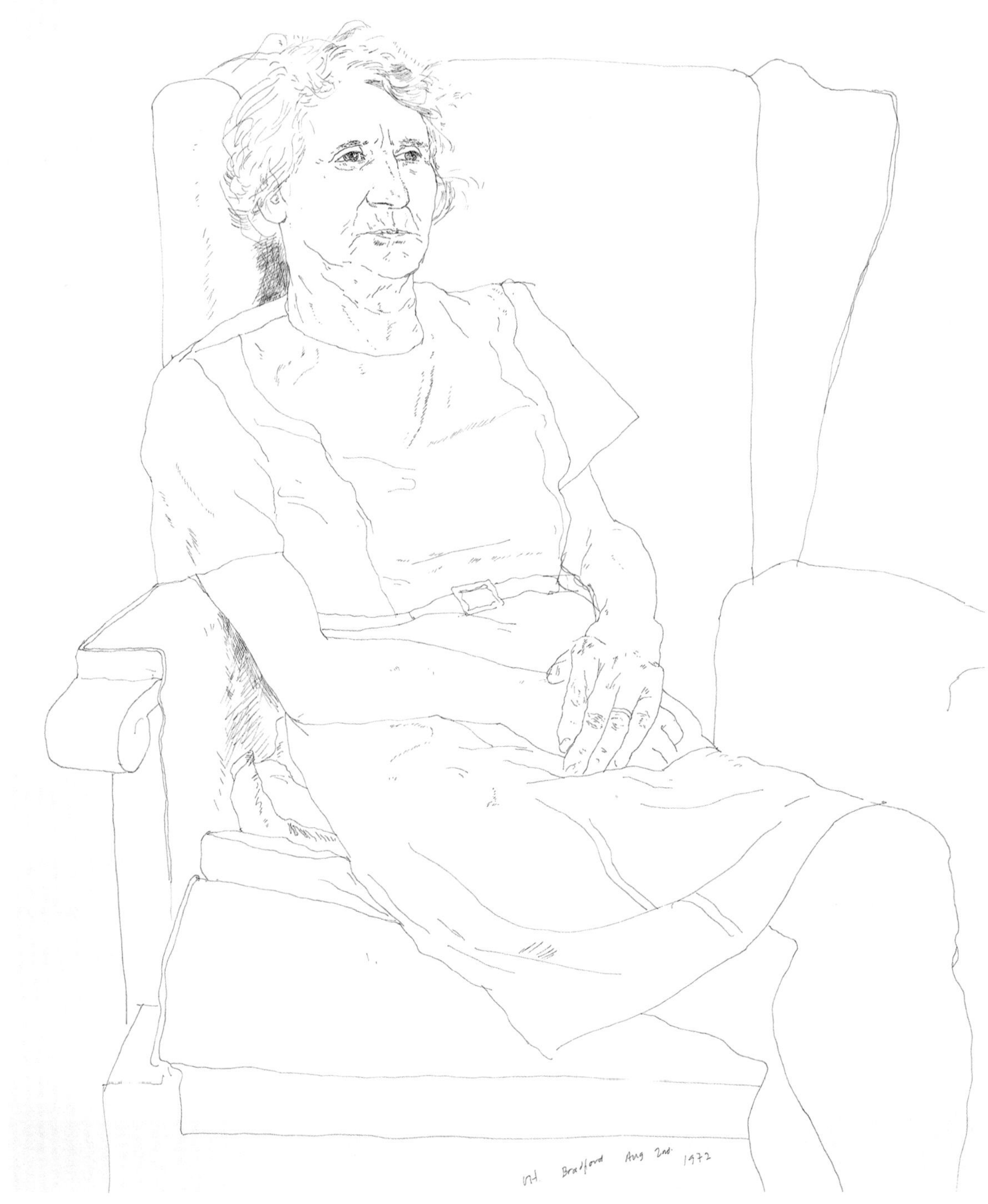


**Portrait of the Artist's Mother, Mrs Laura Hockney, Bradford,** 1972
Tinte auf Papier | Ink on paper,
43,2 × 35,3 cm
Tate: Presented by Klaus Anschel
in memory of his wife Gerty 2004
Inv. N° T11897

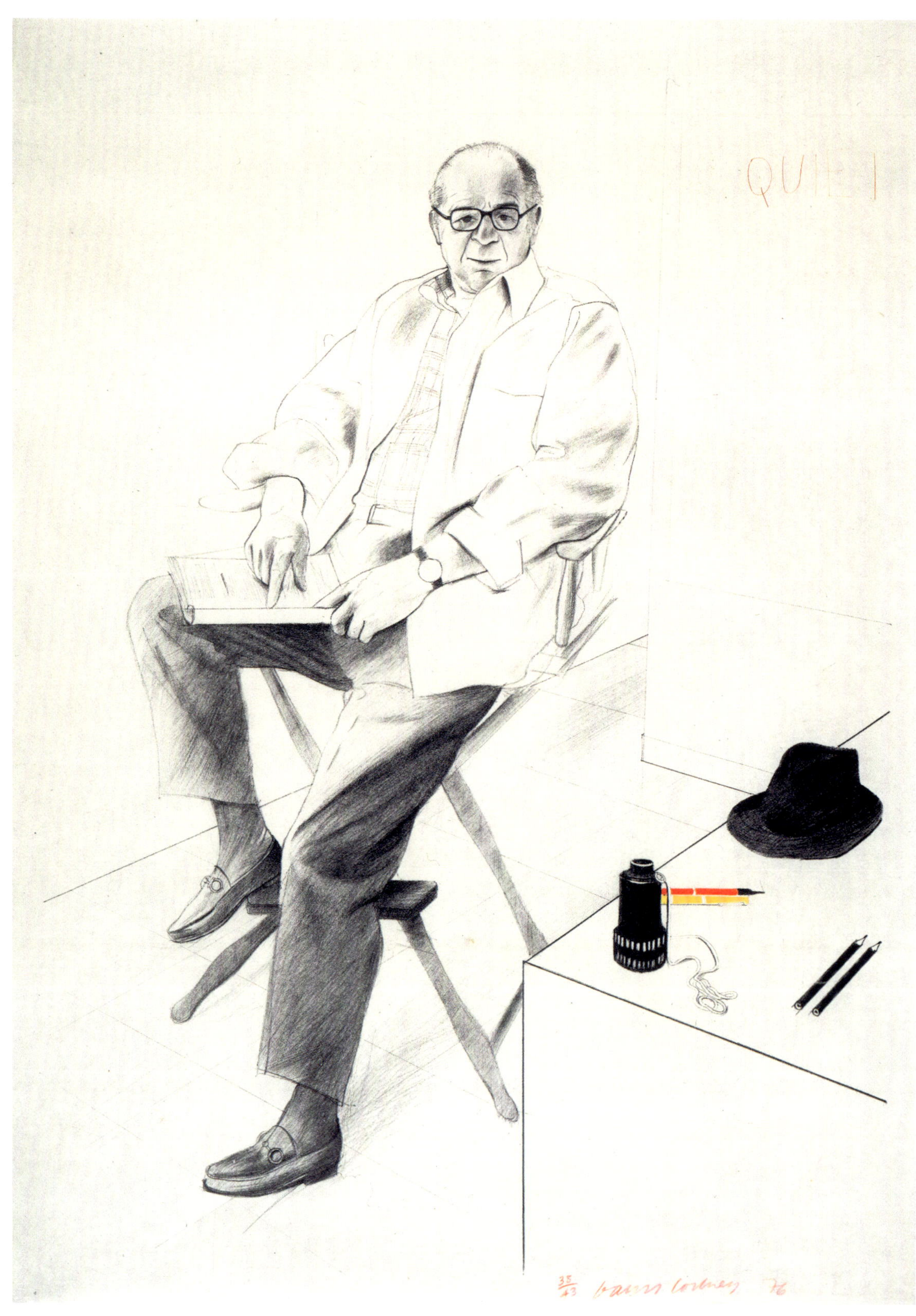

**Billy Wilder,** 1976
Lithografie auf Papier (Auflage von 43) |
Lithograph on paper (Edition of 43),
96,5 × 71,1 cm
Tate: Purchased 1978
Inv. Nº P07239

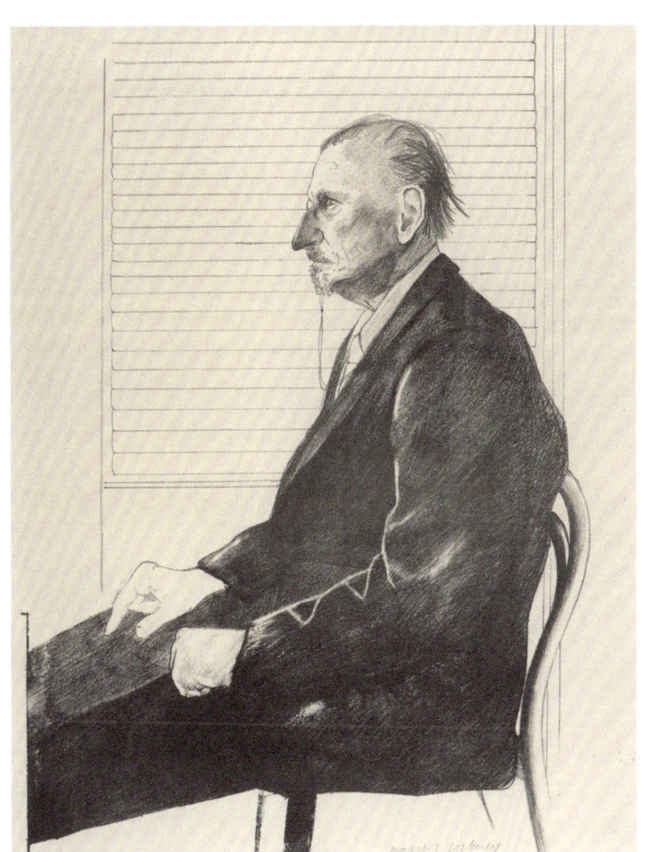

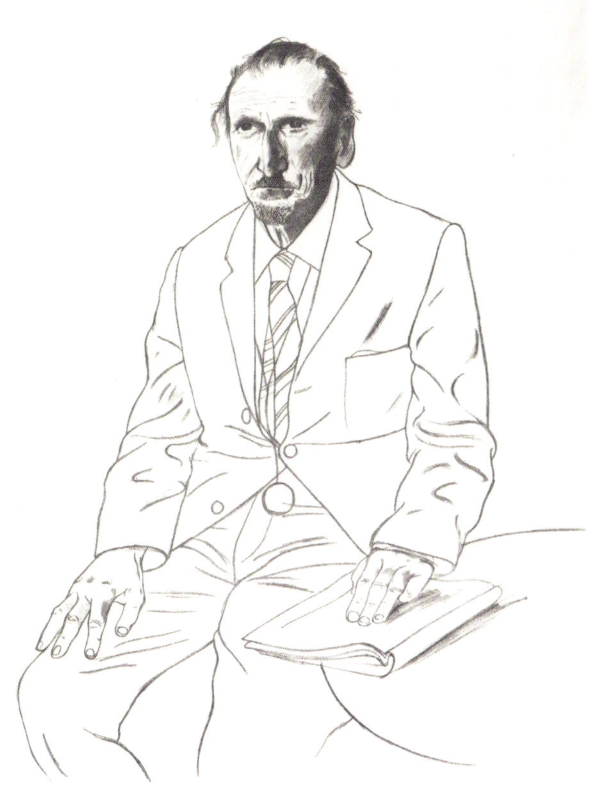

**The Print Collector (Portrait of Felix Man),** 1969
Lithografie auf Papier |
Lithograph on paper,
67 × 53 cm
Tate: Presented by Curwen Studio through the Institute of Contemporary Prints 1975
Inv. N° P06289

**The Connoisseur,** 1969
Lithografie auf Papier (Auflage von 30) |
Lithograph on paper (Edition of 30),
80,6 × 57,5 cm
Tate: Presented by Curwen Studio through the Institute of Contemporary Prints 1975
Inv. N° P06288

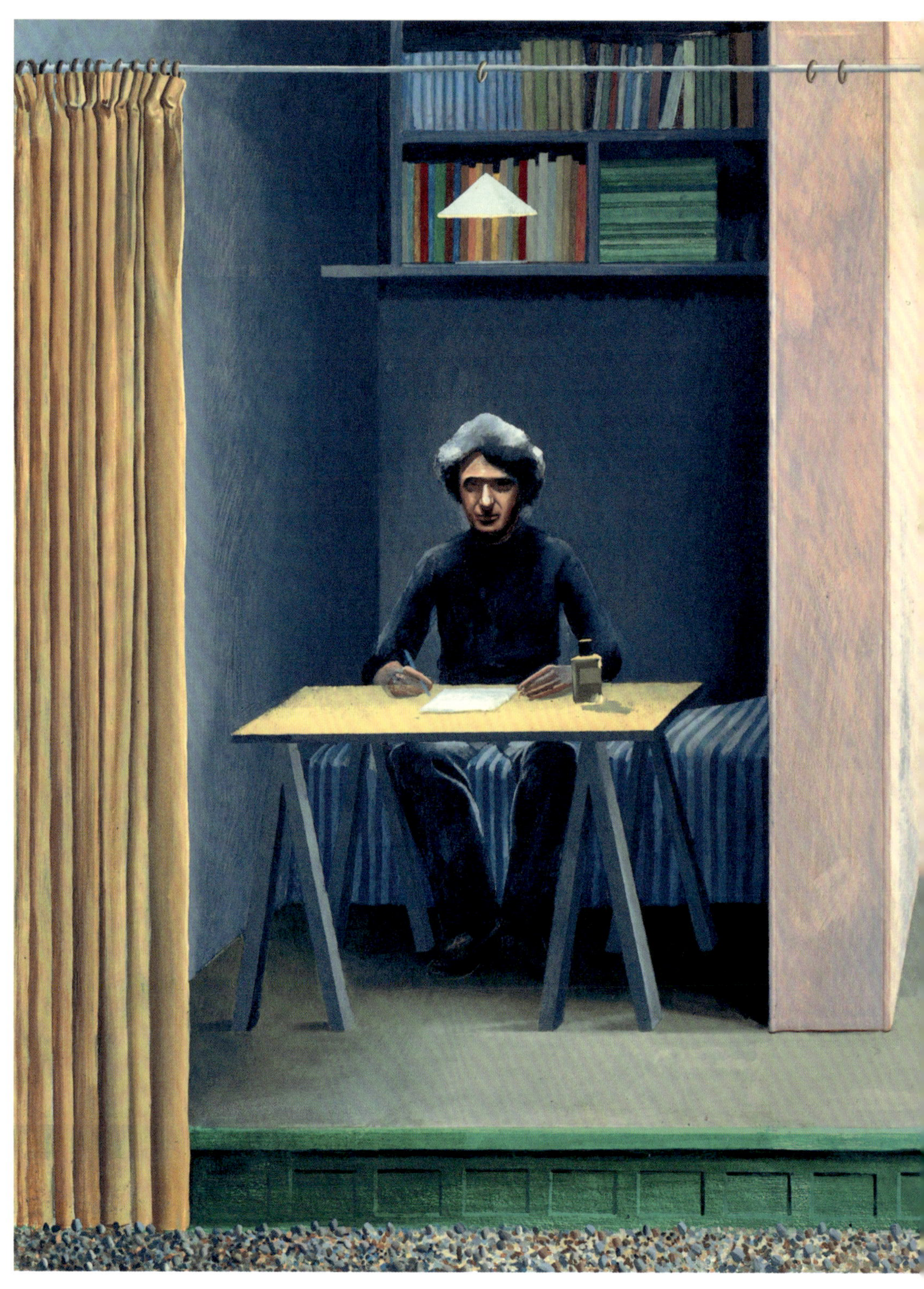

**Shirley Goldfarb and**
**Gregory Masurovsky,** 1974
Öl auf Leinwand | Oil on canvas,
114,6 × 213,4 cm
The Doris and Donald Fisher Collection
at the San Francisco Museum of Modern Art
Inv. N° FC. 566

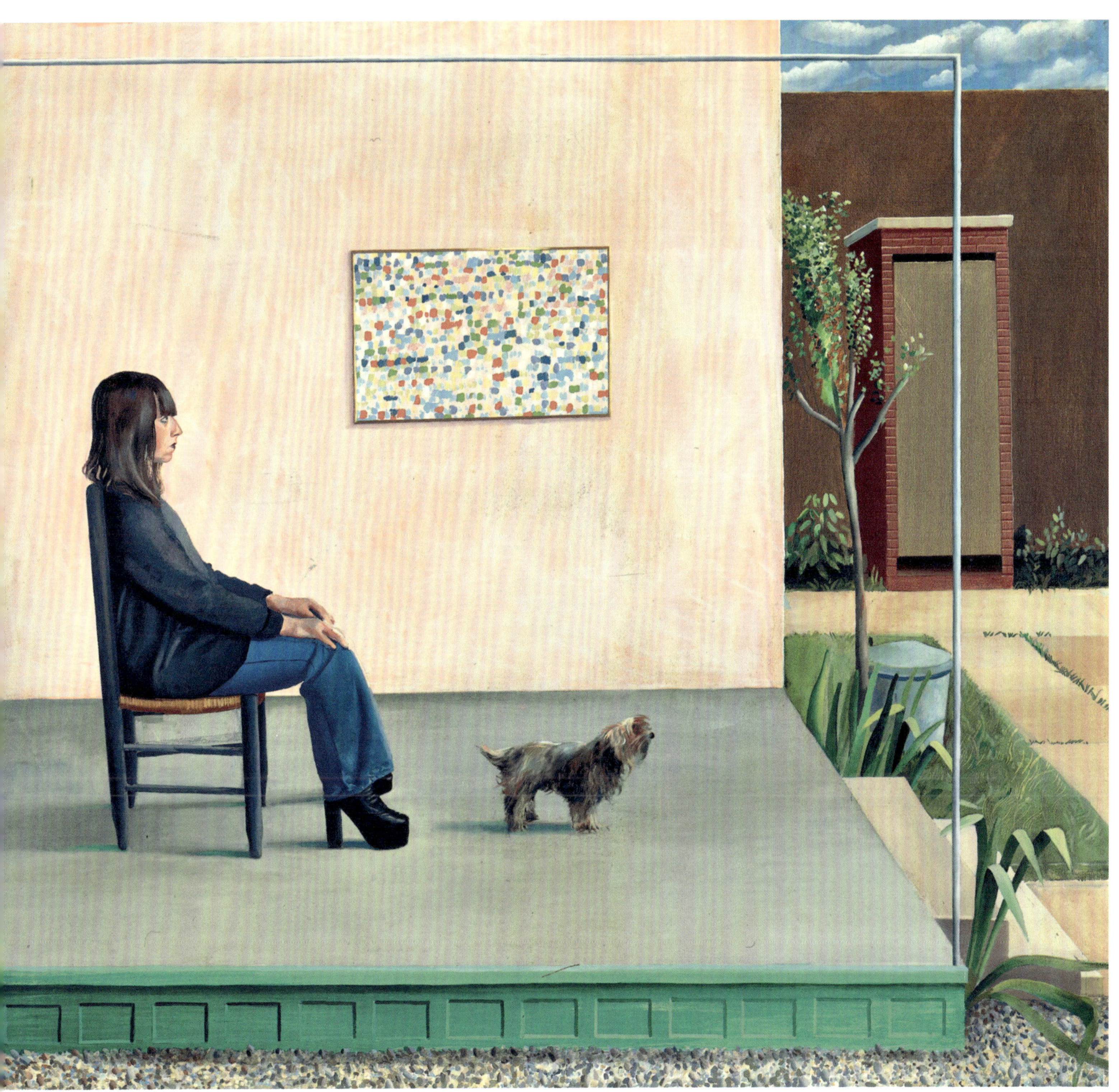

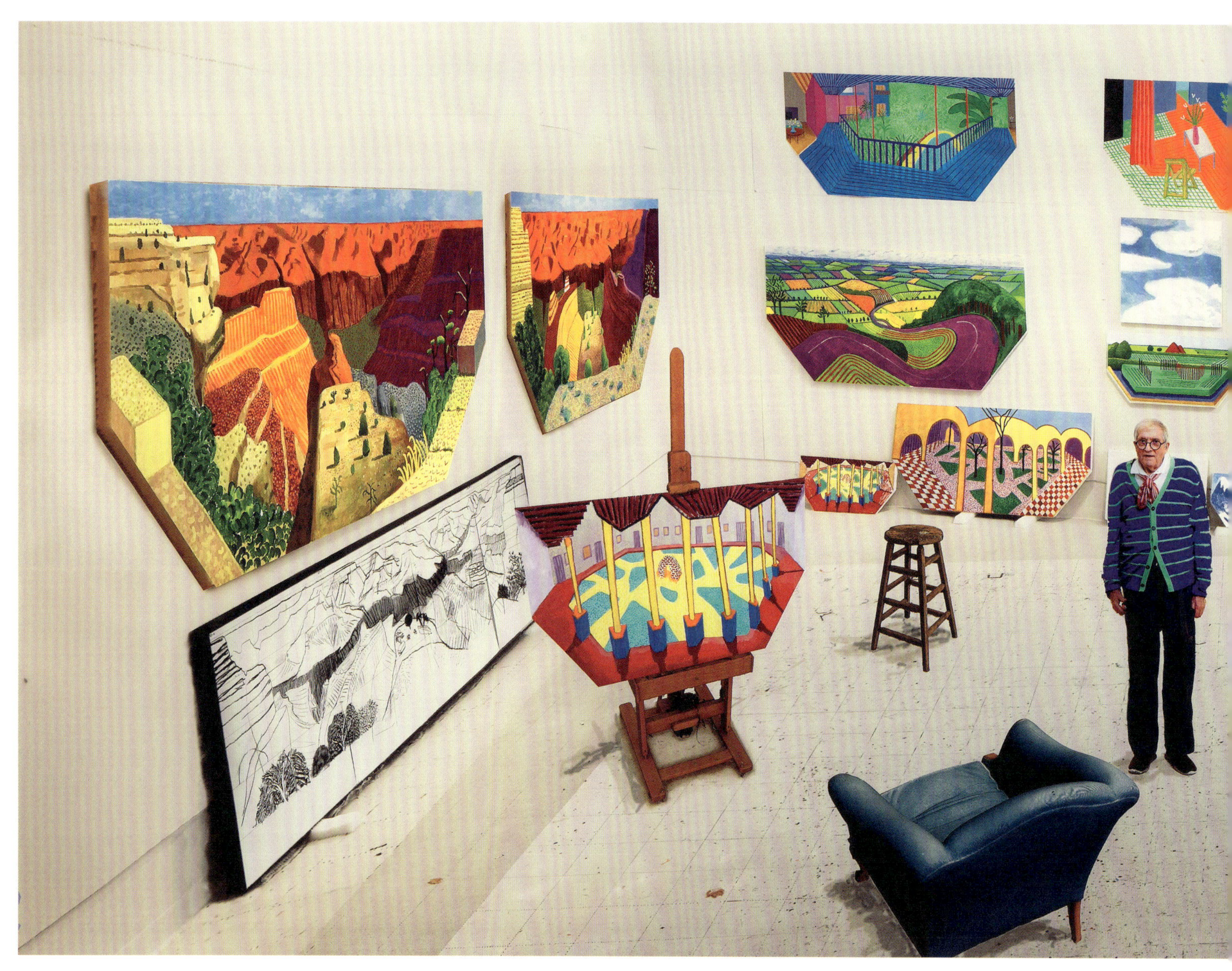

**In the Studio, December 2017,** 2017
Tintenstrahldrucke auf Papier,
montiert auf Aluminium (Auflage 7/12,
Assistenz: Jonathan Wilkinson) |
Inkjet prints on paper, mounted on aluminium
(Edition 7/12, assisted by Jonathan Wilkinson),
278,1 × 760,1 cm
Tate: Presented by the artist 2018
Inv. Nº T15144

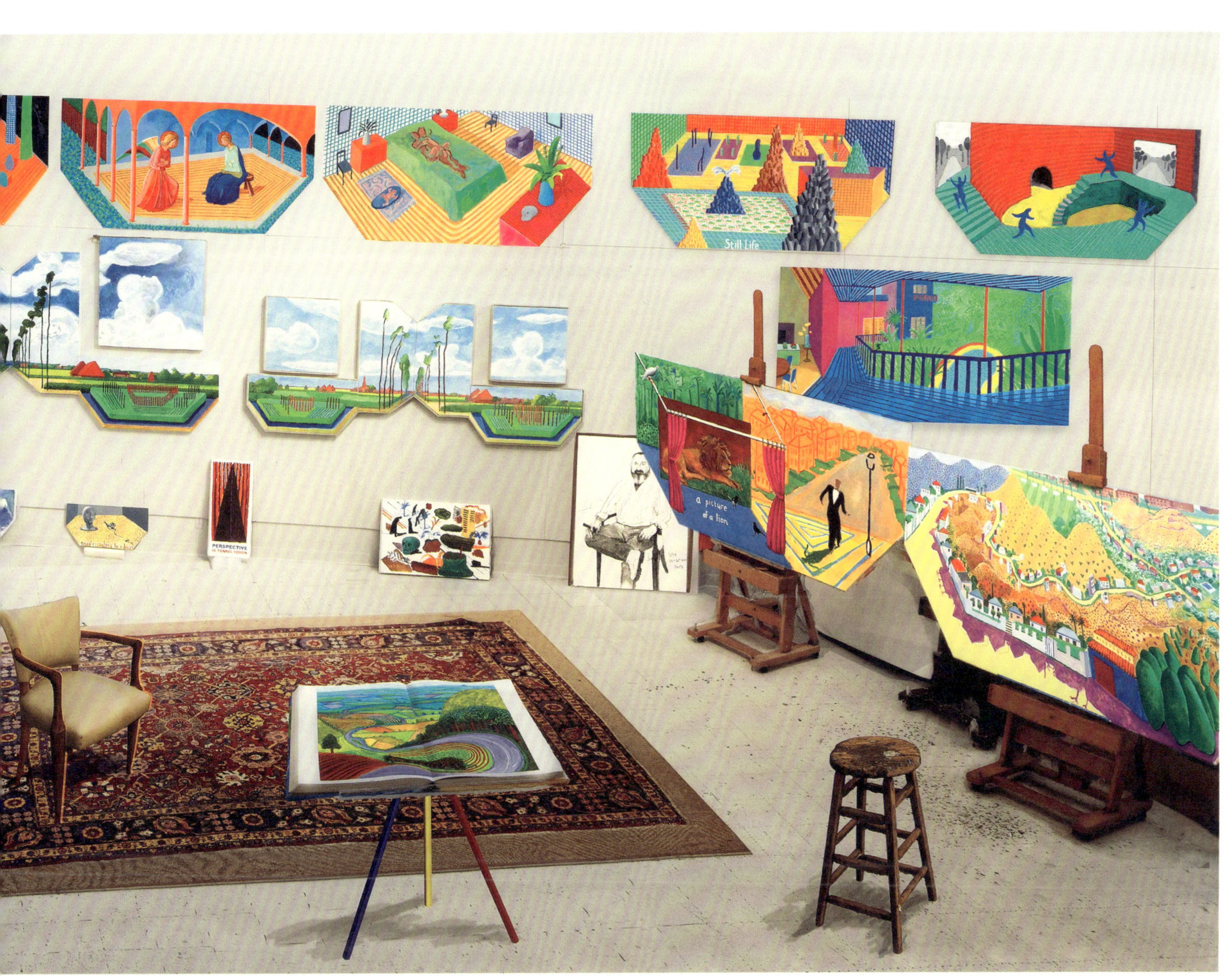
Still Life
PERSPECTIVE
a picture of a lion

27

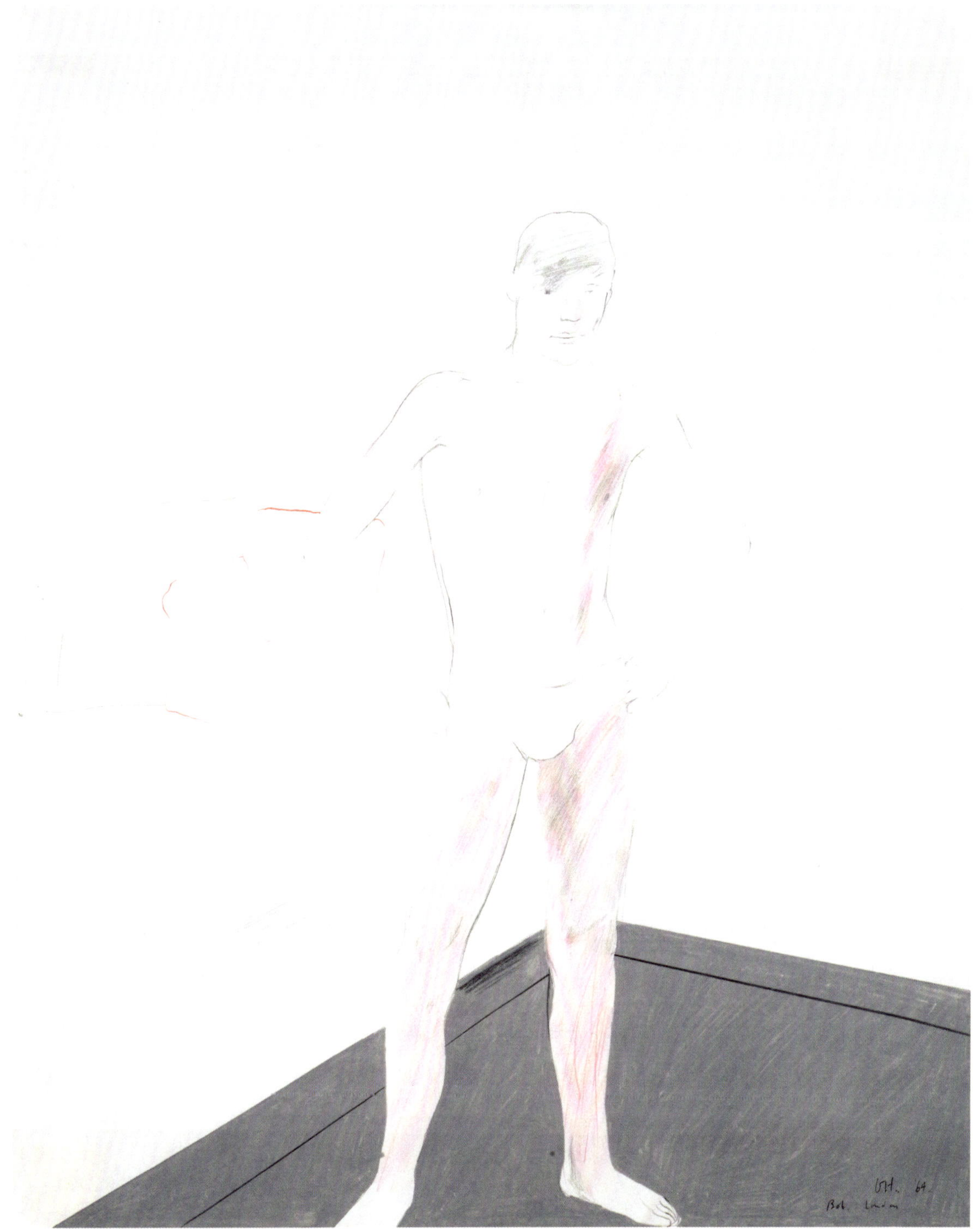

**Bob, London,** 1964
Buntstift auf Papier |
Coloured pencil on paper,
50 × 40,2 cm
Tate: Presented by Klaus Anschel
in memory of his wife Gerty 1997
Inv. N° T07295

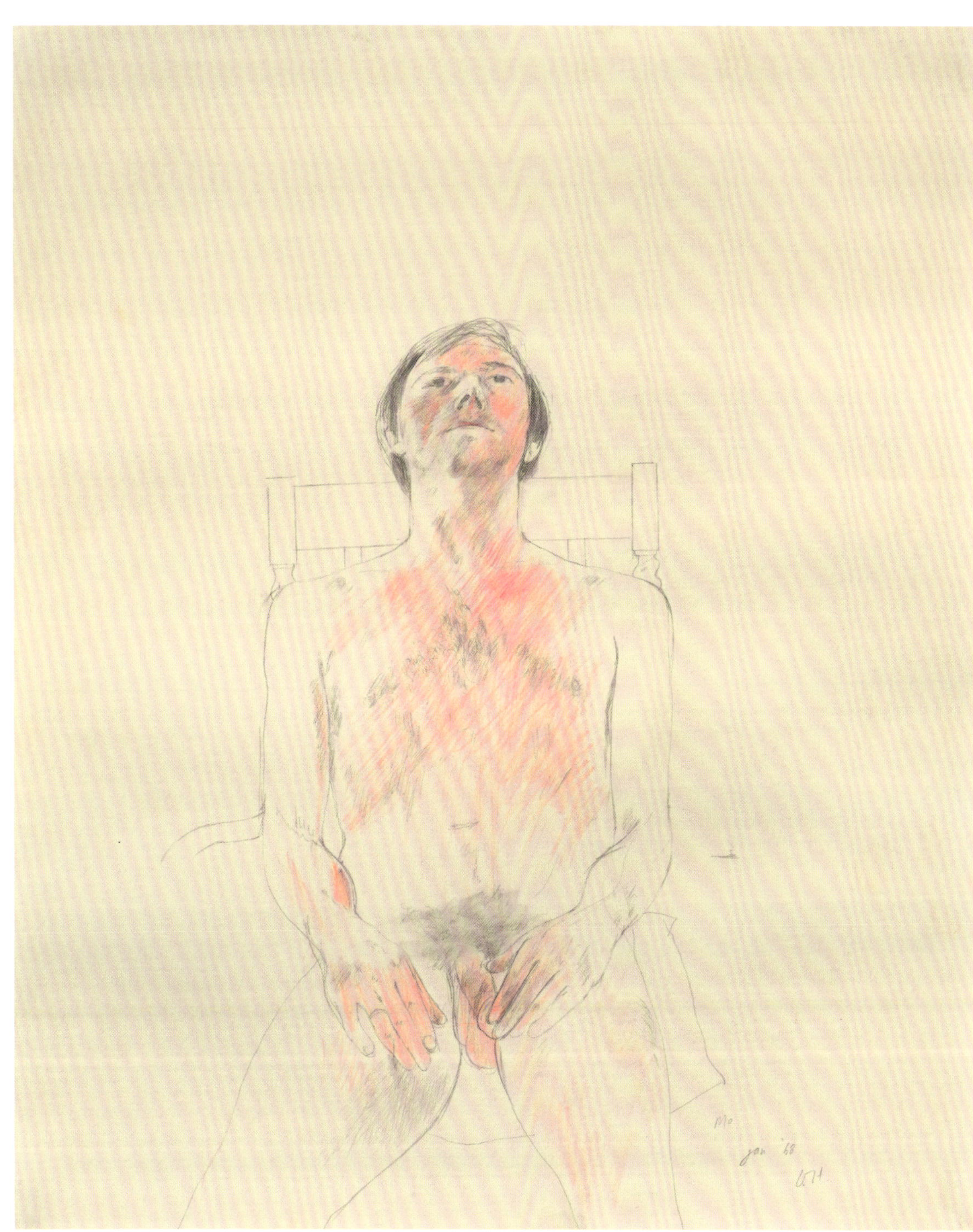

**Mo, Nude,** 1968
Bleistift und Buntstift auf Papier |
Pencil and coloured pencil on paper,
43 × 35,5 cm
Privatsammlung, Köln | Private Collection, Cologne

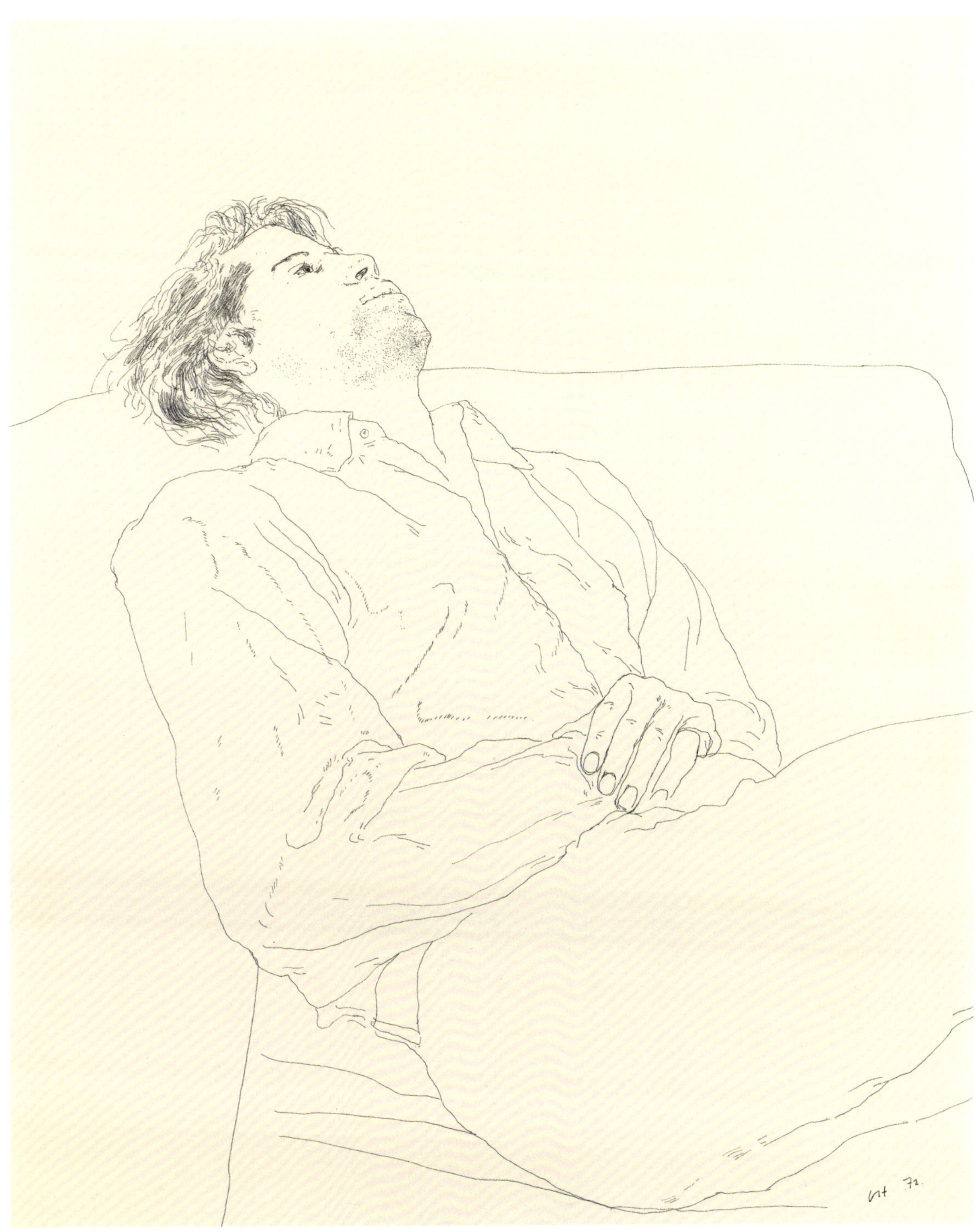

**Peter, Reclining,** 1972
Tusche auf Papier | Ink on paper,
43 × 35,5 cm
Privatsammlung, Köln | Private Collection, Cologne

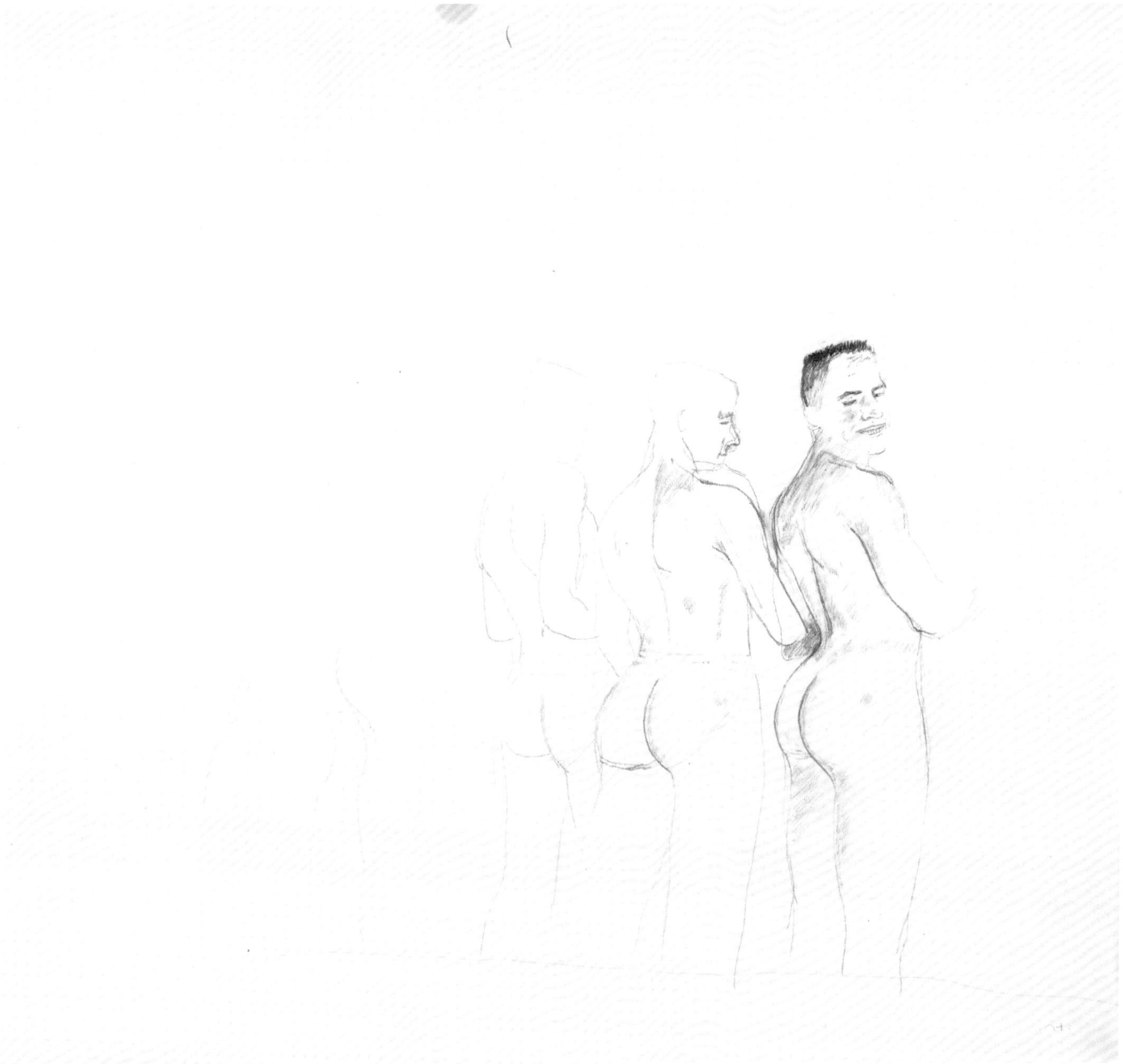

31

**Three Men Under the Shower,** 1965
Bleistift auf Papier | Pencil on paper,
40,5 × 43,8 cm
Privatsammlung | Private Collection

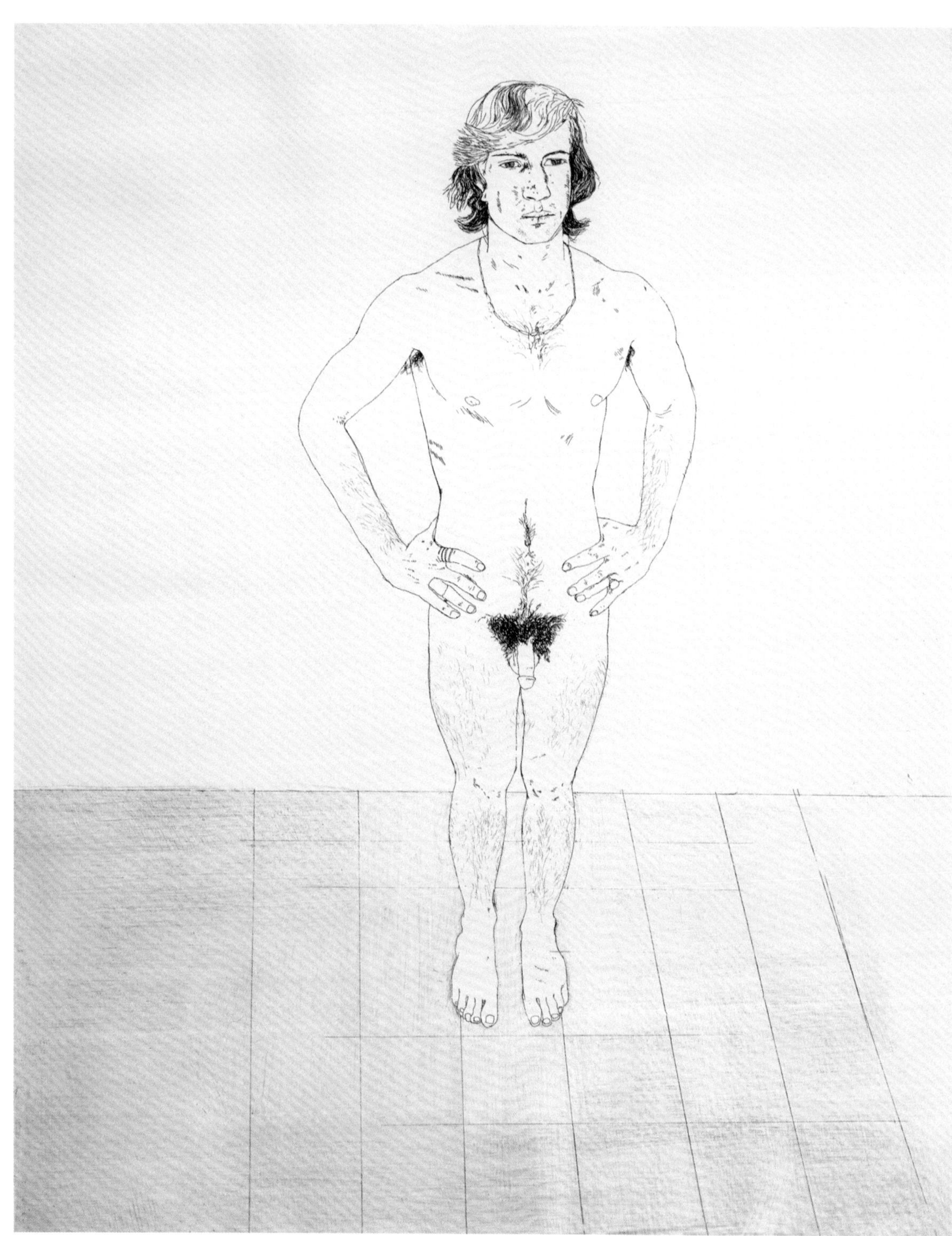

**Peter,** 1969
Radierung (Auflage von 75) |
Etching (Edition of 75),
68,5 × 54,5 cm
Privatsammlung | Private Collection

33

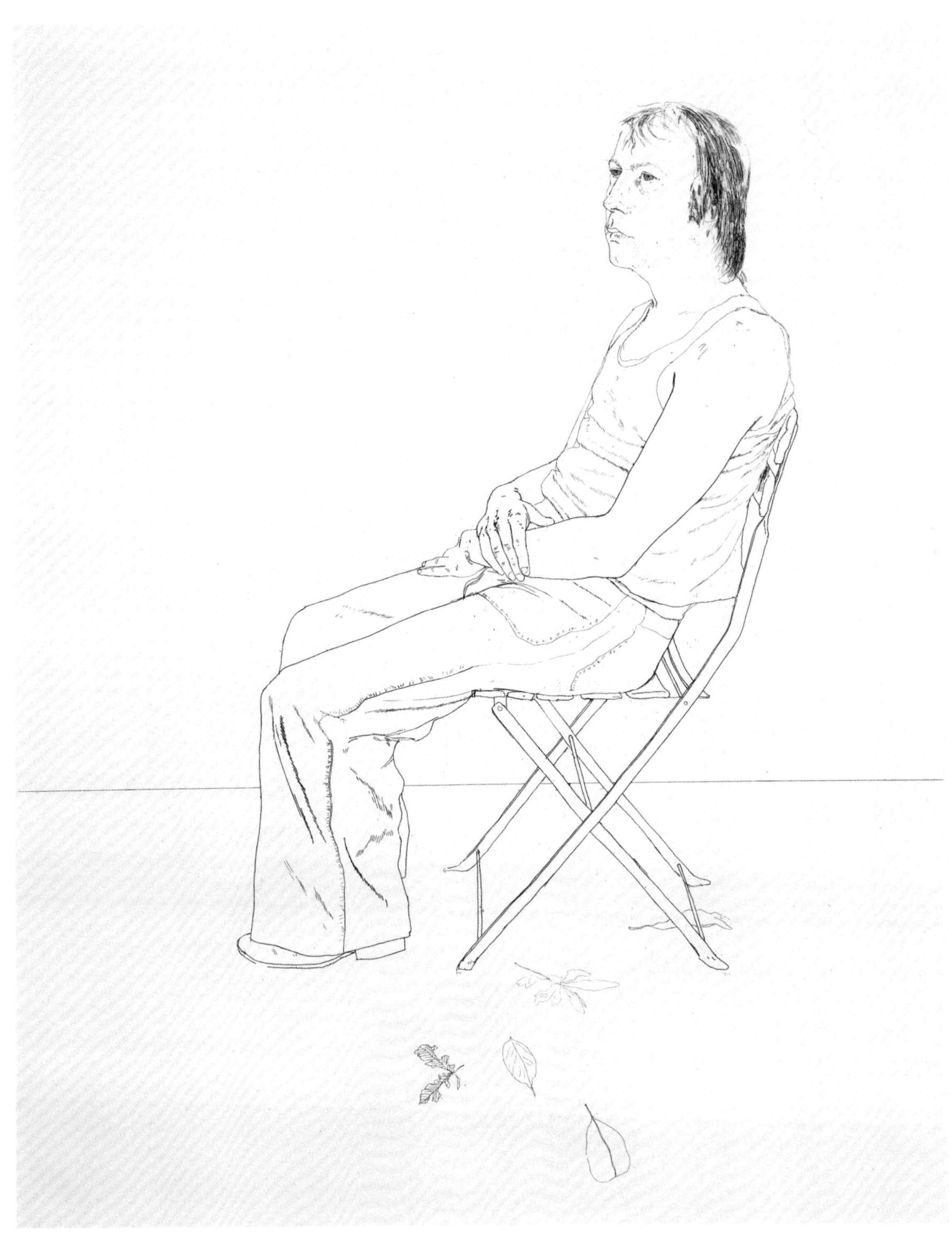

**Mo with Five Leaves,** 1971
Radierung auf Papier (Auflage von 75) |
Etching on paper (Edition of 75),
67,9 × 54 cm
Tate: Purchased 1978
Inv. N° P07238

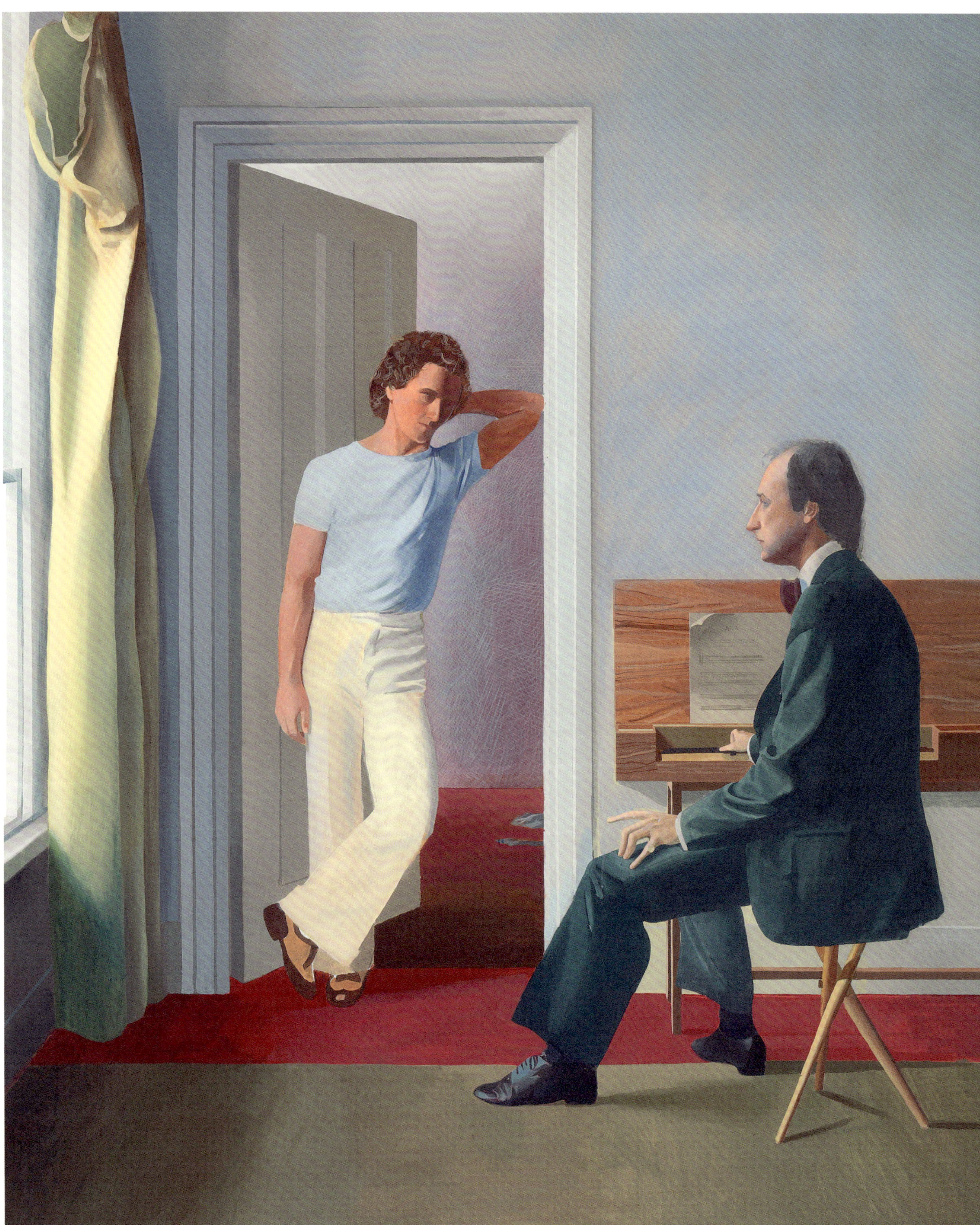

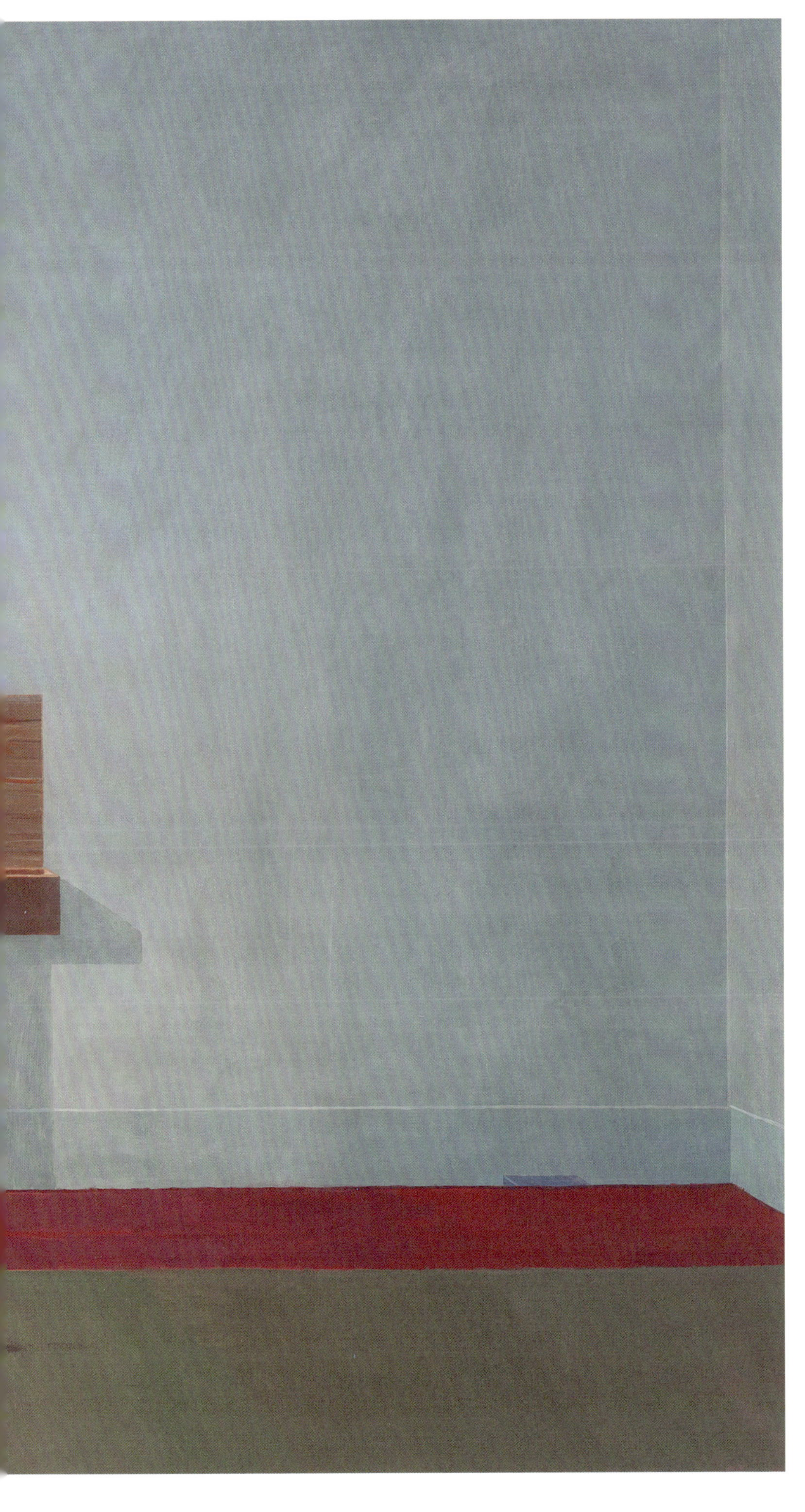

**George Lawson and Wayne Sleep,** 1972–1975
Acryl auf Leinwand | Acrylic on canvas,
212,5 × 300,8 cm
Tate: Presented by the artist 2014
Inv. N° T14098

# Looking Closely. David Hockney im Blick

**Bettina M. Busse, Veronika Rudorfer**

In den vergangenen Jahren wurde David Hockney mit zahlreichen Ausstellungen gewürdigt. Anlässlich seines 80. Geburtstags 2017 machte die umfassende Retrospektive *David Hockney* Station in der Tate Britain in London, im Metropolitan Museum of Art in New York sowie im Centre Pompidou in Paris. 2001 versammelte die retrospektive Schau *David Hockney. Exciting Times Are Ahead* in der Kunst- und Ausstellungshalle der Bundesrepublik Deutschland in Bonn Gemälde aus rund fünfzig Jahren. Neben so umfassenden Retrospektiven widmeten sich Ausstellungen wie *David Hockney. The Arrival of Spring, Normandy, 2020* unter anderem in der Royal Academy of Arts in London, *David Hockney. A Bigger Picture* ebendort oder auch *Hockney Paints the Stage* im Walker Art Center in Minneapolis der Vielfalt von David Hockneys medialen Erkundungen und seiner themenspezifischen Projekte.

David Hockneys Werk wächst bis heute stetig, und seine Auseinandersetzungen mit Porträt, Stillleben, Interieur und Landschaft üben weltweit eine ungebrochene Faszination auf sein Publikum aus. Mit diesen klassischen Gattungen der Kunstgeschichte setzt er sich medial immer wieder neu auseinander – seine künstlerische Praxis ist geprägt von einer schier unendlichen Experimentierfreude und schließt von der Druckgrafik über die Malerei bis zur Fotografie und zu Zeichnungen auf dem iPhone und iPad nahezu jedes mögliche Medium der vergangenen sieben Dekaden mit ein. Diese mediale Offenheit ist für David Hockney geradezu Voraussetzung seiner künstlerischen Produktion, wie er selbst feststellt: „[…] wenn einen zutiefst die Frage fasziniert, wie die Welt wirklich aussieht, muss man zwangsläufig an jedem denkbaren Verfahren interessiert sein, ein Bild herzustellen.“[1] So entsteht ein spannungsreiches Verhältnis zwischen den beinahe traditionell anmutenden Sujets und den immer neuen Medien, in denen David Hockney unter anderem die Landschaften Yorkshires (S. 66–75), seine Familie (S. 17,19), Freundinnen und Freunde (S. 27–29) sowie seine unmittelbare Lebensumgebung (S. 150–151, 153 und 158–159), wie er sie sieht, festhält.

Am Beginn des Arbeitsprozesses steht bei David Hockney immer die eingehende und präzise Betrachtung – und somit der Akt des Sehens selbst. Aus der genauen Beobachtung ergibt sich das Motiv und die Notwendigkeit, es bildlich festzuhalten. Die so entstehenden Bilder setzen ihrerseits wiederum einen neuen Sehprozess in Gang, so Hockney: „Bilder beeinflussen Bilder, aber Bilder bringen uns auch dazu, Dinge zu sehen, die wir sonst vielleicht nicht sehen würden.“[2]

1. David Hockney, zitiert in: Martin Gayford, *A Bigger Message. Gespräche mit David Hockney*, Bern (Piet Meyer Verlag) 2012, S. 11.

2. Ibid., S. 85.

Auf der Suche nach den geeigneten medialen Mitteln dafür lotet David Hockney die Grenzen von Malerei und Zeichnung kontinuierlich aus und erweitert diese Begriffe innerhalb der technischen Möglichkeiten und Bedingtheiten der Fotografie. Zentral ist für ihn dabei der Unterschied zwischen Auge und Kamera: Die Sehweise der menschlichen Augen schließt neben einer geometrischen auch eine subjektiv-psychologische mit ein; die Kamera hingegen bleibt den Gesetzen der Optik verhaftet.[3] Essenziell für den Künstler ist also, *wer* sieht und *wie* gesehen wird. Damit sind seine künstlerischen Arbeiten zutiefst persönliche Zeugnisse der eigenen visuellen Wahrnehmung. Er beschreibt den Vorgang des Sehens – auch in Verbindung mit dem Zeichnen – so: „Man muss hingucken und sich ständig danach fragen, was man sieht. Das Zeichnen lässt einen die Dinge klarer und klarer sehen. Das Bild wandert auf physiologischem Weg durch einen hindurch ins Gehirn, ins Gedächtnis – wo es bleibt –, und es wird dann über die Hände weitergeleitet."[4]

Die Veränderlichkeit der eigenen Wahrnehmung und Perspektive als Konstante seiner künstlerischen Praxis *muss* eine Offenheit und Heterogenität der Stile und Mittel nach sich ziehen. Das rund sieben Dekaden umspannende Werk demonstriert David Hockneys Vielfalt, Erfindungsreichtum und Neugierde und macht anstelle *eines* Stils einen beeindruckenden Pluralismus deutlich – dieses Moment der absoluten künstlerischen Freiheit ist jeder seiner Äußerungen immanent.

Mit starkem Fokus auf seine damals rezenten fotografischen Arbeiten war die bis dato letzte Ausstellung zu David Hockney in Österreich 1996 im Kunst Haus Wien eine Art Momentaufnahme seines Schaffens. Nimmt man die Verbindungen, die sich zwischen dem Künstler und Wien herstellen lassen, in den Blick, übersteigen diese *eine* Ausstellung bei Weitem. So spannt die Malerei des Barock und des Manierismus – prominent vertreten in der Sammlung des Kunsthistorischen Museum Wien – ein starkes Band zwischen den Werken von Jan Vermeer, Caravaggio und seiner Nachfolge, Hans Holbein dem Jüngeren sowie Parmigianino und David Hockney. Nicht nur in seiner vielbeachteten Studie *Secret Knowledge. Rediscovering the Lost Techniques of the Old Masters*[5] geht Hockney den Werken dieser Künstler kompositorisch-perspektivisch auf den Grund, sondern er setzt sich auch in seiner künstlerischen Praxis dezidiert mit Arbeiten der alten Meister bis hin zu jenen Vincent van Goghs (S. 152) und Pablo Picassos auseinander. Einen feinsinnigen künstlerischen Kommentar zu den Themen der perspektivischen Verortung, des Sehens und Gesehenwerdens realisierte David Hockney zudem mit seinem Beitrag zur Ausstellungsreihe *Eiserner Vorhang* in der Wiener Staatsoper für die Saison 2012/2013.[6]

Zehn Jahre nach der Gestaltung seines *Eisernen Vorhangs* ermöglicht die Ausstellung *David Hockney: INSIGHTS. Reflecting the Tate Collection* im Bank Austria Kunstforum Wien nun Einblicke in das so abwechslungsreiche wie konsequente Werk David Hockneys. Zeitlich beginnt die Schau mit Schlüsselwerken aus den frühen Schaffensjahren (S. 173–177), die mit den Grenzen zwischen Figuration und Abstraktion experimentieren. Diese demonstrieren seine kenntnisreiche Auseinandersetzung mit dem damals die Diskurse bestimmenden Abstrakten Expressionismus und der aufkommenden Pop-Art.[7]

3. Zur Unterscheidung zwischen diesen Formen des Sehens äußert sich Hockney in Gayford 2012, S. 53.

4. Ibid., S. 84–85.

5. Deutsche Ausgabe: David Hockney, *Geheimes Wissen. Verlorene Techniken der Alten Meister wieder entdeckt von David Hockney*, München (Knesebeck) 2001 – übersetzt von Bernadette Ott und Rita Seuß.

6. Seit dem Jahr 1998 wird der Brandschutzvorhang der Wiener Staatsoper jährlich von wechselnden Künstlerinnen und Künstlern gestaltet, die von einer Jury ausgewählt werden. Für Abbildungen des *Eisernen Vorhangs* von David Hockney siehe https://www.mip.at/werke/eiserner-vorhang-2012-2013/ [zuletzt besucht am 12.10.2021].

7. Eine Positionierung David Hockneys zum Abstrakten Expressionismus und insbesondere zu Clement Greenbergs Schriften findet sich in Gayford 2012, insbes. S. 47.

Die Ausstellung fokussiert dann auf David Hockneys ab 1964 in Los Angeles entstandene Untersuchungen zur Oberfläche, Textur und Beschaffenheit von Wasser (S. 42–47 und 53–57). Seine Bilder zumeist privater Swimmingpools prägten die visuelle Identität der Stadt entscheidend mit – bis heute ist unsere Vorstellung von Los Angeles untrennbar mit seinen Werken verbunden. Bemerkenswert und folgerichtig zugleich ist, dass David Hockney sich dabei keineswegs auf die Malerei beschränkte, sondern auch mit den Mitteln der Druckgrafik seine visuellen Untersuchungen vorantrieb, deren Ergebnisse er als gleichrangig und autonom gegenüber der Malerei ansieht.

Ebenso ikonisch wie seine *Pool Paintings* wurden David Hockneys Doppelporträts, in denen er in den 1970er-Jahren Familie wie auch Freundinnen und Freunde festhielt (S. 10–21 und 27–35). Wie ambivalent Hockney aber einer bloßen Darstellung der Wirklichkeit mit den Mitteln der Kunst – sei es Fotografie oder naturalistischer Malerei – gegenübersteht, macht er im Folgenden deutlich: „Die meisten Menschen glauben, dass die Welt aussieht wie das Foto von ihr. Ich habe immer unterstellt, dass das Foto fast recht hat. Aber durch das kleine bisschen, um das es fehlgeht, geht es eine Meile fehl. Das ist es, was ich zu ergründen suche."[8] Wenig überraschend, verfolgte er die spezifische Form der Doppelporträts nicht weiter. Vielmehr führte diese *Ergründung* zu dem experimentellen Umgang mit (neuen) Formen der Perspektive, wie in den Farblithografien *Moving Focus* (S. 150–157 und 160–163), in der Fotoserie *40 Snaps of My House, August 1990* (1990, S. 158–159), in den mit Farbe und Licht operierenden Bühnenbildern der 1990er-Jahre sowie in den Gemälden *The First V. N. Painting* oder *The Eleventh V. N. Painting* (beide 1992, S. 143 und 144–145) deutlich wird.

**8.** Ebd.

Die exakte Beobachtung seiner Umgebung führt David Hockney ab den 2000er-Jahren einerseits zu einer Auseinandersetzung mit Landschaften wie jener der Normandie oder des nördlichen Großbritannien, andererseits auf der medialen Ebene zu Bildfindungen mittels iPhone, iPad und simultanen Aufnahmen mit mehreren beweglichen Kameras. Die so entstehenden iPhone- und iPad-Drawings (S. 69–75) wie auch Mehrkanal-Film-Installationen (S. 76–77) belegen den Willen und die Befähigung des Künstlers zur medialen Neuerfindung wie auch zur motivischen Kontinuität in seinem Werk.

David Hockneys Praxis ist ein Arbeiten an und mit den klassischen Gattungen der Kunstgeschichte – stets im Bewusstsein, dass Kunst eben *keine* Darstellung der Wirklichkeit ist oder sein sollte, wie er selbst feststellt: „Ich will damit sagen, dass wir in Wirklichkeit nicht sicher sind, wie die Welt aussieht. Furchtbar viele Leute meinen, wir wissen es, ich aber nicht."[9] Selten in der Kunstgeschichte führte ein Nichtwissen zu einer produktiveren künstlerischen Suche nach möglichen Antworten.

**9.** Ebd.

# Looking Closely: David Hockney in Focus

Bettina M. Busse,
Veronika Rudorfer

Numerous exhibitions have paid tribute to David Hockney over the past years. In 2017, in honour of his eightieth birthday, the comprehensive retrospective *David Hockney* made the rounds from Tate Britain in London to the Metropolitan Museum of Art in New York and the Centre Pompidou in Paris. The 2001 retrospective *David Hockney: Exciting Times Are Ahead* at the Art and Exhibition Hall of the Federal Republic of Germany in Bonn featured paintings spanning approximately fifty years. And in addition to those major surveys, there were also exhibitions – among them *David Hockney: The Arrival of Spring, Normandy, 2020* at the Royal Academy of Arts in London and elsewhere, *David Hockney: A Bigger Picture* at the same venue, and *Hockney Paints the Stage* at the Walker Art Center in Minneapolis – devoted to the artist's widely diverse media explorations and theme-specific projects.

David Hockney's oeuvre continues to grow to this day, and his audience worldwide is as fascinated as ever with his investigations of the portrait, still life, interior, and landscape. Within the framework of an artistic praxis distinguished by the sheer endless pleasure he takes in experimentation, Hockney interrogates these classical art-historical genres again and again in mediums ranging from printmaking and painting to photography and drawings made on an iPhone or iPad – that is, in nearly every conceivable medium of the past seven decades. For Hockney, this openness to different media is virtually the prerequisite for his artistic production, as he himself observes: "But if you are deeply fascinated by what the world really looks like, you are forced to be very interested in any way of making a picture that you come across."[1] The result is a tension-charged relationship between the traditional subjects and the ever new mediums in which the artist captures, among other things, the Yorkshire scenery (pp. 66–75), his family (pp. 17–19) and friends (pp. 27–29), and his immediate everyday surroundings (pp. 150–151, 153 and 158–159) – the way *he* sees them.

1. David Hockney, quoted in Martin Gayford, *A Bigger Message: Conversations with David Hockney*, Thames & Hudson, London 2011, p. 11.

Hockney's working process always begins with thorough and precise observation, and thus with the act of looking itself. It is close contemplation that gives rise to the motif and the necessity of recording it pictorially. This leads to images that, in turn, set new visual processes in motion. As Hockney puts it: "Pictures influence pictures, but pictures also make us see things that we might not otherwise see."[2]

2. Ibid., p. 85.

In his search for the mediums suitable to pursuing this aim, he constantly sounds out the boundaries of painting and drawing, while at the same time broadening them conceptually within the technical possibilities and conditionalities offered by photography. Of key importance to him in this context is the difference between the eye and the camera. Human sight encompasses not only a geometric component but also a subjective psychological one; the camera, on the other hand, cleaves to the laws of optics.[3] The matter of *who* is looking and *how* they are looking is accordingly of fundamental importance to Hockney. And his artworks are thus profoundly personal testimonies to his own visual perception. He describes the process of seeing, also in connection with drawing, as follows: "You have to look and ask questions of what you are seeing all the time. Drawing makes you see things clearer, and clearer, and clearer still. The image is passing through you in a physiological way, into your brain, into your memory – where it stays – it's transmitted by your hands."[4]

3. Hockney talks about the distinction between these different ways of seeing in Gayford 2011, p. 53.

4. Ibid., pp. 84–85.

The changeability of Hockney's own perception and perspective – a constant in his artistic praxis – *inevitably* brings openness and heterogeneity of styles and mediums in its wake. Extending over some seven decades, his oeuvre demonstrates his diversity, inventiveness, and curiosity and reveals not *one* style but a striking pluralism. This element of absolute artistic freedom is inherent to every one of his statements.

The last David Hockney exhibition to take place in Austria to date was at the Kunst Haus Wien in 1996. Focusing strongly on his then recent photographic works, it was something of a snapshot of his artistic approach. Yet the connections between Hockney and the city of Vienna far exceed that *one* exhibition. Baroque and Mannerist painting, for example – both prominently represented in the collection of the Kunsthistorisches Museum Wien – forge strong links between the works of Jan Vermeer, Caravaggio and his followers, Hans Holbein the Younger, Parmigianino, and Hockney. He not only examined the works of these artists from the compositional and perspectival viewpoints in his highly recognized study *Secret Knowledge: Rediscovering the Lost Techniques of the Old Masters,*[5] but persistently explores works by artists ranging from the Old Masters all the way to Vincent van Gogh (p. 152) and Pablo Picasso in his artistic praxis as well. With his contribution to the *Eiserner Vorhang / Safety Curtain* exhibition series at the Vienna State Opera[6] for the 2012/2013 season, he moreover realized a sensitive artistic commentary on the themes of perspectival positioning, seeing, and being seen.

5. David Hockney, *Secret Knowledge: Rediscovering the Lost Techniques of the Old Masters*, Thames and Hudson, London 2006.

6. The fire protection curtain of the Vienna State Opera has featured a composition by a different jury-selected artist every year since 1998. For illustrations of David Hockney's *Safety Curtain 2012/2013*, see https://www.mip.at/en/creations/safety-curtain-2012-2013/ [retrieved on 26.10.2021].

Ten years after his *Safety Curtain*, the exhibition *David Hockney: INSIGHTS. Reflecting the Tate Collection* at the Bank Austria Kunstforum Wien now offers a closer look at an oeuvre as multifarious as it is consistent. The show begins with key examples from the artist's early years (pp. 173–177): works that experiment with the boundaries between the figurative and the abstract and shed light on his well-informed investigation of the two movements that dominated the discourse of the time: Abstract Expressionism and the emergent Pop Art.[7]

7. David Hockney's positions on Abstract Expressionism and in particular the writings of Clement Greenberg are found in Gayford 2011, esp. p. 47.

Then the focus shifts to his examinations of the surface, texture, and consistency of water (pp. 42–47 and 53–57), which he carried out from 1964 onwards in Los Angeles. Depicting, for the most part, private swimming pools, these paintings contributed decisively to shaping the visual identity of that city: to this day, our image of Los Angeles is inextricably linked with Hockney's works. Yet he by no means limited himself to painting – a fact as remarkable as it is logical – but also pursued his visual investigations with the means offered by printmaking to arrive at results he considers on a par with and independent of painting.

The double portraits in which Hockney captured family and friends in the 1970s would prove similarly iconic (pp. 10–21 and 27–35). At the same time, he views the mere depiction of reality using artistic means – whether photography or naturalistic painting – with an ambivalence that is evident when he remarks: "Most people feel that the world looks like the photograph. I've always assumed that the photograph is nearly right, but that little bit by which it misses makes it miss by a mile. This is what I grope at."[8] The fact that he did not continue pursuing the specific form of the double portraits hardly comes as a surprise. That exploration led, rather, to experimentation with (new) forms of perspective, as seen in the colour lithographs *Moving Focus* (pp. 150–157 and 160–163), the photo series *40 Snaps of My House, August 1990* (1990, pp. 158–159), the stage sets of the 1990s – works that operate with colour and light –, and the paintings *The First V. N. Painting* and *The Eleventh V. N. Painting* (both 1992, pp. 143 and 144–145).

8. Ibid.

In the 2000s, Hockney's close observation of his surroundings inspired an investigation of landscapes such as those of Normandy and the northern United Kingdom and, on the level of medium, pictorial invention with the aid of iPhone, iPad, and simultaneous shots with several movable cameras. The resulting iPhone and iPad drawings (pp. 69–75) and multi-channel film installations (pp. 76–77) bear witness to the artist's inventive will and abilities in working with new media, but also to the motivic continuity that distinguishes his oeuvre.

What constitutes David Hockney's artistic praxis is work on and with the classical genres of art history, always with the awareness that art is *not* a depiction of reality, nor should it be, as he himself explains: "I suppose essentially I am saying we are not sure what the world looks like. An awful lot of people think we do, but I don't."[9] Rarely in the history of art has a lack of knowledge led to a more productive artistic search for possible answers.

9. Ibid., p. 11.

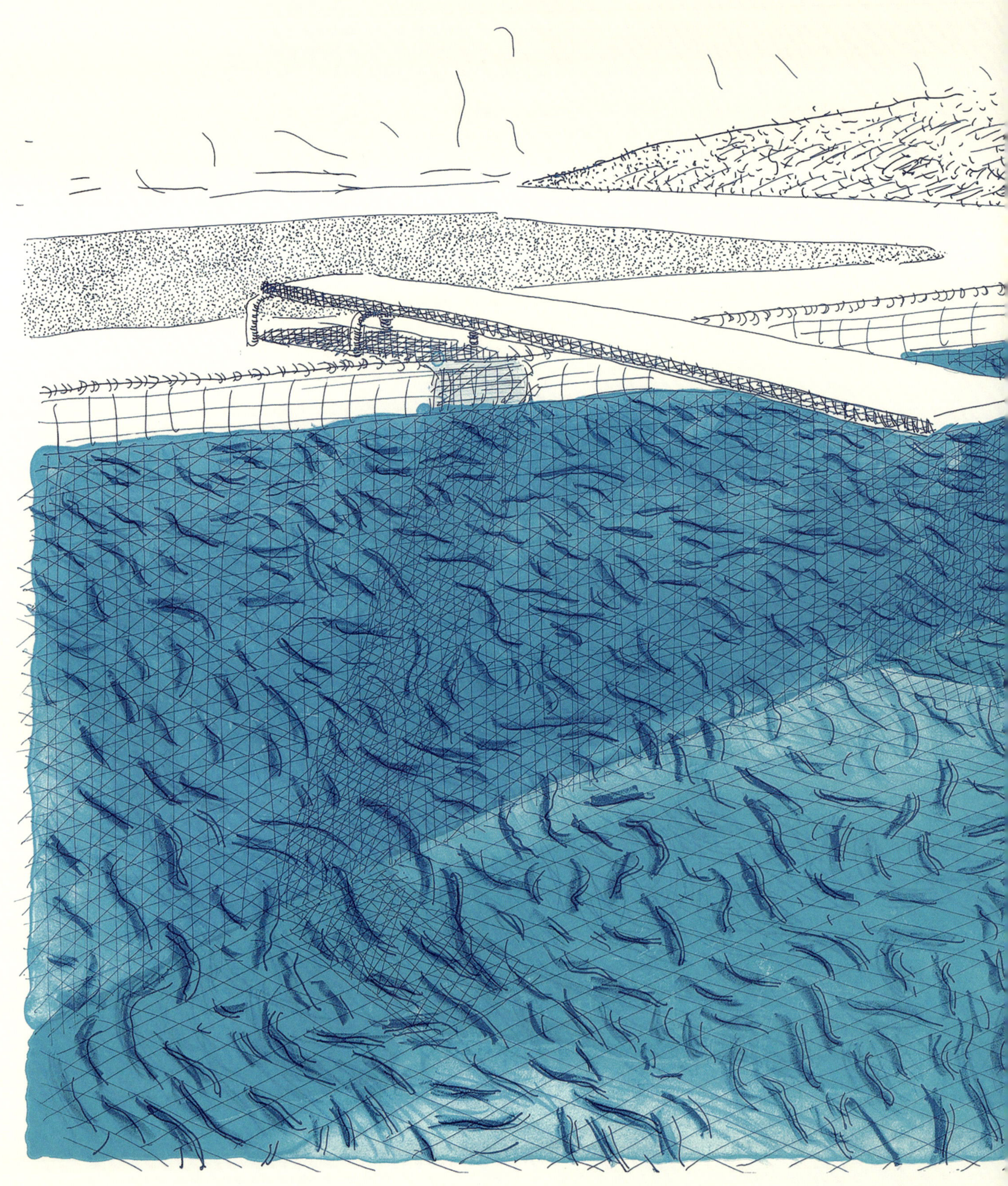
A.P. I

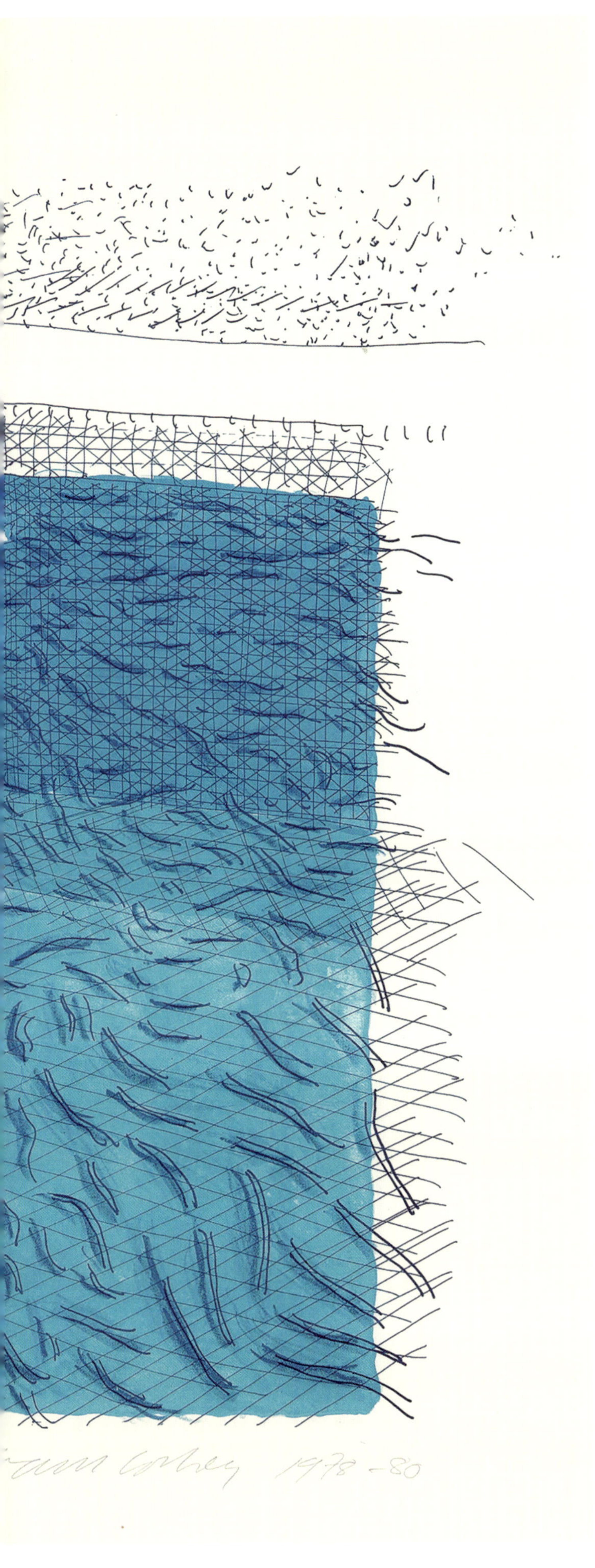

**Lithographic Water Made of Lines, Crayon and Two Blue Washes Without Green Wash,**
1978–1980
Lithografie auf Papier (Auflage von 36) |
Lithograph on paper (Edition of 36),
75 × 86,7 cm
Tate: Presented by Tyler Graphics Ltd in honour of Pat Gilmour, Tate Print Department 1974-7, 2004
Inv. N° P12116

**Two Boys in a Pool, Hollywood,** 1965
Acryl auf Leinwand | Acrylic on canvas,
152,4 × 152,4 cm
Privatsammlung, Belgien | Private Collection,
Belgium

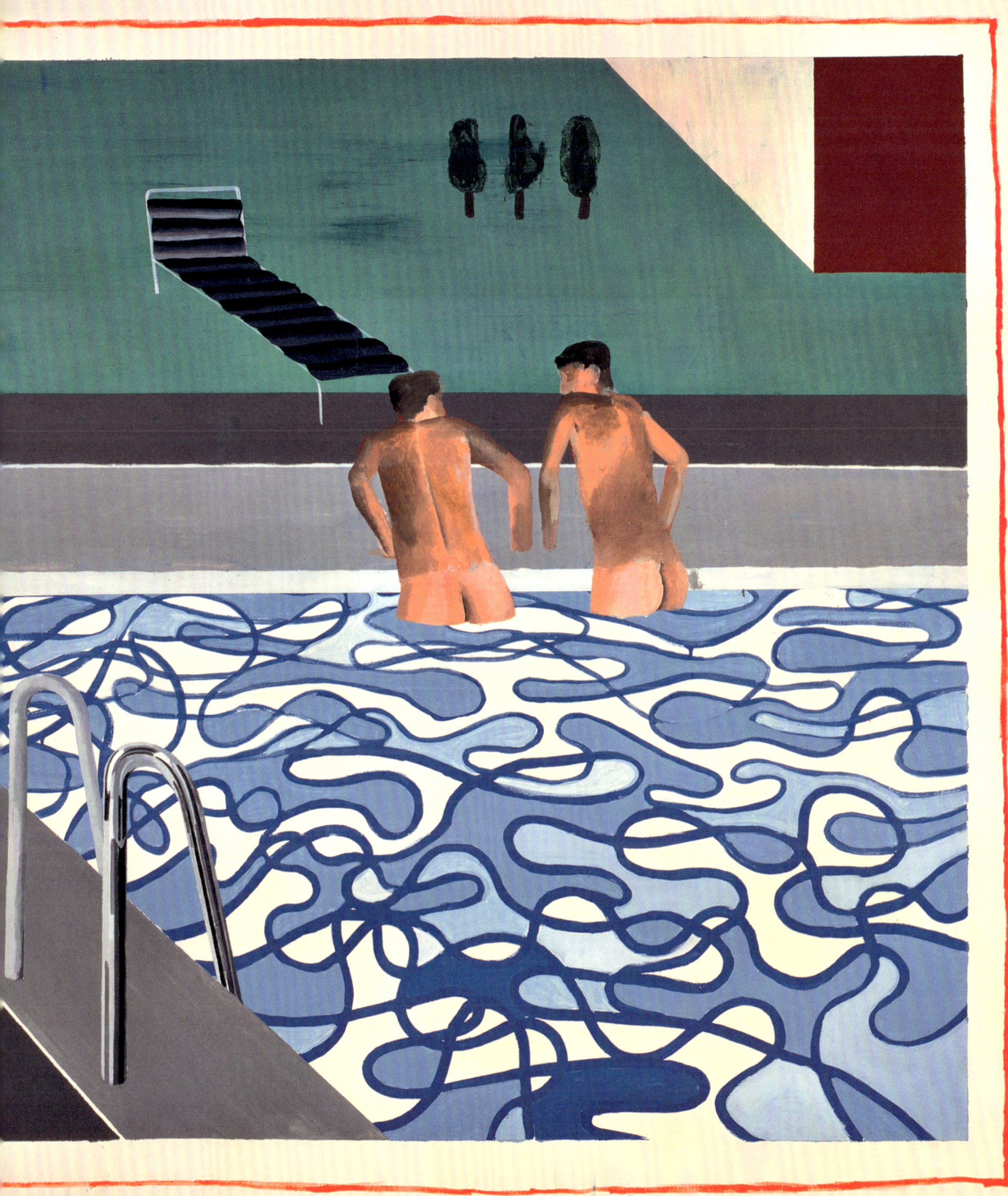

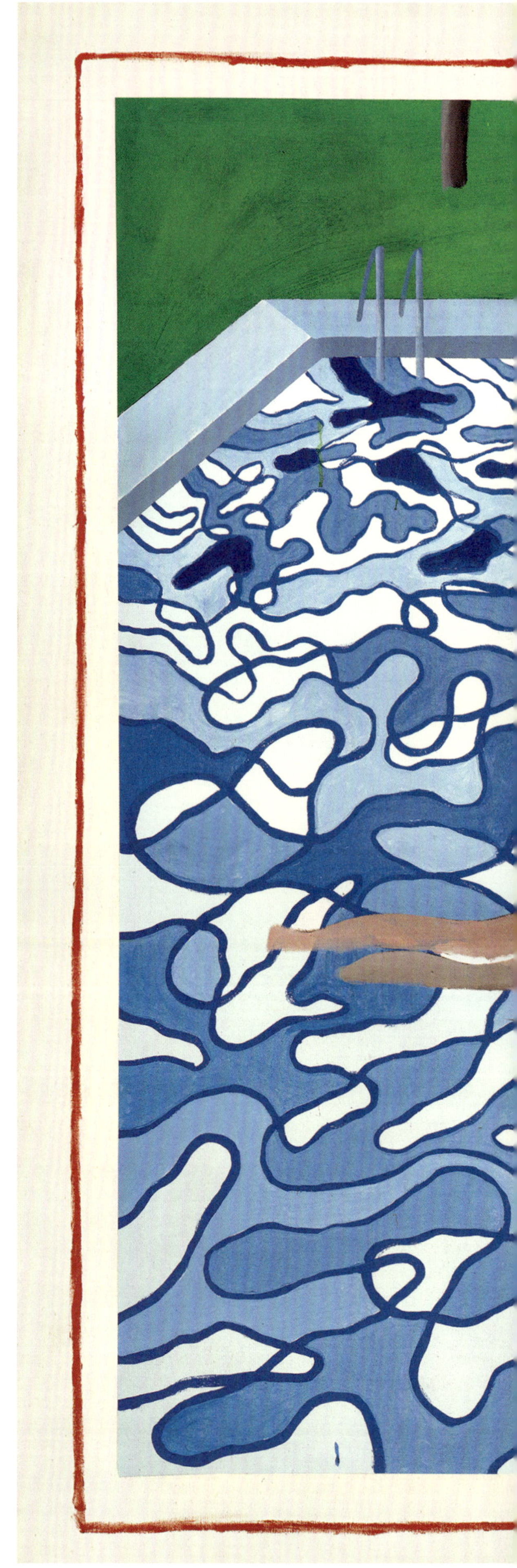

**California Copied From 1965 Painting in 1987,** 1987
Acryl auf Leinwand | Acrylic on canvas, 152,1 × 182,6 cm
Los Angeles County Museum of Art
Genuine gift of David Hockney
Inv. N° M.89.35

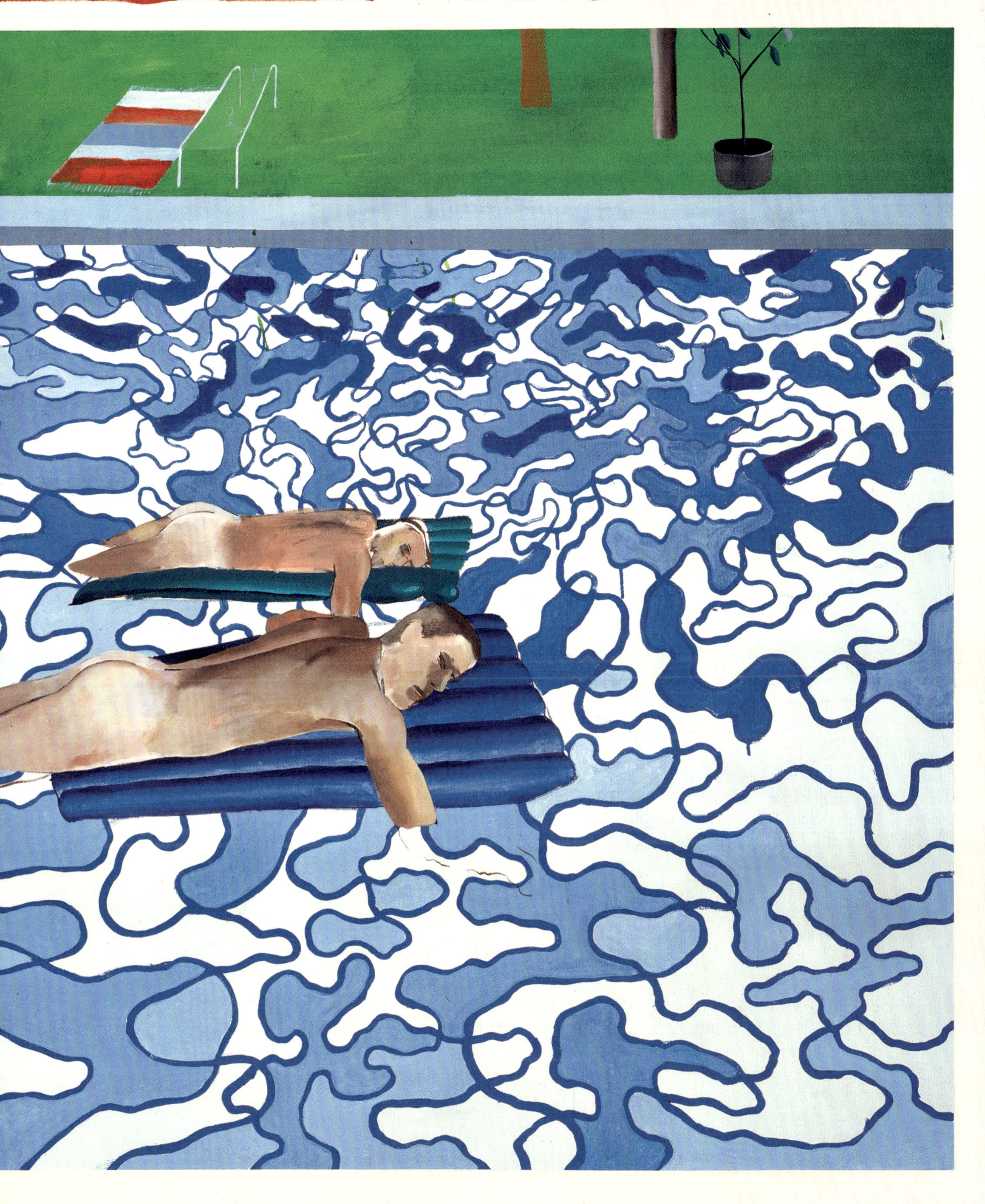

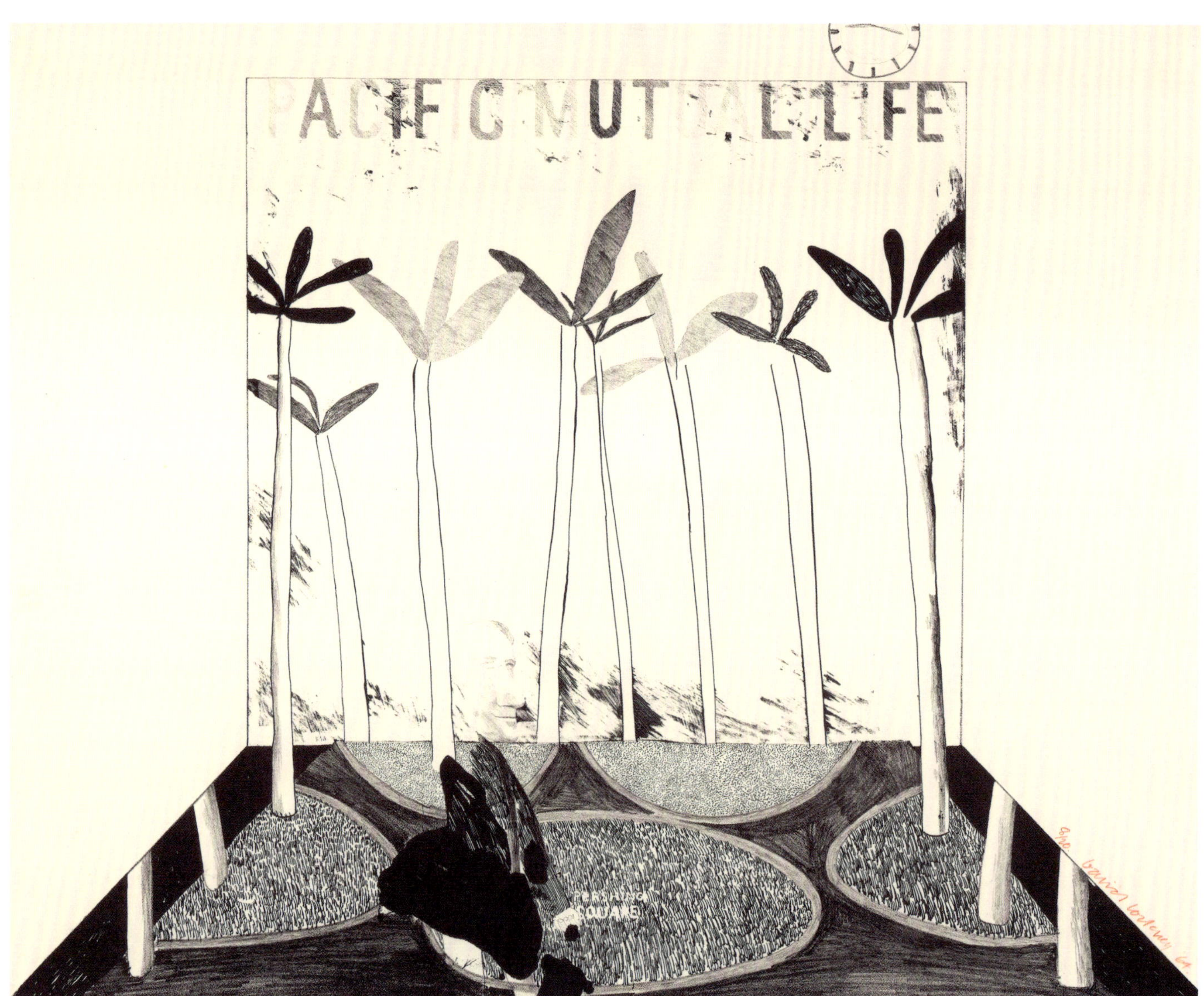

**Pacific Mutual Life,** 1964
Lithografie auf Papier (Auflage von 20) |
Lithograph on paper (Edition of 20),
51,2 × 64 cm
Tate: Presented by Jonathan Cheshire
and Gareth Marshallsea in memory
of Peter Coni 1994
Inv. N° P11379

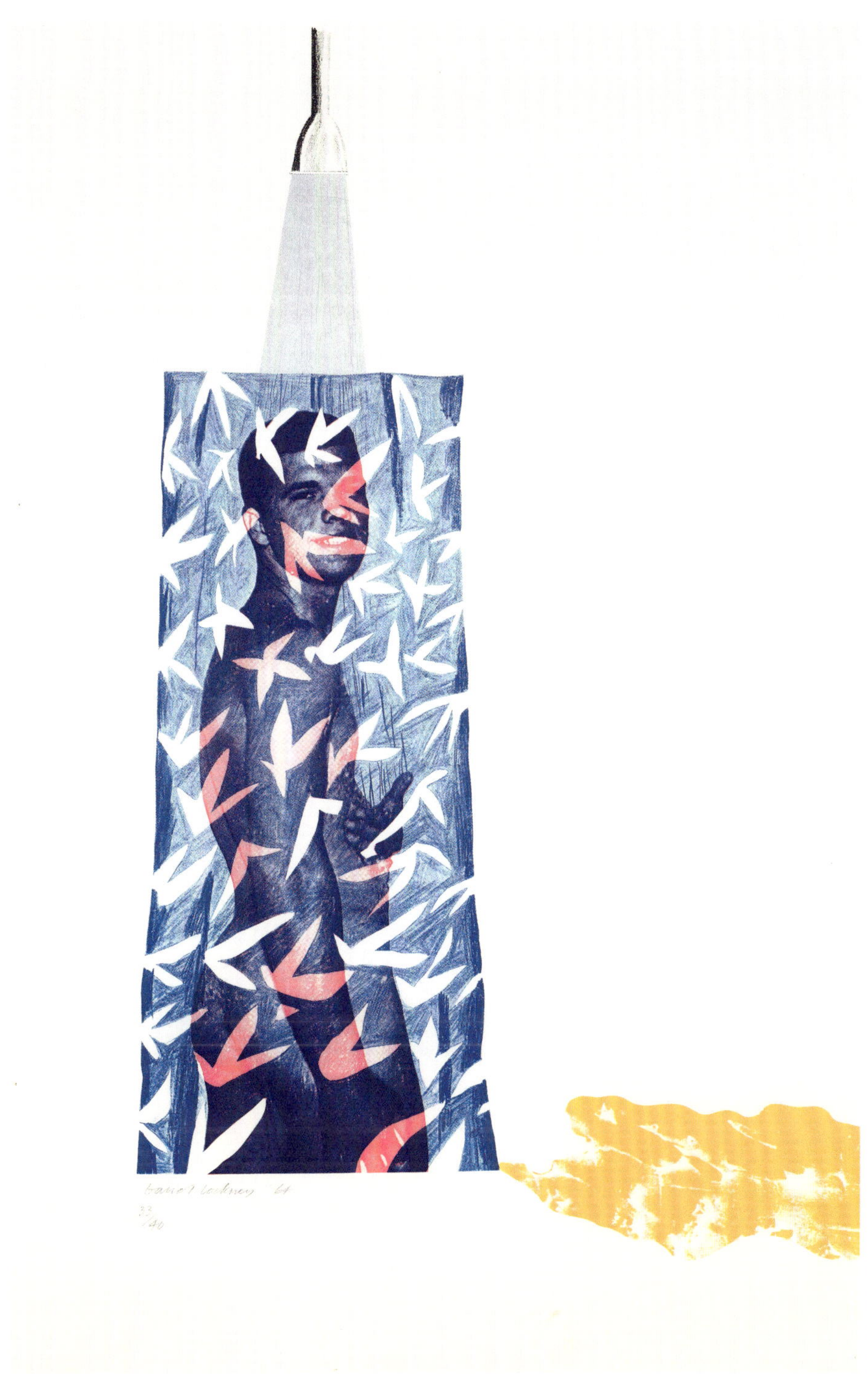

**Cleanliness is Next to Godliness,** 1964
Siebdruck auf Papier | Screenprint on paper,
91,4 × 58,1 cm
Tate: Presented by Rose and Chris Prater
through the Institute of Contemporary
Prints 1975
Inv. Nº P04315

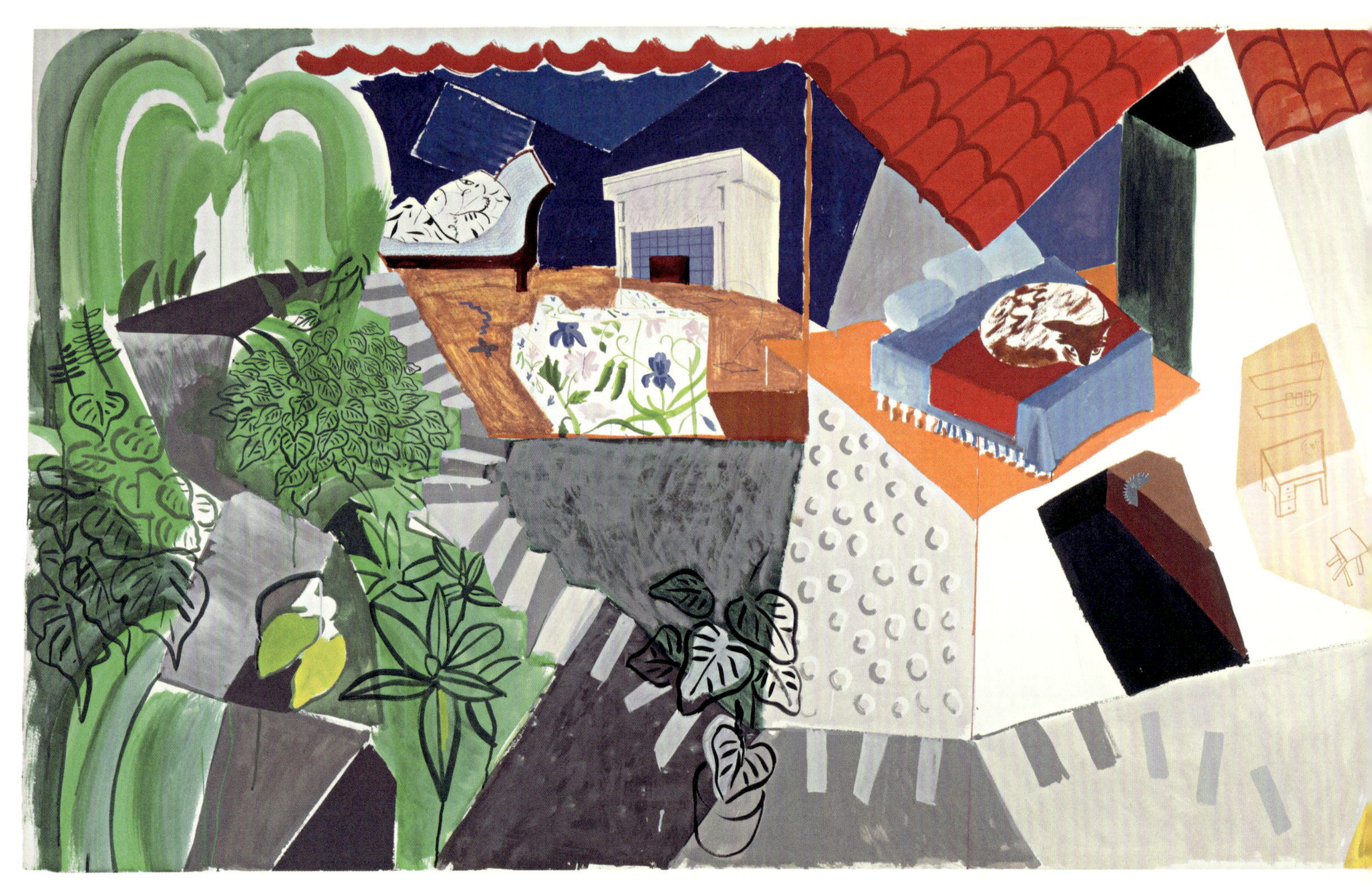

**A Visit with Mo and Lisa, Echo Park, Los Angeles,** 1984
Gouache, Kreide und Bleistift auf zwei Blatt Papier | Gouache, crayon and pencil on two sheets of paper, 154,3 × 513 cm (gesamt)
Privatsammlung | Private Collection

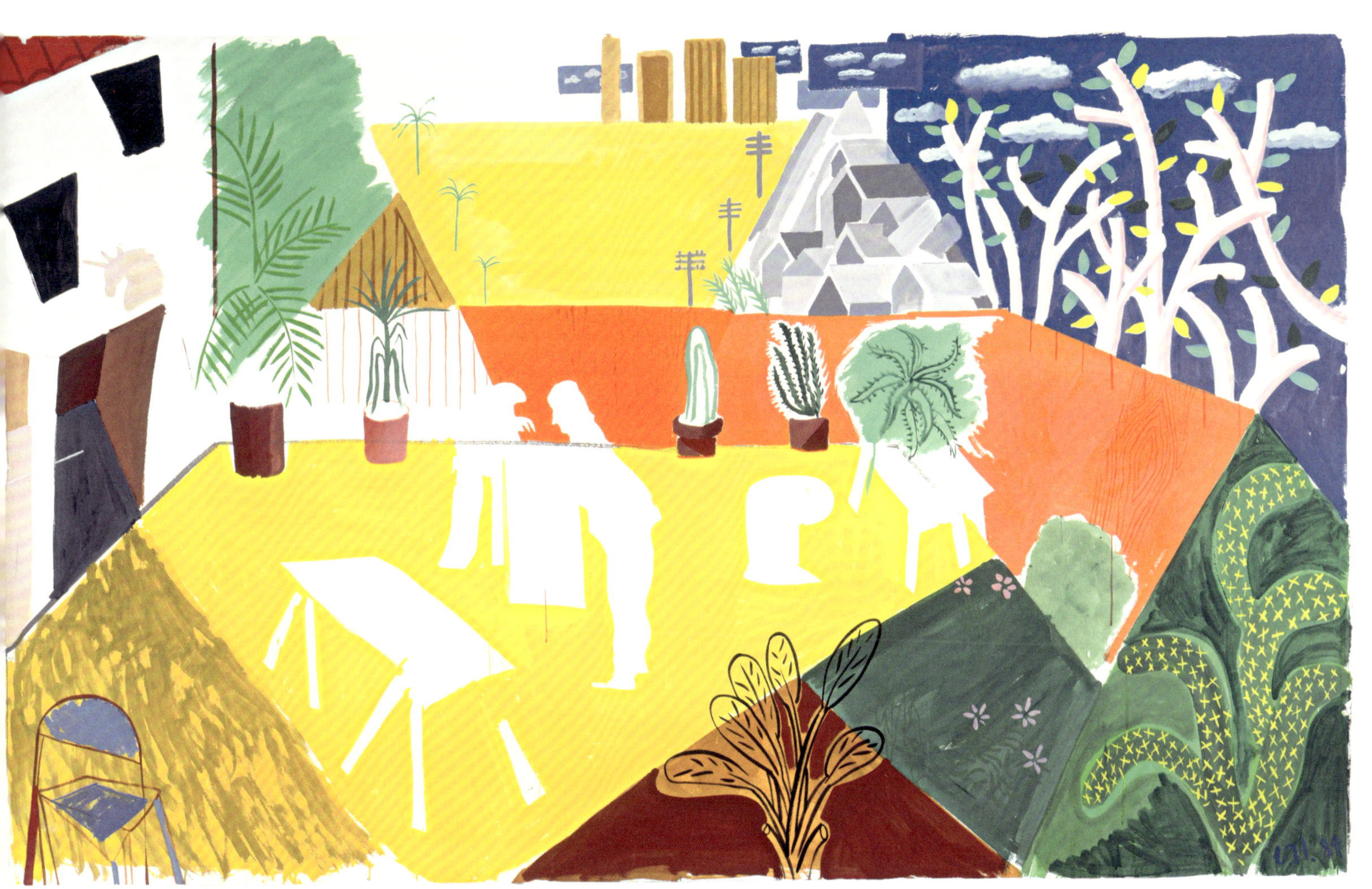

53

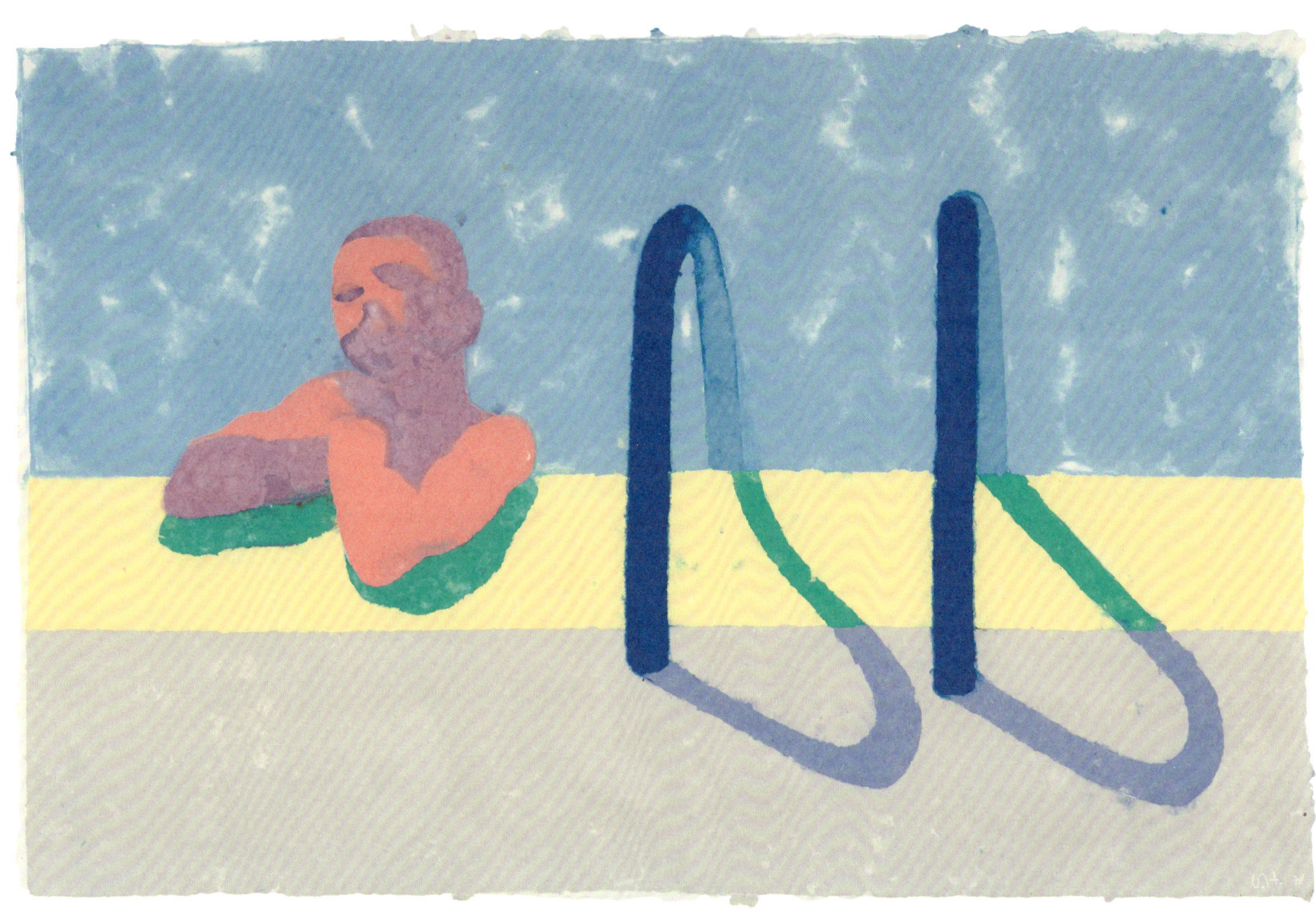

**Gregory in the Pool (Paper Pool 4),** 1978
Handgefärbter und gepresster Zellstoff
(Auflage, Variante E, Unikat) |
Hand-coloured and pressed paper pulp
(Edition, variation E, unique),
81,3 × 127 cm
Privatsammlung | Private Collection

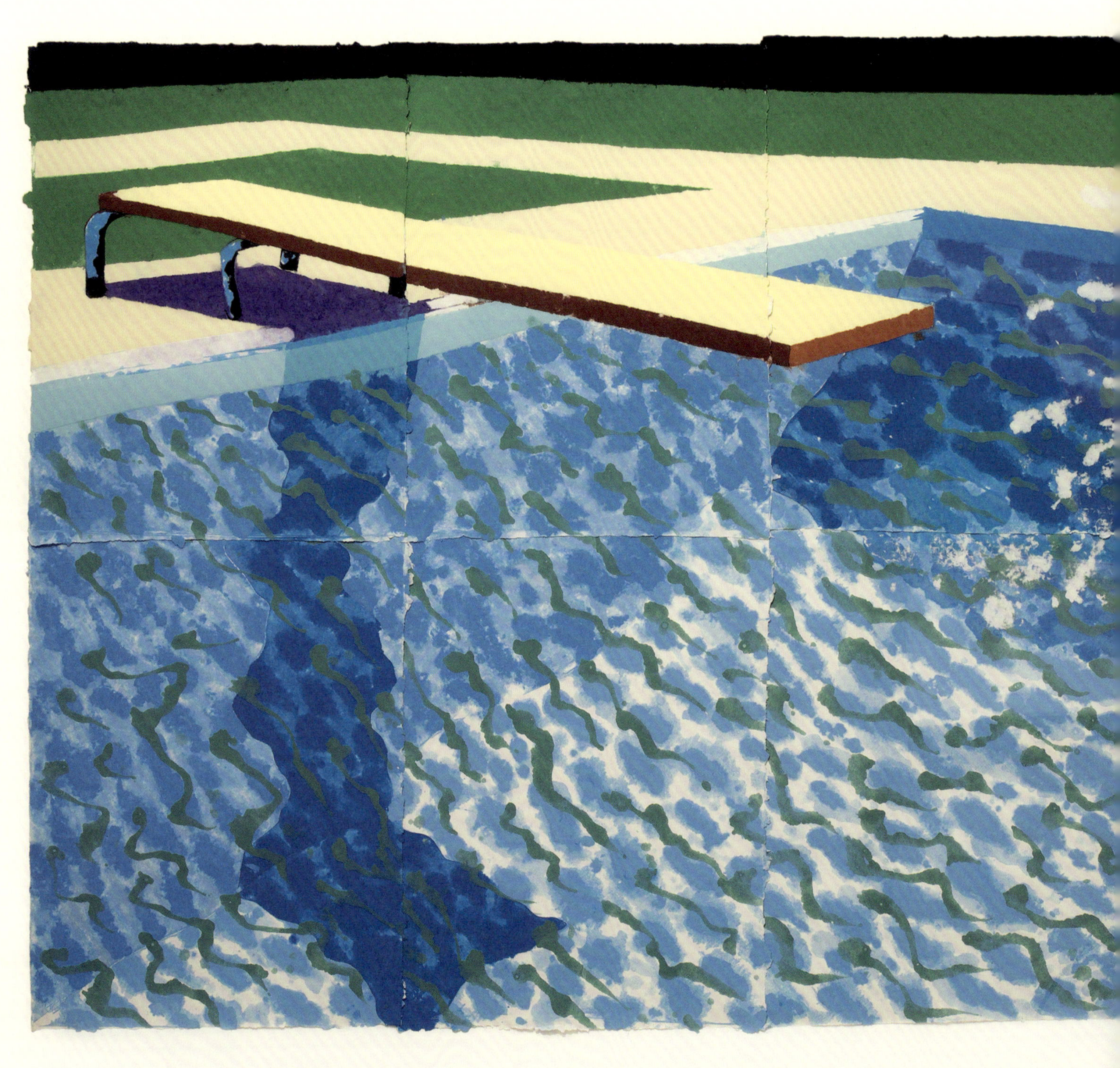

**A Large Diver (Paper Pool 27)**, 1978
Handgefärbter und gepresster Zellstoff |
Hand-coloured and pressed paper pulp,
198,4 × 458,5 cm (gesamt)
San Francisco Museum of Modern Art
T. B. Walker Foundation Fund purchase
Inv. N° 79.18. A-L

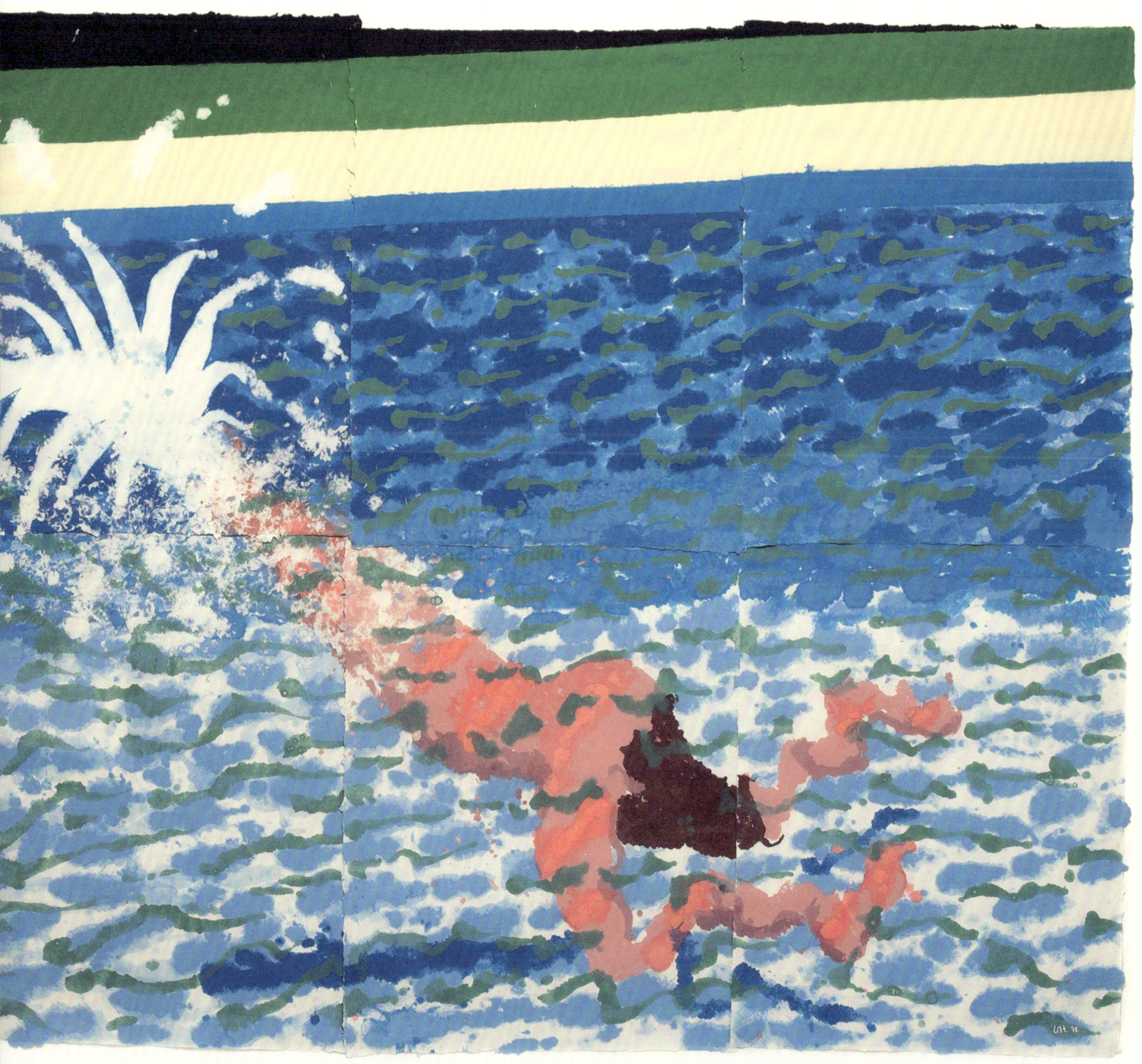

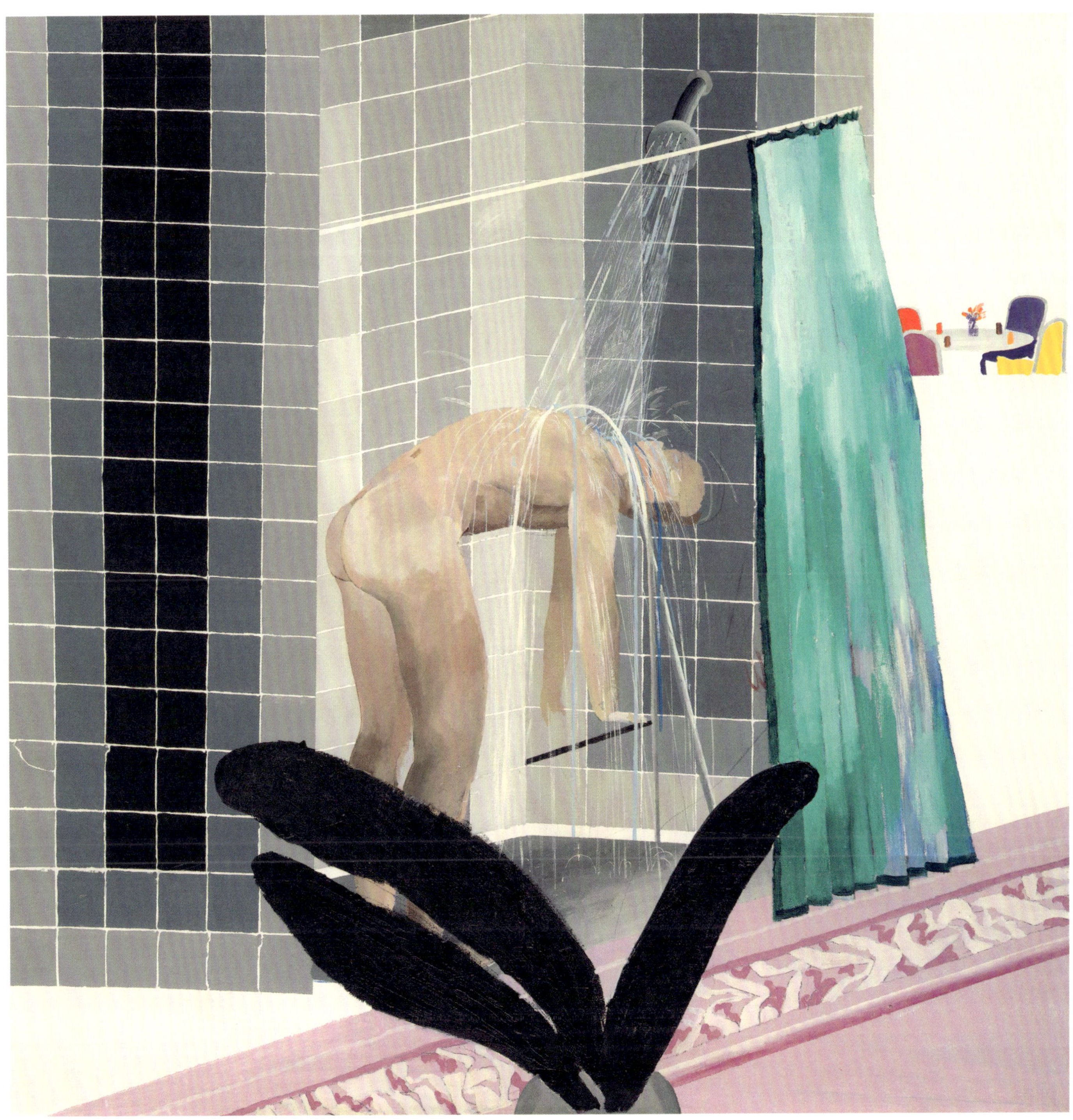

**Man in Shower in Beverly Hills,** 1964
Acryl auf Leinwand | Acrylic on canvas,
167,3 × 167 cm
Tate: Purchased 1980
Inv. N° T03074

Das Werk David Hockneys ist bisher vorrangig von Kunsthistoriker*innen und Kunstkritiker*innen erforscht worden. Wäre das Tableau ein anderes, wenn wir es aus der Perspektive der Medientheorie betrachten würden? Was kann eine kritische Medientheorie zum Verständnis des Hockney'schen Œuvres beitragen, zumal dann, wenn seine aktuellen Verwendungen heutiger Technologien – High Definition Video (HDV), das „Smart“-Phone und das Tablet – mit ins Spiel kommen?

Seit Mitte der 1970er-Jahre ist Hockney mit dem Problem befasst, ganz persönliche Alternativen zur konventionellen Perspektive zu finden (S. 143–163). Beispielhaft zeigt sich dies in seiner Auseinandersetzung mit dem fotografischen Bild. Sein Unbehagen gegenüber der Kamera ist dem ihr eingeschriebenen zentralperspektivischen System geschuldet und der Form des Sehens, das dieses etabliert. „Reine“ Fotografie, wie Hockney die Standardverwendung der Kamera nennt,[1] erzwingt eine einäugige, immobile, fixierte Sichtweise, während sich das Auge im wirklichen Leben ständig bewegt und die Perspektive permanent wechselt. Ein weiteres Problem mit der Fotografie ist ihre zeitliche Instantaneität. Im Unterschied zu einem Gemälde, das den konsekutiven Prozess seiner Entstehung widerspiegelt (die Ablagerung der Farbschichten im Verlauf des Malprozesses), vermag das fotografische Bild die zeitliche Entfaltung nicht einzufangen. Insofern ist die Fotografie für Hockney ein eher unangemessenes Mittel zur Darstellung der komplexen Weise, wie wir die Welt sehen.

1. David Hockney, zitiert in: Martin Gayford, *A Bigger Message. Gespräche mit David Hockney*, Bern (Piet Meyer Verlag) 2012, S. 116.

### Kamerabasierte Arbeiten

Es entbehrt nicht einer gewissen Ironie, dass Hockney zur Erkundung zentraler Elemente seiner eigenen Malpraxis ausgerechnet auf das Medium der Fotografie zurückgriff. Anfang 1982 begann er, mit Fotocollagen zu experimentieren, um der fixierten Perspektive der Kamera und ihrer Instantaneität etwas entgegenzusetzen. Indem er eine Vielzahl zeitversetzter Aufnahmen ein und derselben Szene aus jeweils unterschiedlichem Blickwinkel aneinanderfügte, bot sich ihm die Möglichkeit, die konventionelle fotografische Einzelbildperspektive mit dem Mittel der Collage zu durchbrechen. Multifokalität, die an die mannigfachen, simultanen Blickwinkel des Kubismus erinnert – sie wurde später auch in seine Gemälde und Videos übertragen –, steht für eine subjektive, „verkörperlichte“ Sichtweise. Zudem ermöglicht das Collagieren mehrerer zeitlich *konsekutiver* Aufnahmen, die gelegentlich rasterförmig angeordnet sind, das Nebeneinander von mehr als einem Moment innerhalb eines Mediums, das eigentlich nur einen einzigen Moment kennt.

Im Unterschied zu den Collagen, für die er analoge Kameras verwendete (Polaroid, Spiegelreflexkameras), arbeitet Hockney in seinen Videos mit Digitaltechnik. Für seine riesige collagierte Videoinstallation *The Four Seasons, Woldgate Woods (Spring 2011, Summer 2010, Autumn 2010, Winter 2010)*[2] (2010–2011) montierte er mit seinen Assistenten neun HDV-Kameras an einen auf der Motorhaube eines Land Rovers befestigten Rost. Jede Kamera war in einem leicht versetzten Winkel ausgerichtet, um auf diese Weise eine einzelne saisonale Autofahrt in den Yorkshire Wolds aufzuzeichnen. Die so entstandenen sechsunddreißig Videos werden in einer Installationsansicht präsentiert: Jede Jahreszeit erscheint auf neun fliesenartig angeordneten Monitoren, die an jeweils einer der vier Wände des Ausstellungsraums angebracht sind. Im Gegensatz zum „Standardfilm", einem rein syntagmatischen Ereignis (eine Aufnahme nach der anderen), versetzen die neun Versionen eines jeden saisonalen Moments die Betrachtenden in die Lage, Zeit sowohl *konsekutiv* als auch *simultan* zu erfahren.[3]

2. Siehe https://www.thedavidhockneyfoundation.org/resources/film/the-four-seasons-woldgate-woods-spring-2011-summer-2010-autumn-2010-winter-2010 [aufgerufen am 7.10.2021].

3. Siehe Arthur Kolat, „Essay", in: *David Hockney. Time and More, Space and More …*, hrsg. von der Richard Gray Gallery, Chicago 2018, S. 18. Siehe auch Meredith A. Brown, „Four Seasons", in: Chris Stephens, Andrew Wilson (Hrsg.), *David Hockney*, London (Tate Publishing) 2017, S. 185–190.

## Zwei Arten von Filmpraxis

„Die Digitalfotografie kann uns von einer chemisch erzwungenen Perspektive befreien, wie sie seit 180 Jahren existiert", hat Hockney erklärt.[4] Aus medientheoretischer Sicht ist allerdings kaum einzusehen, wieso analoge fotochemische Medien für die Fortdauer bestimmter visueller Konventionen verantwortlich gemacht werden sollten, denn schließlich gehört es zum Wesen der Filmavantgarde, die Grenzen der vertrauten Praxis des Filmemachens zu erweitern. Vergleicht man *The Four Seasons* mit *31/75 Asyl* (1975) von Kurt Kren, einem Meilenstein des strukturellen Films, so werden zwei prinzipielle künstlerische „Arten von Filmpraxis" sichtbar – einerseits Filme von Künstlerinnen und Künstlern, die in verschiedenen Medien arbeiten (Malerei usw.), aber keine Vollzeitfilmschaffenden sind („artists' film/video"), und andererseits solche, die von Filmemacherinnen und -machern stammen („avant-garde cinema" im eigentlichen Sinne) –, die sich jeweils durch ihre eigenen Produktions-, Distributions- und Ausstellungsformen auszeichnen.[5] Diese Unterscheidung findet auf rezeptionsästhetischer Seite ihren Ausdruck im begrifflichen Gegensatzpaar des „White Cube der Galerie" und der „Black Box des Filmtheaters".

4. David Hockney, zitiert in: Andrew Wilson, „Ways of Looking, And Being in the Bigger Picture", in: Chris Stephens, Andrew Wilson (Hrsg.), *David Hockney* (wie Anm. 3), S. 214–221, hier S. 221.

5. Jonathan Walley, „Modes of Film Practice in the Avant-Garde", in: Tanya Leighton (Hrsg.), *Art and the Moving Image*, London (Tate Publishing) 2008, S. 182–199.

Ähnlich wie Hockneys Video zeigt auch Krens Film die jahreszeitlich bedingte Veränderung von Landschaft mit den Mitteln der „Collage". Die an einundzwanzig Frühlingstagen hintereinander entstandenen Aufnahmen ermöglichen eine simultane Wahrnehmung des zeitlichen Ablaufs. Während Hockney Simultaneität durch mehrere mobile HDV-Kameras erreicht, arbeitete Kren mit einer einzelnen statischen 16-mm-Kamera und einem komplexen Verfahren von Mehrfachbelichtungen. Vor das Objektiv wurde eine Maske aus schwarzem Karton mit fünf Löchern montiert, während einmal pro Tag dasselbe Filmmaterial durch die Kamera lief. Die Mehrfachbelichtungen und die in ihrer Position täglich veränderten Löcher in der Maske führten beispielsweise dazu, dass auf einem Teil des Bildes schneebedeckte Landschaft zu sehen war, auf einem anderen dieselbe Landschaft in schneelosem Grün.

Krens Arbeitsmethode war handwerklich bestimmt und unabhängig (der Filmemacher ist für die Gesamtheit der Produktion verantwortlich), während diejenige Hockneys konzeptuell und kollaborativ (sprich: arbeitsteilig) angelegt ist.

Zudem verfolgen der „artists' film" und das „avant-garde cinema" nicht selten eine andere Idee (beziehungsweise ein anderes Ideal) von Bildqualität. David Hockney geht es in *The Four Seasons* vor allem um klare, fokussierte Bilder, intensive Farbsättigung und einen hohen Grad an Schärfe, was den Einsatz von HDV zum Mittel der Wahl macht.

Die Filmavantgarde hegte seit ihren Anfängen einen tief sitzenden Argwohn gegenüber den mimetischen Möglichkeiten des Films mit seiner „beispiellosen Dimension von ikonischer Genauigkeit", was sie veranlasste, sich gegen die „automatische Produktion exakter Ähnlichkeit" zu wenden und sich stattdessen um „verschwommenere, diffusere Arten des Sehens zu bemühen".[6] Der häufig vorgetragene Einwand, digitale Verfahren seien nichts weiter als das aktuelle Äquivalent des 16-mm-Films, lässt sich kaum aufrechterhalten, wenn man bedenkt, dass es vielen Filmemacherinnen und Filmemachern ja nach wie vor darum geht, den automatischen Hyperrealismus der Kamera bewusst zu mindern, und dies umso mehr, als hochauflösende Abbildungstechnologien heute zum Goldstandard der Konsumkultur geworden sind. Schließlich haben der „artists' film" und das „avant-garde cinema" zwei völlig verschiedene Modelle der Distribution und Ökonomie entwickelt. Der entscheidende Unterschied liegt darin, wie die jeweilige Filmpraxis den Abzug oder die Kopie (print) betrachtet: „Während die beschränkte Zahl von Kopien, die Avantgardefilmemacher herstellen, ihren außerordentlich geringen Budgets geschuldet ist, werden Kopien beim artists' film ganz bewusst verknappt, denn gerade die Knappheit ist es ja, die sie auf dem Kunstmarkt wertvoll macht."[7] Wenn die Reaktion der zeitgenössischen Filmavantgarde auf die zunehmende Konvergenz unserer Medienlandschaft darin besteht, die Vergangenheit dieser Filmpraxis als Ressource für die Gegenwart und die Zukunft zu nutzen, indem sie die Besonderheiten ihres eigenen Mediums zugleich bestätigt und erweitert,[8] reagiert Hockney als Maler dadurch, dass er sich exzessiv der neuesten Technologien bedient, um die Idee der Malerei neu zu beleben. Seine Wahl immer ausgefeilterer Medien scheint nahezulegen, dass es zur Verjüngung der Malerei nur einen Weg gibt, nämlich den technischen Fortschritt. Wenn dem so ist, dann bedienen seine medialen Arbeiten die Werte der Konsumkultur, wenn nicht gar den visuellen Kapitalismus.

## Zeichnen auf einem Stück Glas

In Hinblick auf die Verwendung neuer Werkzeuge sind Hockneys frühe iPhone- und iPad-Zeichnungen (2009–2011, S. 69–75) von besonderem Interesse. Technisch gesehen, ermöglichte die Installation einer App namens *Brushes* auf dem iPhone das Zeichnen mit den Fingern, während auf dem iPad ein Touchpen zum Einsatz kam. Die Ergebnisse – bisweilen eher grafisch und linear, bisweilen eher malerisch und an Aquarelle erinnernd – wurden dem Publikum (nach einer ersten Ausstellung im Originalformat und auf den Originalmedien[9]) als Prints auf Papier in einem sehr viel größeren Format präsentiert als dem Display, auf dem sie entstanden waren, und in limitierter Auflage zum Kauf angeboten.

Von Anfang an gehörten zu Hockneys ständig wiederkehrenden Motiven Landschaften, Blumen, Porträts oder Details des alltäglichen Lebens; vor allem aber gab es gläserne, kristalline Gegenstände wie Aschenbecher, Vasen, Schalen, Flaschen oder Fensterscheiben.[10] Insofern ließe sich eine Verbindung herstellen

6. Erika Balsom, „One Hundred Years of Low Definition", in: Martine Beugnet, Alain Cameron, Arild Fetveit (Hrsg.), *Indefinite Visions. Cinema and the Attractions of Uncertainty*, Edinburgh (Edinburgh University Press) 2017, S. 73–89, hier S. 87.

7. Siehe Anm. 5, S. 187.

8. Siehe Jonathan Walley, *Cinema Expanded. Avant-Garde Film in the Age of Intermedia*, New York (Oxford University Press) 2020, S. 23.

9. *David Hockney: Fleurs fraîches. Dessins sur iPhone et iPad*, Paris: Fondation Pierre Bergé–Yves Saint Laurent, 20.10.2010–30.1.2011.

10. Siehe https://www.hockney.com/works/digital/iphone und https://www.hockney.com/works/digital/ipad [aufgerufen am 7.10.2021].

zwischen Hockneys Wasseraffinität (wie sie sich etwa in seiner bekannten Swimmingpool-Serie zeigt, S. 42–47 und 53–55) und seiner Begeisterung für die Glasoberfläche des neuen Werkzeugs, denn beides – Wasser wie Screen – gehört ja der „Sphäre des Diaphanen" an.[11] Man könnte sogar noch weitergehen und behaupten, in Hockneys Œuvre gebe es eine Art „Flüssigkristalldynamik", die in den spezifischen Flüssigkristalldisplays (liquid crystal displays) des Smartphones und des Tablets konvergiert.

11. Didier Ottinger, „Water, Glass, Screens: the Diaphanous Realm", in: *David Hockney. Pictures of Daily Life. New iPhone and iPad Drawings*, Galeries Lelong & Co., Paris 2018, S. 16.

Trotz seiner technischen Neuheit offenbart der Touchscreen eine gewisse Sehnsucht nach älteren, eher taktilen Schnittstellen, da er auf die elektrische Leitfähigkeit des Fingers reagiert. Im Unterschied zu kamerabasierten Medien, die uns auf Distanz halten, bietet er eine unmittelbare körperliche Interaktion mit dem künstlerischen Werkzeug, was ja auch auf die Malerei zutrifft. Ein weiterer Grund für Hockney, sich dieser Geräte zu bedienen, ist ihre Spontaneität, Schnelligkeit und bequeme Handhabung. Im Gegensatz zu Avantgarde-Filmemacherinnen und -machern war Hockney bei diesen digitalen Arbeiten weniger an arbeitsintensivem Herumbasteln mit seinen Gerätschaften interessiert. Seine eigene Art, „gegen den Apparat zu spielen" und dessen „Automatismus" zu besiegen (wie Vilém Flusser sagen würde), ist in erster Linie konzeptuell.

In Hockneys gesamtem Schaffen bildeten Malerei (und Zeichnen) das Fundament seiner Kunst, nicht Fotografie oder Film. Selbst wenn er kamera- oder screenbasierte Medien erkundet, so bleibt die konzeptuelle Basis seines erweiterten Werks doch die Malerei, die insofern mit Fug und Recht als „painting expanded"[12] bezeichnet werden kann.

12. „Painting expanded" lässt Walleys *Cinema Expanded* (2020) anklingen, der sich in seinem Buch für die Kontinuität künstlerischer Identität ausspricht, selbst wenn der Künstler auf die spezifischen Charakteristiken des Mediums verzichtet, siehe Anm. 8.

David Hockney's work has primarily been investigated by art historians and critics. Would the picture change if we were to adopt a media studies' perspective? What can a critically informed media theory contribute to an understanding of Hockney's *œuvre*, especially when his more recent appropriations of contemporary technology – high-definition video (HDV), the "smart" phone, and the tablet – are involved?

From the mid-1970s on, Hockney has grappled with finding highly personal alternatives to conventional perspective (pp. 143–163). This can be seen in his struggle with the photographic image. His unease with the camera is due to the built-in, single-point perspective it offers the viewer. "Pure" photography, as Hockney calls the standard use of the camera,[1] imposes a one-eyed, immobile, fixed vision, whereas in real life the eye is steadily moving and perspective constantly changing. Another problem with photography is its temporal instantaneity. Unlike painting, which reflects the period of its making (the sedimentation of paint layers over time), the photographic image is unable to capture the unfolding of time. Thus, for Hockney, photography is a less than appropriate means to depict the complex way we see the world.

1. David Hockney, quoted in Martin Gayford, *A Bigger Message: Conversations with David Hockney*, Thames & Hudson, London 2011, p. 116.

### Lens-Based Works

It is not without irony that Hockney resorted to photography in order to explore core elements of his own painting practice. Early in 1982, he began to experiment with photographic collages with which he hoped to counter the camera's fixed viewpoint and instantaneity. By joining together multiple, temporally staggered photographs of a single scene, each taken from a different angle, he found a way of rupturing conventional perspective with photographic means. Multifocality, reminiscent of the cubists' multiple and simultaneous viewpoints – later transposed to his paintings and videos – stands for subjective, embodied vision. Moreover, the collaging of several temporally *consecutive* exposures, sometimes laid out in a neat grid, allowed for the juxtaposition of more than one instant within an otherwise single-instant medium.

In contrast to the collages made with analog equipment (Polaroid, reflex cameras), Hockney's videos rely on digital technology. For his huge, collaged video installation *The Four Seasons, Woldgate Woods (Spring 2011, Summer 2010, Autumn 2010, Winter 2010)*[2] (2010–2011), Hockney and his assistants assembled nine HDV-cameras on a grid attached to the front of a Land Rover. Each camera was aimed at a slightly different angle so as to record a single,

2. See https://www.thedavidhockney-foundation.org/resources/film/the-four-seasons-woldgate-woods-spring-2011-summer-2010-autumn-2010-winter-2010 [retrieved on 7.10.2021].

seasonal road trip in the Yorkshire Wolds. The resulting thirty-six videos are presented in an installation view: in a four-walled space, each wall shows one season, displayed on a tile-like bank of nine monitors. As opposed to "standard film," a purely syntagmatic event (one shot after the other), the nine versions of each seasonal moment enable the viewer to experience time both *consecutively* and *simultaneously*.[3]

3. See Arthur Kolat, "Essay" in: *David Hockney. Time and More, Space and More…*, ed. by Richard Gray Gallery, Chicago 2018, p. 18. See also Meredith A. Brown, "Four Seasons" in: Chris Stephens, Andrew Wilson (eds.), *David Hockney*, Tate Publishing, London 2017, pp. 185–190.

## Two Modes of Film Practice

"Digital photography can free us from a chemically imposed perspective that has lasted for 180 years," Hockney has declared.[4] From a media studies' perspective, however, it is hard to understand why analog photochemical media are to blame for the persistence of certain visual conventions, given the long-standing eagerness of avant-garde film to expand beyond the boundaries of a familiar and "pure" filmmaking practice. The comparison of *The Four Seasons* with *31/75 Asyl* (1975) by Kurt Kren, a landmark piece of Structural Film, sheds light on two artistic "modes of film practice" – on the one hand, films made by artists who might work in various media (painting, etc.) but are not fulltime filmmakers ("artists' film/video"); on the other, those made by filmmakers ("avant-garde cinema" proper). Each mode is marked by its own values of production, distribution and exhibition.[5] This distinction is often expressed in terms of "the white cube of the gallery" and the "black box of the movie theatre."

4. David Hockney quoted in Andrew Wilson, "Ways of Looking, And Being in the Bigger *Picture*" in: Chris Stephens, Andrew Wilson (eds.), *David Hockney*, Tate Publishing, London 2017, pp. 214–221, here p. 221.

5. Jonathan Walley, "Modes of Film Practice in the Avant-Garde" in: Tanya Leighton (ed.), *Art and the Moving Image*, Tate Publishing, London 2008, pp. 182–199.

Not unlike Hockney's video, Kren's film involves the seasonal transformation of landscape by means of "collage." Shot on twenty-one consecutive spring days, it makes possible a simultaneous perception of the passage of time. While Hockney achieves simultaneity via multiple, mobile HDV-cameras, Kren works with a single, static 16mm-camera fitted with a complex, multiple-exposure device. A black cardboard mask with five holes (their positions changing each day) was fixed at the front of the lens. Once a day, the same film stock passed before this contraption. The multiple exposures and the shifting position of the cardboard holes resulted in, for example, one part of the picture being covered in snow and another being bright green.

Kren's working method was craft-based and independent (the filmmaker is responsible for the totality of production), whereas Hockney's is concept-based and collaborative (dependent on the division of labor). Furthermore, the two modes adhere to a different idea(l) of image quality. For artists like Hockney, the goal is utmost clarity and focus, colour saturation and crispness, making HDV the obvious method of choice.

On the other hand, avant-garde filmmakers have shown a nagging distrust in cinema's "unprecedented heights of iconic fidelity," prompting them to turn "against the automatic production of exact likeness, in search of blurrier, smudgier ways of seeing".[6] The argument that digital video is just the contemporary equivalent of 16mm-film does not hold, given many avant-garde filmmakers' ongoing effort to lessen the camera's automatic hyperrealist powers – even more important in our digital age, in which high-tech equipment has become the "gold standard" of consumer culture. Artists' film and avant-garde cinema have also adopted entirely different distributional and economic

6. Erika Balsom, "One Hundred Years of Low Definition" in: Martine Beugnet, Alain Cameron, Arild Fetveit (eds.), *Indefinite Visions. Cinema and the Attractions of Uncertainty*, Edinburgh University Press, Edinburgh 2017, pp. 73–89, here p. 87.

models – most notably in how each of them treats the print. "Whereas the limited number of prints avant-garde filmmakers strike is a function of their extraordinarily low budgets, in artists' film, prints are purposefully scarce, as scarcity is what makes them valuable in the art market".[7] If contemporary avant-garde filmmakers' answer to our period of media convergence is to mine the past for present and future by reaffirming and exceeding the qualities of their own medium,[8] Hockney the painter's answer is to unleash the most recent technical tools in order to revive the idea of painting. His choice of ever more sophisticated media seems to suggest that there is only one direction to rejuvenate painting – namely technological progress. If so, then his media works feed into the values of consumer culture, if not visual capitalism.

7. See note 5, p. 187.

8. See Jonathan Walley, *Cinema Expanded. Avant-Garde Film in the Age of Intermedia*, Oxford University Press, New York 2020, p. 23.

## Drawing on a Piece of Glass

In regards to the adoption of novel tools, Hockney's early iPhone and iPad drawings (2009–2011, pp. 69–75) are of special interest. The artist made use of an app called *Brushes*, which allows for drawing with one's fingers on the iPhone, and with a stylus pen on the iPad. His works in this medium, at times more graphic and linear, at others more painterly, evoking watercolours, are usually presented to the public as prints, after a first exhibition in the original format and media,[9] at scales far larger than the screen on which they were created, and sold in limited editions.

9. *David Hockney: Fleurs fraîches. Dessins sur iPhone et iPad,* Paris: Fondation Pierre Bergé–Yves Saint Laurent, 20.10.2010–30.1.2011.

From the outset, his regular subjects included landscapes, flowers, portraits or details of everyday life; but above all there were crystalline objects such as ashtrays, vases, bowls, bottles or window panes.[10] Thus, a link can be established between Hockney's attraction to water (as in his prominent swimming pool series, for example, pp. 42–47 and 53–55) and his fascination with the new tools' glassy surface, both belonging to the "diaphanous realm".[11] One could go even further and claim a kind of "liquid-crystal dynamic" in Hockney's work, converging in the smartphone and the tablet's liquid-crystal displays.

10. See https://www.hockney.com/works/digital/iphone and https://www.hockney.com/works/digital/ipad [retrieved on 7.10.2021].

11. Didier Ottinger, "Water, Glass, Screens: the Diaphanous Realm" in: *David Hockney. Pictures of Daily Life. New iPhone and iPad Drawings*, Galeries Lelong & Co., Paris 2018, p. 16.

Despite its technical novelty, the touchscreen reveals some nostalgia for older, more tactile interfaces as it responds to the finger's electrical conductivity. Unlike lens-based media, keeping us at a distance, the touchscreen – like painting – offers a direct bodily interaction with the artistic tool. Another reason for Hockney to embrace these devices is their spontaneity, quickness and ease of use. As opposed to avant-garde filmmakers, Hockney was never interested in labor-intensive tinkering with the machine. His own way of "playing against the apparatus" and overcoming its "automatism" (as Vilém Flusser would put it) is primarily conceptual, without giving much thought to its nuts and bolts.

Throughout Hockney's career, painting (and drawing) have been the bedrock of his art, not photography or film. Even when he explores lens-based or screen-based media, the conceptual basis for his expanded work remains painting, and thus can be rightly termed "painting expanded."[12]

12. "Painting expanded" echoes Walley's *Cinema Expanded* (2020), where he argues for the continuity of artistic identity even when the artist dispenses with the medium's specific characteristics, see note 8.

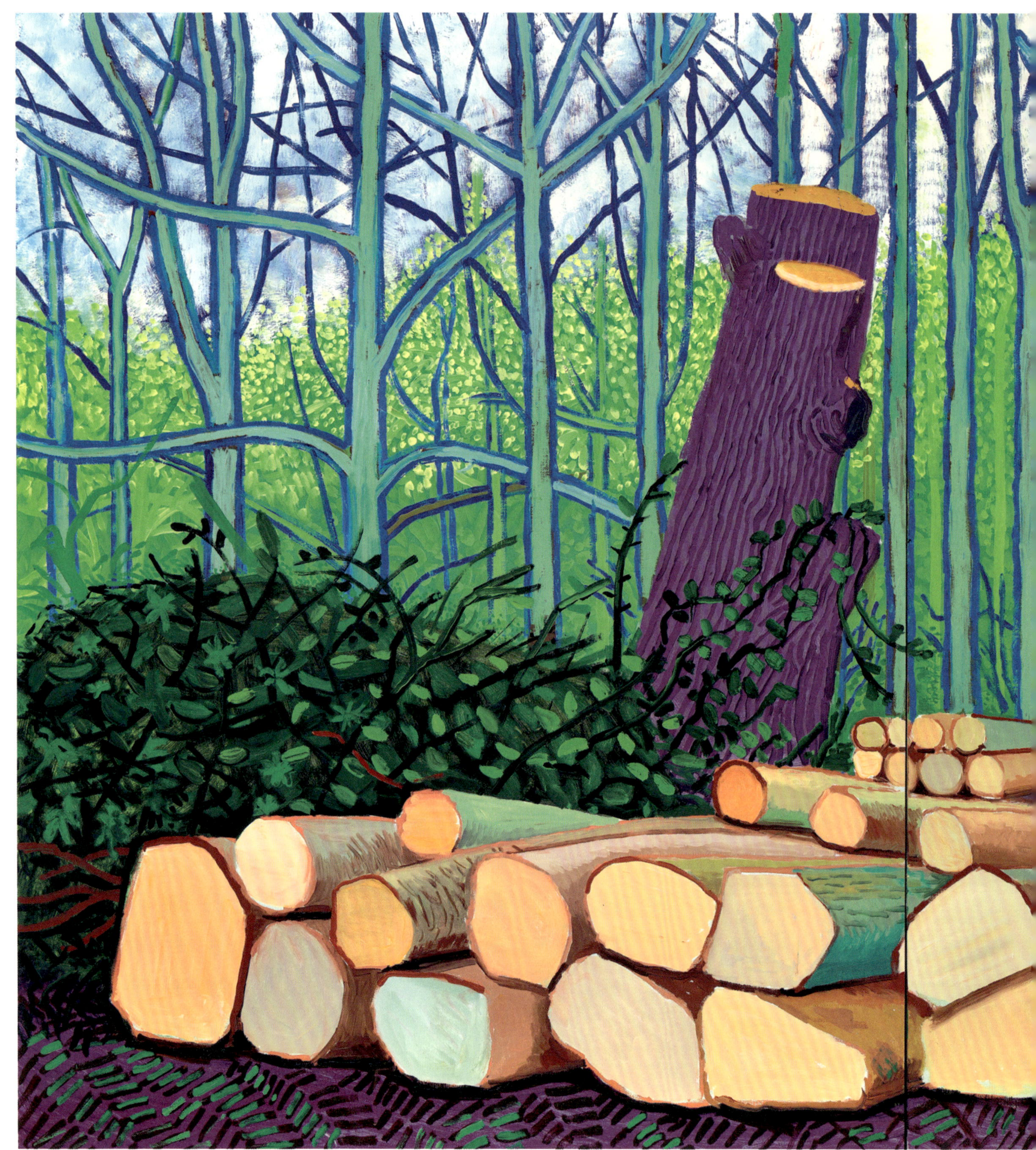

**Felled Trees on Woldgate,** 2008
Öl auf zwei Leinwänden | Oil on two canvases,
152,5 × 244 cm (gesamt)
Sammlung Würth
Inv. Nº 12129

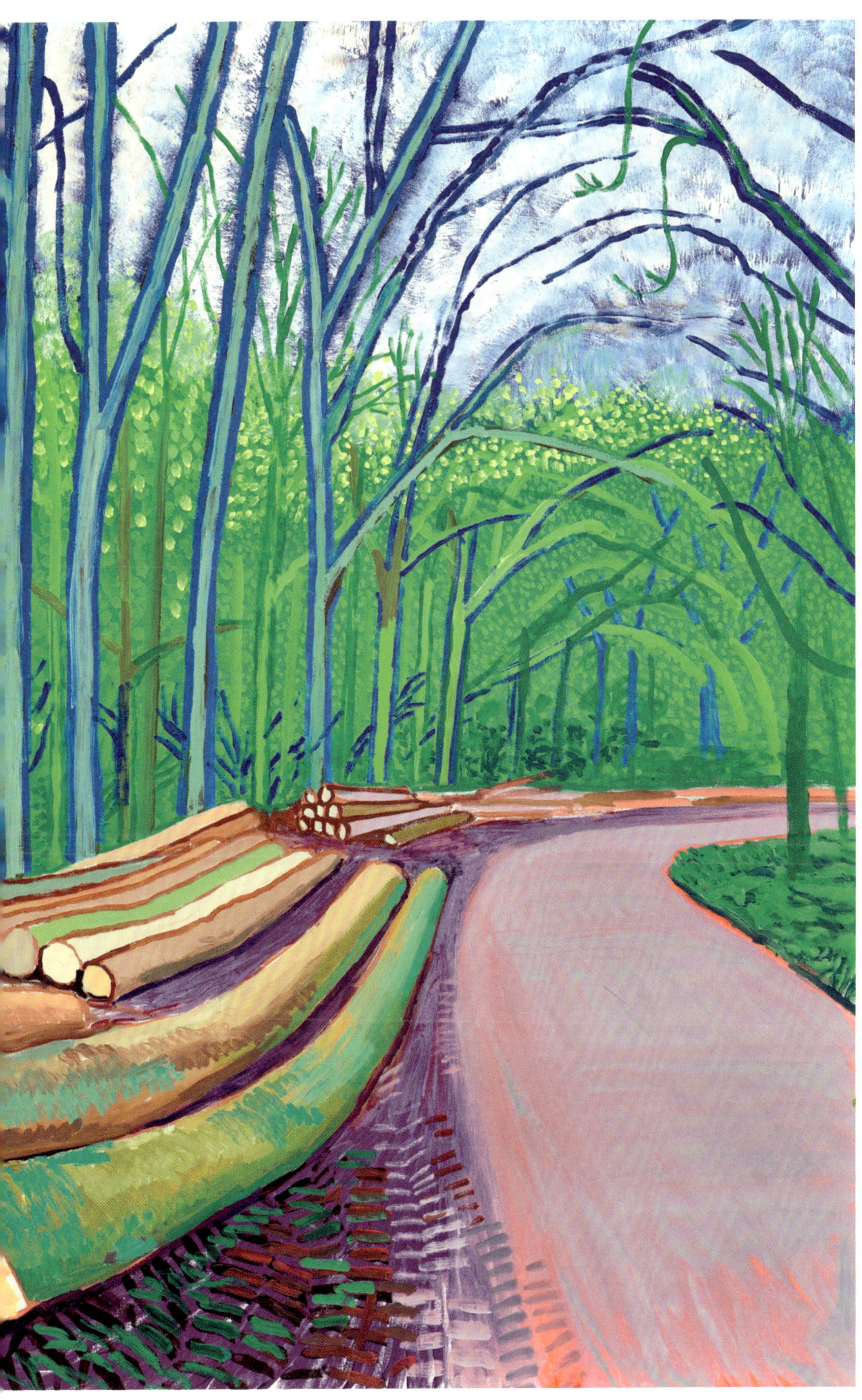

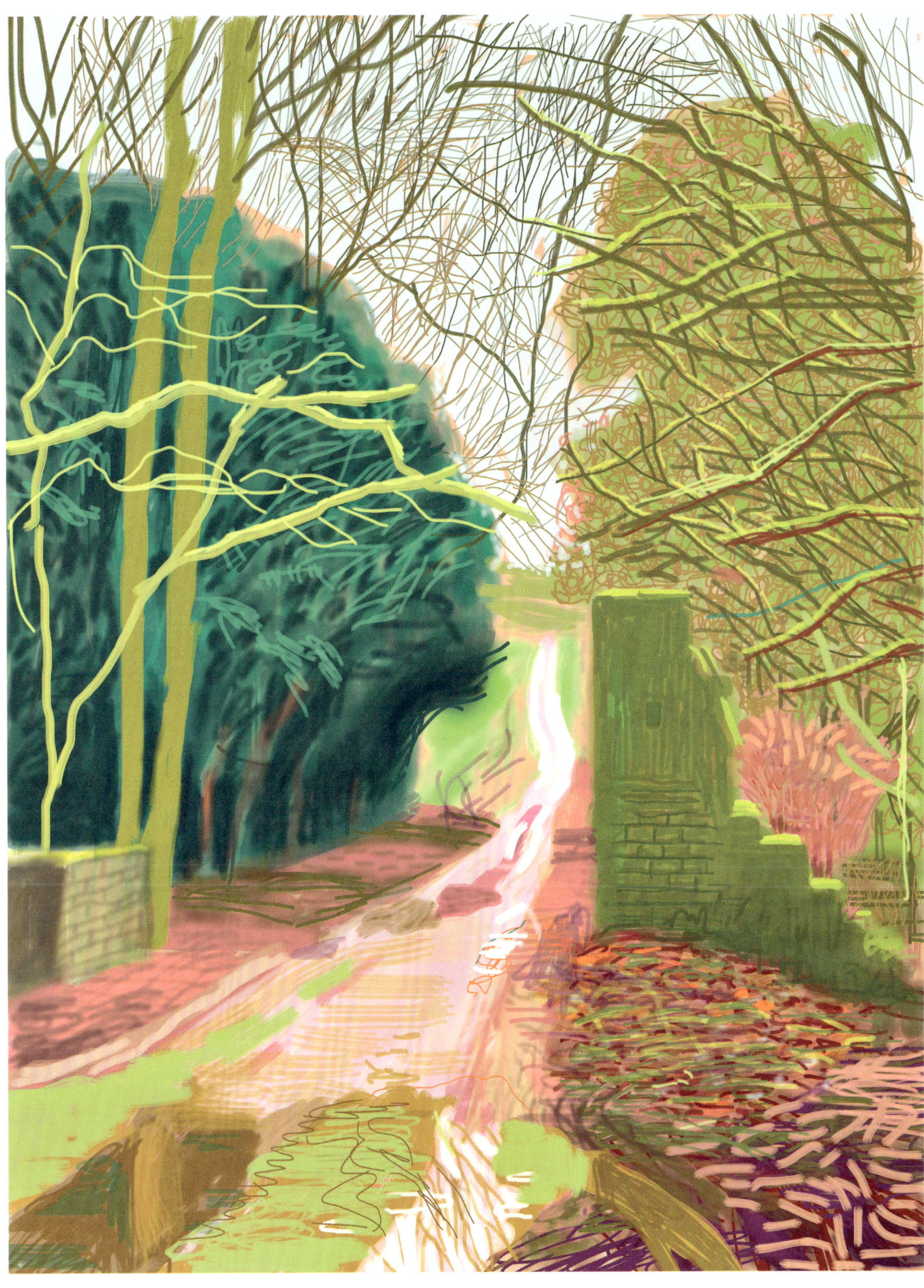

**The Arrival of Spring in Woldgate, East Yorkshire in 2011 (twenty eleven) – 29 January,** 2011
iPad-Zeichnung, gedruckt auf vier Blatt Papier, kaschiert auf vier Blätter Dibond (Auflage 10/10) | iPad drawing, printed on four sheets of paper, mounted on four sheets of Dibond (Edition 10/10),
236 × 178 cm
Vanhaerents Art Collection, Brussels

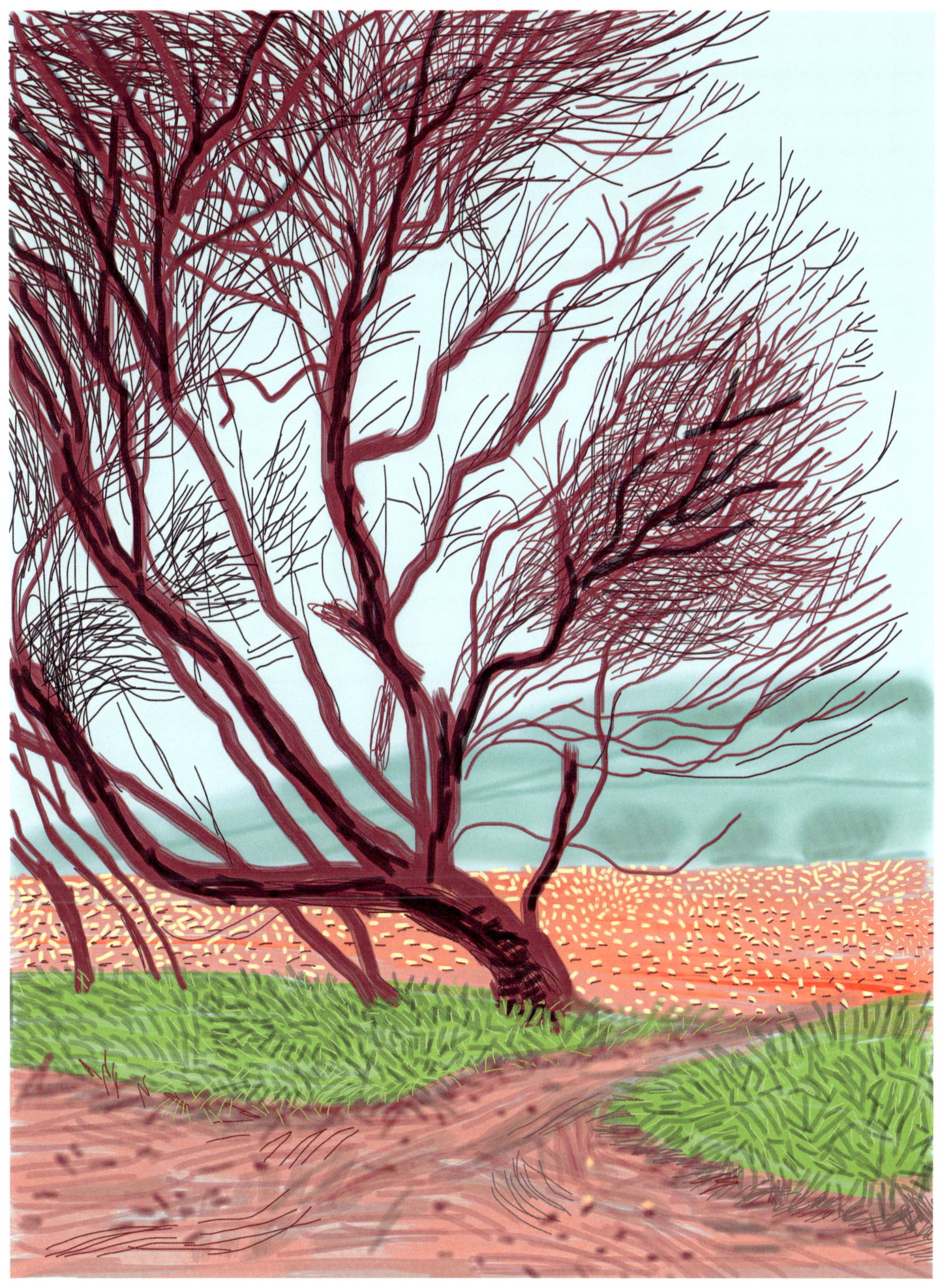

**The Arrival of Spring in Woldgate, East Yorkshire in 2011 (twenty eleven) – 18 March,** 2011
iPad-Zeichenanimation | iPad drawing animation,
variable Dimensionen | various dimensions
Courtesy of the artist

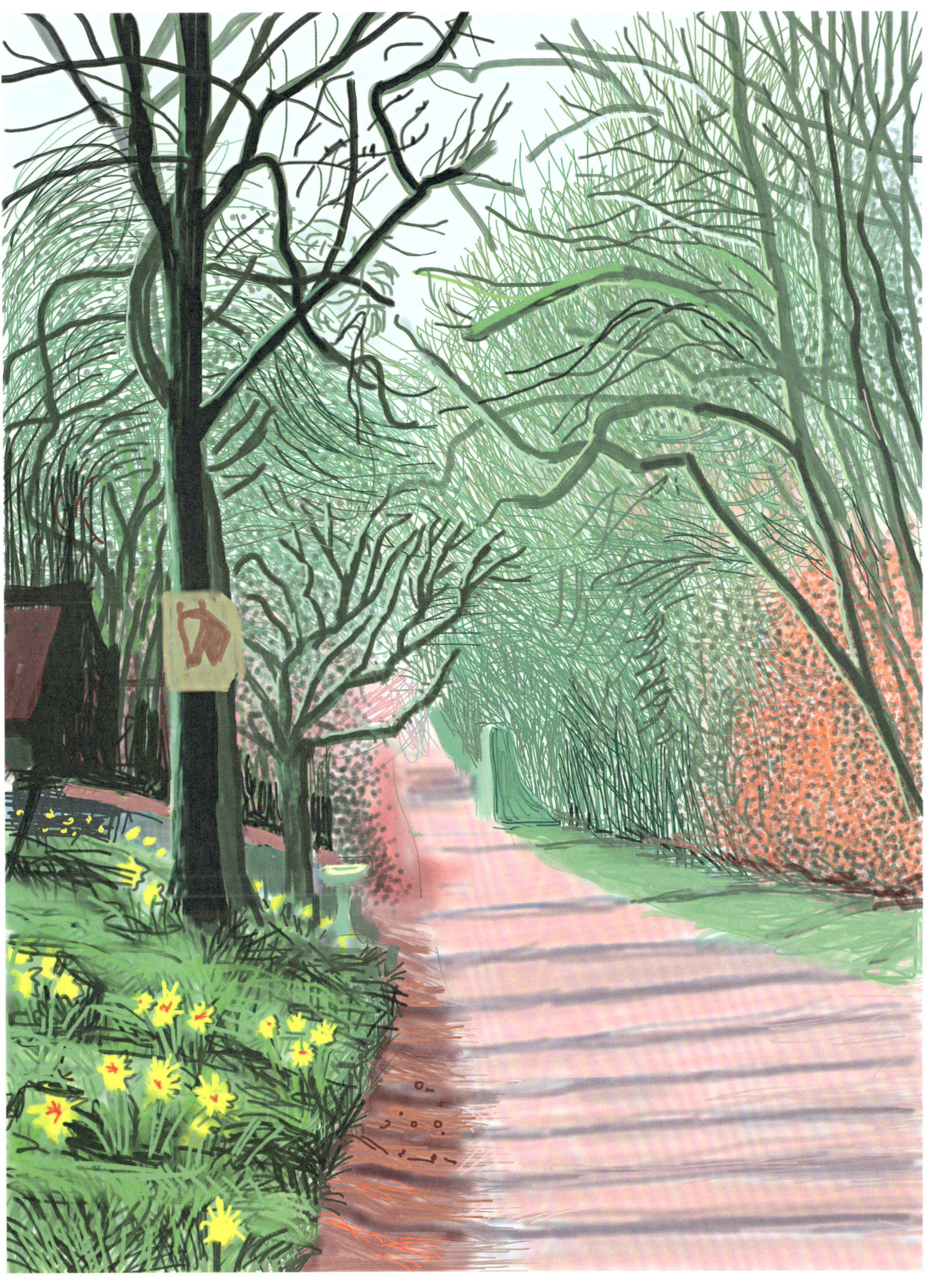

**The Arrival of Spring in Woldgate, East Yorkshire in 2011 (twenty eleven) – 25 March,** 2011
iPad-Zeichenanimation | iPad drawing animation, variable Dimensionen | various dimensions
Courtesy of the artist

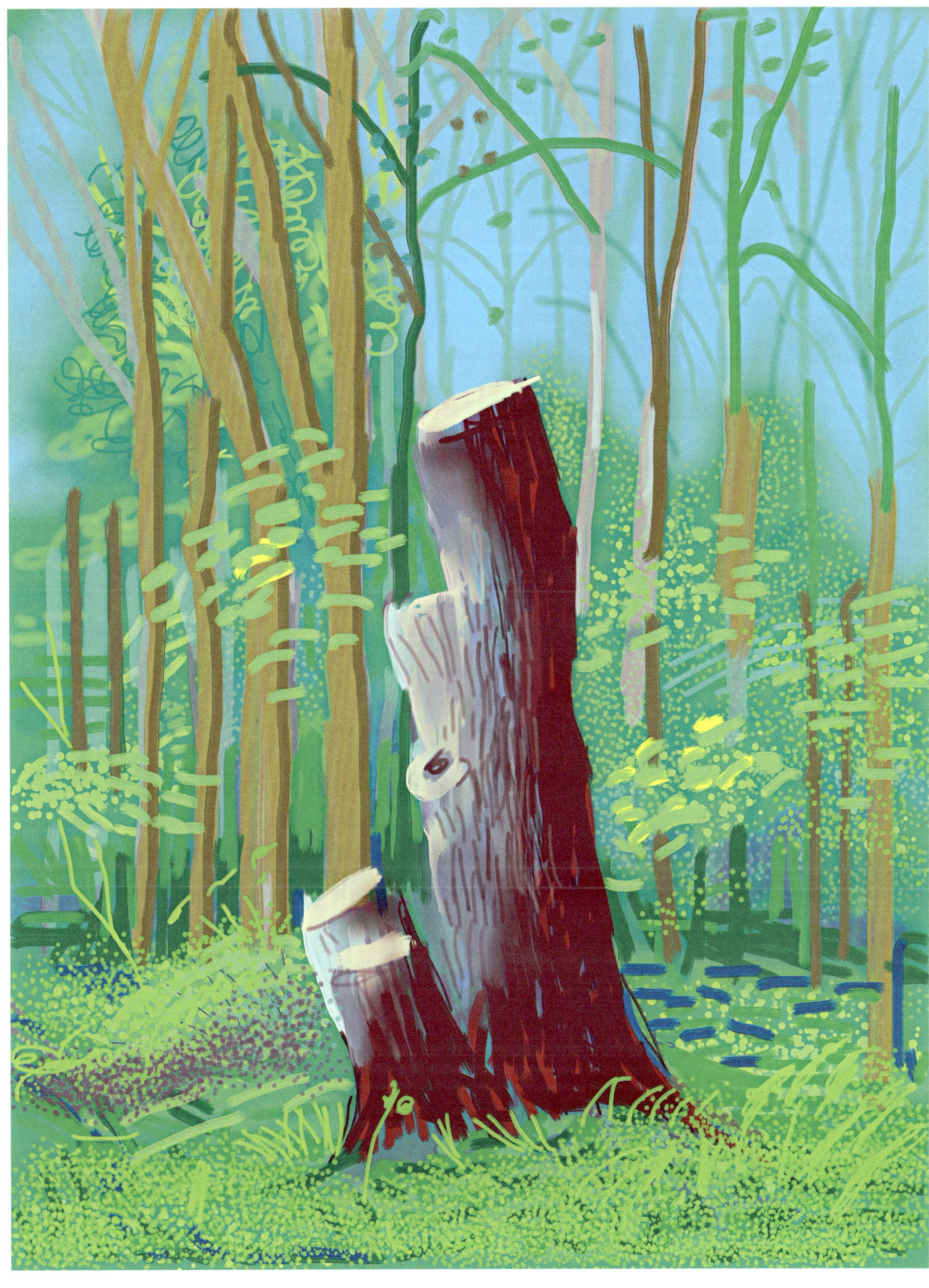

**The Arrival of Spring in Woldgate, East Yorkshire in 2011 (twenty eleven) – 24 April,** 2011
iPad-Zeichenanimation | iPad drawing animation,
variable Dimensionen | various dimensions
Courtesy of the artist

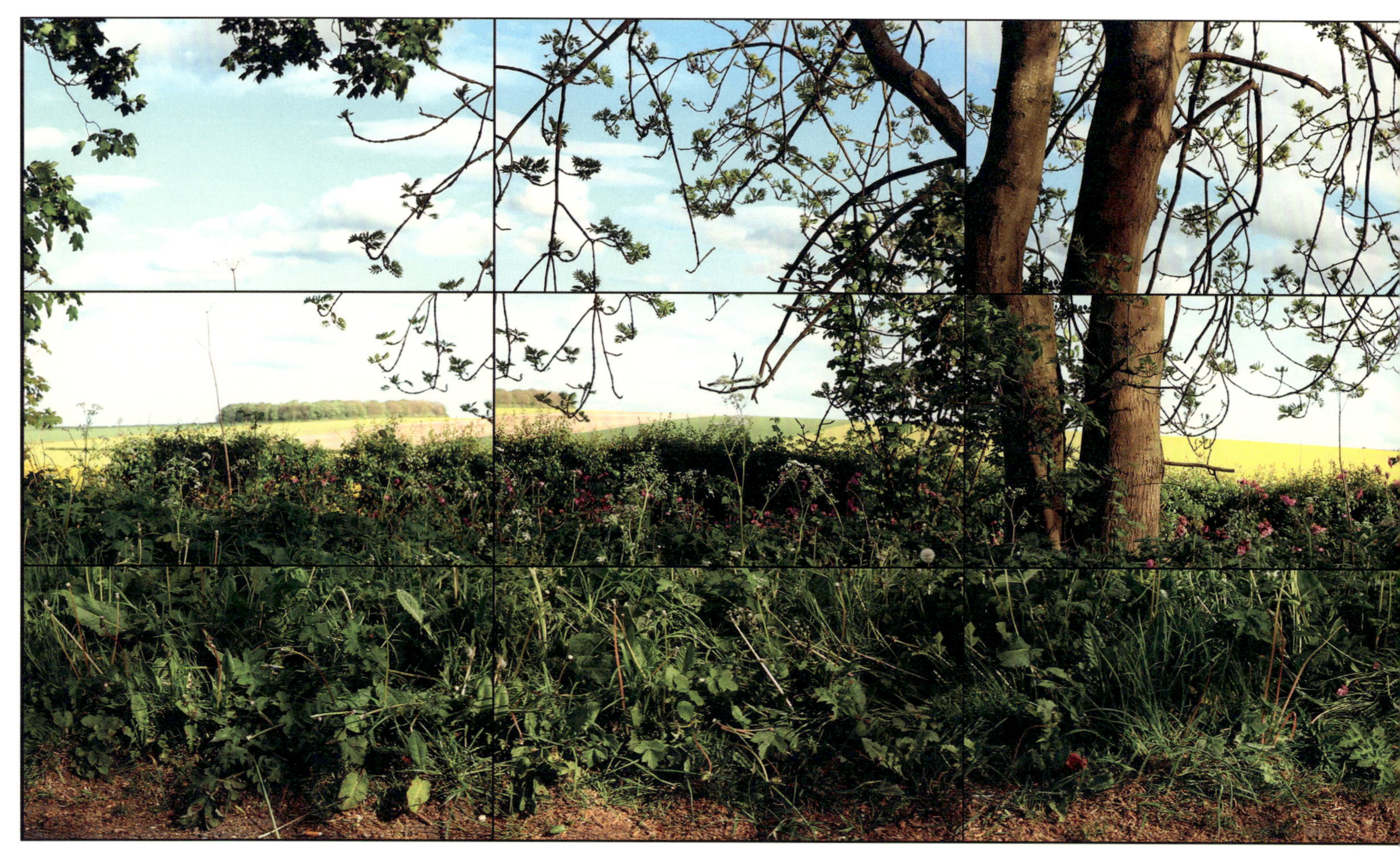

**Seven Yorkshire Landscapes 2011,** 2011
18 digitale Videos, synchronisiert und auf 18 Monitoren präsentiert (Auflage 6/10 + 2 E.A.) | 18 digital videos, synchronized and presented on 18 monitors (Edition 6/10 + 2 A.P.s), 205,7 × 729 × 22,9 cm, Länge | duration: 12'39"
Peress Family Collection
Inv. N° 59566.06

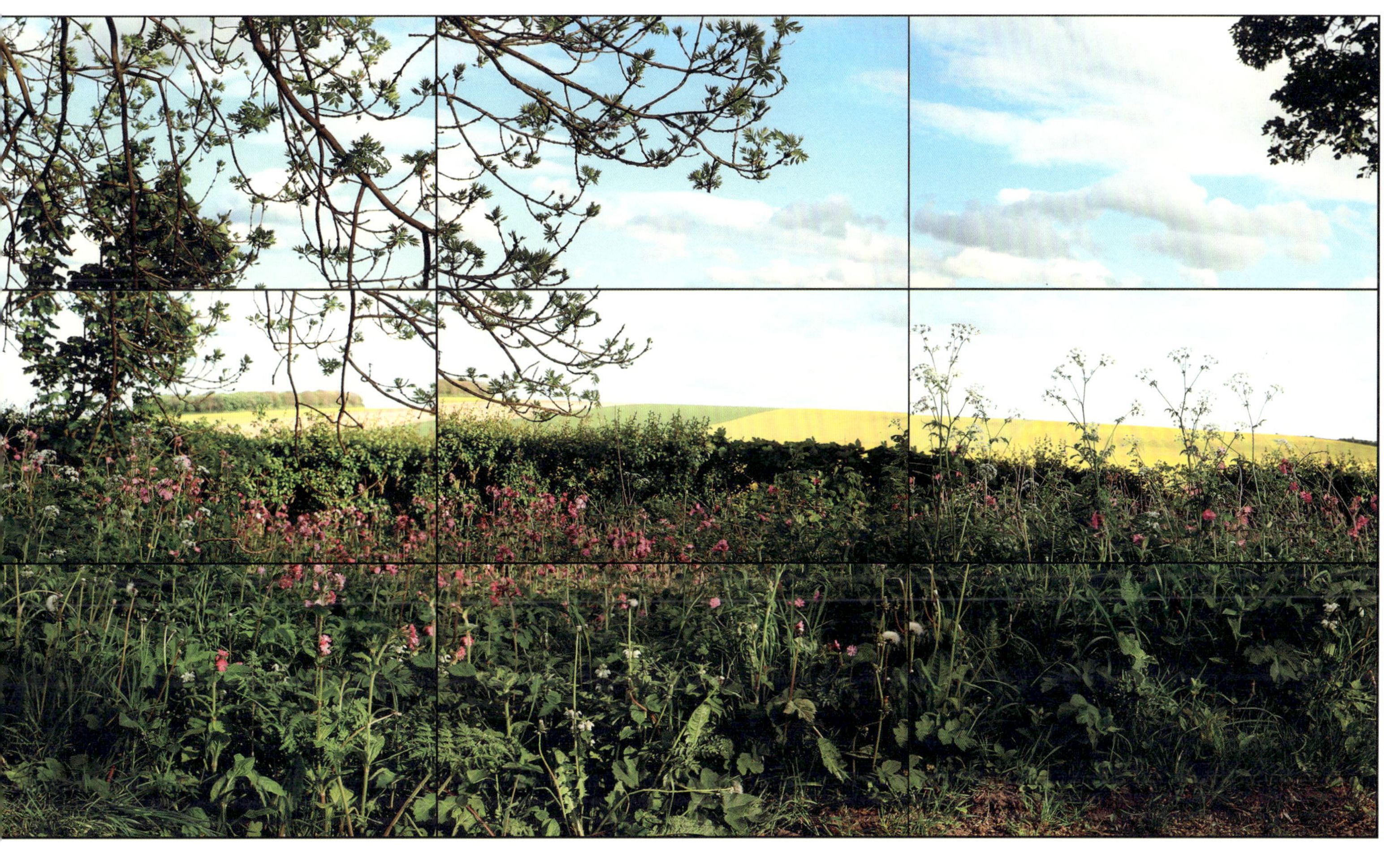

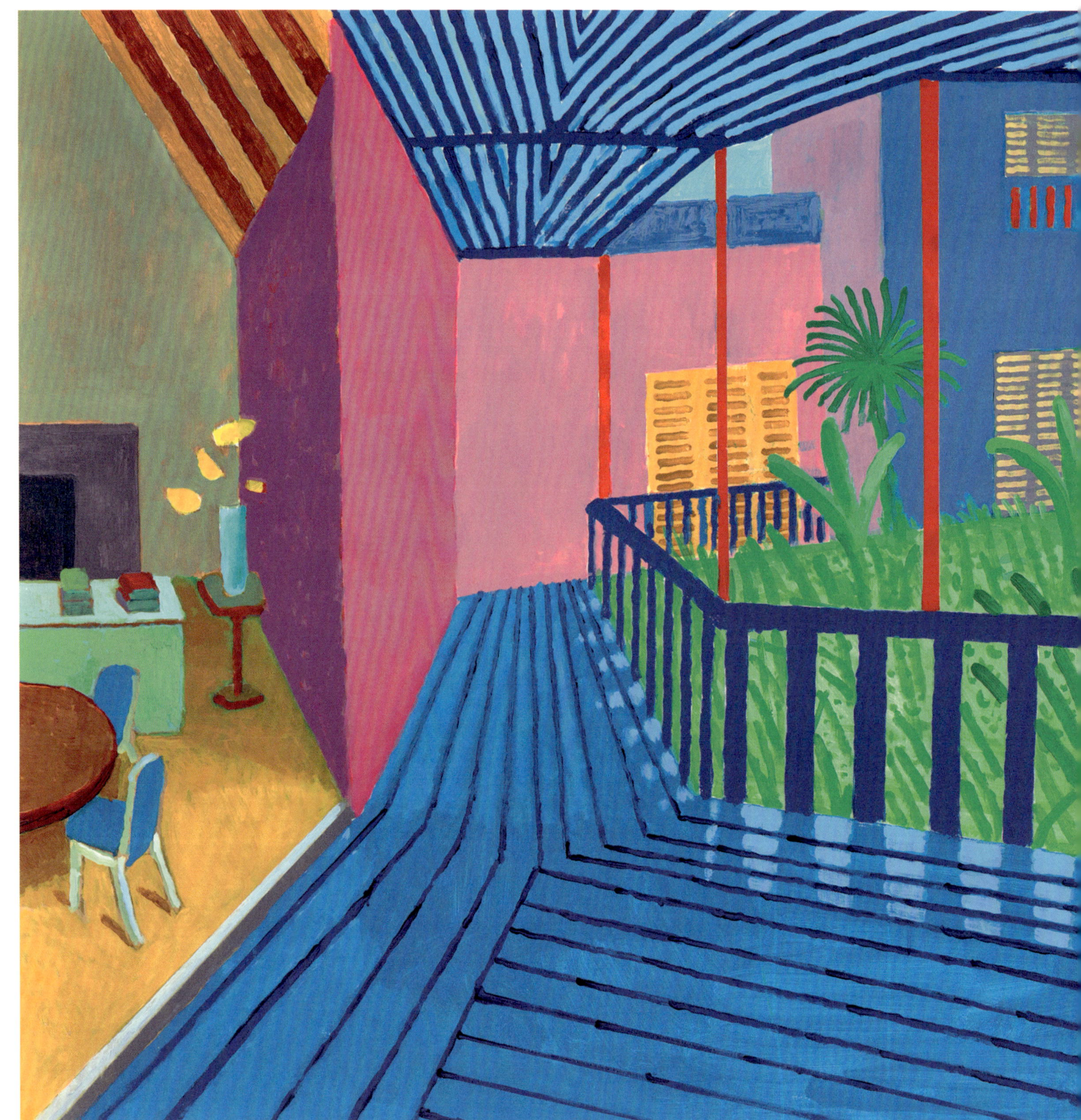

**Interior with Blue Terrace and Garden,** 2017
Acryl auf Leinwand | Acrylic on canvas,
121,9 × 243,8 cm
Privatsammlung, New York |
Private Collection, New York
Inv. N° 88735. Alt # 17A01, PAM 1442

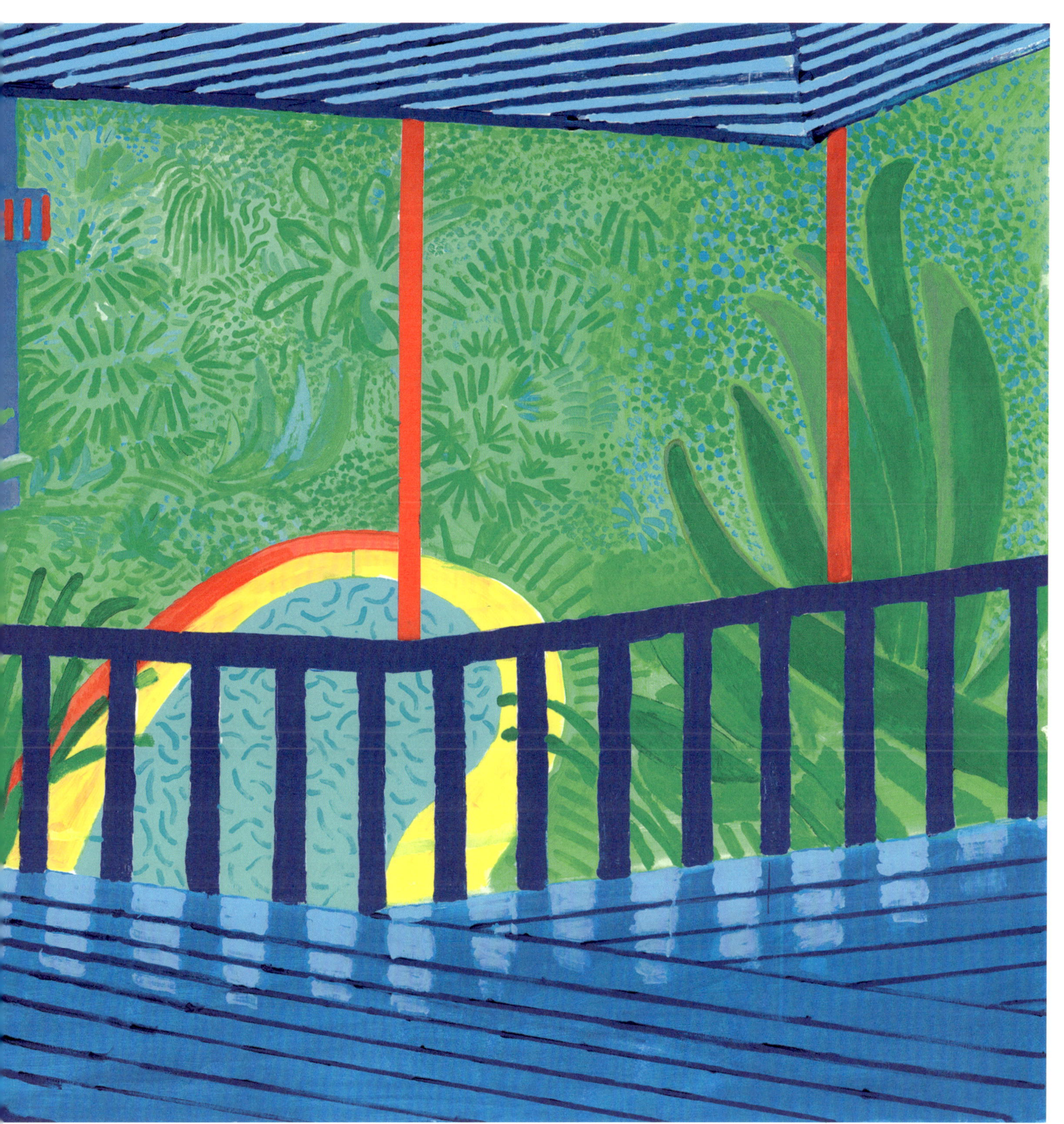

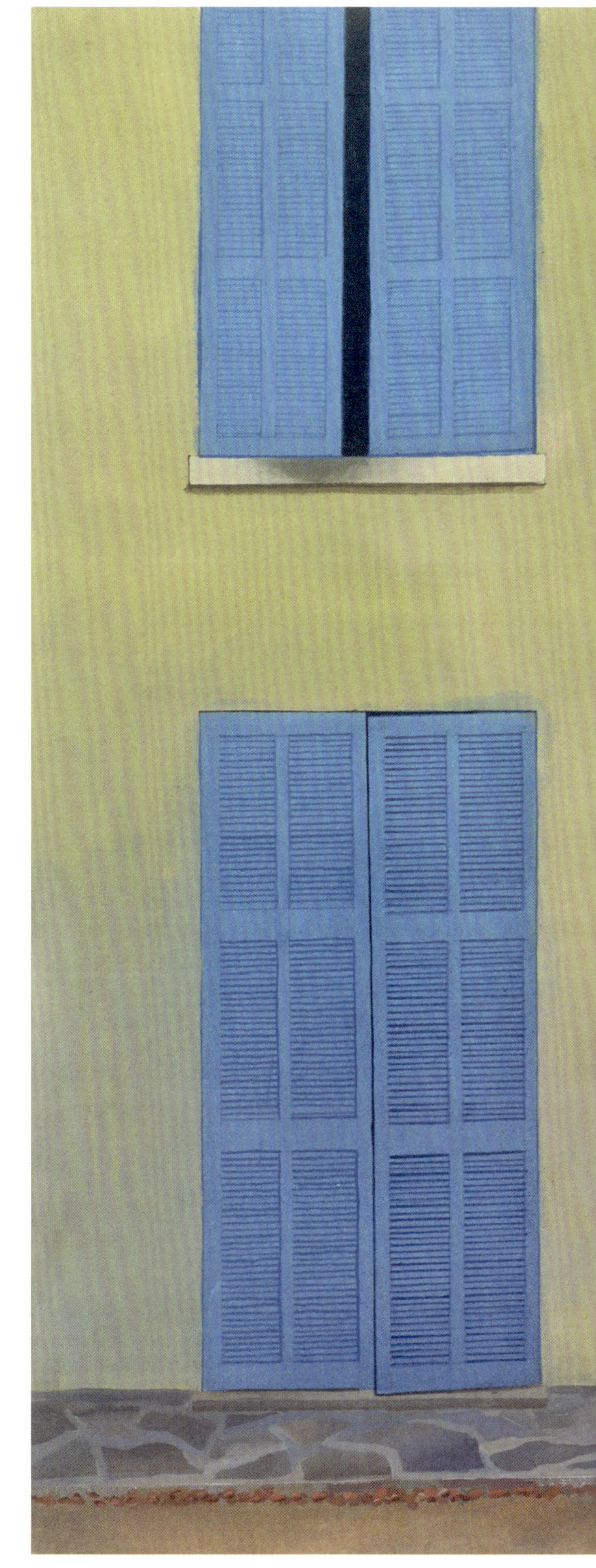

**Two Deck Chairs, Calvi,** 1972
Acryl auf Leinwand | Acrylic on canvas,
123,5 × 154,1 cm
Collection Museum Boijmans Van Beuningen,
Rotterdam
Inv. N° 2808 (MK)

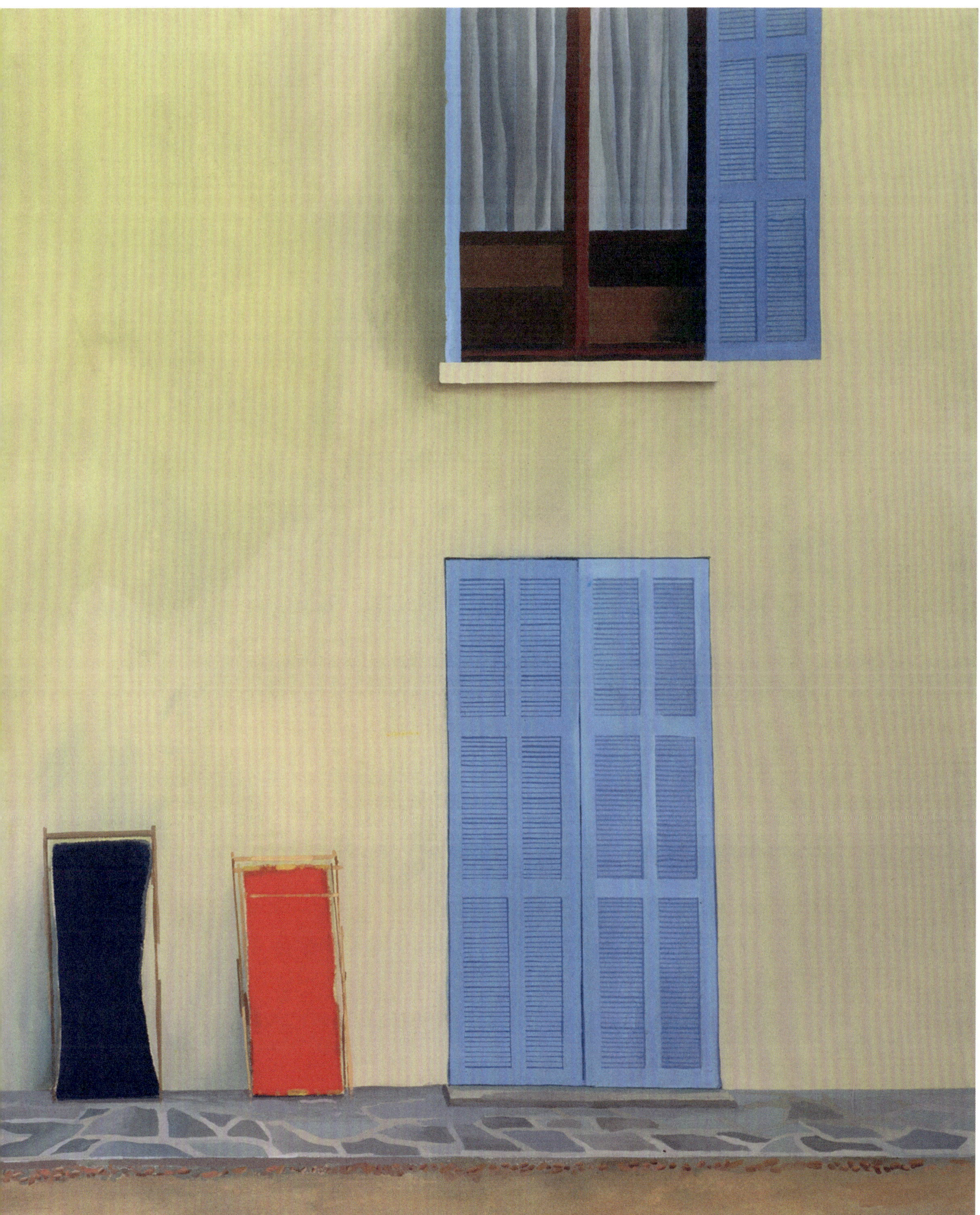

# David Hockney: Eine topografische Annäherung

Ob intime Studien exquisiter Körper oder epische Ansichten ferner Länder – David Hockneys Kunst nimmt uns mit auf eine visuelle Odyssee zu alten und neuen, vertrauten und exotischen, gelebten und imaginären Orten. Bereits in seinen frühesten Werken, die im London der Nachkriegszeit oder in der sexuellen Freizügigkeit und visuellen Dramatik Südkaliforniens angesiedelt sind, vermittelt er anschaulich die sinnliche Freude, die seine Umgebung ihm bereitet, und dasselbe gilt für seine neueren Panoramen, in denen er die Unermesslichkeit des Grand Canyon erfasst oder die Hügel von East Yorkshire in ihrem jahreszeitlichen Wandel dokumentiert (S. 69–75). Die Formen und Sujets sind stets in der unmittelbaren Umwelt des Künstlers verortet ebenso wie in den Figuren, die sie einzeln oder in Gruppen bevölkern und ihr eine menschliche und psychologische Dimension verleihen. So überrascht es kaum zu erfahren, dass Hockney nicht nur seine Porträts, sondern auch seine Landschaften als „Menschen" versteht – ebenso vital, voller Leben und in ständiger Bewegung begriffen wie diese.

Hockney gilt zwar als „*der* südkalifornische Maler par excellence", tatsächlich aber ist er nie allzu lang an einem Ort geblieben. Viele Jahre seines Lebens verbrachte er pendelnd zwischen London und Los Angeles; neue Anregungen und unterschiedliche Sichtweisen findet er jedoch meist auf seinen Reisen, die ihn in größere Fernen führen. Die formalen, historischen und anthropologischen Entdeckungen, die er in anderen Weltregionen machte – in China und Japan ebenso wie im Libanon und in Ägypten, in Norwegen und Spanien –, inspirierten und ermunterten ihn, unsere visuelle Welt aus Zeit, Bewegung und Raum unter neuen Blickwinkeln zu betrachten und zu entziffern. Über mehrere Jahre hinweg hinterfragte Hockney die Konventionen der Bildgebung, etwa in Ansichten wie *In The Studio, December 2017* (2017, S. 24–25), einer ambitionierten Fotostudie vom Interieur seines eigenen Ateliers hoch oben in den Hollywood Hills, ehe ihn seine Vorliebe für neue Medien und neue Gefilde vor mehreren Jahren bewog, von Kalifornien in die Normandie umzusiedeln. Um den Einzug des Frühlings festzuhalten, stand er früh auf und protokollierte grafisch den Wandel der Jahreszeiten und ihre Entfaltung als Narrativ in Echtzeit und *en plein air.* So erinnern uns seine detailliert gemalten und gezeichneten Landschaften in diesen turbulenten Zeiten immer wieder an die unaufhörliche wundersame Regeneration unserer Naturwelt. Blickt man auf die Anfänge seiner Karriere zurück, so wird deutlich, dass Hockneys Örtlichkeiten stets integraler Bestandteil seiner visuellen Erkundungen waren. Die intensive Auseinandersetzung mit der Frage der adäquaten Darstellung veranlasst den Künstler immer wieder, sich neuen Medien und Territorien zuzuwenden. Vor diesen Hintergrund richtet dieser Essay sein Augenmerk darauf, wie Hockneys Reisen und Auslandsaufenthalte in den 1960er-Jahren die Entwicklung seiner Arbeitspraxis beeinflussten. „Orte“ betrachtet er ebenso als Muse wie auch als Raum für die künstlerische Neuerfindung, um Themen wie Identität, Migration und Sexualität zu erörtern. Untersucht werden soll, auf welche Art und mit welchem Komplexitätsgrad Hockney subtile oder unbestimmbare Verbindungen in die Rhythmen und Muster einflocht, die seine erlebten Erfahrungen zu Beginn seiner Karriere prägten. Dieser Essay zeichnet die rasche Entwicklung einiger häufig wiederkehrender visueller Modi und Mittel des Künstlers vom Grafischen und Diagrammatischen zum Szenischen und Emblematischen nach, angefangen von der gestischen Abstraktion über konstruierte Realitäten bis hin zu Stadtlandschaften des Post-Pop. Dabei werden Hockneys „Topografien“ dieser Zeit nicht einfach als Ergebnis statischer Betrachtung dargestellt, sondern vielmehr als komplexe Synthese von Realität, Appropriation und Fantasie, die seinen Wunsch kennzeichnen, Dinge so einzufangen, wie sie heute gesehen und erinnert werden.

## Zur Definition eines neuen Bildes

*The Third Love Painting* (1960, S. 180–181) ist ein grob ausgeführtes Gemälde, das gestische Pinselführung mit Graffiti verbindet und den Trubel und die Entrechtung der innerstädtischen Bevölkerung ebenso heraufbeschwört wie das wachsende Bewusstsein des Künstlers für die in London aufkommende Subkultur queerer Treffpunkte. Trotz der bewusst nichtrealistischen Darstellung ist das codierte Repertoire an Wörtern und phallischen Formen dennoch insofern in der Realität verankert, als es auch in einer Welt von Zeichen und Formen am Leben festhält. Das Werk, das bereits jene abstrakten Formen erkennen lässt, die Hockney als Propaganda für queere Liebe bezeichnete, entstand zur Zeit seiner Ankunft in London im Herbst 1959, wo er am Royal College of Art ein weiterführendes Studium begann. Diese Erfahrung war eine Offenbarung für einen Künstler aus dem Norden Englands, von dem die Metropole „sehr weit weg“ schien.[1] Im Gegensatz zu *Woman with a Sewing Machine* (1954, S. 179) und anderen Darstellungen des häuslichen Arbeiter*innenlebens im Stil des Sozialistischen Realismus – einem Sujet, das während seiner Ausbildung an der Bradford School of Art (1953–1957) bevorzugt gelehrt wurde – begann Hockney nach 1960 mit einer Reihe von Gemälden, in denen er eine komplexe Vielfalt formaler und rhetorischer Mittel verwendete. So verband er abstrakte Passagen mit bestimmten Bildmotiven, die er aus Fotografien oder anderen Kunstwerken übernahm, um aufreizend voyeuristische Reisen durch persönliche Beziehungen, Situationen und private Räume zu unternehmen. Diese Werke sind Ausdruck einer neuen Generation von Kunstschaffenden, die das traditionelle Landschaftsgenre von ihrer Themenliste verbannt hat, und als solche schöpfen sie teils direkt aus dem Leben und teils aus anderen Quellen, um die Vorherrschaft der abstrakten Malerei zu brechen und eine neue Form der urbanen Kultur zu reflektieren.

1. David Hockney, zitiert in: Martin Gayford, *A Bigger Message. Gespräche mit David Hockney*, Bern (Piet Meyer Verlag) 2012, S. 136.

Hockneys sehr eigene Methode der Darstellung von Orten, Objekten und Figuren zeigt sich auch in *Tea Painting in an Illusionistic Style* (1961, S. 109), dem letzten von drei Bildern, die von der unverkennbaren rot-schwarzen Verpackung der Typhoo-Teebeutel, dem Lieblingstee seiner Mutter, inspiriert waren. Dieses durch und durch englische Symbol kann als ironischer Kommentar zu der seinerzeit vorherrschenden Begeisterung für Importe aus den USA verstanden werden: Der Typhoo-Slogan „The tea that puts the ‚T' in Britain" spielt mit der Standarderklärung aller Britinnen und Briten, warum sie in heiklen Situationen gern eine Tasse Tee trinken. Dazu Hockney: „Ich ging immer sehr früh ins Royal College of Art ... bevor Lyons in South Kensington geöffnet hatte, und machte mir selbst meinen Tee ... es war immer Tee von Typhoo, der Lieblingsmarke meiner Mutter ... Die Teepackungen stapelten sich genauso wie die Dosen und Tuben mit Farben ... und ich dachte mir, dass das für mich in gewisser Hinsicht ein Stillleben ist ... Da stand eine Packung Typhoo-Tee, eine ganz gängige, beliebte Teemarke, also habe ich sie als Motiv hergenommen. So nah bin ich der Pop-Art nie wieder gekommen."[2]

2. David Hockney, zitiert in: Nikos Stangos (Hrsg.), *David Hockney by David Hockney*, London (Thames & Hudson) 1976, S. 63f.

Mit dem vertrauten Design der Teepackung und ihrer typischen Form verleiht Hockney seinem Bild ein Element, das die behagliche Atmosphäre seines Zuhauses in Bradford versinnbildlicht, und vermittelt uns durch die speziell konstruierte Leinwand den Eindruck, dass wir ein Bild der Welt betrachten, aber nicht die Welt selbst. Die in einem Raum von beklemmender Enge sitzende Figur, die die gesellschaftliche Außenseiterrolle des Künstlers verdeutlicht, wurde vielfach in Bezug auf Hockneys Homosexualität interpretiert, doch die Präsentation des Gemäldes in der Ausstellung *Young Contemporaries* von 1962 ebnete ihm den Weg in die etablierte Kunstwelt. Sein dandyhaftes Auftreten und seine Identität als Künstler aus der nordenglischen Arbeiterklasse galten jetzt – zumal in der Boulevardpresse – als Insignien eines Aufsteigers, der ein neues ikonoklastisches Bild großstädtischen Lebens geschaffen hatte. Diese Stilisierung des Künstlerkörpers zu einem starken Symbol Londons sollte bis weit in die 1960er-Jahre hinein andauern, auch wenn Hockney selbst Großbritannien zunehmend den Rücken kehrte.

## A Marriage of Styles – Eine Verbindung von Stilen

Hockneys Wunsch nach stärkerer Figuration und emotionalerem Gehalt in seinen Bildern zeigt sich in einem vage autobiografischen Gemälde, zu dem er durch seine erste Italienreise im Dezember 1961 angeregt wurde. Im Gegensatz zu früheren Werken, in denen sich hinter traumartigen Fantasien eine brutalere Realität verbirgt, dokumentiert *Flight Into Italy – Swiss Landscape* (1962, S. 102–103) die merkwürdige Erfahrung einer Landschaft, die auf der Reise des Künstlers durch die Alpen auf dem Weg nach Florenz sowohl flüchtig gesehen als auch imaginiert wurde: „Besonders habe ich mich auf die Alpen gefreut und mir gedacht: Ich werde die Alpen sehen, die sind doch ein richtiges Sujet für ein Bild: Berglandschaften in den Alpen. Ich liebe die Düsternis des Nordens ebenso sehr wie die Sonne des Mittelmeers und Kaliforniens, und ich stellte mir vor, wie die nebligen Alpen mich richtig ergreifen würden. Aber leider habe ich sie nicht gesehen."[3]

3. Ibid., S. 87.

In *Flight Into Italy – Swiss Landscape* halten sich Persönliches und Objektives die Waage, zugleich wird das Problem thematisiert, wie eine Landschaft darzustellen ist, ohne naturalistisch zu sein. Das Gemälde zeigt eine Schweizer Bergkette auf unterschiedliche Arten und in verschiedenen Repräsentationsmodi: von den aus Geografiebüchern bekannten geschichteten Farbbändern und der Farbfeldmalerei über die Darstellung der Berghöhe und den vogelperspektivischen Blick auf die Straße bis hin zum collagierten Ausschnitt eines Berggipfels aus einer Postkarte und einem flüchtig gemalten, für die Gegend typischen Haus im Chalet-Stil. Auf der Fahrt durch die Region, bei der der Künstler die beeindruckende Landschaft um sich her kaum wahrnimmt und vom Rücksitz des Morris-Vans seines Freundes lediglich den Blick auf ein oder zwei Berge erhascht, erkennen wir nach und nach die ironischen Anspielungen des Bildes, die nicht nur Hockneys Reise grafisch als Landkarte und szenisch durch die Zeit vermitteln, sondern auch daran erinnern wollen, dass unsere Vorstellungen und Erwartungen darüber, wie eine fremde Landschaft auszusehen hat, von visuellen Klischees geprägt sind. Insofern könnte man *Flight Into Italy – Swiss Landscape* als ein Bild begreifen, das mit kultureller Repräsentation spielt und den Wert des tatsächlichen Erlebens eines Ortes hinterfragt, indem es die flüchtige und somit „unechte" Erfahrung des Künstlers als Readymade-Landschaft wie eine Souvenirpostkarte für all jene präsentiert, die sie nicht mit eigenen Augen sehen können. Wenig später ging Hockney dazu über, seine Reisen mithilfe einer Kamera festzuhalten, wobei er Architektur und Menschen knipste wie jeder andere Tourist auch: „Das ist wie der visuelle Beweis der eigenen Existenz", sagte er einmal, „wie eine Dokumentation der eigenen Zeit."[4]

Hockneys anhaltendes Interesse, die Grenzen zwischen Realität, Fiktion und Kunstfertigkeit zu verwischen, zeigt sich auch in den Werken, die er schuf, nachdem er im Sommer 1962 von seiner zweiten Europareise nach London zurückgekehrt war, deren letzte Etappen ihn nach München und Westberlin geführt hatten. Die Faszination, die Berlin auf ihn ausübte, verdankte sich den berühmten Romanen Christopher Isherwoods und ihren Schilderungen des trotzigen Vorkriegshedonismus in den dortigen Cafés, Bars und Bordellen. Diese Reise rückt Hockney in den Kontext jener komplexen, sich ständig verlagernden Geografien exilierter queerer Männer, die sich in den 1960er-Jahren mehr und mehr zu den modernen Subkulturen Nordeuropas hingezogen fühlten. Dies steht im Gegensatz zur traditionell homoerotisch geprägten Kultur der Länder des südlichen Mittelmeerraums mit ihren Verweisen auf die griechische Liebe und ihre idealisierten Darstellungen der klassischen Antike – eine Idee, die Hockney in *Renaissance Head* (1963, S. 96–97) unterwandert.[5] Vor diesem Hintergrund könnte man andere Bilder wie *Berlin: A Souvenir* (1962–1963) mit den abstrahierten Gruppierungen männlicher Akte unter dem Schriftzug „BERLIN" und *The Berliner and the Bavarian* (1962, S. 104), in dem stereotype Vertreter dieser Regionen gegenübergestellt werden, als Porträts einer Stadt verstehen, deren legendäre Kultur von Freiheit und Dekadenz in der Wirklichkeit von der politischen Unsicherheit des Kalten Kriegs überschattet wurde. Die historischen Museen Berlins boten dem Künstler jedoch unerwartete Anregungen, und sie bilden die Grundlage mehrerer Gemälde, in denen er sich mit Ruhe und Bewegung auseinandersetzt und die Beziehung zwischen zwei Figuren komplex gestaltet. Wie sich der Künstler erinnerte: „Irgendwie kann ich ein Museum nie im selben Tempo wie die anderen Besucher besichtigen, und als ich mit Jeff [Goodman] im Pergamon-Museum war, wurden wir getrennt. Plötzlich sah ich ihn dann neben einer ägyptischen Skulptur stehen, die er allerdings nicht beachtete, weil er gerade in etwas anderes an der Wand vertieft war. Beide Figuren schauten in dieselbe Richtung, und ich fand es amüsant, dass sie auf den ersten Blick wie vereint wirkten."[6]

Aus dieser Erinnerung heraus entstand als erstes Gemälde *The First Marriage (A Marriage of Styles I),* (1962, S. 105), in dem Jeff und die anonyme Skulptur wie ein Ehemann und seine Frau wirken. Darin spielt Hockney mit der kurzzeitig

**4.** David Hockney, zitiert in: „David Hockney", in: *Andy Warhol's Interview,* Juli 1972, o. S. Von der Verfasserin eingesehen in den Pressemappen der Tate.

**5.** Eine umfassendere Abhandlung zur Geschichte queerer Migration findet sich in Paul Melia, „Showers, Pools and Power", in: Paul Melia (Hrsg.), *David Hockney*, Manchester und New York (Manchester University Press) 1995, S. 50–52.

**6.** Wie Anm. 2, hier S. 89.

glaubhaften, aber doch unscharfen Beziehung der beiden Figuren und kontrastiert unterschiedliche visuelle Stile. Anders als beim naturalistischen Ansatz einer die Wirklichkeit nachbildenden Darstellung, in der jedes Detail der betreffenden Szene gezeigt wird, ließ der Maler hier einen Großteil der Leinwand leer und verzichtete auf alle Kohärenz schaffenden Elemente, sodass sich unser Blick allein auf den seiner Ansicht nach wesentlichen Aufmerksamkeitsgehalt richtet. Wie in den *Illustrations for Fourteen Poems from C. P. Cavafy* (1966, S. 126–133), die auf den Erlebnissen des Dichters in Alexandria beruhen, aber ins moderne Beirut verlegt wurden, wohin Hockney für vorbereitende Studien reisen konnte, transportieren die eingefügten Requisiten – unter anderem weißer Sand, eine Palme und ferne Berge – die Figuren von Berlin in eine neue, uneindeutig exotische Umgebung, wodurch das Gemälde vom realen Leben in eine erdachte oder erfundene Bilderwelt und wieder zurück gewendet wird.

## Das gelobte Land

Die dunklen verschmierten Stellen und Farbflecken in Hockneys Gemälden aus der trübseligen Zeit nach Aufhebung der Rationierungen in London fehlen in den Radierungen, die mit den befreienden Folgen seiner ersten Amerikareise im Sommer 1961 in Zusammenhang stehen. In den drei Monaten, die der Künstler in New York verbrachte, verband er sein Interesse an der Stadt rasch mit sexuellem Vergnügen und der Suche nach einer kathartischeren, aufgeschlosseneren Kultur: „Die schiere Energie der Stadt faszinierte mich. Alles war erstaunlich sexy und unglaublich leicht. Die Menschen waren wesentlich offener, ich fühlte mich völlig frei. New York war rund um die Uhr in Betrieb. Greenwich City hatte nie geschlossen, die Buchhandlungen blieben die ganze Nacht auf, sodass man in ihnen stöbern konnte, das schwule Leben war viel stärker organisiert, und ich dachte mir: ‚Das ist genau der richtige Ort für mich.'"[7]

Das erste in Amerika entstandene Werk Hockneys, die kleine Radierung *My Bonnie Lies Over the Ocean* (1961–1962, S. 183) verbindet grafische Symbole, Schrift und ein populäres Volkslied, um etwas anzudeuten, das Bildern im Grunde unmöglich ist: eine Fahrt über ein gewaltiges Meer, das den Künstler von seiner Heimat trennt, sowie Situationen und Beziehungen, und das alles innerhalb einer einzigen statischen Darstellung. Ähnlich erzählen die sechzehn Tafeln des Radierungszyklus *A Rake's Progress* (1961–1963, S. 118–125) eine autobiografische Geschichte über die Erfahrung des Künstlers bei seiner Ankunft in New York. Für den amerikanischen Pop-Art-Künstler Andy Warhol (1928–1987), dessen Leben und Arbeit als Synonym für die Metropole gelten kann (und der 1972 mit Hockney ein Gespräch für sein Magazin *Andy Warhol's Interview* führte), repräsentieren Hockneys episodenhafte Begegnungen mit der kulturellen Ikonografie, die er in den Tafeln namentlich benennt – seien es das Chrysler Building und der Madison Square Garden oder die Figuren des öffentlichen Lebens auf den Straßen der Stadt wie Prediger, Entertainer und Wahlkämpfer –, die metaphorischen Wandlungen, die Hockney durchlebte, während er im amerikanischen Wohlleben aufging, „und zwar mit der erklärten Absicht", wie Warhol betonte, „dass man, wenn es ein Leben zu leben gibt, dieses genau so leben soll".[8] Die gängige Meinung, New York sei eine Stadt der unbegrenzten Möglichkeiten, wird in Hockneys künstlerischer Reaktion allerdings hinterfragt: Sie lässt – bestätigt durch die Details seiner erzählenden

**7.** David Hockney, zitiert in: Christopher Simon Sykes, *Hockney: The Biography. 1937–1975*, Bd. I, London (Century) 2011, S. 95f.

**8.** Wie Anm. 4, o. S.

Bilder – eine ganz anders geartete Realität erahnen, nämlich diejenige einer von sozialen Grenzen und ökonomischer Ungerechtigkeit geprägten Stadt, die er ironisierend mit dem Elend vergleicht, das der britische Maler William Hogarth in den 1730er-Jahren in London dokumentierte: „Du sprichst von einer Version des Rake's Progress, die ich nur machte, weil New York mich so sehr an das London des 18. Jahrhunderts erinnert hat, und zwar insofern, als die Menschen dort einfach auf der Straße zu sterben schienen, ohne dass es irgendwen gekümmert hätte. In England dagegen, wenn dort einer auf der Straße starb, dann holte man einen Krankenwagen, setzte ihm eine Suppe vor und legte ihn in einen Saal, und alles war gut… Es erinnerte mich wirklich an Hogarth, und als ich wieder in England war, beschloss ich, eine moderne Version davon zu machen."[9]

9. Wie Anm. 4, o. S.

Auch Hockneys erste Begegnung mit Südkalifornien im Jahr 1963 und seine Entscheidung im darauffolgenden Jahr, Los Angeles zu seiner zweiten Heimat zu machen, wurde vorwiegend durch die Wunschvorstellungen des Künstlers von einer besonderen Art der Freiheit und einem auf Glamour, Sonnenschein und Sex ausgerichteten Gefühlsleben bestimmt. Aufgrund dieser Bilder, die in den Jahren rasanter urbaner Expansion, unaufhaltsamen Bevölkerungswachstums und rasch zunehmenden Tourismus entstandenen sind und die mit ihren Sujets – Palmen, Rasensprenger, junge Männer unter Duschen, Swimmingpools und modernistische Architektur – den reinen Hedonismus zelebrieren, galt Hockney schließlich als derjenige Künstler, der Kalifornien gleichsam „erfunden hat"(S. 42–57). Der Ruf, die visuelle Identität der Stadt definiert zu haben, war endgültig besiegelt, als der Architekturkritiker Reyner Banham Hockneys berühmtes Gemälde *A Bigger Splash* (1967) als Covermotiv für sein 1971 erschienenes Buch *Los Angeles: The Architecture of Four Ecologies* verwendete. Was Hockney in die Stadt gelockt hatte, waren die Literatur und die zwielichtigen illustrierten Magazine – die er auch von Kalifornien nach London importierte –, und kaum in Los Angeles angekommen, gab er zu Protokoll, was ihm dort auffiel: „… es gab keine Bilder von Los Angeles. Niemand wusste damals, wie die Stadt aussieht. Als ich da war, wurden etliche Schnellstraßen erst noch fertig gebaut. Ich weiß noch, dass ich in meiner ersten Woche dort eine Auffahrt zu einem Freeway sah, die in die Luft führte, und plötzlich kam mir der Gedanke: ‚Mein Gott, diese Stadt braucht ihren Piranesi. Los Angeles könnte seinen eigenen Piranesi haben, also, hier bin ich!'"[10]

10. David Hockney, zitiert in: Marco Livingstone, *David Hockney*, New York (Thames & Hudson) 1981, S. 70.

Hockneys Übersiedlung nach Los Angeles brachte eine unmittelbare Veränderung mit sich: Er begann die Formen und den Charakter seiner neuen Umgebung so zu malen, wie sie sich in einem ganz bestimmten Moment darstellten, und zwar nicht schematisch oder durch die Verbindung unterschiedlicher Ideen und Anregungen aus Büchern, sondern vielmehr in einem unverhohlen naturalistischen Stil, der sich durch klare Linien und schnurgerade leuchtende Farbstreifen auszeichnet. Nachdem er dazu übergegangen war, seine neue Umgebung auch zu fotografieren, sah er sich mit der Herausforderung konfrontiert, das Wasser und die reflektierenden Oberflächen, die ihm in vielen Aspekten des Lebens in Kalifornien begegneten, malerisch darzustellen: der verschwenderische Umgang der Bevölkerung mit Wasser, der ihm ins Auge stach, ob in Duschen und Pools oder bei Rasensprengern, sowie die minimalistischen, luxuriösen Werkstoffe, die er allenthalten in der städtischen Architektur und in Interieurs bemerkte. *Cleanliness is Next to Godliness* (1964, S. 49), *Water Pouring into*

*Swimming Pool, Santa Monica* (1964) und *Drawing for 'Glass Table with Objects'* (1964) sind einige Beispiele für die Art von Bildern, in denen das Thema des Wassers und seiner Flüchtigkeit schier unendliche Möglichkeiten bot, Farbe, Tiefe und Bewegung festzuhalten.

War es dem Künstler in New York darum gegangen, die soziale Realität der Stadt zu dokumentieren, so erkennen manche Kritikerinnen und Kritiker in seinen Los-Angeles-Bildern einen Prozess der Verdinglichung, in dem gefilterte Erfahrungen im Widerspruch stehen zu dem, was wir als unmittelbare Wahrnehmung und Realität sehen. Dies zeigt sich in Hockneys formalem Kunstgriff, die Freiluftmotive mit einem weißen Rand zu umgeben (S. 44–47), wie bei einer Fotografie, die das Künstliche des Bildes betonen soll; die Handlungen werden nicht an einem spezifischen Ort verankert, sondern in einem ganz bestimmten Moment festgehalten. Diese Haltung rückt auch dadurch ins Blickfeld, dass Hockney der physischen Struktur von Los Angeles offenbar jedes Gemeinschaftsgefühl und jeden gesellschaftlichen Kontext abspricht, vielmehr fungieren seine isolierten Formen als Zeichen für Leere, Einsamkeit und Abwesenheit. Die Lithografie *Pacific Mutual Life* (1964, S. 48), die sich durch den Schriftzug ebenso auszeichnet wie durch den umgebenden Himmel und die Palmen, die das knapp umrissene, fast körperlose Gebäude einrahmen, schildert die Enttäuschung des Künstlers, der auf der Suche nach der umtriebigen Schwulenszene auf dem Pershing Square eigens nach Downtown fuhr, nur um festzustellen, dass das Leben, das er dort anzutreffen hoffte, gar nicht stattfand. In Hockneys Stadtansichten von Los Angeles werden die Straßen und Gebäude auf eine Ansammlung geradliniger Striche und minimalistischer Gitter reduziert – nach Ansicht von Rosalind Krauss eine Kunst, die „sich von der Natur abgewendet hat" –, womit er womöglich die Frage aufwerfen möchte, inwieweit sich die Straßen und Stadtviertel überhaupt voneinander unterscheiden.[11] Vor diesem Hintergrund könnte man die Menschen, die Hockneys Los-Angeles-Bilder bevölkern – von den beiden unbekleideten Schwimmern auf ihren Luftmatratzen in *California Copied From 1965 Painting in 1987* (1987, S. 46–47) bis zu *Man in Shower in Beverly Hills* (1964, S. 57) –, lediglich als die Körper junger, vom Künstler mit voyeuristischem Blick fetischisierter Kalifornier interpretieren, deren markante Gesäßbacken in den Mittelpunkt unserer Aufmerksamkeit gerückt werden. Dabei sind sie in seltsam abwesenden oder unpersönlichen Situationen festgehalten und wirken verdinglicht, als gehörten sie niemandem – entblößt und bar jeder Persönlichkeit, Individualität oder Umgebung.[12]

**11.** Andrew Causey, „Mapping and Representation", in: Paul Melia (Hrsg.), *David Hockney*, Manchester und New York (Manchester University Press) 1995, S. 99.

**12.** Ibid., S. 102.

Ende der 1960er-Jahre entwickelte sich Hockneys Werk zu einer noch naturalistischeren Darstellung von Figuren in häuslichen Interieurs, in denen Licht und Raum zunehmend atmosphärisch dargestellt wurden. Er unternahm auch weiterhin ausgedehnte Reisen, kehrte nach New York zurück und fuhr nach Japan, Südostasien, Deutschland und Frankreich, ehe er sich 1973 in Paris niederließ. Sein nomadisches Leben und seine Beschwörung von Orten befassen sich scheinbar mit etwas sehr Gewöhnlichem, das aber in eine ganze Bandbreite formaler, emotionaler und experimenteller Kräfte eingebettet ist. Dieses erstaunliche Œuvre aus den ersten zehn Jahren seiner Karriere bekräftigt nicht zuletzt die Überzeugung des Künstlers, dass Bilder uns dabei helfen, die Welt wahrzunehmen, auf dass wir sie dann entsprechend unserer jeweiligen kulturellen Zugehörigkeit, Erfahrung und Identität deuten können.

# Mapping David Hockney

Helen Little

Through intimate studies of exquisite bodies or epic vistas of distant lands, David Hockney's art takes us on visual odysseys to places old and new, familiar and exotic, lived and imagined. From his earliest works rooted in the milieu of postwar London or in the sexual freedom and visual drama of southern California to his more recent panoramas that grasp at the incalculability of the Grand Canyon or map the hillsides of East Yorkshire with seasonal precision (pp. 69–75), Hockney's pictures speak vividly to the sensual delights he finds in his surroundings. With forms and subjects as firmly rooted in the artist's immediate environment as in the isolated groups of figures that often charge it with a human and psychological dimension, it is perhaps unsurprising to discover that Hockney considers both his landscapes and portraits as "people", equally vital, full of life and constantly moving.

Despite his popular personification as "*the* painter of southern California", Hockney has in fact never stayed in one place for too long. Having for many years divided his time between London and Los Angeles, he always finds new stimulation and different ways of looking when he travels further afield, and the formal, historical and anthropological discoveries he has made in other places – from China to Japan, Lebanon to Egypt, Norway to Spain – have provided rich stimuli, prompting new ways of looking and deciphering our visual world of time, movement and space. After spending several years interrogating pictorial conventions in panoramas such as *In The Studio, December 2017* (2017, pp. 24–25) – an ambitious photographic study of the interior of the artist's studio high up in the Hollywood Hills –, Hockney's predilection to seek out new mediums and terrains is evidenced in his recent relocation from California to Normandy, France. Rising early to capture the arrival of spring, Hockney recently dedicated himself to charting the changing seasons *en plein air* as they unfold as a narrative in real time, his forensically painted and drawn rural landscapes a crucial reminder in this turbulent era of the constant and wondrous regeneration of the natural world. Looking back to the very start of his career, it becomes clear that Hockney's localities have always been integral to his visual investigations. As the artist's preoccupation with representation continues to move into new mediums and territories, this essay draws attention to how Hockney's travels and periods living abroad shaped the development of his practice during the 1960s. Taking "place" as both a muse and site for artistic reinvention with which to problematise issues of identity, migration and sexuality, it considers the complex ways Hockney wove subtle or intangible relationships into the rhythms and patterns that shaped his lived experience at the outset of his career. From gestural abstraction, constructed realities and post-Pop cityscapes, it charts the rapid development of some of the artist's recurring visual modes and devices from the graphic and diagrammatic to the scenic and emblematic. In doing so, it presents Hockney's "topographies" of this period not simply as the product of static observation but as a complex synthesis of reality, appropriation and fantasy that form his commitment to capturing things as they are seen and remembered today.

## Towards the definition of a new image

*The Third Love Painting* (1960, pp. 180–181) is a coarsely painted image, combining gestural brushwork and scribbled graffiti redolent of the noise and disenfranchisement of inner-city dwellers and the artist's growing awareness of London's burgeoning subculture of queer meeting places. Deliberately non-realist, its coded repertoire of words and phallic shapes is rooted in reality: clinging to life in a world of marks and shapes. As part of the artist's emerging repertoire of abstracted forms he described as propaganda for queer love, this painting marks Hockney's arrival in London as a postgraduate student at the Royal College of Art in the autumn of 1959, a revelatory experience for an artist hailing from the north of England from where the metropolis seemed "a long, long, way away"[1]. In contrast to *Woman with a Sewing Machine* (1954, p. 179) and other socialist realistic images of working class domestic life he had been encouraged to make at Bradford School of Art (1953–1957), after 1960 Hockney began to make a series of pictures incorporating a complex range of formal and rhetorical devices, blending passages of abstraction with found imagery from photographs or other works of art to offer tantalisingly voyeuristic journeys through personal relationships, situations and private spaces. As part of a new generation of artists who excluded the traditional genre of landscape from their list of subjects for art, these works can be said to take something partly from life and partly from other sources to push against the dominance of abstract painting and reflect a new kind of urban culture.

1. David Hockney, quoted in Martin Gayford, *A Bigger Message: Conversations with David Hockney*, Thames & Hudson, London 2011, p. 136.

Hockney's idiosyncratic approach to rendering places, objects and figures is also evident in *Tea Painting in an Illusionistic Style* (1961, p. 109), the last of three pictures inspired by the distinctive red and black packets of his mother's favourite tea, a symbol of Englishness that can be seen as an ironic comment on the prevalent fascination with American imports and whose slogan "The tea that puts the 'T' in Britain" plays on the nation's stock response of making a cup of tea in a crisis. As the artist described: "I used to go into the Royal College of Art very early in the morning ... before Lyons had opened in South Kensington, and I used to make my own tea in there ... it was always Typhoo tea, my mother's favourite ... The tea packets piled up with the cans and tubes of paint ... and I just thought, in a way it's like still-life paintings for me ... There was a packet of Typhoo tea, a very ordinary popular brand of tea, so I used it as a motif. This is as close to pop art as I ever came."[2]

2. David Hockney, quoted in Nikos Stangos (ed.), *David Hockney by David Hockney: My Early Years*, Thames & Hudson, London 1977, pp. 63–64.

Taking the tea packet's familiar design and shape to invest his picture with something that represented the familiarity and comfort of his family home in Bradford, Hockney's construction of a shaped canvas gives the impression that we are looking at a picture of the world but not at the world itself. Despite its many queer readings into the seated figure occupying an oppressive space asserting the artist's position as an outsider in wider society, this painting's appearance in the 1962 *Young Contemporaries* exhibition launched Hockney's entry into the mainstream art world. Here, the artist's dandyish appearance and identity as a northern working-class artist were cited with increasing currency in the popular press to map a newly aspirational and iconoclastic image of metropolitan life. This fashioning of the artist's body as a potent symbol of London would continue well into the 1960s even as Hockney became increasingly absent from Britain.

## A Marriage of Styles

Hockney's aspiration to introduce greater figuration and emotional investment into his pictures is present in a loosely autobiographical painting inspired by the artist's first trip to Italy in December 1961. In contrast to his earlier paintings in which dreamlike fantasies conceal harsher realities, *Flight Into Italy – Swiss Landscape* (1962, pp. 102–103) documents a strange experience of a landscape both seen and imagined as the artist travelled through the Alps en route to Florence, Italy: "I was especially looking forward to the Alps and I thought, I'm going to see the Alps, and here's a real subject to make a picture of: mountain landscapes in the Alps. I love Gothic gloom as much as Mediterranean or Californian sun, and I thought the misty Alps would be a great thrill. But unfortunately I didn't see them."[3]

3. Ibid., p. 87.

Keeping the personal and objective highly in check and addressing the problem of how to paint a landscape without being naturalistic, *Flight Into Italy – Swiss Landscape* presents a Swiss mountain range in different ways and modes of representation: from the bands of colour riffing on geography books and colour field painting denoting the elevation of the mountain range and bird's eye view of the road to a collaged cut out of a mountain peak taken from a postcard and a loosely painted, vernacular chalet-style building. As Hockney travels through the region largely oblivious to the impressive landscape around him, glimpsing only one or two of the mountains from the back of his friend's Morris van, we begin to appreciate the ironies at play in this picture that not only attempts to evoke Hockney's journey diagrammatically as a map and scenically through time but commemoratively in the way it draws on visual clichés based on pre-existing notions and expectations of what foreign landscapes look like. We might, therefore, think of *Flight into Italy – Swiss Landscape* as a picture that plays with cultural representation and questions the value of original experience of a place, taking the artist's fleeting and therefore "inauthentic" experience and presenting it as a ready-made landscape like a tourist postcard for those who are not able to see it for themselves. Hockney would soon start to use a camera to document his travels, taking snaps of architecture and people like an ordinary tourist: "It's really like visual proof of one's existence," he remarked, "like a record of your time."[4]

4. David Hockney, quoted in "David Hockney", in *Andy Warhol's Interview*, July 1972, unpaginated. Consulted by the author in Tate Press Clippings.

Hockney's interest in blurring the boundaries of reality, fiction and artifice continues in a body of work he made after returning to London from his second European trip in the summer of 1962, the last leg of which took him to Munich and West Berlin. Attracted to Berlin via Christopher Isherwood's famous novels chronicling the defiant pre-war hedonism of its cafés, bars and brothels, the trip positions Hockney within a set of complex, shifting geographies of exiled queer men who by the 1960s were becoming drawn to the modern subcultures of northern Europe. This is in contrast to the traditionally homoeroticised Latin culture of the southern Mediterranean with its references to Greek love and idealised images of classical antiquity – a notion Hockney subverts in *Renaissance Head* (1963, pp. 96–97).[5] On that basis, one might think of other paintings such as *Berlin: A Souvenir* (1962–1963) with its abstracted groupings of male nudes captioned by the word "BERLIN" and *The Berliner and the Bavarian* (1962, p. 104) that contrasts stereotypical figures encountered in these regions as portraits of a city whose legendary culture of freedom and decadence was in reality obscured by the political instability of the Cold War. The historical museums of Berlin, however, offered Hockney an unexpected stimulus, forming the basis of several paintings exploring stillness and movement and complicating the relationship between two figures. As the artist recalled: "I never seem to be able to go around a museum at the same pace as everybody else, and when I went to the Pergamon Museum with Jeff [Goodman] we got separated. Suddenly I caught sight of him standing next to an Egyptian sculpted figure, unconcerned about it because he was studying something on the wall. Both figures were looking the same way, and it amused me that in my first glimpse of them they looked united."[6] The first painting to emerge from this recollection, *The First Marriage (A Marriage of Styles I)* (1962, p. 105) casts Jeff and the anonymous sculpture as man and wife, playing on their briefly plausible yet tenuous relationship and contrasting visual styles. Unlike naturalism's lens-like approach to capturing every detail of a given scene, Hockney has left the major part of this canvas unpainted, editing out any coherent elements to allow our eyes to focus on what he believes to be the key areas for our attention. As in *Illustrations for Fourteen Poems from C.P. Cavafy* (1966, pp. 126–133) based on the poet's experiences of Alexandria but recast to modern Beirut where Hockney was able to travel to make preparatory studies, the introduction of pictorial props including white sand, a palm tree and distant mountain range transports the figures from Berlin to a new and ambiguously exotic setting, flipping the painting from real life to invented or fantasy imagery and back again.

5. For a fuller account of this history of queer migration see Paul Melia, "Showers, Pools and Power" in Paul Melia (ed.), *David Hockney*, Manchester University Press, Manchester and New York 1995, pp. 50–52.

6. See note 2, p. 89.

## The Promised Land

The murky smears and stains of colour in the paintings Hockney made in the post-rationing dinginess of London are absent from a body of etchings tied to the liberating effect of the artist's first trip to America in the summer of 1961. Spending three months in New York, Hockney very quickly linked his interest in the city with sexual pleasure and his search for a more cathartic, hospitable culture: "I was taken by the sheer energy of the place. It was amazingly sexy, and unbelievably easy. People were much more open, and I felt completely free. The city was a total twenty-four-hour city. Greenwich city was never closed, the bookshops were open all night so you could browse, the gay life was much more organised, and I thought, 'this is the place for me.'"[7] The first work Hockney made in America, the diminutive etching *My Bonnie Lies Over the Ocean* (1961–1962, p. 183), blends graphic mapping, text and popular music to suggest an action that pictures cannot really have: of a journey across a vast ocean separating the artist from home, and of situations and relationships all

7. David Hockney, quoted in Christopher Simon Sykes, *Hockney: The Biography. 1937–1975, Volume I*, Century, London 2011, pp. 95–96.

contained in a static image. Likewise, the sixteen plates that make up the suite of etchings *A Rake's Progress* (1961–1963, pp. 118–125) tell an autobiographical story of the artist's immersive experience of New York. For the American Pop artist Andy Warhol (1928–1987), whose life and work is synonymous with the city (and who interviewed Hockney for his magazine *Andy Warhol's Interview* in 1972), Hockney's episodic encounters with the cultural iconography namechecked throughout the plates, from the Chrysler Building and Madison Square Garden to the preachers, entertainers and campaigners of the city's street life, represent the metamorphic changes Hockney underwent as he indulged in the good life of America "with the resolution," Warhol asserted, "that if there's one life to live, live it thusly."[8] This prevalent view of New York as a city of opportunity is questioned in Hockney's response – confirmed by the details of his narrative images – hinting at a deeper reality of a city scarred by social barriers and economic injustice which he compares to the deprivation of London chronicled by the British artist William Hogarth in the 1730s: "You're talking about a version of Rake's Progress which I did only because New York reminded me so much of 18th century London in that, you know, people seemed to die on the street and nobody seemed to care. Whereas in England, you know, if you were dying on the streets, they'd send an ambulance around and they'd bring you some soup and put you in a hall and everything would be alright ... It did remind me of Hogarth and when I went back to England, I decided to do a modern version of it."[9]

8. See note 4, n.p.

9. See note 4, n.p.

Similarly, Hockney's first encounter with southern California in 1963 and his adoption of Los Angeles as his second home the following year have largely been cast through the lens of fantasy and the artist's pursuit of a particular kind of freedom and emotional life centred around glamour, sunshine and sex. Created during a time of rapid urban expansion, population growth and tourism, Hockney's pleasure-seeking pictures of the city's palm trees, lawn sprinklers, boys in showers, swimming pools and modernist houses have fashioned him as the artist who "invented" California (pp. 42–57). This reputation for having defined the city's visual identity was sealed when the architecture critic Reyner Banham selected Hockney's celebrated painting *A Bigger Splash* (1967) for the cover of his book *Los Angeles: The Architecture of Four Ecologies* published in 1971. Having been drawn to the city through literature and the seedy illustrated magazines he imported from California to London, Hockney immediately set out to chronicle what he found there: "... there were no paintings of Los Angeles. People then didn't know what it looked like. And when I was there, they were still finishing up some of the freeways. I remember seeing, within the first week, a ramp of freeway going into the air, and I suddenly thought: 'My God, this place needs its Piranesi; Los Angeles could have a Piranesi, so here I am!'"[10]

10. David Hockney, quoted in Marco Livingstone, *David Hockney*, Thames & Hudson, New York 1981, p. 70.

An immediate change in Hockney's work after his relocation to Los Angeles is that he began to paint the forms and character of his new environment as seen in specific moments in time, executed in a straightforwardly naturalist style characterised by crisp lines and rectilinear bands of bright colour rather than schematically or through the blending of disparate ideas and things he saw in books. Having begun to take photographs of his new environment, a particular concern became the challenge of how to depict the water and reflective surfaces

Hockney encountered in many aspects of Californian life, from what he noted as Californians' exuberant use of water in showers, pools and sprinklers to the minimal, luxurious materials he found in the city's architecture and interiors. *Cleanliness is Next to Godliness* (1964, p. 49), *Water Pouring into Swimming Pool, Santa Monica* (1964) and *Drawing for 'Glass Table with Objects'* (1964) are examples of the kind of work for whom the subject of water and transience provided endless possibilities to capture its colour, depth and movement.

Unlike the artist's commitment to register the social reality of New York, critics have drawn attention to a process of objectification at play in Hockney's Los Angeles pictures in which distilled experiences remain at odds with what we perceive as immediate perception and reality. This is suggested by the formal device of enclosing the artist's outdoor subjects within white borders (pp. 44–47), like a photograph that insists on the artificiality of the image, freezing their actions in a moment in time rather than rooting them in a specific location. This position also comes to the fore in the way Hockney denies any sense of community or social context in the physical fabric of Los Angeles, his isolated forms operating as signs for empty and lonely absences. Identified as much by its graphic signage, surrounding sky and palm trees that frame the sparsely delineated building devoid of volume, *Pacific Mutual Life* (1964, p. 48) recounts the artist's disappointment at having travelled downtown in search of the bustling gay scene of Pershing Square, only to find it lacking the life he hoped to find there. Reducing the streets and buildings of Los Angeles to a series of rectilinear lines and minimalist grids deemed by Rosalind Krauss a kind of art that has "turned its back on nature'", Hockney's cityscapes seem to question if one street or part of the city is distinguishable from another.[11] On that basis, one might think of the people who populate Hockney's Los Angeles paintings, from the two nude swimmers lounging on inflatable lilos in *California Copied From 1965 Painting in 1987* (1987, pp. 46–47) to *Man in Shower in Beverly Hills* (1964, p. 57) as the bodies of young Californians fetishized by the visiting artist, their prominent buttocks presented as the focus of our attention in strangely absent or impersonal situations, objectified as if belonging to no one – dislocated and devoid of personality, individuality or environment.[12]

**11.** Andrew Causey, "Mapping and Representation", in Paul Melia (ed.), *David Hockney*, Manchester University Press, Manchester 1995, p. 99.

**12.** Ibid., p. 102.

By the end of the 1960s, Hockney's work had moved towards even greater naturalism in scenes of figures in domestic interiors invested with increasingly atmospheric representations of light and space. He also continued to travel extensively, returning to New York and voyaging to Japan, Southeast Asia, Germany and France, before settling in Paris in 1973. Forming a remarkable body of pictures from the first ten years of his career, Hockney's itinerant existence and evocations of places seem to take something very ordinary but embed it in a range of formal, emotional and experiential forces. Above all, they assert the artist's belief that pictures can make us see the world, which we can then interpret according to our own cultural affiliations, experiences and identities.

**Renaissance Head,** 1963
Öl auf Leinwand | Oil on canvas,
122 × 122 cm
CAM – Fundação Calouste
Gulbenkian, Lisbon
Inv. Nº PE 216

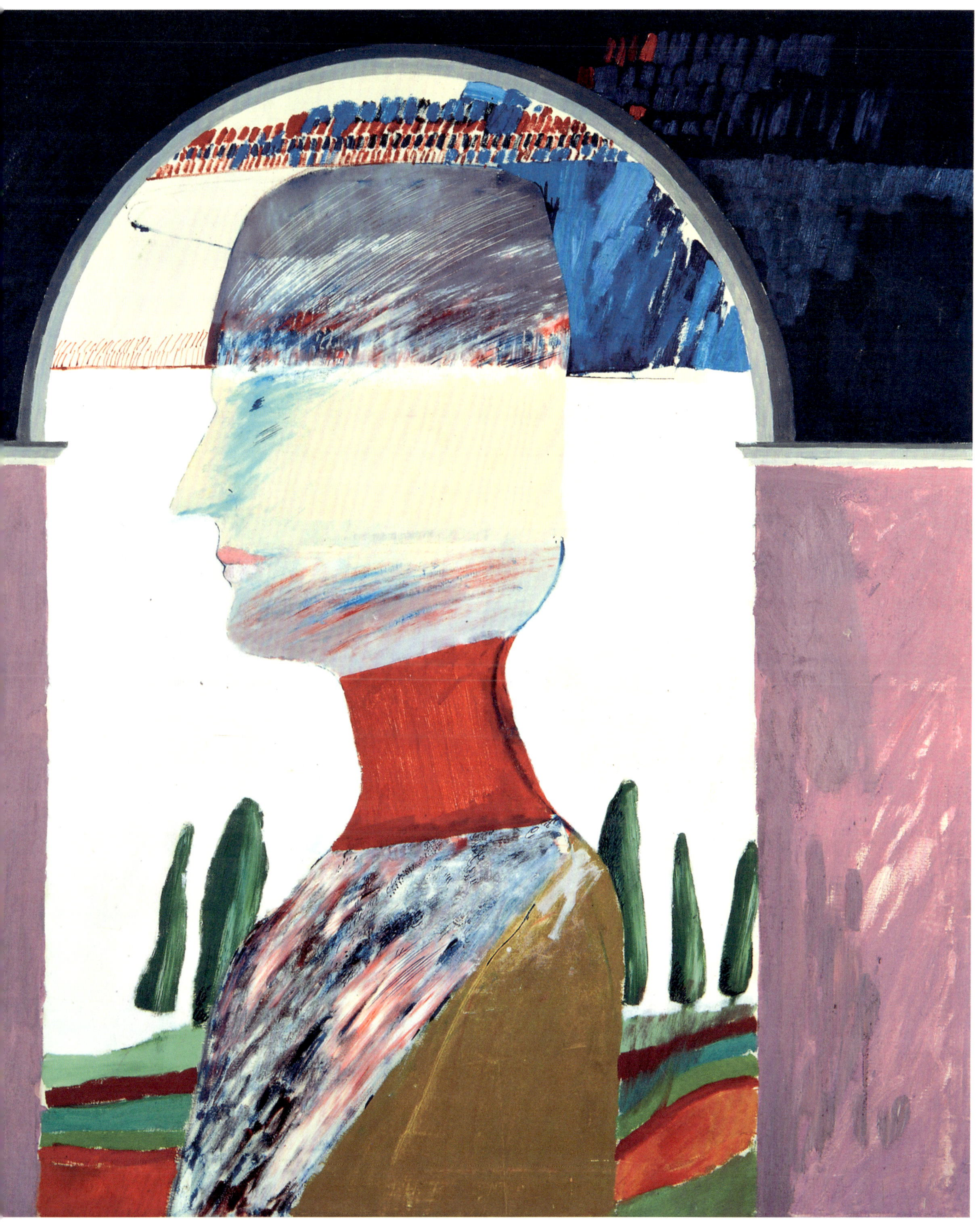

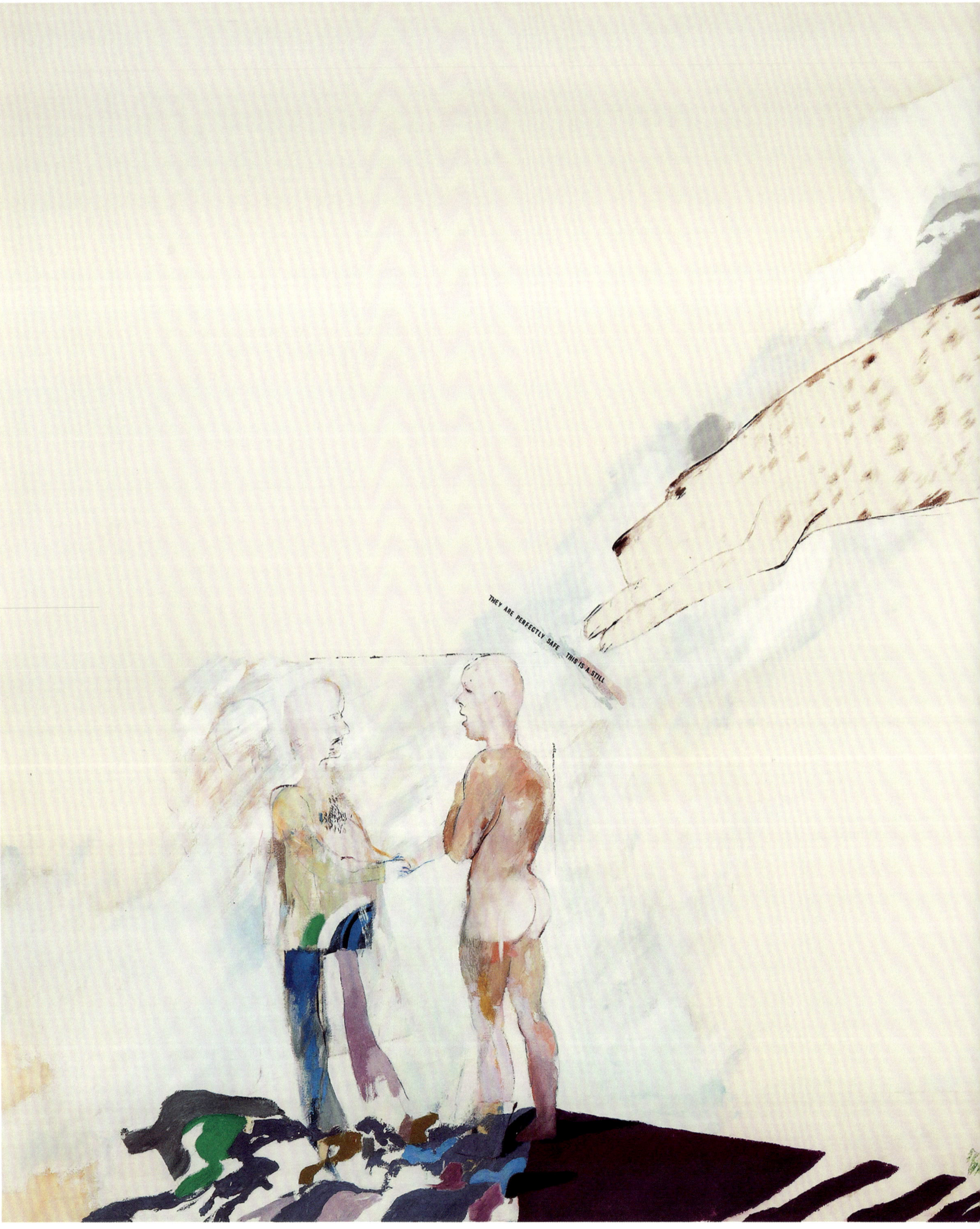
THEY ARE PERFECTLY SAFE
THIS IS A STILL

**Picture Emphasizing Stillness,** 1962
Öl und Letraset auf Leinwand |
Oil and Letraset on canvas,
157,5 x 182,8 cm
Museu Coleção Berardo, Lisbon
Inv. N° UID 102-269

**In Memoriam: Cecchino Bracci,** 1962
Öl auf Leinwand | Oil on canvas,
213,3 × 91,4 cm
Museo Nacional Thyssen-Bornemisza, Madrid
Inv. N° 584 (1978.12)

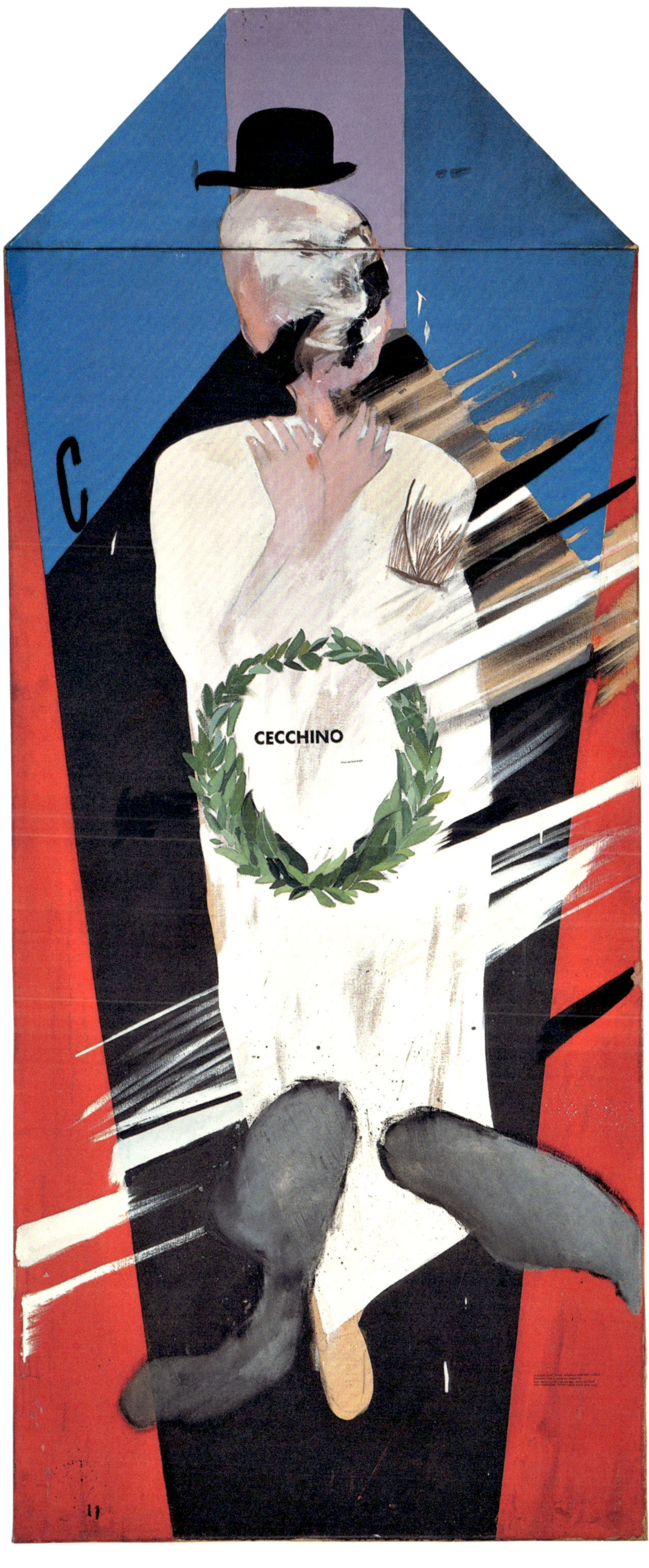
C
CECCHINO

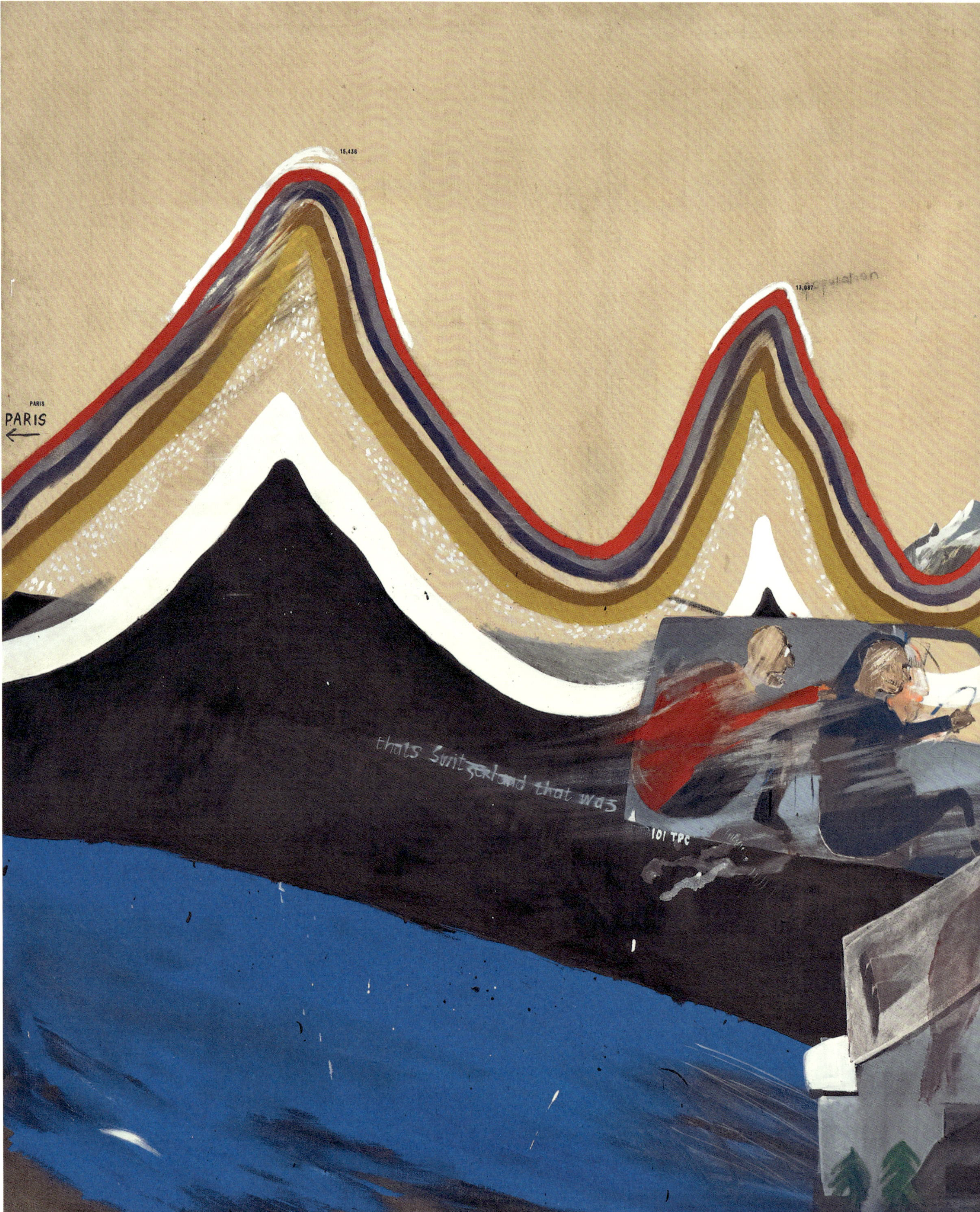
15,436
13,087
PARIS
PARIS
thats Switzerland that was
101 TPC

**Flight into Italy – Swiss Landscape,** 1962
Öl auf Leinwand | Oil on canvas,
182,9 × 182,9 cm
Kunstpalast, Düsseldorf
Inv. N° 0.1981.1

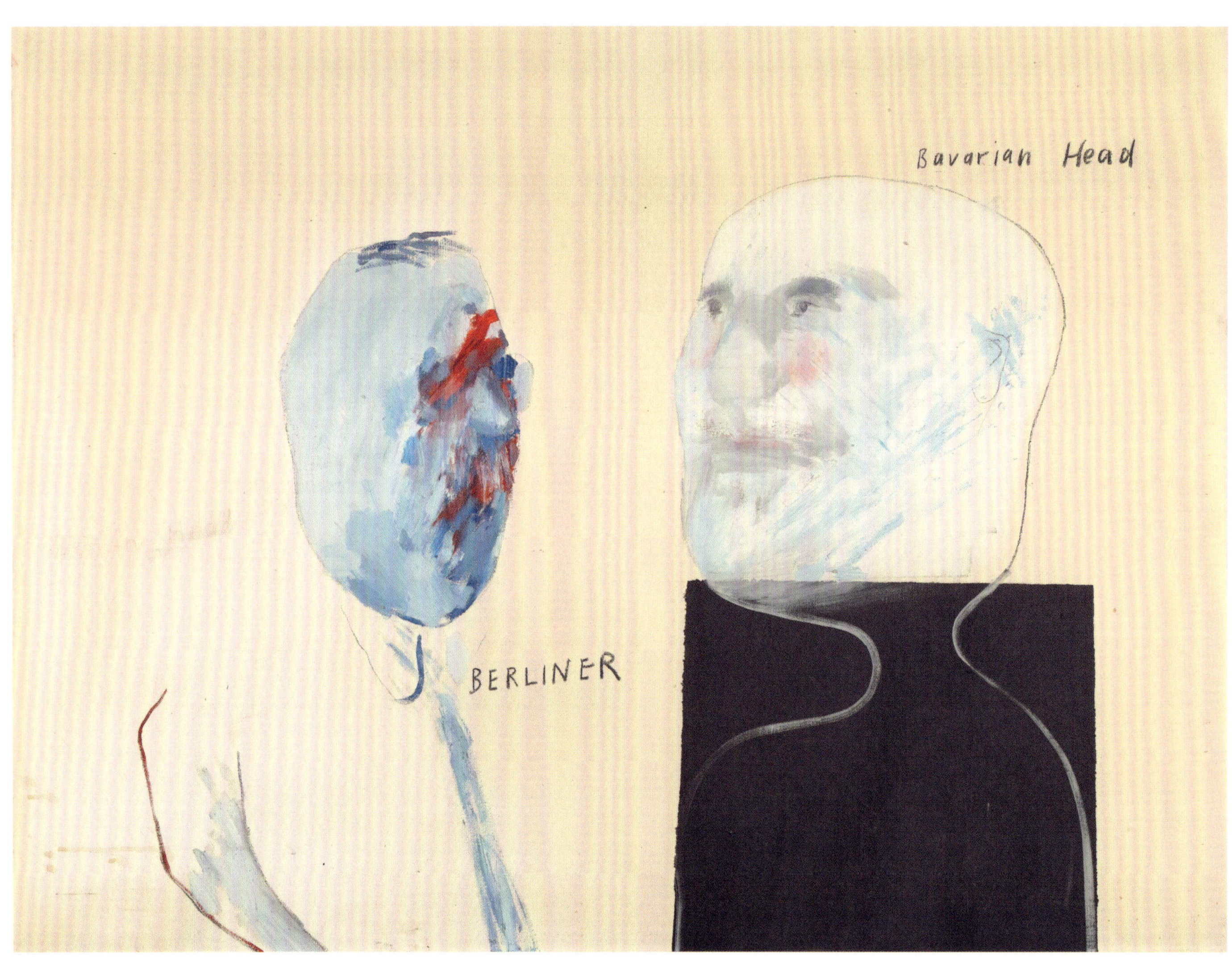


**The Berliner and the Bavarian,** 1962
Öl auf Leinwand | Oil on canvas,
92,1 × 122,6 cm
Tate: Accepted by HM Government in lieu of inheritance tax on The Estate of Frith Banbury and allocated to the Tate Gallery 2009
Inv. N° T12883

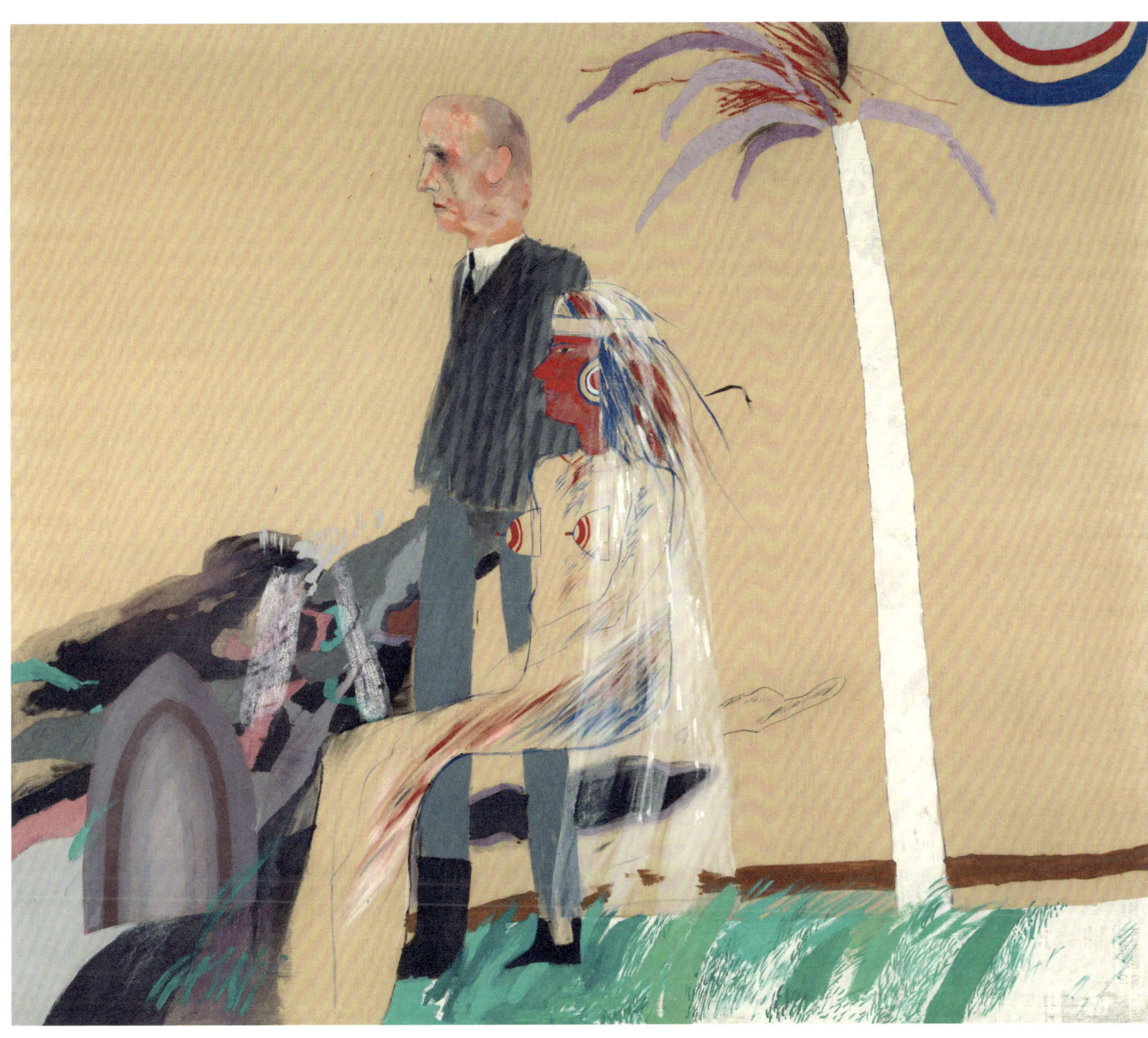

**The First Marriage (A Marriage of Styles I),** 1962
Öl auf Leinwand | Oil on canvas,
182,9 × 214 cm
Tate: Presented by the Friends of the Tate Gallery 1963
Inv. N° T00596

**Man Stood in Front of his House with Rain Descending (The Idiot),** 1962
Öl auf Leinwand | Oil on canvas,
243 × 152,5 cm
Collection S.M.A.K., Stedelijk Museum voor Actuele Kunst, Gent
Inv. N° 701

107

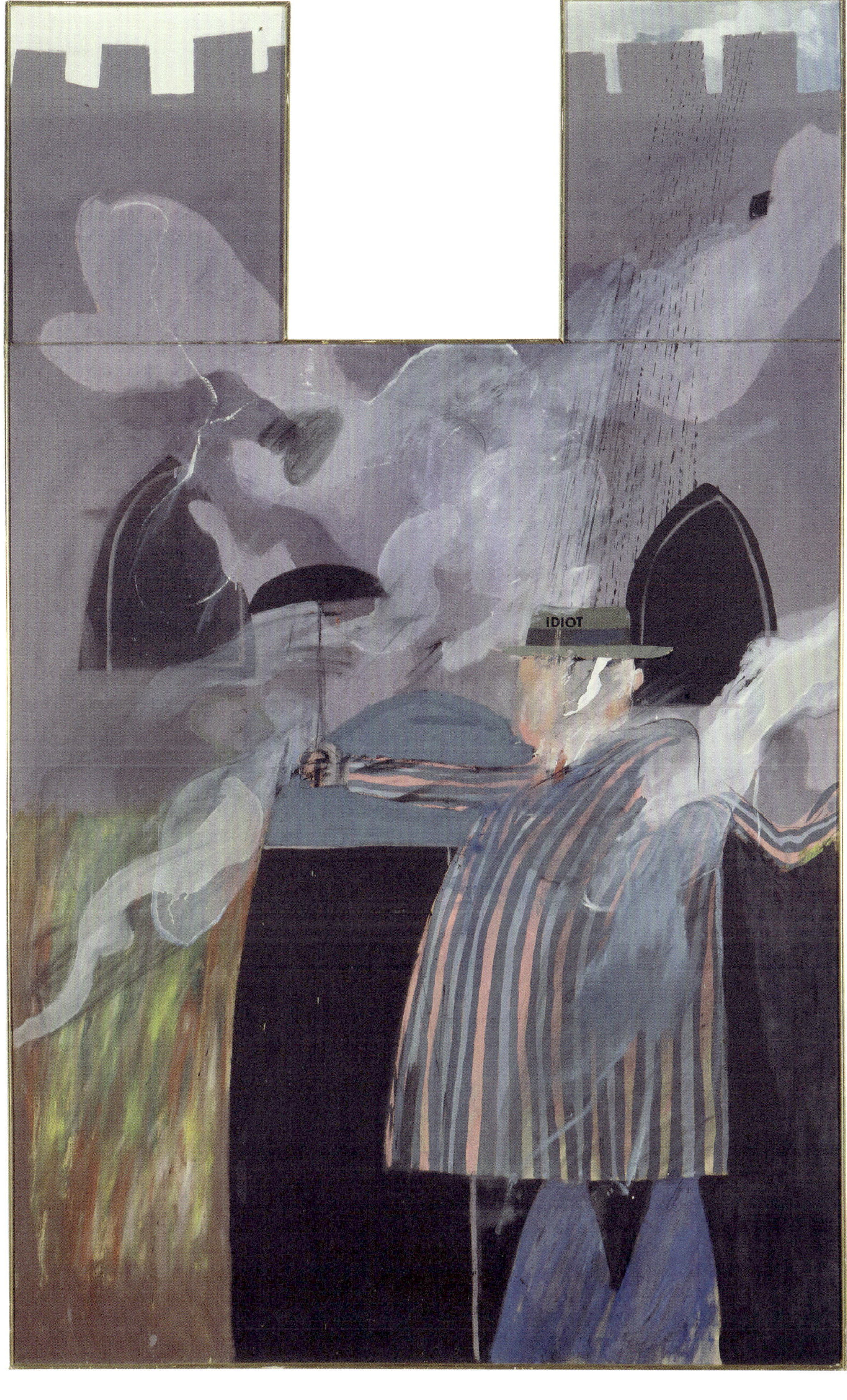

**Tea Painting in an Illusionistic Style,** 1961
Öl auf Leinwand | Oil on canvas,
232,5 × 83 cm
Tate: Purchased with assistance
from the Art Fund 1996
Inv. N° T07075

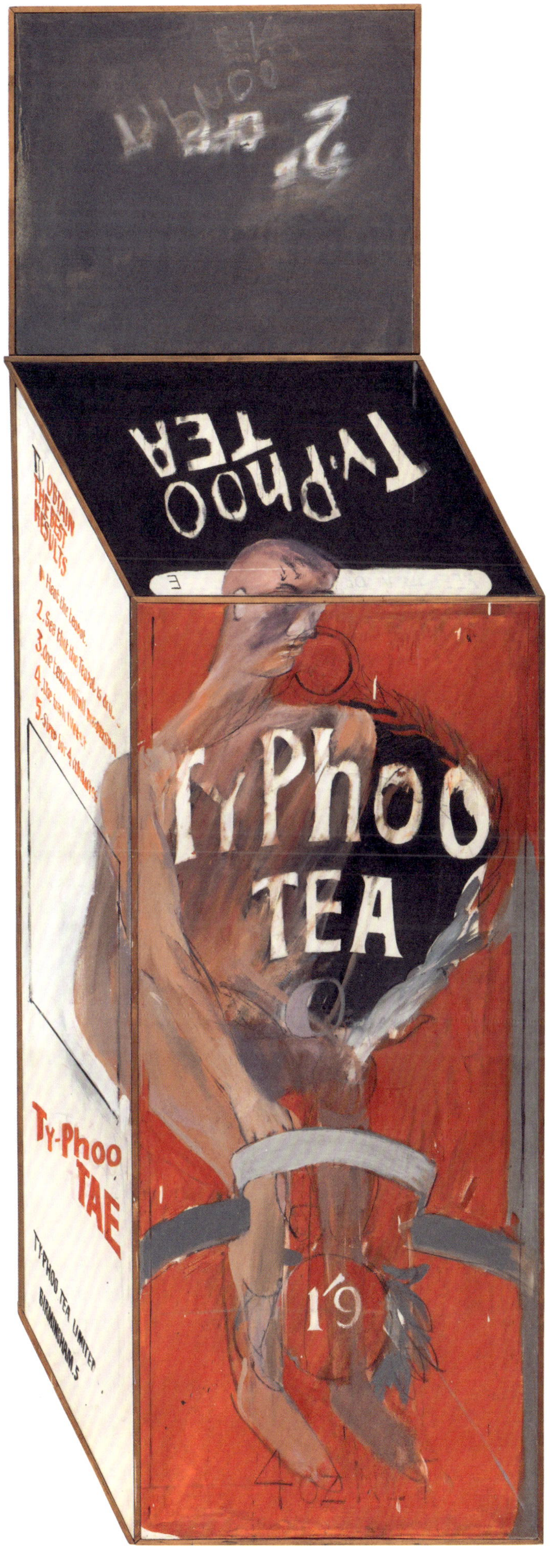
Ty.Phoo TEA
TO OBTAIN THE BEST RESULTS
TyPhoo TEA
1'9
Ty-Phoo TAE
TYPHOO TEA LIMITED
BIRMINGHAM.5

# Hockney druckt

Jan Svenungsson

In verschiedenen Gesprächen, die ich in letzter Zeit geführt habe, habe ich immer wieder die Rede auf Hockney gebracht. Hast du eine Meinung? Welche? Mehrere Künstlerinnen und Künstler aus meinem Freundeskreis antworteten etwa so: „Früher dachte ich, ich mag seine Arbeiten nicht, aber heute gefallen sie mir." Einige sagten, seine Druckgrafik sei das Beste, was er geschaffen hat. Ein Schriftsteller lobte Hockneys Buch von 2001, *Secret Knowledge. Rediscovering the Lost Techniques of the Old Masters.*[1] Das entsprach auch voll und ganz meiner eigenen Meinung. Dann stellten wir beide fest, dass wir in der Frage, ob seine zentrale Hypothese korrekt sei oder nicht, ganz gegensätzlicher Auffassung waren. Hockney wird von allen dafür bewundert, dass er nie stehengeblieben ist. Eine meiner Studierenden sagte mir, er sei ihr Lieblingskünstler, und dass in der Malklasse, in der ihr Freund studiert, alle heimlich ein Hockney-Buch bereithielten für den Fall, dass der Inspiration mal wieder auf die Sprünge geholfen werden muss. Während ich mich in Hockneys Druckgrafik vertiefe, verstehe ich diese jungen Malerinnen und Maler absolut. Seine druckgrafischen Arbeiten sind einfach von einer so gehaltvollen Qualität. Sie inspirieren mich, selbst Bilder zu machen, anstatt darüber zu lesen oder zu schreiben.

Hockney ist ein großartiger Geschichtenerzähler. Die Interviews, die ich von ihm lese, sind alle ausgesprochen sympathisch. Wenn er spricht, so scheint mir, versucht er immer, aus dem Moment heraus *logisch* zu argumentieren und nie einfach nur zu wiederholen, was erwartet wird. In seinem Werk sehe ich ein Vor und Zurück zwischen einem Interesse für Narratives und Beziehungen sowie eine Leidenschaft für intensive Beobachtung und dafür, wie diese dann in Bildern umgesetzt werden kann. Wie versetzt man die Betrachtenden in die Lage, die eigene Erfahrung durch anschauliche Darstellung zu teilen? Das mag sehr elementar klingen: Ist dies nicht genau das, was die meisten Künstlerinnen und Künstler tun? Oberflächlich betrachtet vielleicht. Für Hockney ist dieser Anspruch – dieses Problem – seit etwa siebzig Jahren die treibende Kraft hinter seiner nicht nachlassenden Produktivität, und hat Begleiterscheinungen der unterschiedlichsten Art gezeitigt: visuelle, technische, soziale, befreiende. Deshalb ist es nur folgerichtig, dass Hockney eine große Leidenschaft für die Rolle und Bedeutung der *Werkzeuge* entwickelt hat. Er ist außerordentlich sachkundig, was Methoden und Techniken betrifft, die Kunstschaffende der Vergangenheit benutzten, und er selbst sucht ständig nach neuen (technischen) Mitteln die ihm helfen können, seinen Zielen näher zu kommen. Mit welchen Techniken der Bildproduktion überträgt und verwandelt man die multisensoriale Informationsmenge, die das Gehirn durch Beobachtung erhält, in eine

**1.** Deutsche Ausgabe: David Hockney, *Geheimes Wissen. Verlorene Techniken der Alten Meister wieder entdeckt von David Hockney,* München (Knesebeck) 2001 – übersetzt von Bernadette Ott und Rita Seuß.

künstlerische Darstellung? Ist man auf eine Geschichte oder auf eine Momentaufnahme aus oder auf ein Mittelding aus beiden? Soll der Prozess reibungslos vonstattengehen oder Friktionen enthalten? Wie geht man mit Tiefenschärfe und Perspektive um? Wie kompensiert man den Verlust von Auflösung und Details? Wie wählt und berücksichtigt man all die akustischen, olfaktorischen, intellektuellen, psychologischen und physiologischen Stimuli, die neben den visuellen ja auch vorhanden sind, während man beobachtet und denkt? Das alles ist völlig unmöglich, wenn man die Rolle der Werkzeuge und Techniken nicht mitreflektiert. Jedes künstlerische Werkzeug hat seine eigenen Beschränkungen und Eigenarten. Die traditionellen Drucktechniken haben viele. Das macht sie besonders attraktiv.

Bereits 1954, als 17-jähriger Student an der Bradford School of Art, hatte Hockney beeindruckende Farblithografien geschaffen, aber seine erste wichtige Phase als Druckgrafiker begann 1961 während seiner Studienzeit am Londoner Royal College of Art. Es fehlte ihm an Geld für Leinwände und Farben, während in der Druckwerkstatt Materialien, wie er herausfand, kostenlos erhältlich waren. Inspiriert von William Hogarths achtteiliger Gemäldeserie *A Rake's Progress* (1732–1734), von denen dieser selbst im Jahr darauf Kupferstichversionen angefertigt hatte, nahm er ein gleichnamiges Projekt mit Radierungen in Angriff (S. 118–125). Während Hogarths Kupferstiche genaue Kopien der Gemälde waren (seinerzeit – das heißt vor Erfindung der Fotografie – die einzige Möglichkeit, ein Gemälde in Druckform zu veröffentlichen), benutzte Hockney das Medium der Radierung für eine freie Re-Imagination der Hogarth'schen Themen. Er verlagerte die Geschichte ins heutige New York (er hatte die Stadt gerade erstmals besucht) und verlieh der zentralen Figur sein eigenes Aussehen. Alle sechzehn Blätter der Serie wurden von jeweils nur einer Platte gedruckt, die er mit Strichätzung und Aquatinta bearbeitet hatte. In jedem Bild ist ein isolierter Teil der Darstellung mit roter Tinte gedruckt, der Rest in Schwarz. Die Entscheidung des Künstlers, alle Radierungen nach demselben Muster zu gestalten, gab ihm die Möglichkeit zur freien bildnerischen Erfindung *innerhalb* dieser Beschränkungen. Die Radierungen wurden 1963, ein Jahr nach seinem Studienabschluss, veröffentlicht. Auch heute noch, sechzig Jahre später, wirken sie bemerkenswert frisch.
In einem weiteren Radierungsprojekt aus den 1960er-Jahren – den Illustrationen zu C.P. Cavafys *Fourteen Poems* (S. 126–133) – liegt der Schwerpunkt auf der unverblümten Darstellung zweier männlicher Liebhaber, die exquisit in durchgehenden, nackten Linien gezeichnet sind. Wie radikal diese Radierungen gewirkt haben müssen, wird umso deutlicher, wenn man bedenkt, dass sie 1966 veröffentlicht wurden, also zu einer Zeit, als homosexuelle Beziehungen in Großbritannien noch unter Strafe standen.

Bereits von Anfang an war Hockney mit seinem Werk bemerkenswert erfolgreich. Anders als Hogarth zweihundert Jahre zuvor war er nie darauf angewiesen, Druckgrafik zu produzieren, um mit seiner Arbeit veröffentlicht zu werden. Stattdessen müssen es wohl bestimmte Aspekte der drucktechnischen Methoden gewesen sein, die seinen Schaffensprozess immer wieder von Neuem getriggert haben. Von 1954 bis 1995 veröffentlichte David Hockney mehr als dreihundert Editionen mit Radierungen und Lithografien. Diese Projekte reichen in ihrer Bandbreite von sehr direkten, einfachen Drucken bis zu außerordentlich komplexen Lithografien, die mit über vierzig Platten hergestellt wurden.

Radierung und Lithografie bieten einzigartige Alternativen zur Zeichnung und Malerei. Mechanisch gesehen muss es nicht viel anders sein als mit einem Stift oder Pinsel auf Papier zu arbeiten. Psychologisch gesehen ist es das aber auf jeden Fall. Wenn man an einer Zeichnung oder einem Gemälde arbeitet, sieht man das Bild im Moment des Entstehens genau vor sich. Arbeitet man aber auf einem Stein oder einer Platte für einen Druck, bekommt man nur einen eingeschränkten Eindruck davon, wie das Bild werden wird. Es ist seitenverkehrt, und wenn Farben mit im Spiel sind, muss man sie sich vorstellen. Erst wenn die Entwürfe geprooft sind, wird man sehen, ob das Bild tatsächlich so geworden ist, wie man es geplant hat. Falls nicht, kann man die Entwürfe modifizieren und es noch einmal versuchen. Jede Drucktechnik bringt ihre speziellen Herausforderungen mit sich, welche die Praxis und das Denken des Künstlers beeinflussen und für das Publikum jeweils spezifische Merkmale bereithalten. Hockney hat kaum Siebdrucke gemacht. Ganz offensichtlich fühlt er sich von der Kombination aus Möglichkeiten und Beschränkungen, die dieser Technik innewohnen, nicht stimuliert. Holz- oder Linolschnitte hat er überhaupt nicht gemacht. Analogdrucke herzustellen ist eine sehr haptische Angelegenheit. Man arbeitet mit Platten, Steinen und Transferfilmen, verwendet Nadeln und Stäube, Tinten und Säuren und ist auf klapprige alte Druckerpressen und andere Gerätschaften angewiesen. Nicht selten braucht man auch fremde Hilfe. Einer der großartigen Aspekte der Druckgrafik ist ja gerade der, dass die Zusammenarbeit mit anderen zum integralen Bestandteil des Verfahrens wird. Bei Hockney waren es langjährige Beziehungen, die ihn – unter anderem – mit dem Radierspezialisten Maurice Payne und dem Lithografen Ken Tyler verbanden. Seit den 2000er-Jahren hilft ihm der Computerexperte Jonathan Wilkinson, sich mit digitalen Arbeitsmethoden vertraut zu machen. Alle diese langjährigen Mitarbeiter haben ihm auch für zahlreiche Porträts Modell gesessen.

Von Anfang an hat sich Hockney mit zwei Arten von Motiven beschäftigt: Menschen und Orte. In der Frühphase konzentrierte sich seine Beobachtung von Menschen öfter auf Beziehungen, die in Narrative integriert wurden. Mit der Zeit etablierte sich eine Praxis des Einzelporträts in Form von Zeichnungen, Drucken und Gemälden, bei der einige enge Freundinnen und Freunde im Laufe mehrerer Jahrzehnte Hunderte Male dargestellt wurden. Seine frühen Bilder von Örtlichkeiten stellten hauptsächlich städtisches Ambiente dar – heute sind es rurale Landschaften. Ein Ort kann in Serien wiederholt werden, die ihn bei unterschiedlichem Wetter oder zu verschiedenen Jahreszeiten zeigen. Wiederholung ist das Entscheidende, sowohl bei Porträts als auch bei Landschaften. Nur durch Wiederholung lässt sich der Vorgang des Beobachtens vertiefen.

Während seines gesamten künstlerischen Schaffens hat sich Hockney immer wieder dafür begeistert, neue Werkzeuge des Bildermachens zu entdecken. Für eine gewisse Zeit kann das Mittel sogar den Zweck bestimmen. Neben seinen gründlichen Erkundungen traditioneller Drucktechniken gab es in den 1980er-Jahren auch eine intensive Phase, in der er Druckgrafik mit seinem Faxgerät machte (die er im selben Moment einem ganzen Freundeskreis weiterleitete – wie ein Instagrammer *avant la lettre*). Dann fand er heraus, dass er komplexe Drucke auch zu Hause mithilfe seines Canon-Farbkopierers herstellen konnte. Das riesige Gerät hatte eine eigene Tonerkartusche für jede Farbe, die jeweils einzeln nacheinander gedruckt werden mussten. 1986 produzierte Hockney auf dem Canon 33 Editionen seiner stolz als „home-made prints" bezeichneten Arbeiten. Aus weiteren Experimenten mit verschiedenen Techniken entstanden Fotocollagen (S. 158–159) und Bilder aus Papierbrei (S. 53–55).

Seit etwa fünfzehn Jahren eignet sich Hockney die digitalen Werkzeuge des Bildermachens mit derselben Leidenschaft an, die er früher für ihre analogen Gegenstücke aufgebracht hat. Diese Begeisterung entwickelte sich parallel zu einem intensiven Fokus auf das Malen von Pleinair-Landschaften in Öl zu verschiedenen Jahreszeiten – ganz nach altmodisch impressionistischer Art. Zunächst experimentierte er an seinem Desktop-Computer mit Photoshop für Porträts, und ab 2009 verwendete er eine App namens *Brushes* auf seinem neuen iPhone. Schon bald zeichnete er auch auf seinem Mobiltelefon permanent nach dem Leben. Und auch an diesen digitalen Werken ließ er einen ausgewählten Kreis von Freunden teilhaben, indem er ihnen täglich die Dateien direkt vom Handy aus schickte. Als das iPad auf den Markt kam, rüstete er sofort auf (S. 69–75).

Im Januar 2011 sah ich in Paris zufällig die erste Ausstellung dieser Bilder. Alle Exponate wurden auf denselben Geräten gezeigt, auf denen sie auch produziert worden waren, will heißen, das, was wir in der Galerie zu sehen bekamen, entsprach genau dem, was Hockney bei der Herstellung der Bilder gesehen hatte. Angesichts der nebeneinander aufgereihten Geräte wirkte die ganze Ausstellung allerdings etwas zu stark dominiert von den Designentscheidungen der Firma Apple. Wenig später ging Hockney dazu über, seine digitalen Bilder stattdessen auf hochwertigen Tintenstrahldruckern zu produzieren (S. 69). Die Hintergrundbeleuchtung des Bildschirms war jetzt nicht mehr vorhanden. Ein gewisser Trennungseffekt, wie er für traditionelles Drucken typisch ist, kam damit wieder zur Geltung.

Hockneys zunehmende Vertrautheit mit digitalen Methoden führte zu Videolandschaftsporträts auf mehreren synchronisierten Monitoren (S. 76–77) und in den letzten Jahren zu einer Serie „fotografischer Zeichnungen", bei denen es sich um digitale Fotocollagen von Menschengruppen im Studio handelt, die konträre Perspektiven kombinieren. Auch heute noch lässt sich Hockney vom Computerwerkzeug in seinen vielfältigen Varianten zu dem inspirieren, was er schon immer leidenschaftlich gern getan hat: seine Beobachtungen von Menschen und Orten in Bilder umzusetzen.

David Hockney stellt stets seine Neugier in den Vordergrund. Betrachtet man sein Gesamtwerk, so ist es – naturgemäß – heterogen: Abenteuer ohne Risiko wäre ja auch ein Widerspruch in sich. Doch in seinen vielen aufeinanderfolgenden Projekten offenbart sich – insbesondere in den druckgrafischen Arbeiten – eine wahre Fundgrube an *Möglichkeiten*. Möglichkeiten, dasselbe immer und immer wieder und jedes Mal neu zu tun, jedes Mal die Welt mit weit geöffneten Augen zu betrachten. In dieser Hinsicht ist er ein großes Vorbild, für uns alle.

# Hockney making prints

I have mentioned David Hockney in various conversations lately. Do you have an opinion? What is it? Several artist friends answered something along the lines of: "I used to think I don't like him, but now I do." Some said the prints are his best work. A writer praised Hockney's 2001 book *Secret Knowledge: Rediscovering the Lost Techniques of the Old Masters*. I agreed wholeheartedly. He and I then realized we have opposite views on whether its central hypothesis is correct or not. Everyone admires how Hockney has never stopped. One of my students told me he is her favourite artist. She went on to say that in the painting class where her boyfriend studies, all students have a Hockney book stashed away – for those moments when inspiration needs to be replenished. While I absorb myself in Hockney's printmaking, I understand these young painters perfectly. The prints have such a generous quality. They make me want to make pictures, instead of reading or writing about it.

Hockney is great at telling stories. The interviews I read are all engaging. It seems to me that when he speaks, he always tries to *make sense* in the moment, and never simply to repeat the expected. In his work I see a back and forth between an interest for narrative and relationships, and a passion for intense observation and how it can be translated into picture. How do you enable the viewer to truly share your experience through *depiction*? That may sound very basic: Isn't this what most artists do? On the surface, perhaps. For Hockney, this ambition – this problem – has been the driving force behind his relentless activity for some seventy years. It has produced all sorts of side effects along the way: visual, technical, social, liberating. It follows that Hockney is ardent about the role of tools. He is deeply knowledgeable about methods and technologies used by artists in the past and he himself is constantly looking for new tools which can help him further his aims. Just how do you translate and transmute the multisensorial array of information that observation inputs to your brain – into a depiction, using picture-making technology? Do you aim for story or snapshot or something in between? Do you want the process to be smooth or have friction? How do you deal with depth of field and perspective; how do you compensate for loss of resolution and detail; how do you select and take account of all the aural, olfactory, intellectual, psychological and physiological stimuli which are present alongside the visual, while you are observing and thinking? There is no way you can do this while ignoring the role of tools and technology. Every picture-making tool has its limitations and quirks. Traditional printmaking techniques have many. This makes them attractive.

Already as a 17-year-old at the Bradford School of Art in 1954, Hockney made impressive colour lithographs, but his first major printmaking period began in 1961 while a student at the Royal College of Art. Short on money for canvas and paint, he learned material was freely available in the print workshop. He soon embarked on an etching project (pp. 118–125) inspired by William Hogarth's eight-painting series *A Rake's Progress* from 1732–1734, which Hogarth himself had made engravings of the following year. While these engravings were careful copies of the paintings (reflecting the fact that this was the only way to publish a painting before the invention of photography), Hockney used the medium of etching for a free-wheeling reimagining of Hogarth's themes. He set the story in present-day New York (which he had just visited) and gave the central character his own likeness. All sixteen prints in the series were printed from single plates, for which line etching and aquatint was used. In each image, one isolated part of the picture is printed with red ink, the rest in black. Deciding that all etchings share the same configuration offered the artist a free pass at pictorial invention within these restraints. The etchings were published in 1963, one year after his graduation. They look strikingly fresh today, sixty years later. In another etching project from the sixties, the illustrations to C. P. Cavafy's *Fourteen Poems* (pp. 126–133), the focus is on direct depiction of two boy lovers. They are exquisitely drawn in single, naked lines. The impact of these etchings becomes even more striking when you learn they were published in 1966: gay love was still criminalized in Great Britain.

From early on Hockney has been remarkably successful with his work. He never *needed* to make prints to publish it, unlike Hogarth more than two hundred years earlier. Instead, there must have been aspects to the printmaking methods which triggered his creative process, again and again. From 1954 to 1995, David Hockney has published more than three hundred editions of etchings and lithographs. These projects cover the range from very direct and straightforward prints to hugely complex lithographs made from over forty plates.

Etching and lithography offer unique alternatives to drawing and painting. Mechanically, it doesn't have to be much unlike using a pen or brush on paper. Psychologically, it is. When you make a drawing or painting you see the image exactly as it is, at that moment. When you work on templates for a print, you only partially see what will become your picture: it is reversed, and if colours will be involved, you have to imagine them. Only when your templates have been proofed will you see if your picture has turned out as planned. If it has not, you can modify the templates and try again. Every printing technique poses particular hurdles to be negotiated, which influence the experience and thinking of the maker and offer specific characteristics to the viewer. Hockney has hardly made any screenprints. Apparently, this technique's combination of possibilities and hurdles doesn't stimulate him. He has made no woodcuts or linocuts at all. Making analogue prints is very tactile. You work on plates and stones and transfer films, use needles and dust, inks and acids and you depend on cranky old presses and other machinery. You often need help. One of the great aspects of printmaking is the way collaboration becomes integrated in the process. In Hockney's case there have been longstanding relationships with, among others, the etching specialist Maurice Payne and the lithographer Ken Tyler. From the 2000s, the computer expert Jonathan Wilkinson has been assisting Hockney's immersion in digital methods of working. All longstanding collaborators have sat for numerous portraits.

Two types of subject matter follow Hockney since the very beginning: people and places. Early on, his observation of people was more often focused on relationships and integrated into narratives. Over time a practice of single portraiture has been established in the form of drawings, prints and paintings, where some close friends have been depicted hundreds of times over several decades. Early pictures of places were primarily urban – today they are rural landscapes. One site may be repeated in a series, showing it in different weathers or seasons. Repetition is key, both for portraits and landscapes. Only through repeating the act of observation can you deepen it.

Throughout his time as an artist, Hockney has been happy to let himself be carried away upon discovering new picture-making tools. For a while, the new means may inspire the ends. Beside his deep forays into traditional printmaking, he had an intense period in the 1980s making prints with his fax machine (instantaneously distributing them to a circle of friends, like an Instagrammer before his time). He then discovered he could make complex prints at home using his Canon colour copier. The huge machine had separate cartridges for each colour, which had to be printed one at the time. Hockney produced thirty-three editions of what he proudly labeled "home-made prints" on the Canon in 1986. Other tool-based adventures have resulted in photo collages (pp. 158–159) and paper pulp pictures (pp. 53–55).

For the last fifteen years or so, Hockney has embraced digital picture-making tools with the same fervour earlier reserved for their analogue counterparts. This enthusiasm has developed in tandem with an intense focus on painting landscapes in oil *en plein air*, like an old-fashioned impressionist observing the seasons. He first experimented with using Photoshop on his desktop computer for portraits, then in 2009 began using an app called *Brushes* on his new iPhone. Soon he was constantly drawing from life on his phone. Again he shared his work with a circle of friends, sending them digital files directly from the phone, every day. When the iPad was released he immediately upgraded (pp. 69–75).

In January 2011, I happened to see the first exhibition of these pictures, in Paris. All images were displayed on the same devices on which they had been made, which meant that what we saw in the gallery was exactly similar to what Hockney had been seeing as he made the pictures. Yet, with rows of devices, the exhibition felt dominated by Apple's design choices. Soon after, Hockney began printing his digital pictures on high-end inkjet printers instead (p. 69). The screen's backlight was gone. A certain separation effect, typical of traditional printmaking, had been re-introduced.

Meanwhile, Hockney's ever increasing familiarity with digital methods has inspired multiple-screen video portraits of landscapes (pp. 76–77) and in the last few years a series of "photographic drawings", which are digital photographic collages of groups of people in the studio, employing contradictory perspectives. At this point in time, the computer tool in its many itinerations keeps inspiring Hockney to do what he has always been passionate about: translating his observations of people and places into pictures.

David Hockney follows his curiosity as if nothing else matters. When you look at the totality of his work, it is uneven – of course. Adventure without risk is an oxymoron. Yet among the many projects following one another – print projects in particular –, there is a treasure trove of possibilities displayed. Possibilities for doing the same thing again and again, each time new, each time looking at the world with eyes wide open. His is an example, for us all.

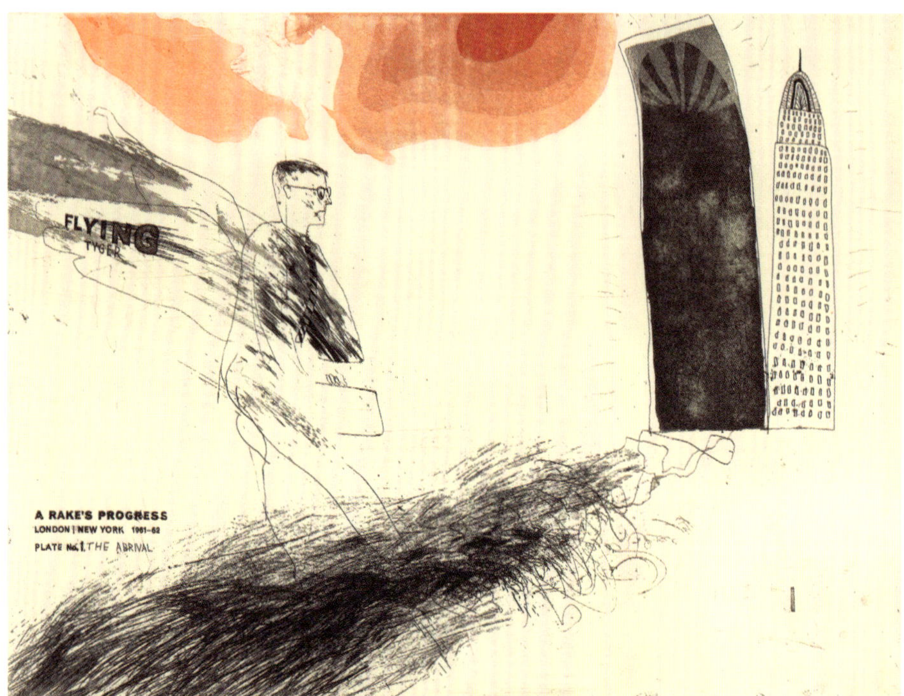


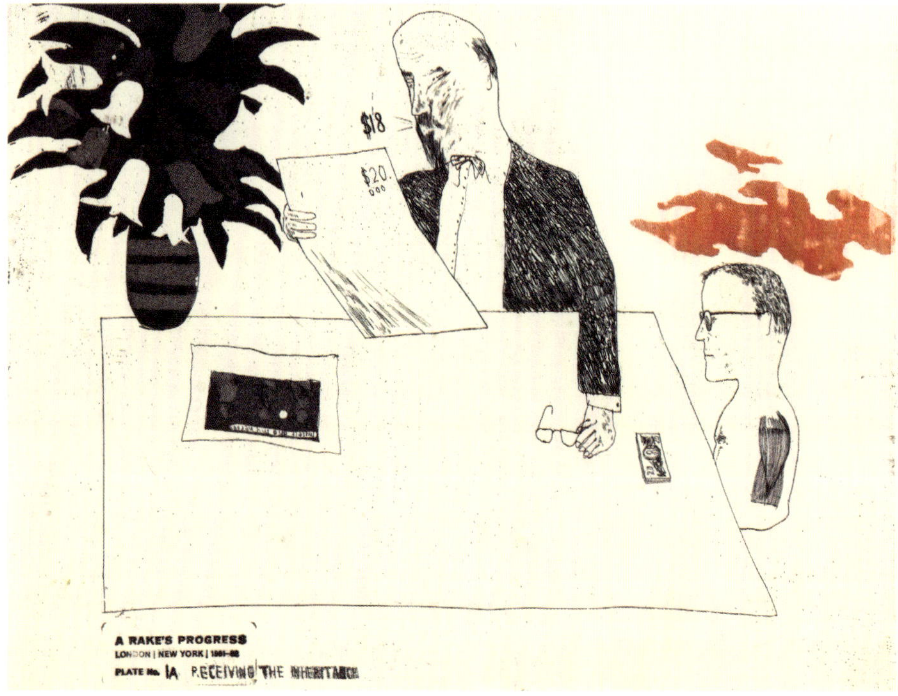


**1. The Arrival** aus | from
**A Rake's Progress,** 1961–1963
Radierung und Aquatinta auf Papier (Auflage von 50) | Etching and aquatint on paper (Edition of 50), 30 × 40 cm
Tate: Purchased 1971
Inv. N° P07029

**1a. Receiving the Inheritance** aus | from
**A Rake's Progress,** 1961–1963
Radierung und Aquatinta auf Papier (Auflage von 50) | Etching and aquatint on paper (Edition of 50), 30 × 40 cm
Tate: Purchased 1971
Inv. N° P07030

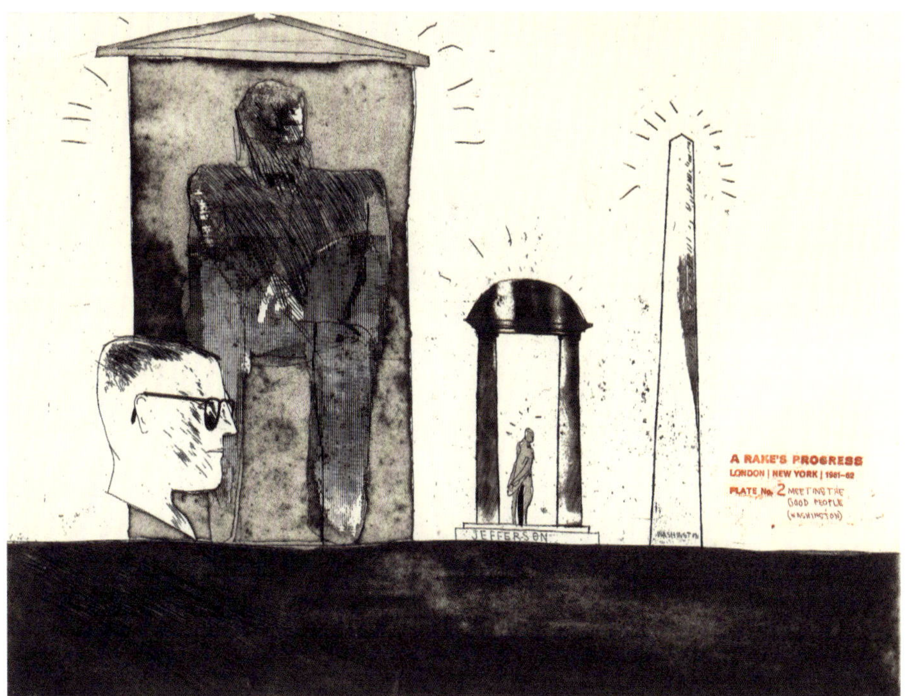


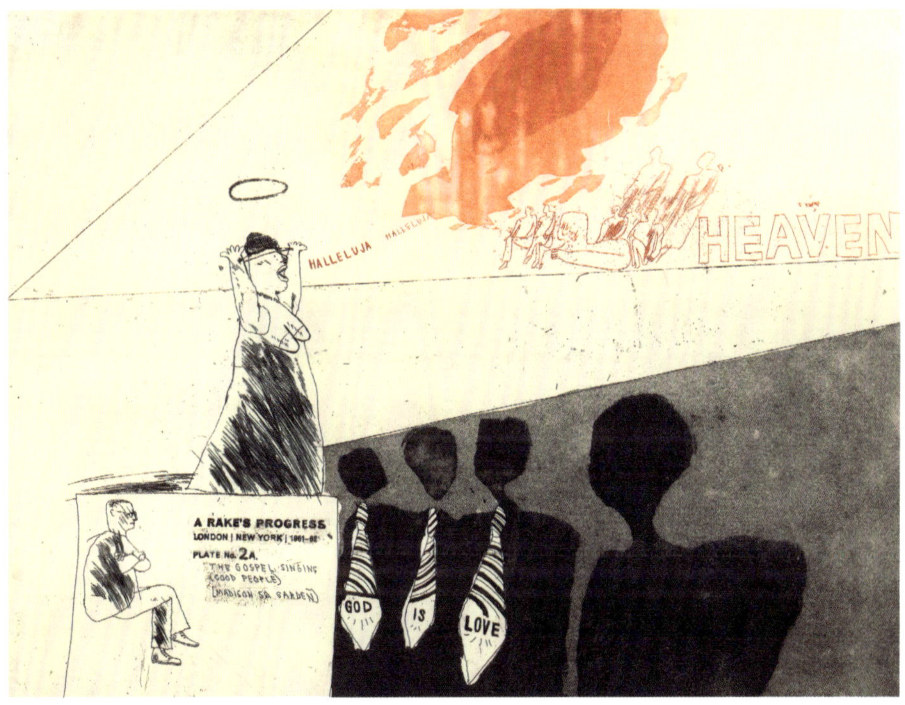


**2. Meeting the Good People (Washington)**
aus | from **A Rake's Progress,** 1961–1963
Radierung und Aquatinta auf Papier (Auflage von 50) | Etching and aquatint on paper (Edition of 50),
30,2 × 40,3 cm
Tate: Purchased 1971
Inv. N° P07031

**2a. The Gospel Singing (Good People) Madison Square Garden** aus | from **A Rake's Progress,** 1961–1963
Radierung und Aquatinta auf Papier (Auflage von 50) | Etching and aquatint on paper (Edition of 50),
30,4 × 40,2 cm
Tate: Purchased 1971
Inv. N° P07032

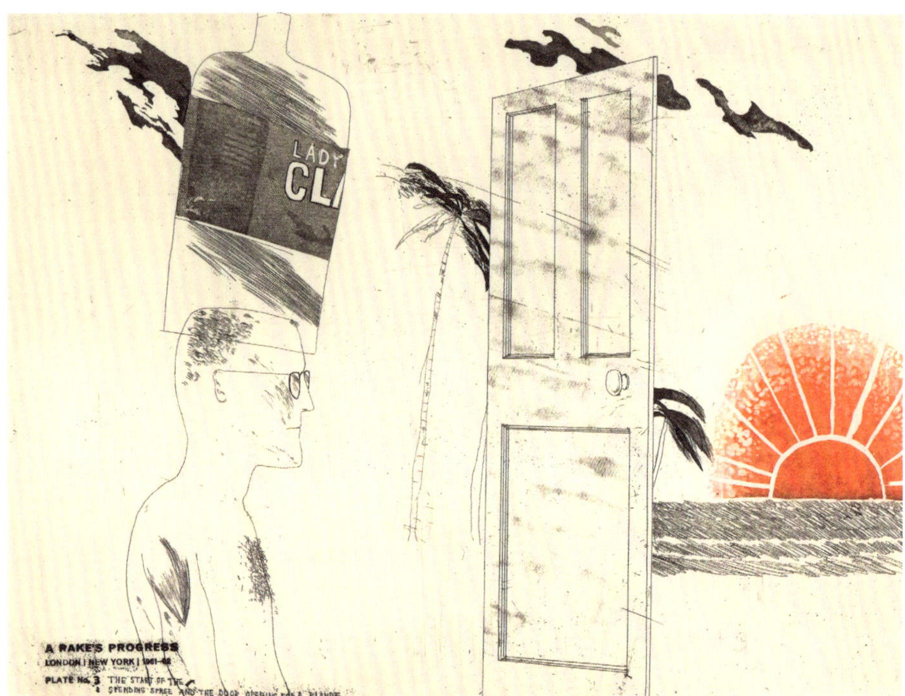


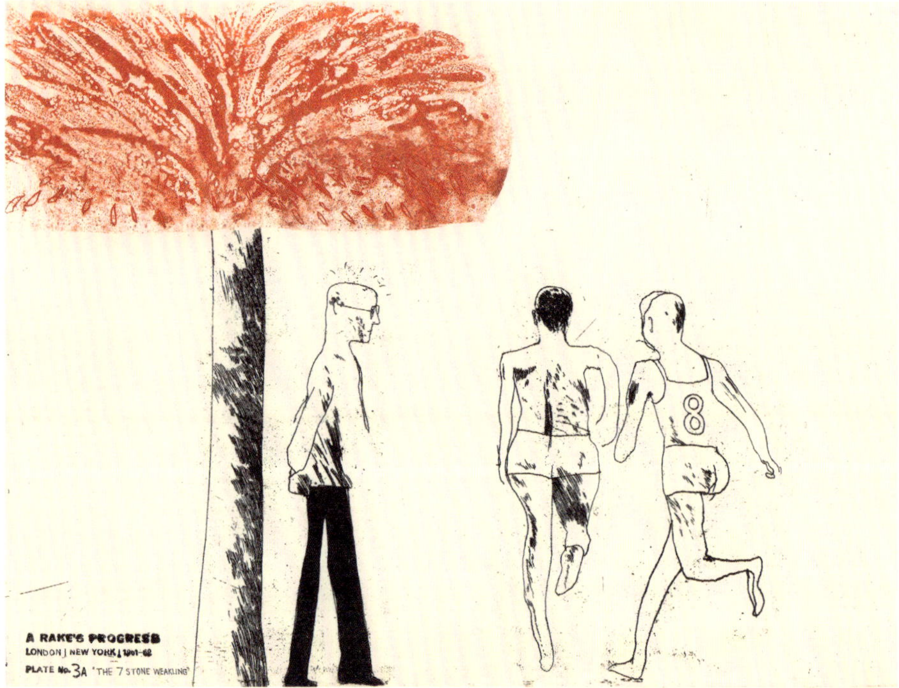


**3. The Start of the Spending Spree and the Door Opening for a Blonde** aus | from **A Rake's Progress,** 1961–1963
Radierung und Aquatinta auf Papier (Auflage von 50) | Etching and aquatint on paper (Edition of 50), 30,2 × 40 cm
Tate: Purchased 1971
Inv. N° P07033

**3a. The Seven Stone Weakling** aus | from **A Rake's Progress,** 1961–1963
Radierung und Aquatinta auf Papier (Auflage von 50) | Etching and aquatint on paper (Edition of 50), 30 × 40 cm
Tate: Purchased 1971
Inv. N° P07034

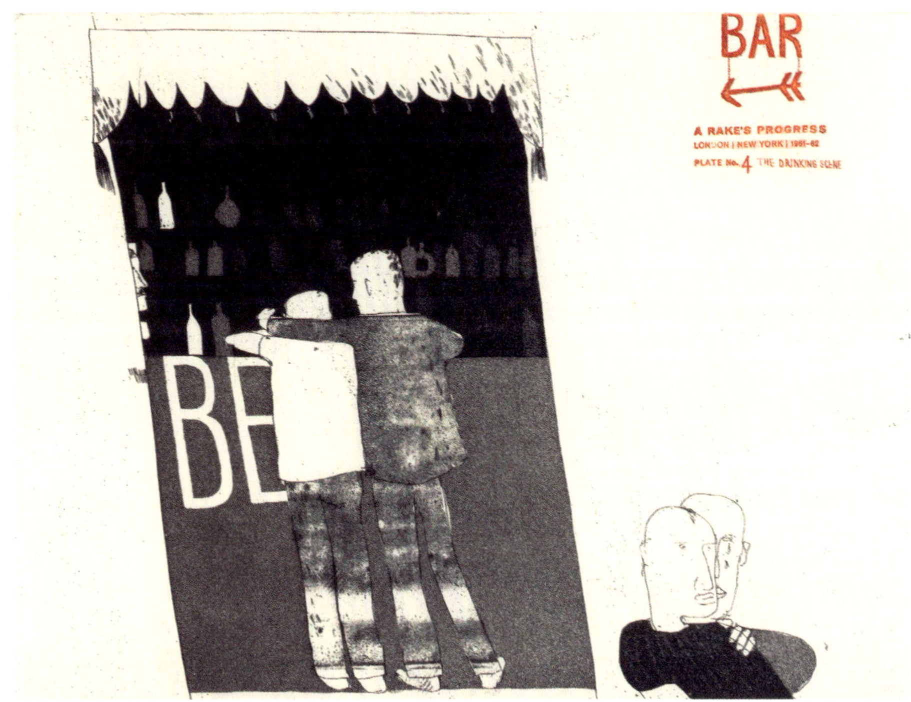


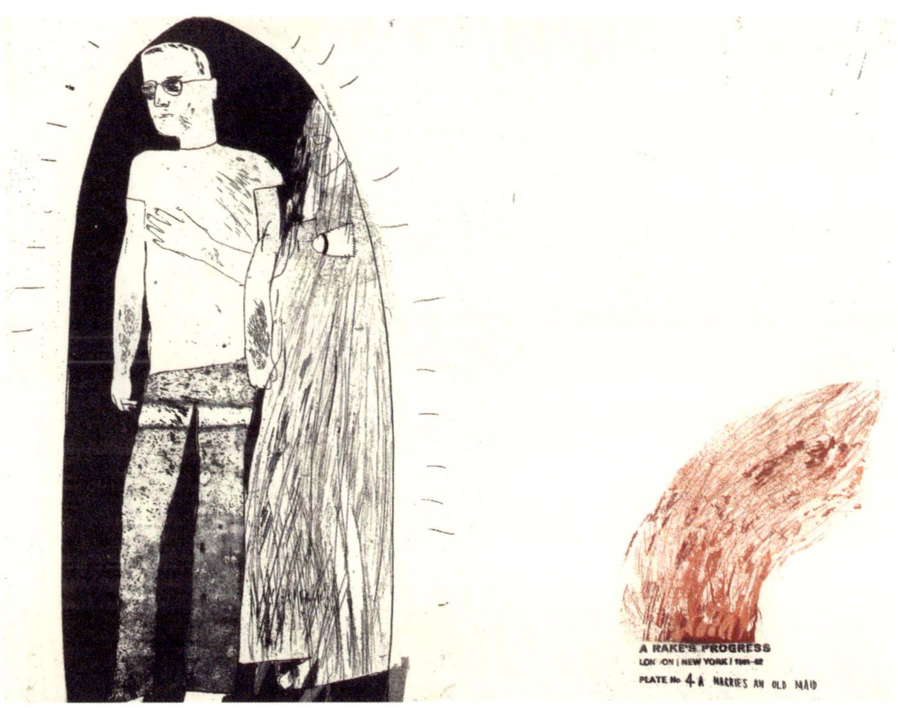


**4. The Drinking Scene** aus | from
**A Rake's Progress,** 1961–1963
Radierung und Aquatinta auf Papier (Auflage von 50) | Etching and aquatint on paper (Edition of 50), 29,5 × 40 cm
Tate: Purchased 1971
Inv. Nº P07035

**4a. Marries an Old Maid** aus | from
**A Rake's Progress,** 1961–1963
Radierung und Aquatinta auf Papier (Auflage von 50) | Etching and aquatint on paper (Edition of 50), 30 × 40 cm
Tate: Purchased 1971
Inv. Nº P07036

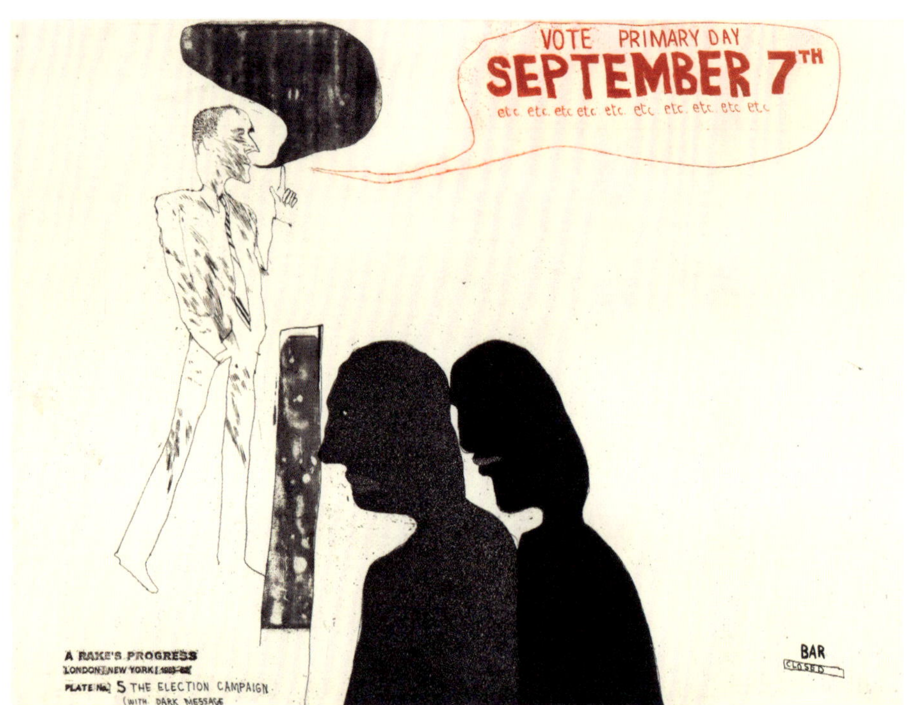


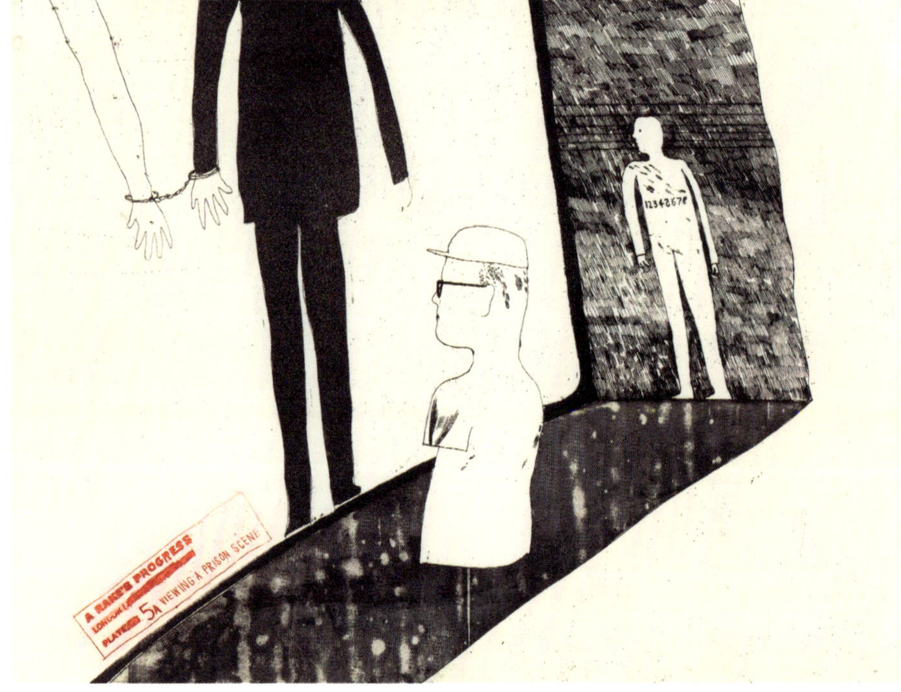


**5. The Election Campaign (with Dark Message)** aus | from **A Rake's Progress,** 1961–1963
Radierung und Aquatinta auf Papier (Auflage von 50) | Etching and aquatint on paper (Edition of 50), 30 × 40 cm
Tate: Purchased 1971
Inv. N° P07037

**5a. Viewing a Prison Scene** aus | from **A Rake's Progress,** 1961–1963
Radierung und Aquatinta auf Papier (Auflage von 50) | Etching and aquatint on paper (Edition of 50), 30 × 40 cm
Tate: Purchased 1971
Inv. N° P07038

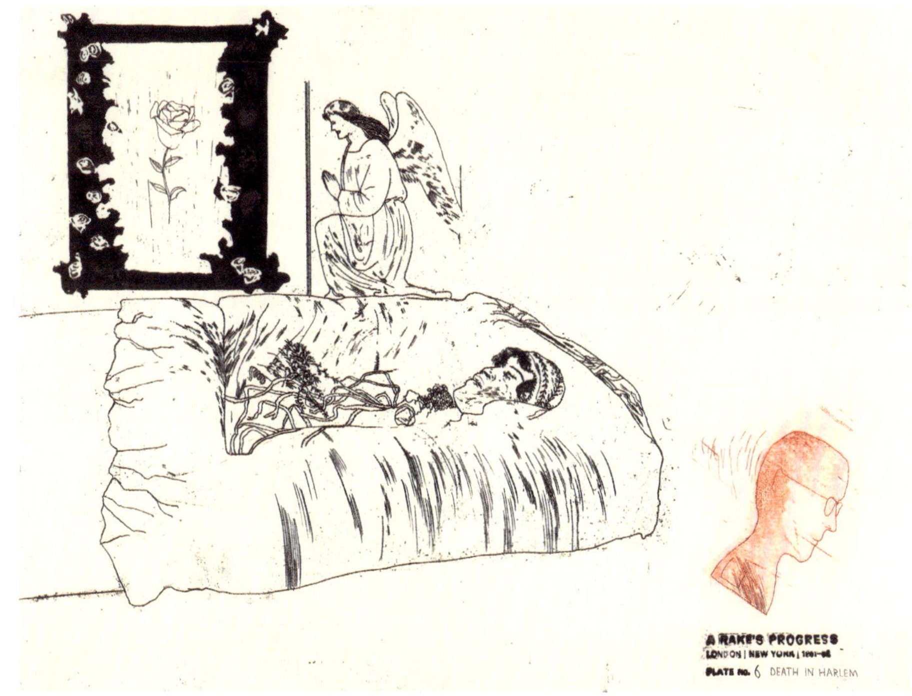


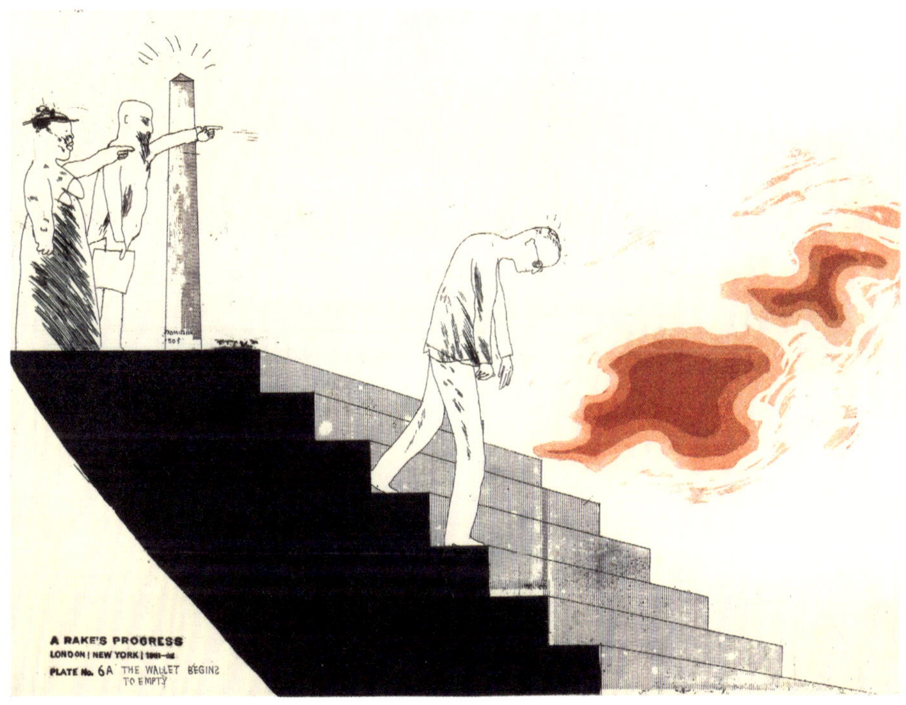


**6. Death in Harlem** aus | from
**A Rake's Progress,** 1961–1963
Radierung und Aquatinta auf Papier (Auflage von 50) | Etching and aquatint on paper (Edition of 50), 30 × 40 cm
Tate: Purchased 1971
Inv. N° P07039

**6a. The Wallet Begins to Empty** aus | from
**A Rake's Progress,** 1961–1963
Radierung und Aquatinta auf Papier (Auflage von 50) | Etching and aquatint on paper (Edition of 50), 30 × 40 cm
Tate: Purchased 1971
Inv. N° P07040

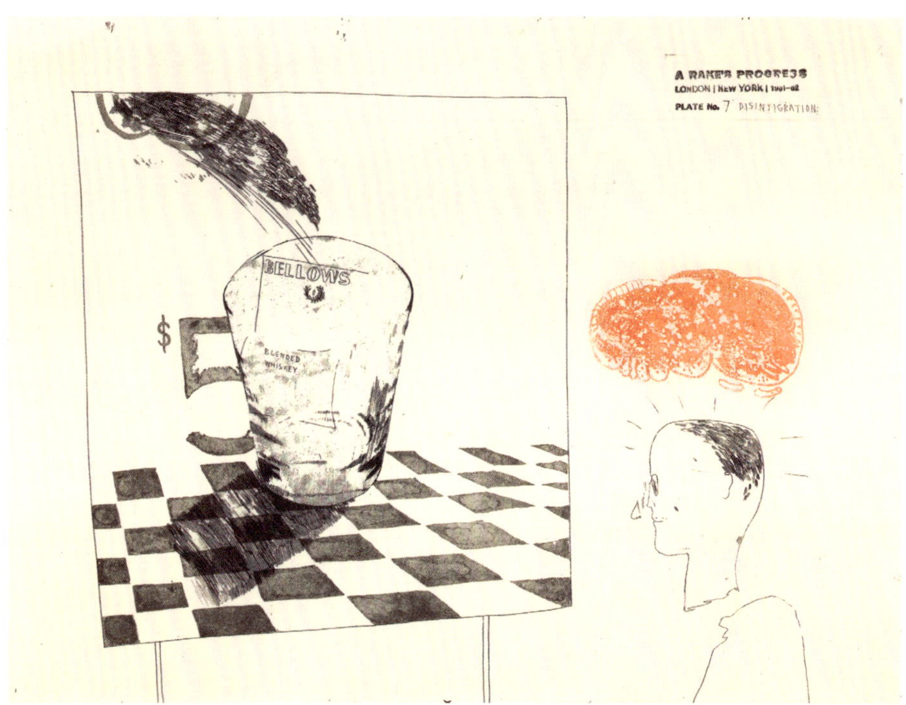


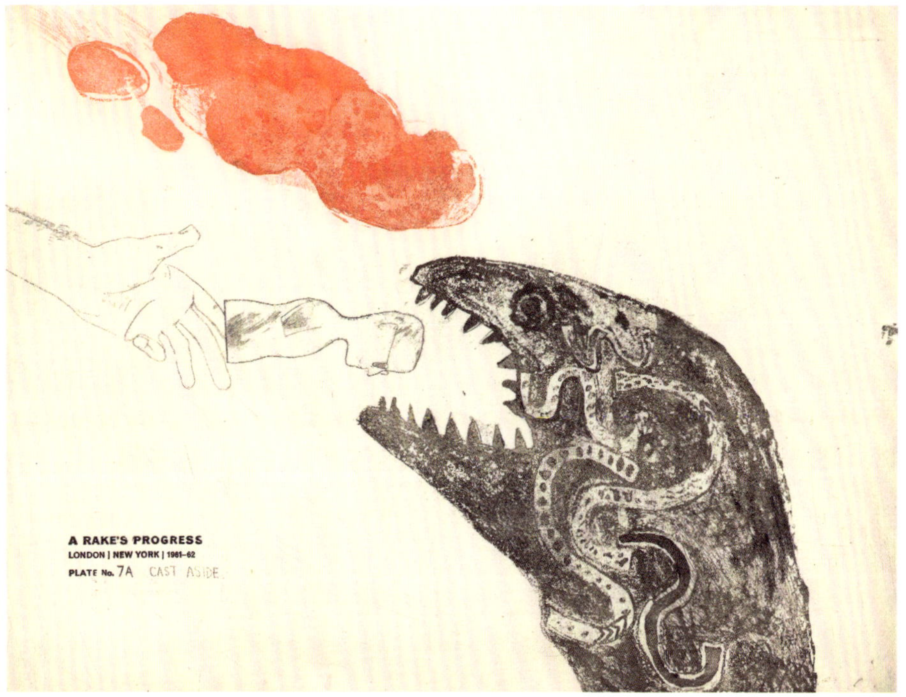


**7. Disintegration** aus | from
**A Rake's Progress,** 1961–1963
Radierung und Aquatinta auf Papier (Auflage von 50) | Etching and aquatint on paper (Edition of 50), 30 × 40 cm
Tate: Purchased 1971
Inv. N° P07041

**7a. Cast Aside** aus | from
**A Rake's Progress,** 1961–1963
Radierung und Aquatinta auf Papier (Auflage von 50) | Etching and aquatint on paper (Edition of 50), 30 × 39,7 cm
Tate: Purchased 1971
Inv. N° P07042

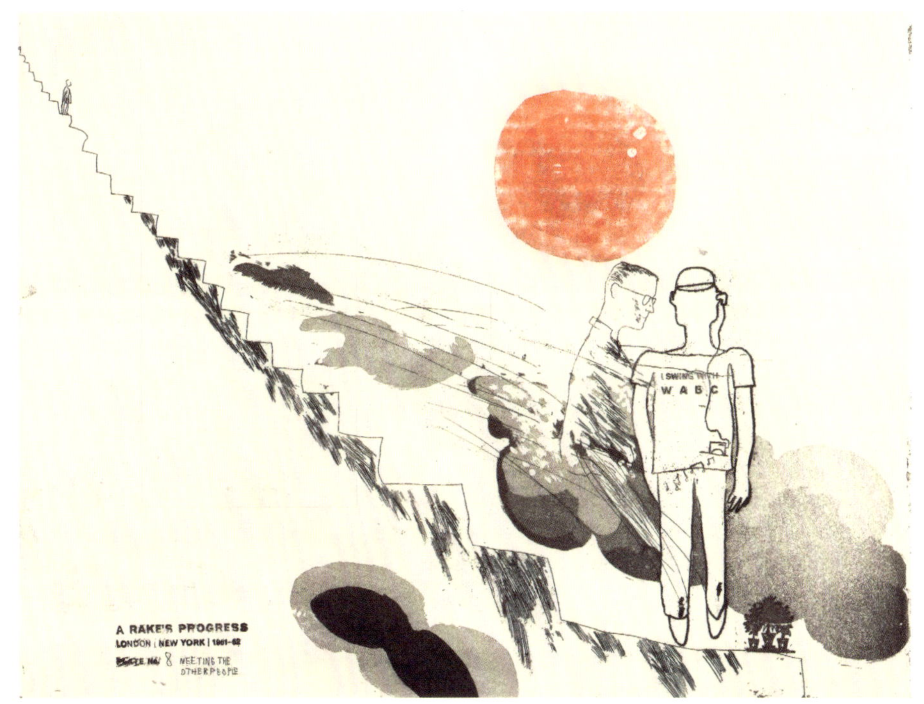


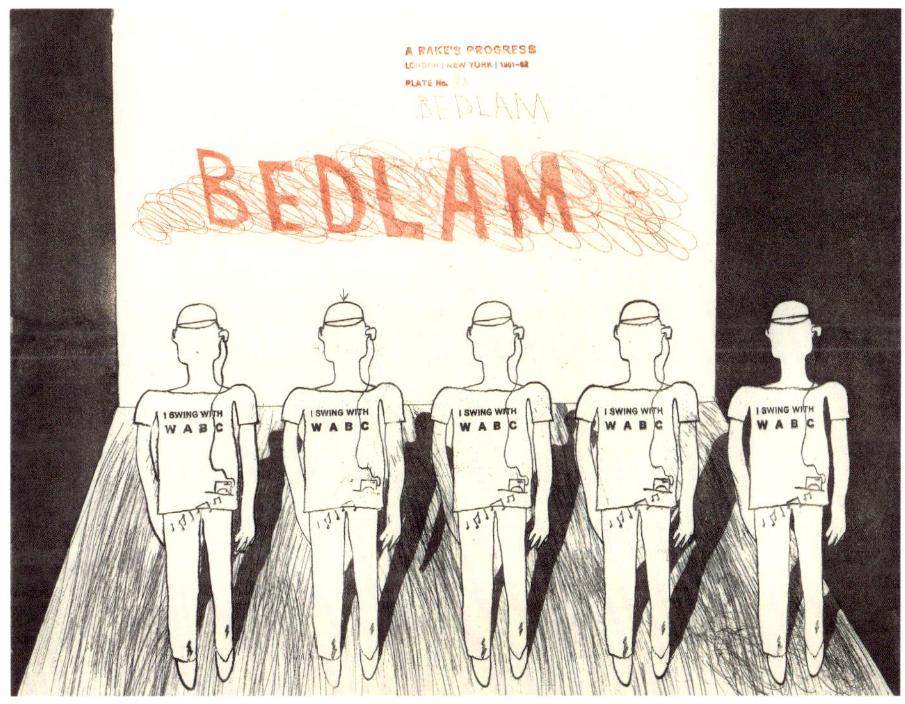


**8. Meeting the Other People** aus | from
**A Rake's Progress,** 1961–1963
Radierung und Aquatinta auf Papier (Auflage von 50) | Etching and aquatint on paper (Edition of 50), 30 × 40 cm
Tate: Purchased 1971
Inv. N° P07043

**8a. Bedlam** aus | from
**A Rake's Progress,** 1961–1963
Radierung und Aquatinta auf Papier (Auflage von 50) | Etching and aquatint on paper (Edition of 50), 30,5 × 40,6 cm
Tate: Purchased 1971
Inv. N° P07044

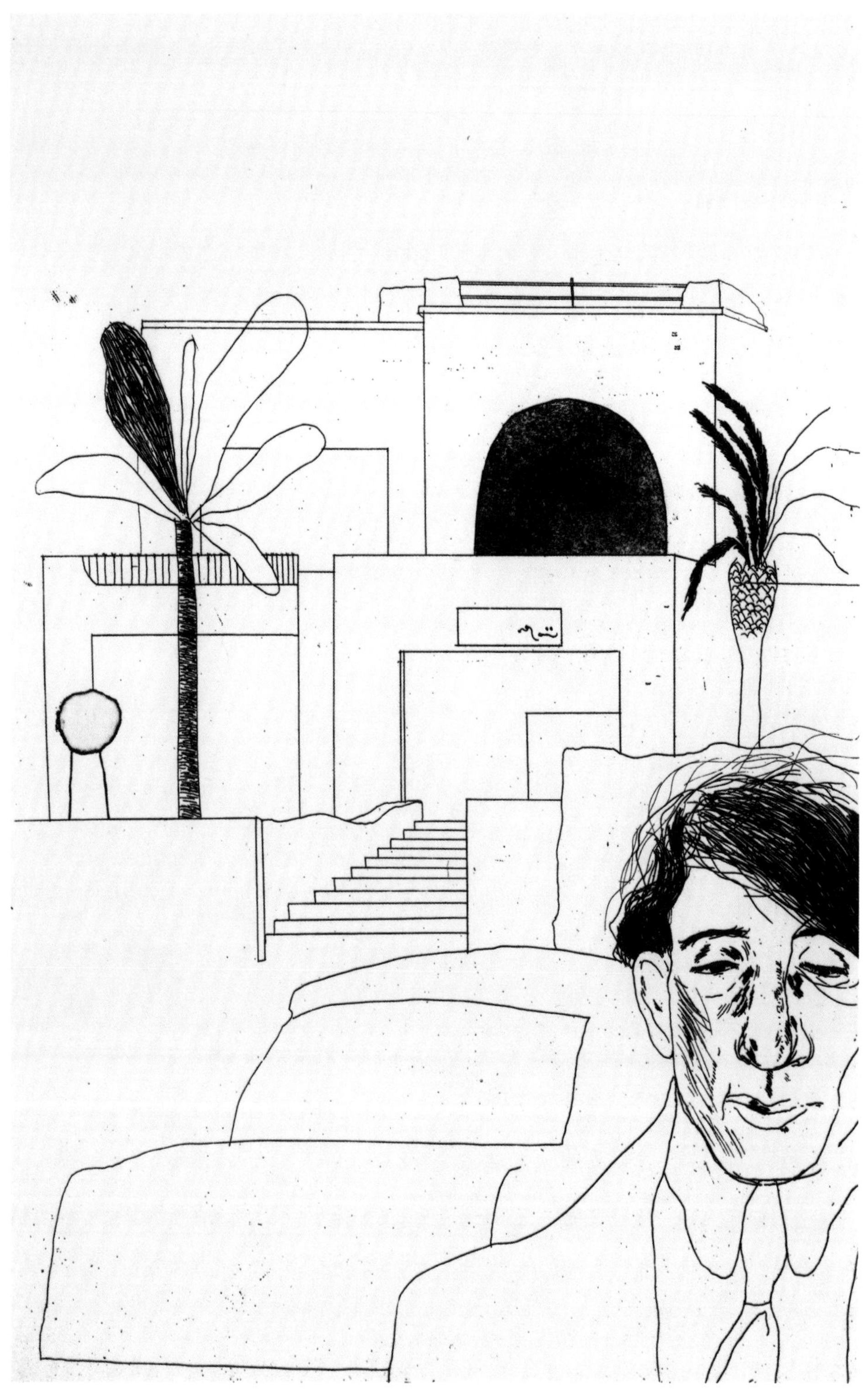

**Portrait of Cavafy II** aus | from **Illustrations for Fourteen Poems from C. P. Cavafy,** 1966
Radierung und Aquatinta auf Papier |
Etching and aquatint on paper,
34,5 × 22,3 cm
Tate: Purchased 1992
Inv. N° P7757

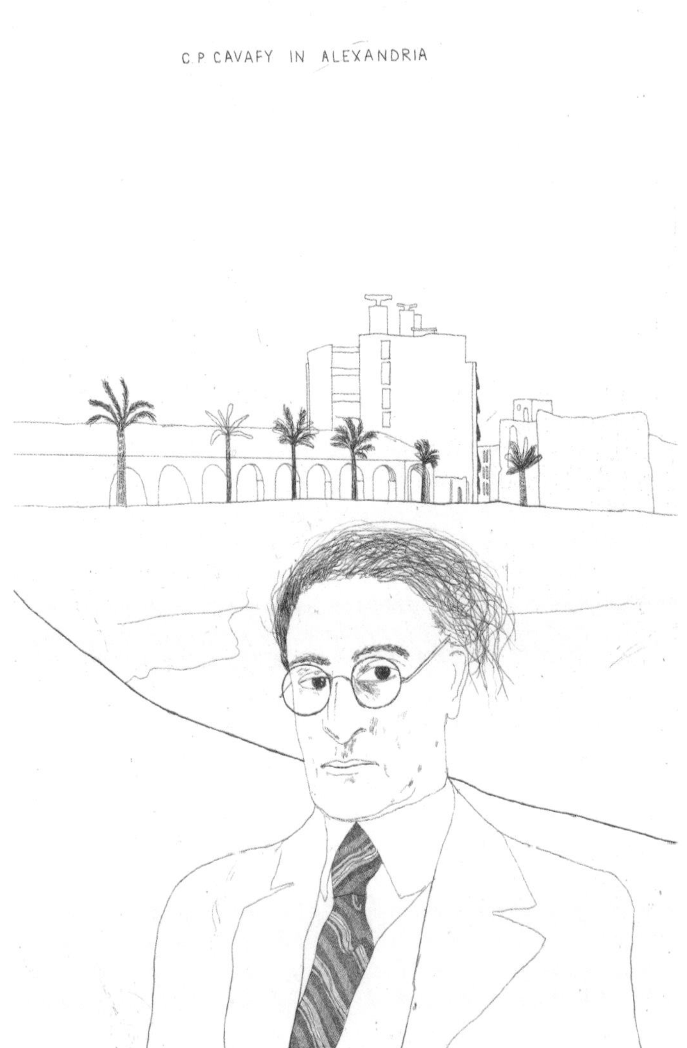


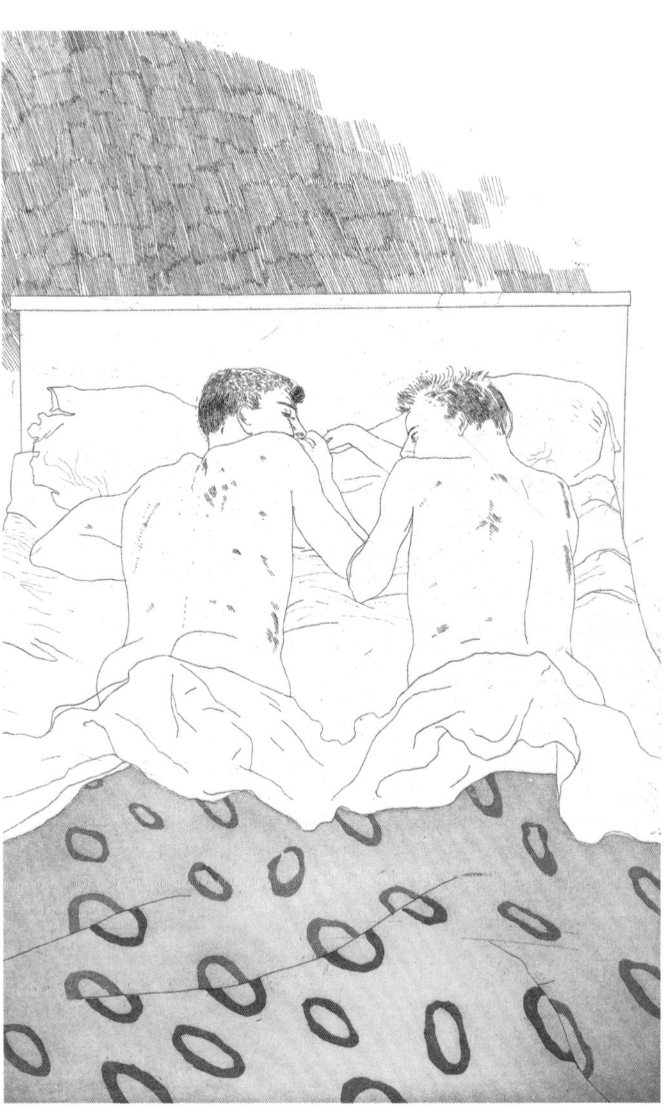

**Portrait of Cavafy in Alexandria**
aus | from **Illustrations for Fourteen Poems from C. P. Cavafy,** 1966
Radierung und Aquatinta auf Papier | Etching and aquatint on paper,
34,5 × 22,3 cm
Tate: Purchased 1992
Inv. N° P77563

**Two Boys Aged 23 or 24**
aus | from **Illustrations for Fourteen Poems from C. P. Cavafy,** 1966
Radierung und Aquatinta auf Papier | Etching and aquatint on paper,
34,5 × 22,3 cm
Tate: Purchased 1992
Inv. N° P77564

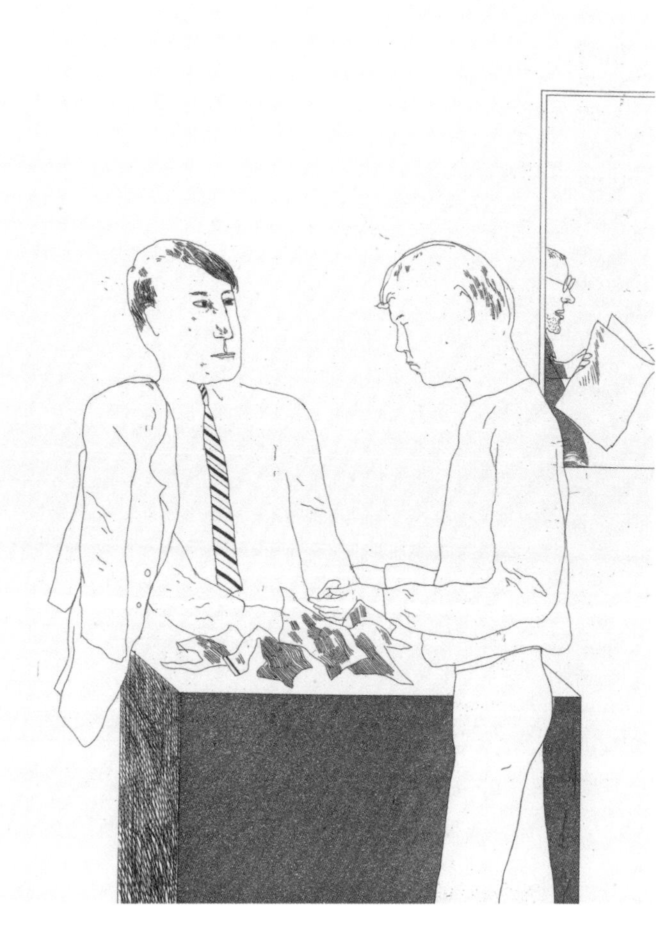

**He Enquired After the Quality** aus | from **Illustrations for Fourteen Poems from C. P. Cavafy,** 1966
Radierung und Aquatinta auf Papier | Etching and aquatint on paper, 34,5 × 22,3 cm
Tate: Purchased 1992
Inv. N° P77565

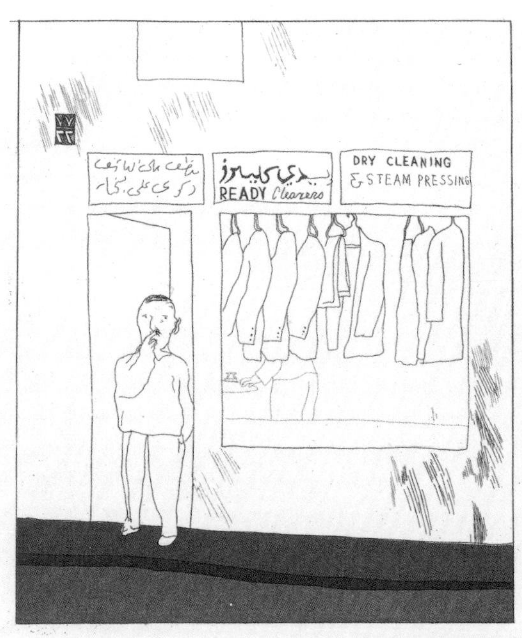


**To Remain** aus | from **Illustrations for Fourteen Poems from C. P. Cavafy,** 1966
Radierung und Aquatinta auf Papier | Etching and aquatint on paper, 34,5 × 22,3 cm
Tate: Purchased 1992
Inv. N° P77566

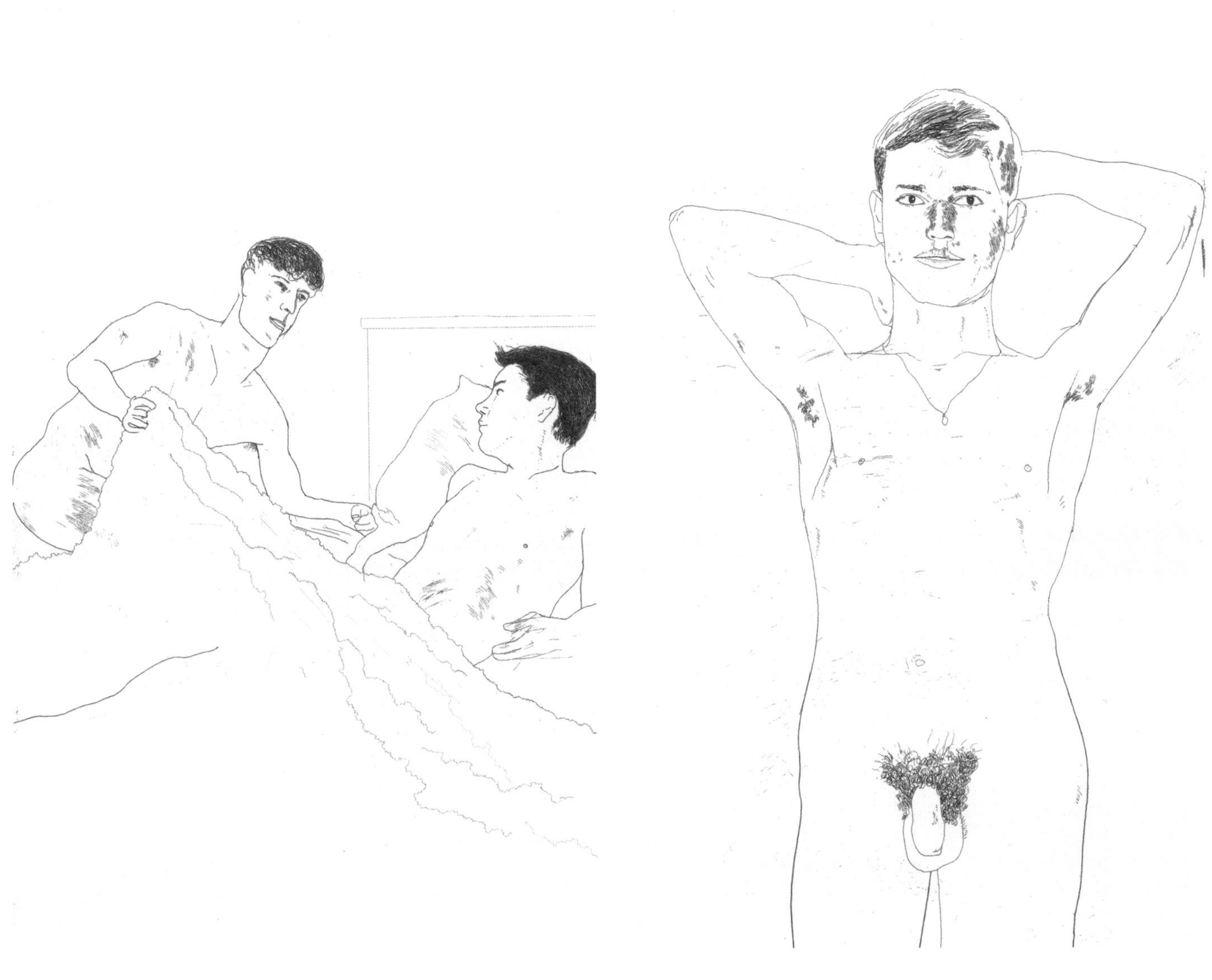

**According to the Prescriptions of Ancient Magicians** aus | from **Illustrations for Fourteen Poems from C. P. Cavafy,** 1966
Radierung auf Papier | Etching on paper, 34,5 × 22,3 cm
Tate: Purchased 1992
Inv. N° P77567

**In an Old Book** aus | from **Illustrations for Fourteen Poems from C. P. Cavafy,** 1966
Radierung auf Papier | Etching on paper, 34,5 × 22,3 cm
Tate: Purchased 1992
Inv. N° P77568

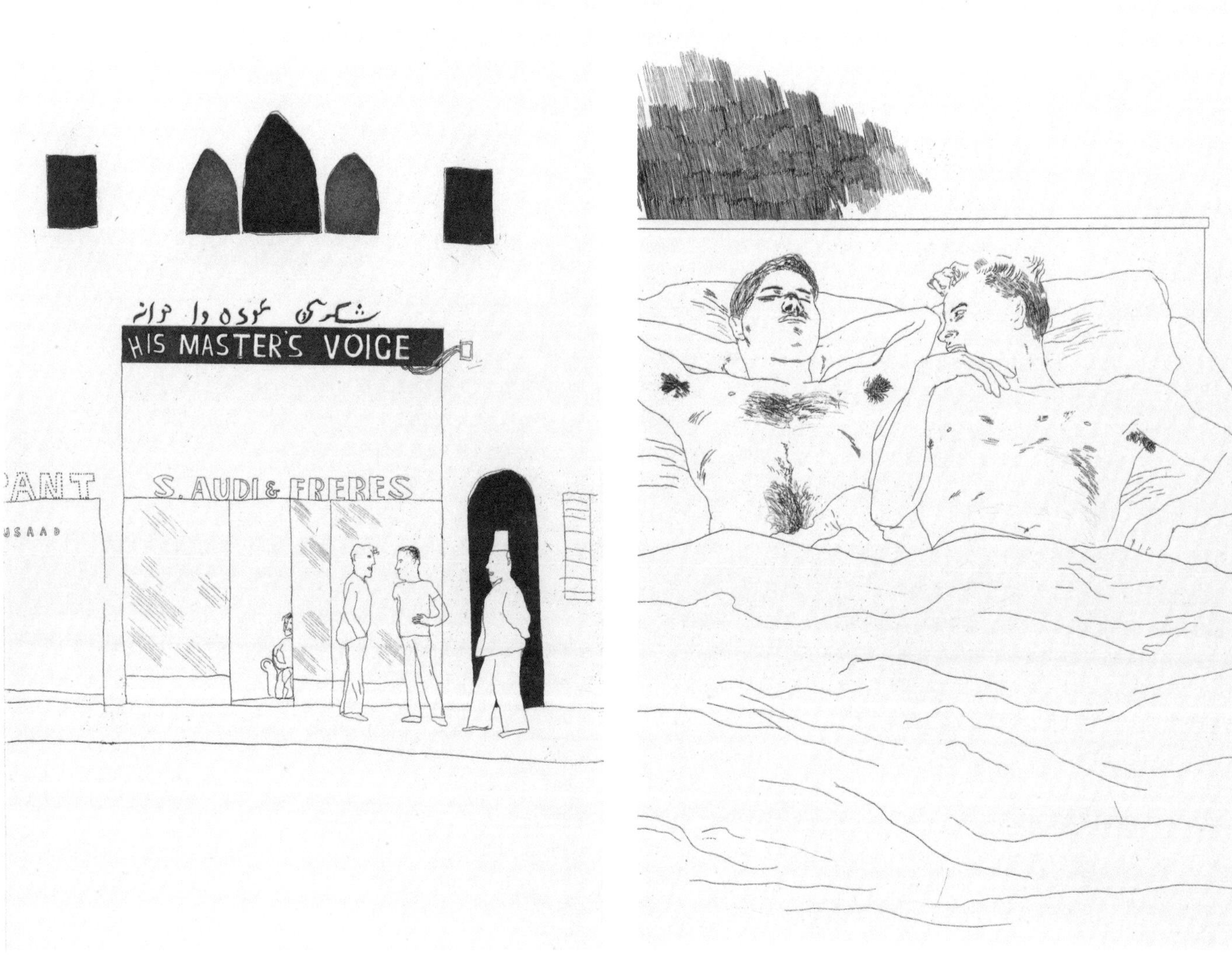


**The Shop Window of a Tobacco Store** aus | from **Illustrations for Fourteen Poems from C. P. Cavafy,** 1966
Radierung und Aquatinta auf Papier |
Etching and aquatint on paper,
34,5 × 22,3 cm
Tate: Purchased 1992
Inv. N° P77569

**In the Dull Village** aus | from **Illustrations for Fourteen Poems from C. P. Cavafy,** 1966
Radierung und Aquatinta auf Papier |
Etching and aquatint on paper,
34,5 × 22,3 cm
Tate: Purchased 1992
Inv. N° P77570

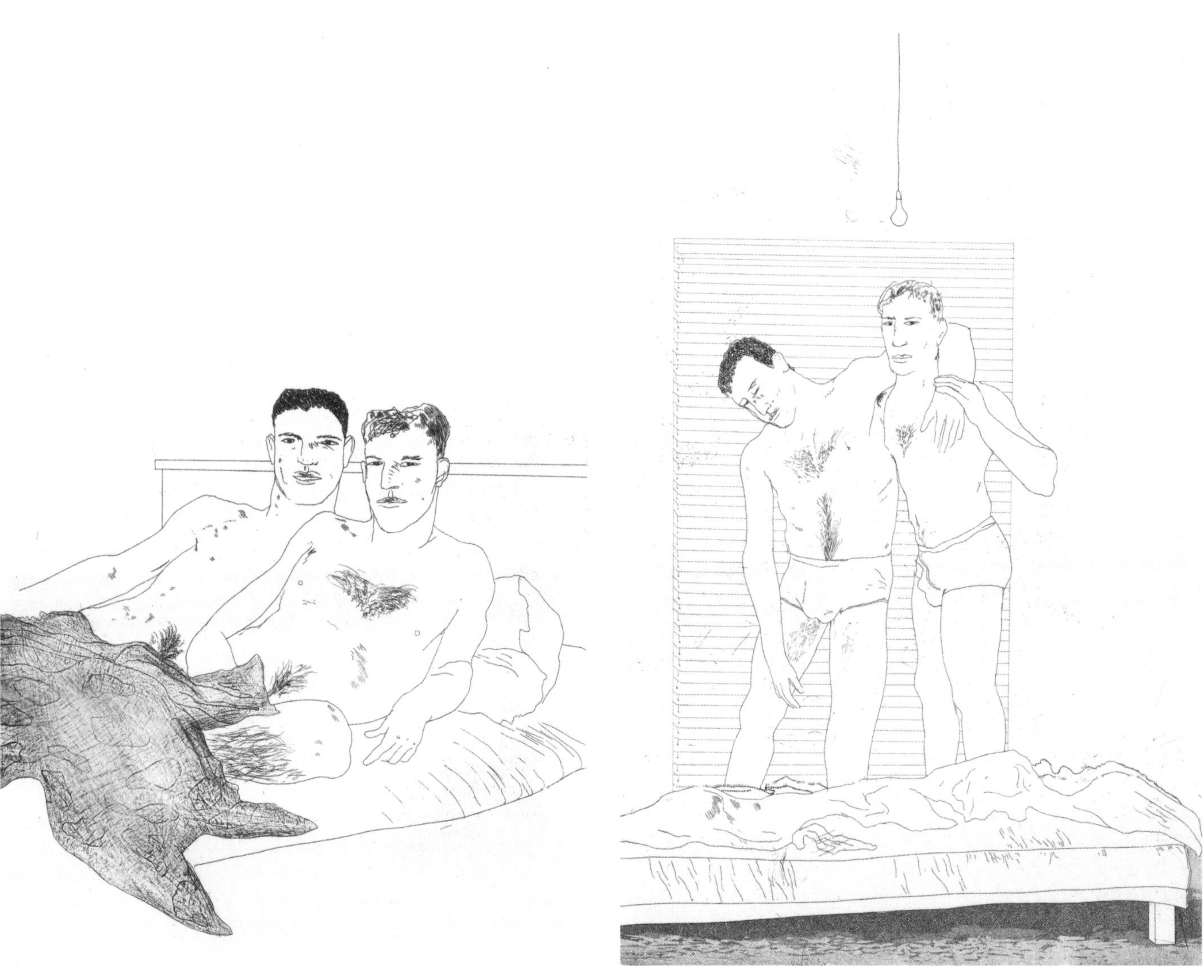

**The Beginning** aus | from **Illustrations for Fourteen Poems from C. P. Cavafy,** 1966
Radierung und Aquatinta auf Papier |
Etching and aquatint on paper,
34,5 × 22,3 cm
Tate: Purchased 1992
Inv. N° P77571

**One Night** aus | from **Illustrations for Fourteen Poems from C. P. Cavafy,** 1966
Radierung und Aquatinta auf Papier |
Etching and aquatint on paper,
34,5 × 22,3 cm
Tate: Purchased 1992
Inv. N° P77572

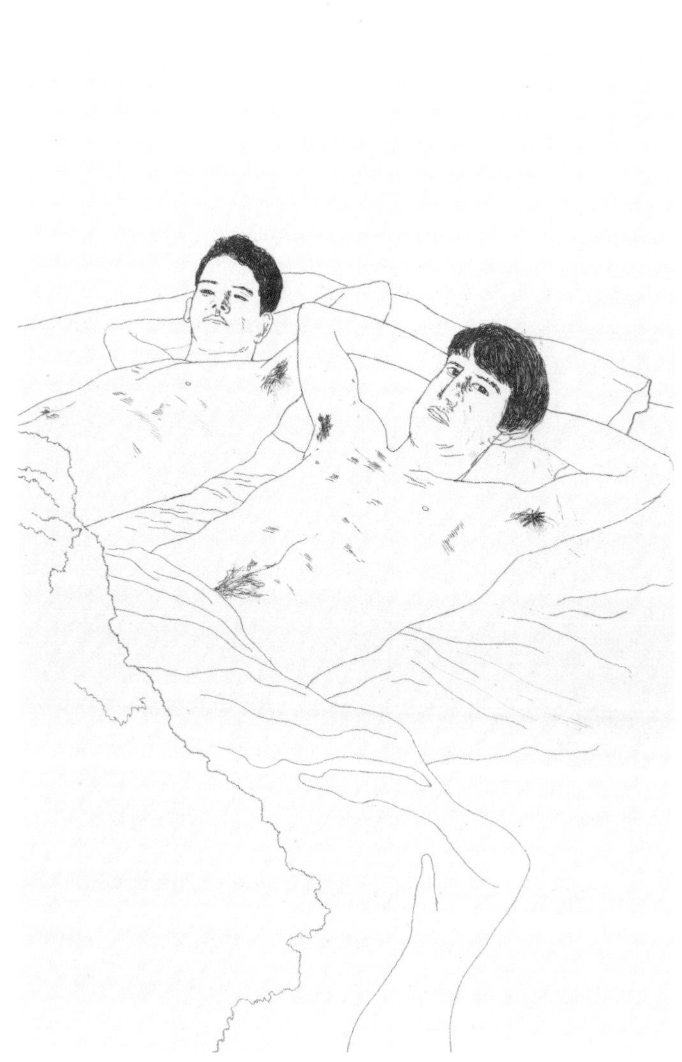

**In Despair** aus | from **Illustrations for Fourteen Poems from C. P. Cavafy,** 1966
Radierung auf Papier | Etching on paper,
34,5 × 22,3 cm
Tate: Purchased 1992
Inv. N° P77573

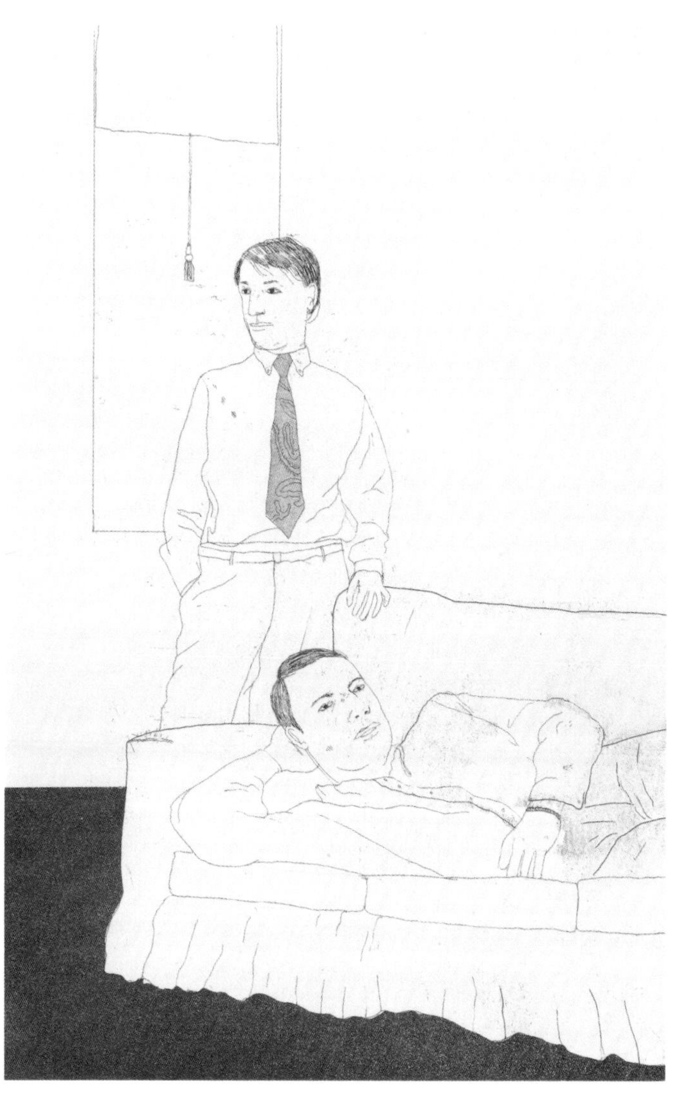

**Beautiful and White Flowers** aus | from **Illustrations for Fourteen Poems from C. P. Cavafy,** 1966
Radierung und Aquatinta auf Papier | Etching and aquatint on paper,
34,5 × 22,3 cm
Tate: Purchased 1992
Inv. N° P77574

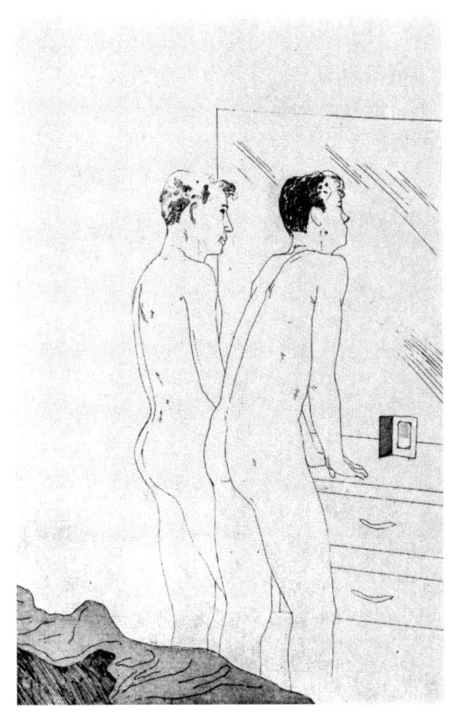

**Quartet,** 1966
Radierung auf Papier | Etching on paper,
33 × 22,8 cm
Privatsammlung | Private Collection

Larissa Kikol



# Die unangestrengte Hand oder Das große Lockerlassen

Der Abstand ist da. Mehr als 20 Jahre im 21. Jahrhundert lassen allmählich Charakteristika erkennen, und zwar von einer postmodernen Malerei des 20. Jahrhunderts oder, noch spezifischer, der 1960er- bis 1980er-Jahre, und von heute, einer Gegenwartsmalerei dieses Jahrhunderts. Im Nachhinein betrachtet blieben viele Künstlerinnen und Künstler ihrer Zeit verhaftet, was nicht die Qualität ihrer Arbeit mindert, aber ihnen tiefere Wurzeln in einem historisch enger gesteckten Kontext verleiht. Dagegen wirken Werke anderer Kunstschaffender heute noch so aktuell wie damals, vor allem ästhetisch und stilistisch tragen sie ein Vakuum an Frische in sich, das ohne Verluste über die weitere Malereientwicklung standhält. David Hockney zählt zu ihnen. Doch woran liegt das?

Dass Hockney in erster Linie in der Pop-Art verortet wird, ist nur eine Einstiegshilfe in sein Werk. Weitere Stileinflüsse lassen sich bei Jean Dubuffet und den Buchstabenbildern wie auch bei der Graffiti-Art-Brut finden, in der Neuen Figuration, in einem distanzierten Realismus, der von einer Edward-Hopper-Atmosphäre subtil ins Komische umschlägt, in der naiven Malerei, der gestisch-naturalistischen Darstellungsform, bei kindlichen Kritzelzeichen und in surrealen Tendenzen. Nachweise lassen sich dafür viele anführen. Die kindlichen Kritzeleien oder Smileys entdeckt man im Detail, zum Beispiel rieselt Hockney sie auf seinen iPad-Zeichnungen wie Puderzucker zwischen die Landschaft (S. 69–75). Das Surreale drückt sich in knallig-chemischen Farben einiger Baumstämme (S. 66–67), Häuser oder Hügel aus sowie in einer kubistisch getürmten Landschaftsbebauung oder in einer nach Belieben gebogenen, geglätteten oder aufgebrochenen Architektur. Naive Formsprachen wendet er mal bei Baumblättern, Straßen oder bergähnlichen Objekten an. Gestisch-naturalistisch entstehen andere Landschaftsgemälde mit vielen Ästen – oder auch Porträts.

Hockney lässt sich stilistisch nicht einfangen, er scheint es auch gar nicht zu wollen. Entscheidend ist, dass er diese verschiedenen Stile nicht bedient, sondern sich vielmehr ihrer bedient. Er nutzt sie je nach Laune und Motiv, spielt sie gegeneinander aus, manchmal sogar in ein und demselben Werk, und bleibt gegenüber jedweder Stilzuschreibung locker. Er scheint nichts er- oder ausfüllen zu wollen. Darin liegt das stilistisch Charakteristische begründet, das am besten alles zusammenfasst und seine Position beschreibt: das Lockerbleiben, das Spielende.

Dem zugrunde liegt eine Struktur, die sich durch die meisten seiner Werke zieht: sein Pinselstrich. Um ihn besser zu begreifen, lohnt es sich, Hockneys Hand zu beobachten. Auf den Landschaftsgemälden und den dazugehörigen Making-of-Videos erkennt man den einzelnen Strich am genauesten: Bei der Entstehung bleibt die Linienplatzierung eine ungefähre, die sich erst in späterer Kombination mit anderen Linien und Farbflächen zu einer genaueren, figürlichen Linie transformiert.[1] Die langen Pinsel hält Hockney am Stielende, sodass die Kontrolle über die Pinselhaare, also die exakte Führung, geringer ist.[2] Der Pinselkopf schwingt über der Leinwand leicht aus, sein Auftreffen auf der Bildoberfläche lässt sich somit nicht auf den Millimeter genau bestimmen. Eine konkretere Platzierung wäre besser möglich, würde man den Pinsel weiter unten anfassen. Doch Hockney zeichnet keine exakten Linien für eine illusionistische oder hyperrealistische Malerei. Auf seinen Bildern erkennt man stets, wie sie gemacht sind, aus großer Nähe bleibt die Linie eine autonome Linie, keine Werkzeuglinie, die einzig der figürlichen Darstellung diente. Hinzu kommt, dass Hockney auch noch selbst Abstand zur Leinwand hält, eine halbe Armlänge oder gerade so weit, dass die Zigarette in der anderen Hand das Bild nicht beschädigen kann.

1. Siehe https://www.youtube.com/watch?v=UVBYfTr8BRQ [zuletzt besucht am 30.8.2021].

2. Ebd.

Nach Martin Gayford übersetzt Hockney alles, was er sehe, in Linien, Punkte, Farbkleckse und Pinselstriche, also in Zeichen. Den Drang, dies zu tun, sieht Gayford bereits in Hockneys Kindheit. Auch Hockney selbst spricht über dieses Vergnügen und den Spaß daran, den er schon früh entdeckte.[3] Gayford erkennt in den sehr großen Gemälden freie, kalligrafische und auch rasche Pinselstriche.[4] Hockney verweist auf Inspirationen aus der chinesischen Malerei, aber auch auf Einflüsse von Pablo Picasso, „das heißt, die Pinselstriche sind alle sichtbar“ und kämen kräftiger aus dem Arm.[5] Die Beschreibungen „rasch“ und „kräftig aus dem Arm“ mögen im Zweifel auf Stellen der sehr großen Bilder zutreffen, jedoch würde ich sie als dem Format geschuldet ansehen und nicht als David Hockneys stilistisches Hauptcharakteristikum betrachten.

3. David Hockney, zitiert in: Martin Gayford, *A Bigger Message. Gespräche mit David Hockney*, Bern (Piet Meyer Verlag) 2012, S. 34.

4. Ibid., S. 65.

5. Ebd.

Werden allerdings einzelne Flächen dichter mit Farbe bestrichen, beispielsweise bei einem Weg, geschieht dies mit etwas mehr Nachdruck. Grob wird der Pinsel in verschiedene Richtungen hin und her gestoßen, nachgerade unelegant werden seine Borsten aufgedrückt und verbogen.[6] So heftig wie bei den Neoexpressionisten geht es dabei aber nicht zu, gleichwohl erlaubt es diese Maltechnik, vom Abstrakten, also von losen Linien und Flächenarrangements in einem weißen, schwebenden Bildraum, in das Figürliche überzuschwingen.

6. Siehe Zeichnung 5/46, https://www.hockney.com/works/digital/iphone [zuletzt besucht am 30.8.2021].

Des Öfteren sieht man bei David Hockney einzelne Linien, in denen weniger Druck und Schnelligkeit liegen. David Hockney ist kein Action-Painter, kein abstrakter Expressionist und auch kein neuer alter Wilder. Seine Linien fungieren nicht als Barometer für unterbewusste Emotionen, es geht nicht um individuellen Ausdruck oder um die Sichtbarkeit von Kraft und Temperament des Körpers. Schnelligkeit, Matsch und Spontaneität wären ebenso unpassende Parameter.

Manche Linien scheinen sogar zögerlich und langsam aufgetragen. Anderenorts ist der Strich kritzelig, auch das liegt an dem langen Holzstiel und seiner distanzierten Handhabung. Ohne den direkten körperlichen und vitalen Druck wirkt die Hand vermeintlich unmotiviert, lustlos, ohne besondere Anstrengung. Das klingt negativ, und in den meisten Fällen mag es einen unbeabsichtigten Qualitätsmangel bedeuten, der zu schlechteren Bildergebnissen führt. Nicht jedoch bei David Hockney; statt einer tatsächlichen Unmotiviertheit handelt es sich natürlich um eine stilistisch gewollte Als-ob-Haltung.

Übrigens lässt sich ein ähnliches Strichcharakteristikum auch in Zeichnungen von Egon Schiele, Andy Warhol oder dem jüngeren britischen Kollegen David Shrigley finden. Bei Letzterem liegt die ästhetische Qualität ebenfalls in einer scheinbar ungelenken, unmotivierten Hand. Im Gegensatz dazu stehen die Pinselstriche von Vincent van Gogh. Im Vergleich heben sich Hockneys Linien sehr viel spielerischer und unabhängiger vom Bildmotiv ab, sie bleiben sturer in ihrer Autonomie. Seine unmotivierte Hand führt zu einer autonomen Linie, die nicht eine gefühlte Landschaftsatmosphäre widerspiegelt, sondern ihr Eigenleben behält. Ändert sie die Richtung, auch mal öfter in kürzeren Abständen, wie bei einem knöchrigen Ast, scheint er gerade mal Daumen und Zeigefinger ein wenig zu bewegen und den Pinsel dadurch zu rollen.[7] Dabei werden Hand, Arm oder Körper kaum bewegt. Auch das wirkt fast lustlos, ein Touch von „Hingerotztem", von „Wenn es denn sein muss" entsteht. Statt schöner, expressiver oder engagierter Linien malt er sture, unabhängige Linien, die etwas Ungelenkes und Schelmisches in sich tragen. Das Ganze lässt sie lässig wirken, unangestrengt. Was auf den ersten Blick nach Alterssteifheit aussieht, entpuppt sich nicht nur als Kühnheit, sondern als eine zeitgenössische Coolness, die sich nicht mehr bemühen oder anstrengen muss. Denn sie kann ohnehin alles – mit einer leichten Daumenbewegung je nach Laune zwischen zwei Zügen an der Zigarette. Auf einigen Werken spitzt sich das Lockere noch weiter zu, dann tritt das Verspielte in aller Klarheit hervor. Besonders in den digitalen Zeichnungen manifestiert sich diese verspielte Klarheit in Abstraktion und einer beinahe kindlichen Zeichensprache. Auf der iPhone-Zeichnung *Untitled, 510* (2009) wird die Sonne zu einem Strichknäuel, in dem gedellte Kritzellinien zu jeder Seite hin ausschlagen. Auf *Untitled 165* (2009) vollzieht sich die freie Transformation durch verbeulte, schiefe Strichmännchen, krumme Ausmalungen und betont dilettantisch wirkende Raummarkierungen. Hockney übertreibt, oder besser gesagt: Er lässt sich gehen, in den Spaß der kindlichen Kritzelei als totale Konsequenz der Lockerheit und der unangestrengten Hand.

Die Malerei ist sein Spielfeld, und das nicht nur auf dem iPhone. Zwar zeigt es sich in den digitalen Werken am unmittelbarsten, doch in Wirklichkeit liegt das Spielerische in seinem gesamten Werk verborgen.

Das „bigger" als roter Faden mit Augenzwinkern ist ein cleverer Schachzug. Auch der Wiederholungszwang von Motiven und Themen lässt sich als künstlerische Spielanleitung deuten. Statt von Werkserien oder Werkphasen könnte man auch von wechselnden Spielregeln sprechen. Mal ist es Natur in Grün, Blau und Braun, mal tragen die Landschaften laute, surreale Farben, und mal halten sich Aquarelle fast nur in Grautönen. Angefangen bei den Skizzenbüchern, die jeweils unter anderen ästhetischen und stilistischen Aufgabenstellungen entstehen, bis hin zu großen Serien wie den Poolbildern, den Fotocollagen oder den Porträts in den Innenräumen entpuppt sich der Begriff „Werkphase" als weniger zutreffend. Arbeiten, die sich untereinander stark ähneln und sich von anderen Gruppen wiederum stark absetzen, lassen sich trotzdem nicht als eine werkimmanente Notwendigkeit, als eine Abgeschlossenheit oder als eine

7. Siehe Zeichnung 27/46, https://www.hockney.com/works/digital/iphone [zuletzt besucht am 30.8.2021].

Phase ohne Parallelen erkennen. Die meisten werden zu unterschiedlichen Zeiten wieder aufgegriffen, weitergeführt, verändert und zugunsten anderer Serien wieder pausiert. Schnelle, eindeutige Wechsel und ein umfassendes Ansetzen verschiedener Stile, Techniken und Motive entsprechen vielmehr dem Spielen nach immer anderen, selbst erfundenen beziehungsweise selbst auferlegten Spielregeln.

Was David Hockney daher in Wahrheit betreibt, sind Meisterspiele. Er stellt sich immer neuen Handicaps, neuen Anforderungen, neuen Findungen seiner bildästhetischen und bildwissenschaftlichen Auseinandersetzung und Forschung. Dabei verbeißt er sich nicht, sondern spielt das Spiel des Bildermachens virtuos wie kein anderer. Gerade dieses spielerische Hin-und-her-Pendeln verhindert, dass er sich in einem wie auch immer gearteten Zeitgeist verfängt. Wie der Pinsel, der sich nicht bis in die Spitze kontrollieren lässt, bleibt auch David Hockney in stilistischer Hinsicht über die Jahrzehnte hinweg locker.

# The Effortless Hand or The Great Letting Go

Larissa Kikol



The distance is there. Now, more than two decades into the twenty-first century, the characteristics of postmodern painting in the twentieth century are gradually starting to emerge, or more specifically, of painting from the 1960s to the 1980s, and indeed of contemporary painting of this century. In retrospect, many artists remain caught in their time; while this does not impact the quality of their work, it roots them more deeply in a narrower historical context. Other artists' work feels as contemporary today as ever, retaining an aesthetic and stylistic freshness that endures, undiminished by painting's developmental trajectory. David Hockney is one such artist. But what is his secret?

Hockney may be characterized first and foremost as a pop artist, but this is merely an access ramp to his work. Other influences on his style can be found in Jean Dubuffet and art brut's sinuous alphabet paintings, as well as in art brut graffiti, in new figuration, in a distanced realism where Edward Hopper atmospherics are subtly infused with humour, in naïve painting, in gestural, naturalistic forms of expression, in childlike doodling and surrealist tendencies. Evidence for all of this abounds. The childlike doodling and smileys are there in the details; Hockney scatters them like icing sugar all over his iPad drawings, for example (pp. 69–75). The surreal finds expression in the gaudily chemical colours of a number of tree trunks (pp. 66–67), houses or hills as well as in towering cubistic landscape formations or architectural constructions that are bent, smoothed or broken up at will. He might apply naïve formal language here and there for tree leaves, streets or mountain-like objects, and use gestural naturalism in other landscape paintings with lots of branches – or in portraits.

Hockney is impossible to pin down stylistically, and he seems to like it that way. The point is that he does not so much adhere to these various styles as help himself to them. He uses them as the mood takes him, or on the prompting of certain subject matter, playing one off against the other, sometimes within the same painting, forever unperturbed by attempts to pigeonhole him. He seems to feel no obligation to fill any role or fulfil any expectation. And therein lies the stylistic characteristic that best sums up his work and describes his position: relaxed and playful at all times.

Much of this rides on a structure that is evident in almost all of his works: his brushstroke. To better understand it, you need to observe Hockney's hand. The individual brushstrokes are most visible in his landscape paintings and the accompanying making-of videos: the initial line placement remains approximate, only transforming into a more precise, figurative line in combination with other lines and areas of colour later on.[1] Hockney holds the long brush at the end of its handle, to reduce his ability to control the brush hairs.[2] The head of the brush swings slightly over the canvas, its contact with the image surface impossible to determine with millimetre precision. To do this would require holding the brush further down. But Hockney does not draw exact lines to create illusionistic or hyper-realistic paintings. His paintings always reveal how they were made; at close range the lines retain their autonomy, they are not tool lines used solely for figurative representation. Hockney also keeps a distance from the canvas itself, half an arm's length or just far enough away to prevent the cigarette in his other hand from doing any damage.

According to Martin Gayford, Hockney translates everything he sees into lines, dots, daubs of paint and brushstrokes – signs in other words. The urge to do this, Gayford believes, lies in Hockney's childhood. Hockney himself also talks about the pleasure and the fun he discovered here at an early age.[3] Gayford sees "quick, free, calligraphic brushstrokes" in the largest paintings.[4] Hockney talks about being inspired by Chinese painting, but also about the influences of Pablo Picasso, "meaning the marks are all visible" and are "boldly made with the arm."[5] The descriptions "quick" and "boldly made with the arm" could possibly apply to areas in the very large paintings, but I personally would attribute this to the format rather than consider it a predominant characteristic of Hockney's style. Yet when individual areas are coated more densely with paint, on a path for example, more vigour is certainly applied. The paintbrush is crudely pushed around in various directions, its bristles unceremoniously pressed and bent.[6] Things never get as out of hand as they might with the neo-expressionists, yet this painting technique allows the artist to spill over from the abstract – loose lines and surface arrangements in a white, floating pictorial space – into the figurative.

Often in David Hockney's works you see individual lines executed with less pressure and speed. David Hockey is no action painter, no abstract expressionist and no old *Neue Wilde*. His lines do not function as barometers of subconscious emotions, nor are they made in the service of individual expression or to reveal the power and temperament of the body. So speed, sludge, and spontaneity would be similarly ill fitting as parameters.
Some lines even seem to have been made hesitantly and slowly. In other places the brushstroke is shaky, another consequence of the long wooden handle held at the end. Without direct physical and vital pressure, the hand probably feels unmotivated, lethargic, lacking effort. That sounds negative, and in most cases it could well result in an unintended quality deficit and inferior image quality. With David Hockney, however, this betrays no actual lack of motivation but is, of course, a stylistically intentional as-if stance.

Incidentally, a similar quality of mark can be found in the drawings of Egon Schiele, Andy Warhol and Hockney's younger British colleague, David Shrigley. In the latter's case the aesthetic quality also comes from a seemingly awkward, unmotivated hand. Vincent van Gogh's brushstrokes stand at the opposite end of this spectrum. By contrast, Hockney's lines stand out much more playfully and independently from the pictorial subject and remain more stubbornly autonomous. His effortless hand gives rise to an autonomous line that does not reflect the felt atmosphere of a landscape, but retains a life of its own.

1. See https://www.youtube.com/watch?v=UVBYfTr8BRQ [retrieved 30.8.2021].
2. Ibid.
3. David Hockney, quoted in Martin Gayford, *A Bigger Message: Conversations with David Hockney*, Thames & Hudson, London 2011, p. 34.
4. Ibid., p. 65.
5. Ibid.
6. See drawing 5/46, https://www.hockney.com/works/digital/iphone [retrieved on 30.8.2021].

If it changes direction, or does so multiple times at shorter intervals as when describing a bony branch, all Hockney does is to roll the brush a little between his thumb and forefinger, barely moving his hand, arm or body.[7] This too feels almost lethargic, as if accompanied by an "if I have to" and a sigh. Instead of beautiful, expressive or committed lines, he paints wilful, independent lines with an air of awkwardness and mischief to them. The overall effect feels casual, effortless. What at first glance might be mistaken for the stiffness of age turns out to be not only nerve, but also a contemporary coolness that no longer has to try or make an effort. Because it can do it all anyway – with a mere flick of the thumb, between puffs on a cigarette.
In a number of works this laissez-faire becomes even more pronounced, and gives way to outright playfulness. Particularly in the digital drawings this playful clarity manifests itself in abstraction and an almost childlike sign language. In the iPhone drawing *Untitled, 510* (2009) the sun becomes a bundle of marks, a flurry of bent, scribbled lines radiating outwards in every direction. In *Untitled 165* (2009) the free transformation is consummated through a lumpy, malformed stick figure, untidy colouring-in and deliberately amateurish-looking spatial delineation. Hockney is exaggerating, or more to the point: he's letting himself go, revelling in the fun of childish doodling as the ultimate consequence of relaxation and an effortless hand.

Painting is his playing field, and not just on the iPhone. Although it is most immediately apparent in the digital works, in reality playfulness lurks in every corner of his oeuvre.

The running gag with "bigger" is a clever gambit. The compulsion to repeat imagery and themes can also be interpreted as a set of artistic rules of the game. Rather than making "series of works" or "phases", one could also talk about changing the rules of the game. Sometimes it is nature in green, blue and brown, sometimes the landscapes appear in brash, surreal colours, and sometimes the watercolours are *almost* limited to shades of grey. Starting with the sketchbooks, each of which is created under different aesthetic and stylistic conditions, and on to major series like the pool paintings, the photo collages or the portraits in interiors, the term "phase" seems to make little sense. Works that are strongly similar to one another and thus strongly different to other groupings are nevertheless impossible to pinpoint as an inherent necessity in the oeuvre, as a self-contained episode, or a phase without parallels. Most of them are picked up again at different times, taken further, changed or put on hold again in favour of other series. Rapid, unambiguous changes and a comprehensive application of different styles, techniques and imagery instead spring from playing by ever-changing, self-invented or self-imposed rules of the game.

David Hockney, then, is really a grandmaster at play, forever presenting himself with new handicaps, new challenges for himself, new findings from his aesthetic, pictorial investigations and research. But he doesn't get lost in all of this, but plays the image-making game with unparalleled virtuosity. And it is this playful movement back and forth that prevents him getting caught in any one particular zeitgeist. Like the brush that won't be entirely controlled, David Hockney himself remains stylistically unconstrained from one decade to the next.

7. See drawing 27/46, https://www.hockney.com/works/digital/iphone [retrieved 30.8.2021].

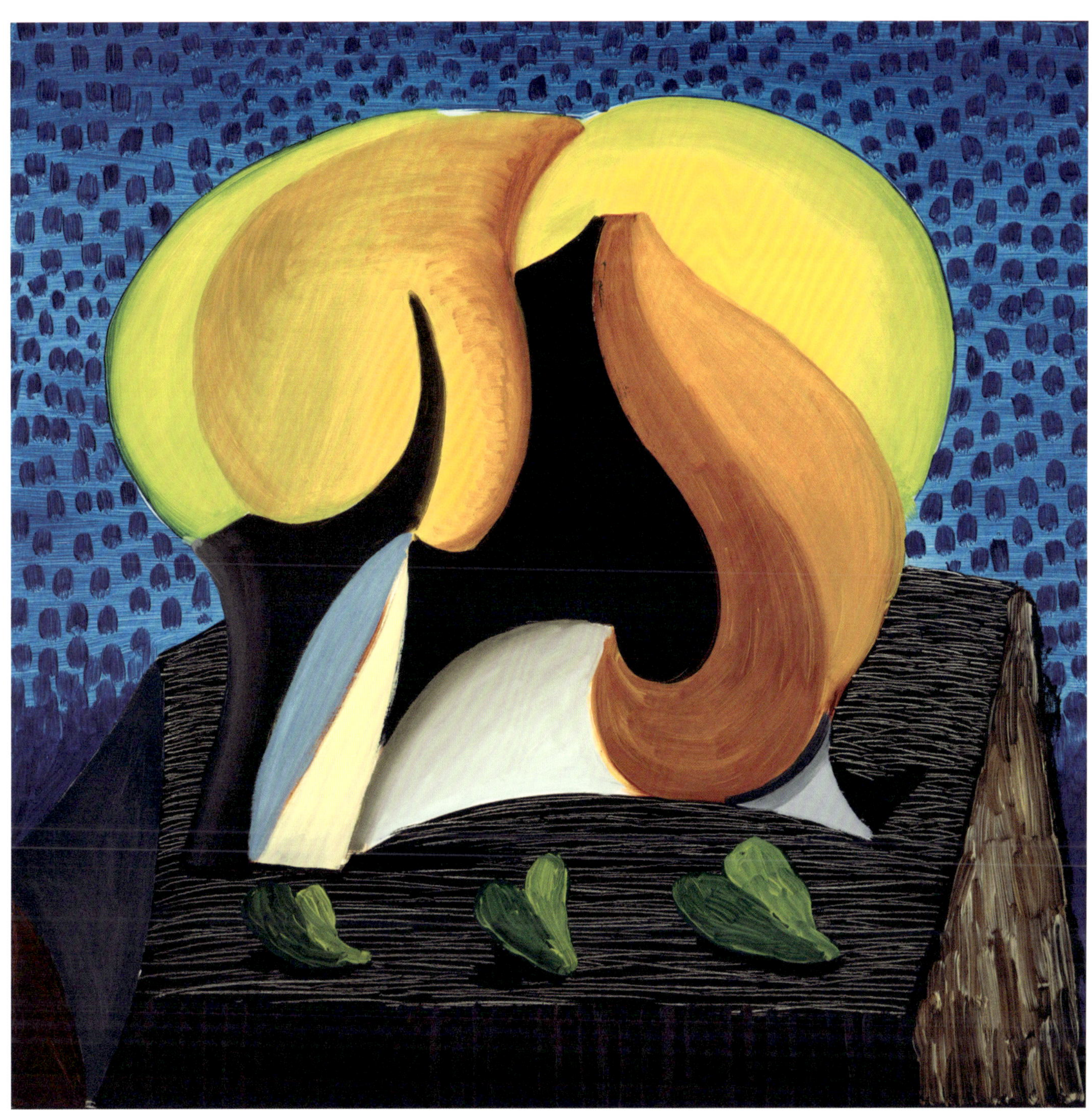

**The First V. N. Painting,** 1992
Öl auf Leinwand | Oil on canvas,
61 × 61 cm
Peress Family Collection
Inv. N° 72845

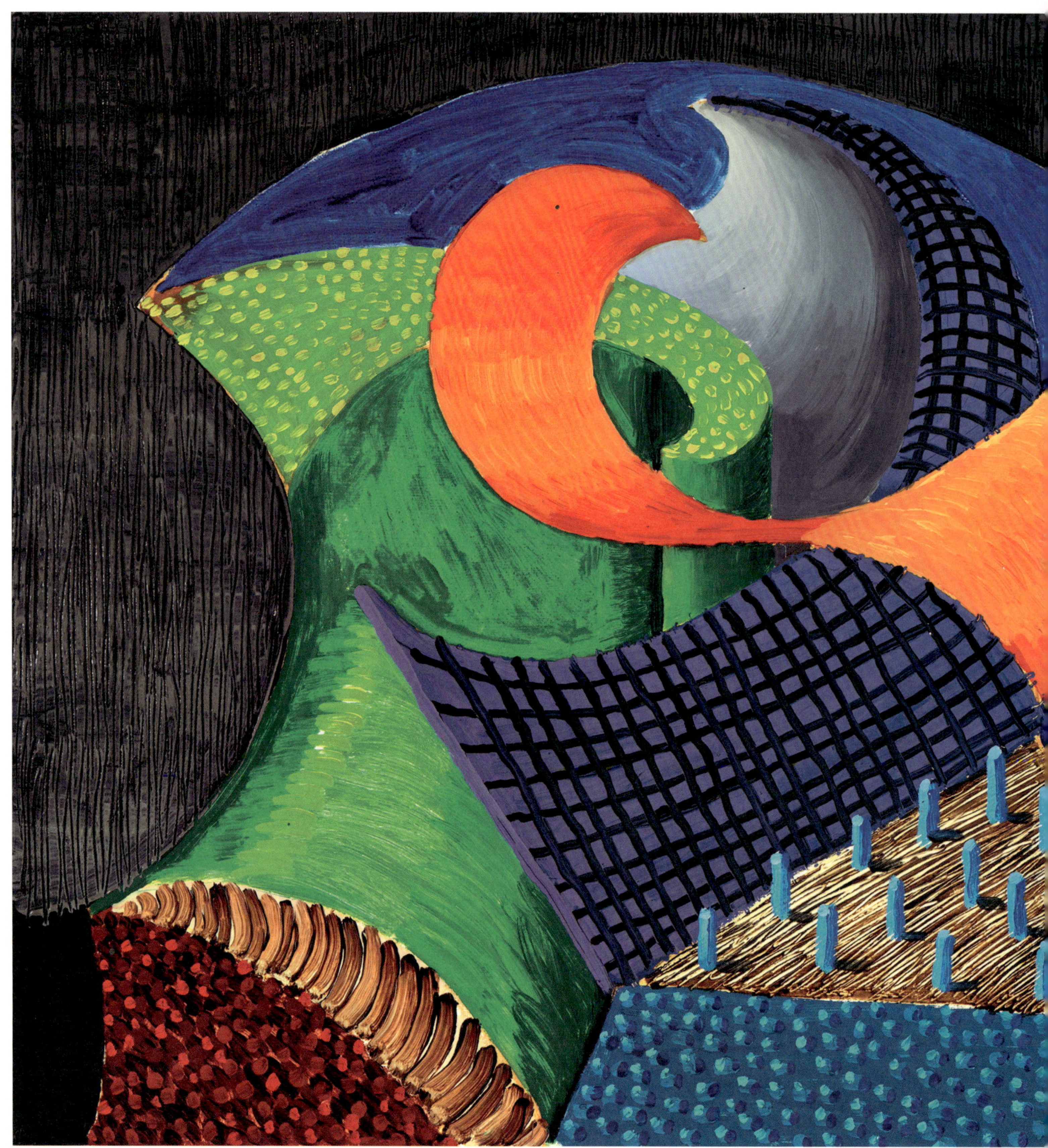

**The Eleventh V. N. Painting,** 1992
Öl auf Leinwand | Oil on canvas,
61 × 91,45 cm
The David Hockney Foundation

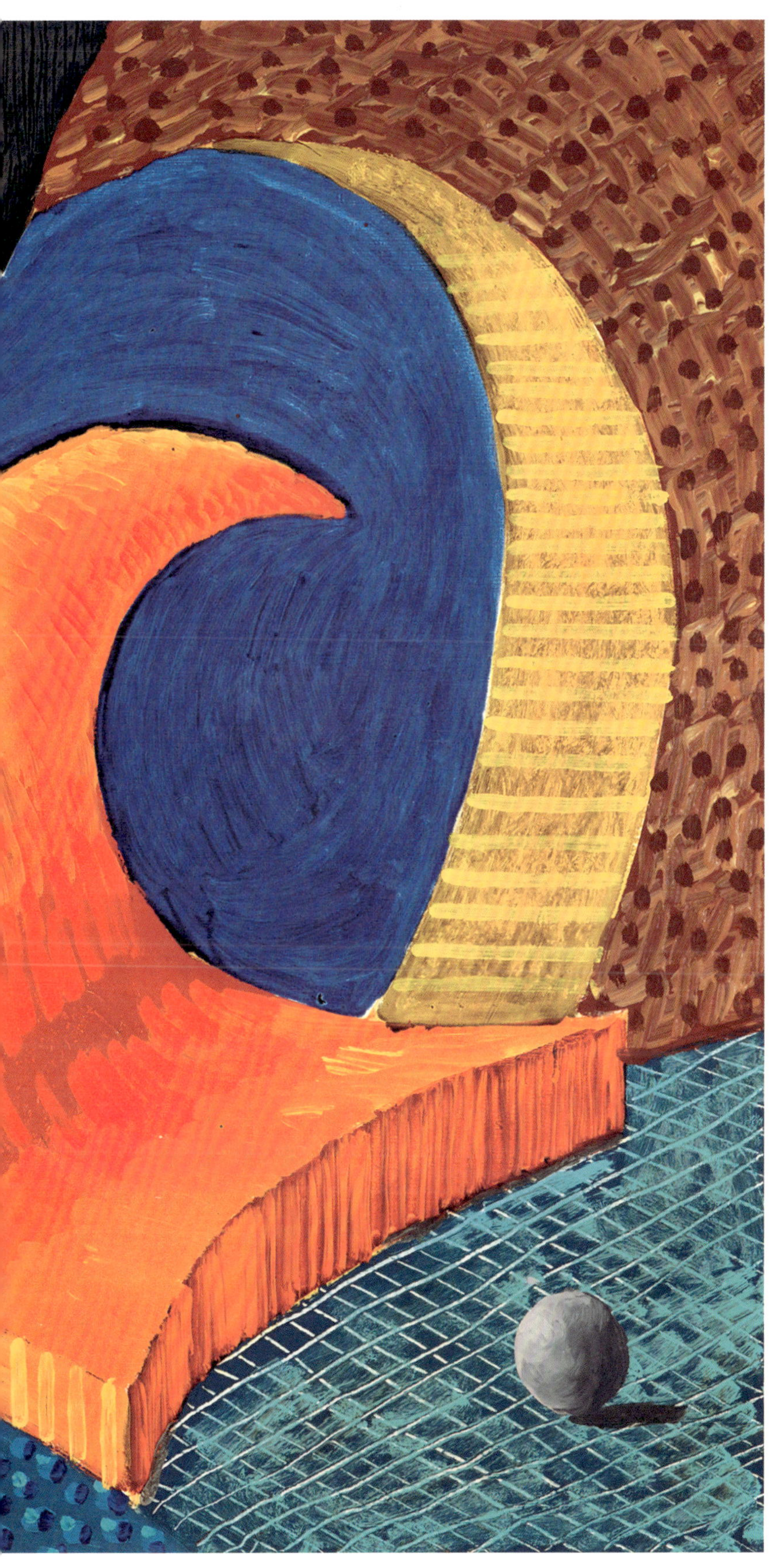

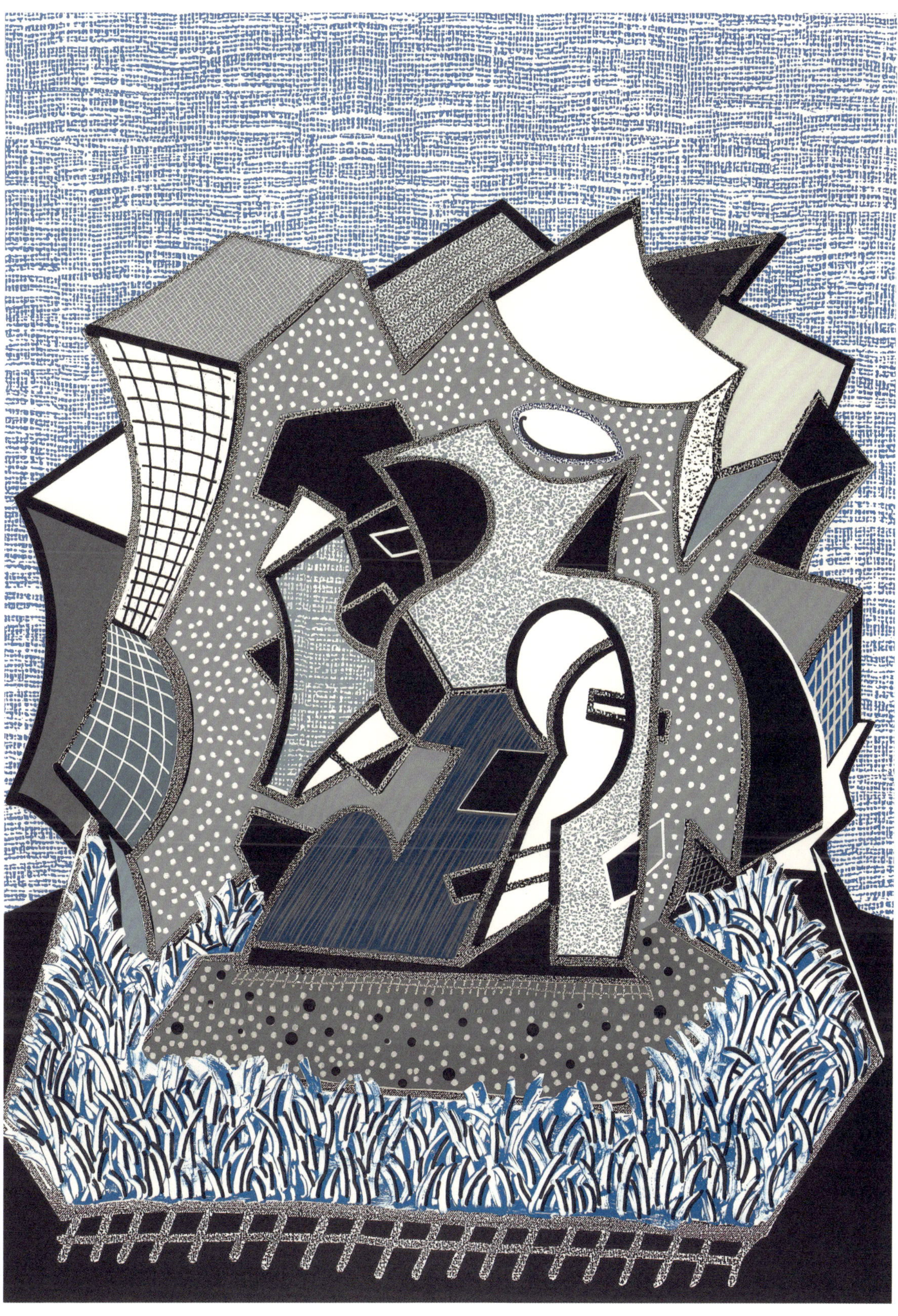

**Eine (Part I),** 1991
Lithografie auf Papier (Auflage von 35) |
Lithograph on paper (Edition of 35),
113,5 x 80,7 cm
Tate: Presented by the artist 1993
Inv. N° P20134

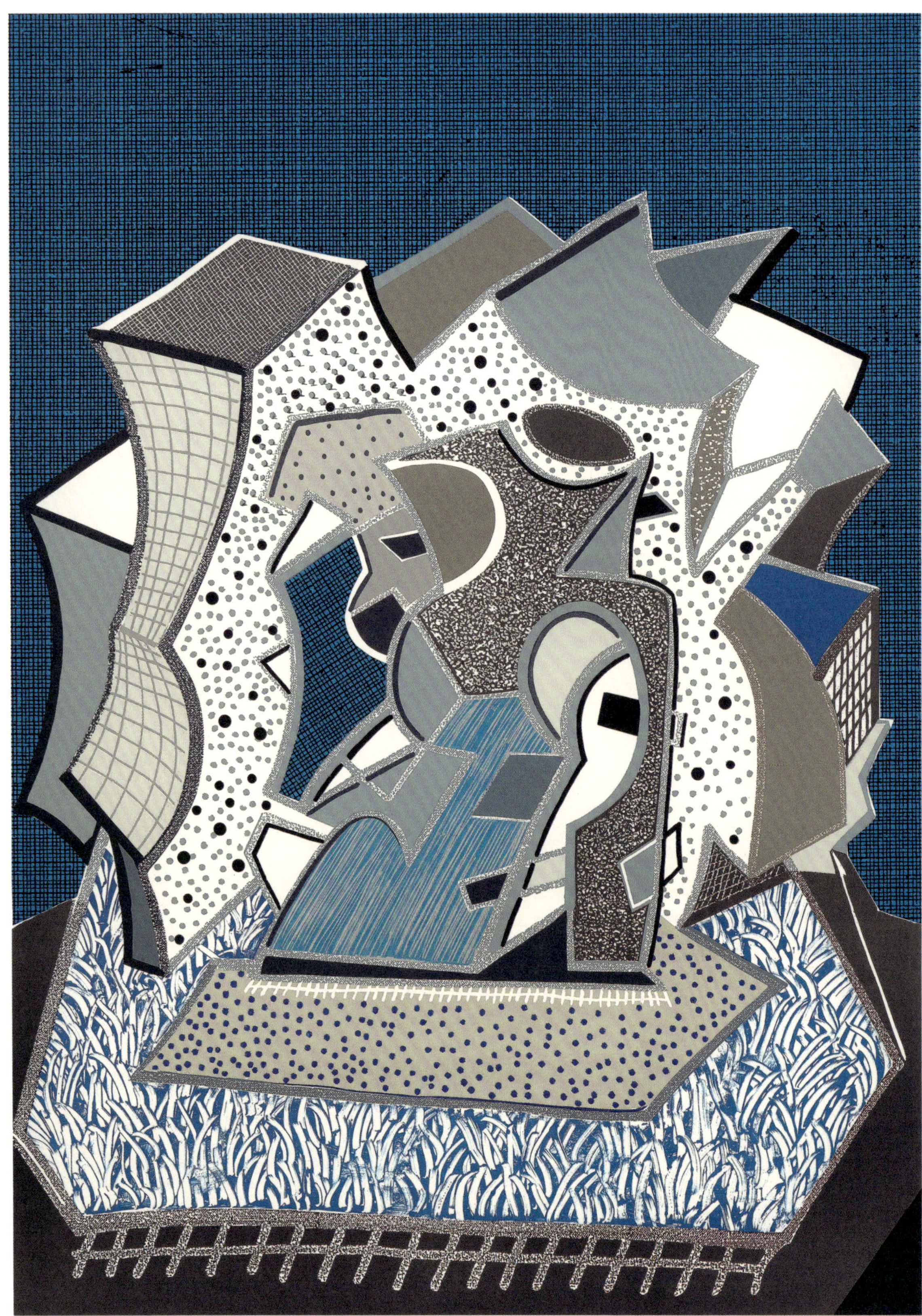

**Deux (Second Part),** 1991
Lithografie auf Papier (Auflage von 35) |
Lithograph on paper (Edition of 35),
113,5 × 80,7 cm
Tate: Presented by the artist 1993
Inv. N° P20138

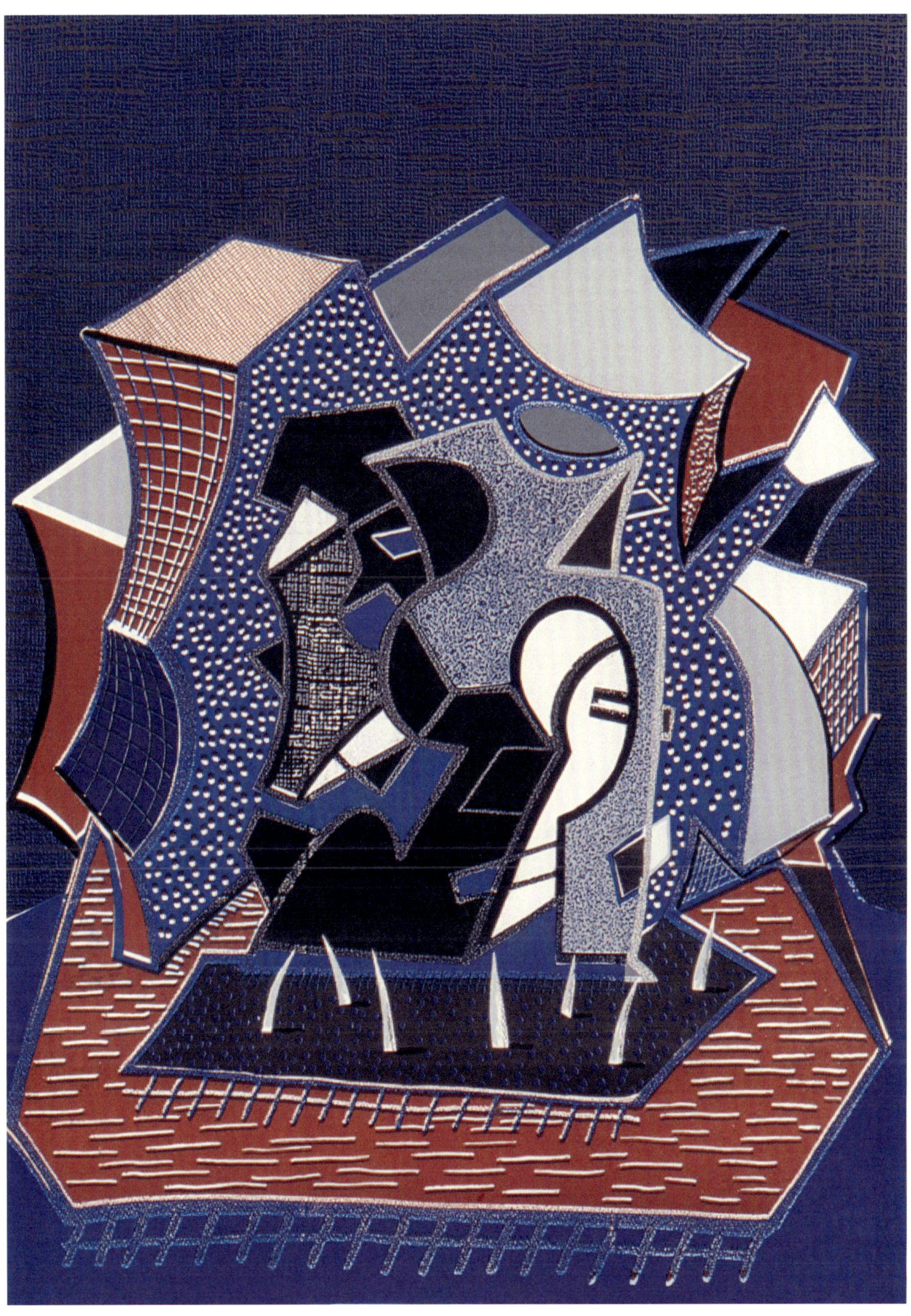

**Tres (End of Triple),** 1990
Lithografie auf Papier (Auflage von 35) |
Lithograph on paper (Edition of 35),
113,5 × 80,7 cm
Tate: Presented by the artist 1993
Inv. N° P20133

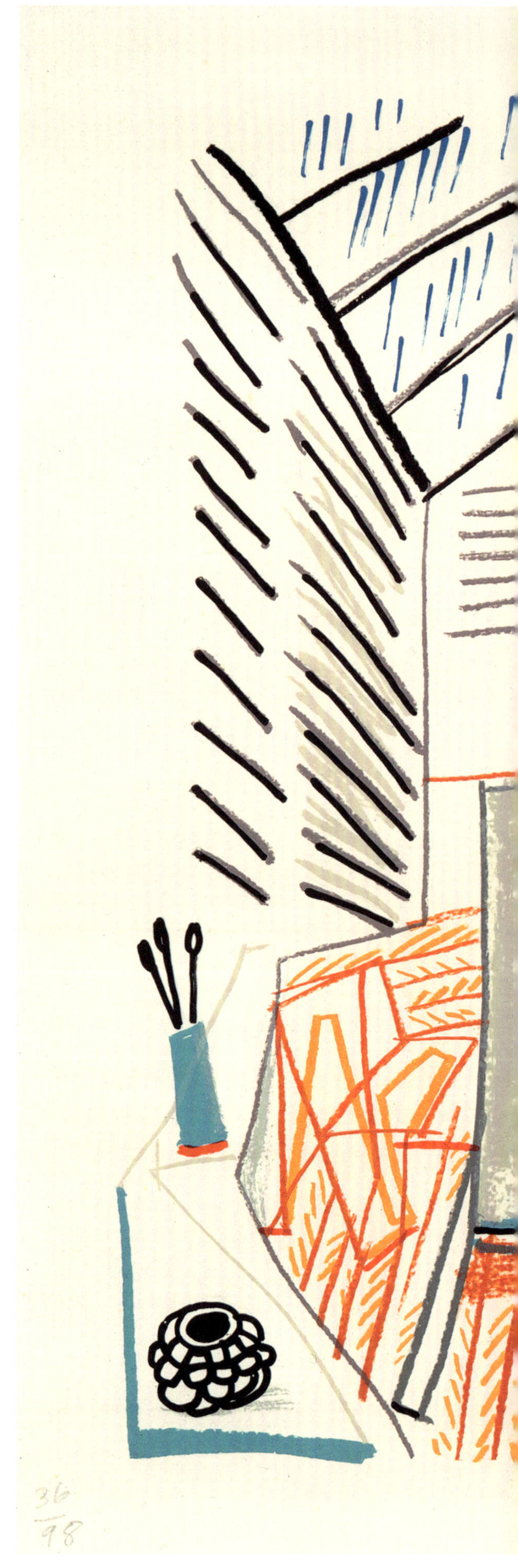

**Pembroke Studio with Blue Chairs and Lamp,** 1984
Lithografie auf Papier (Auflage von 98) |
Lithograph on paper (Edition of 98),
48 × 56 cm
Tate: Presented by the artist 1993
Inv. Nº P20111

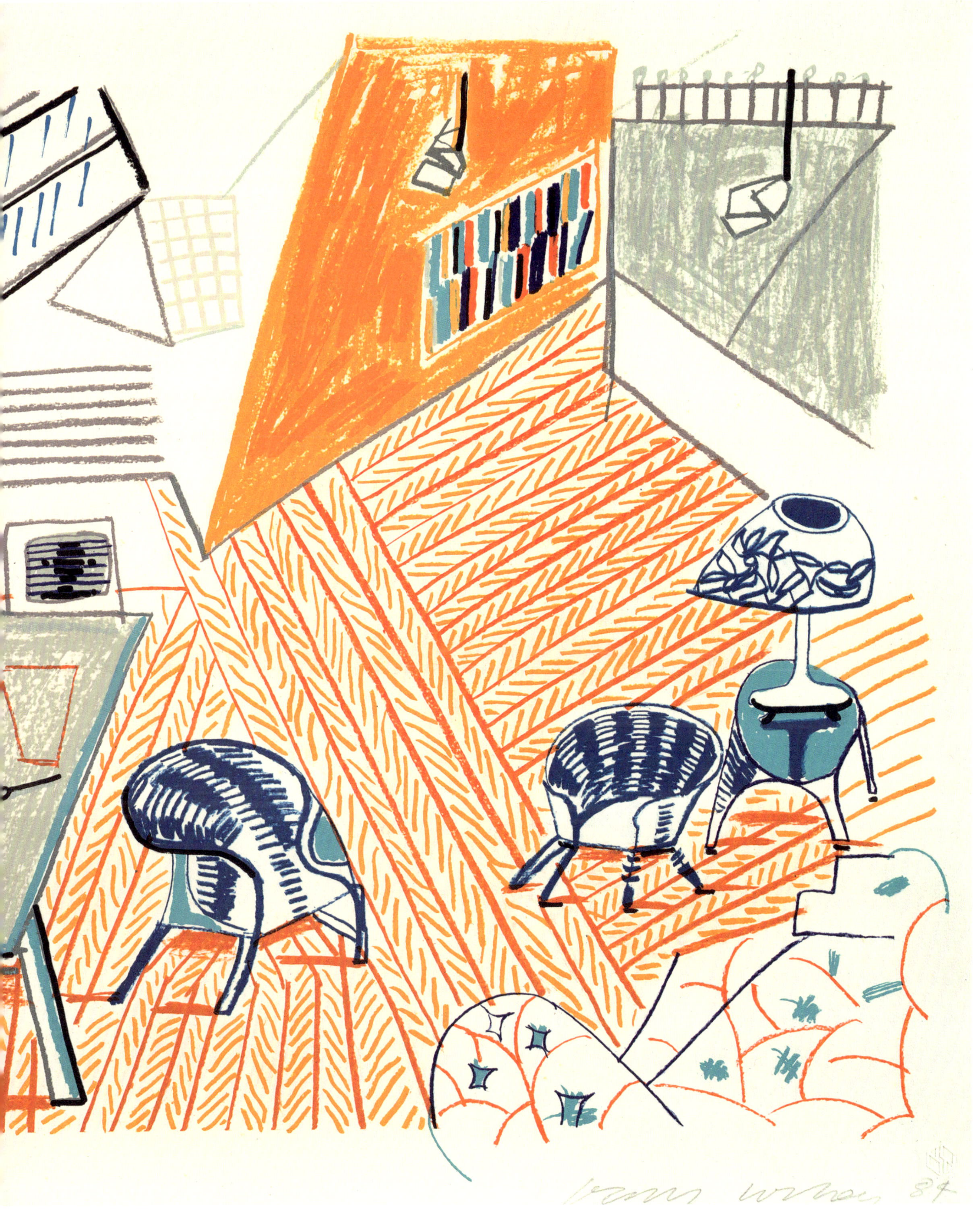

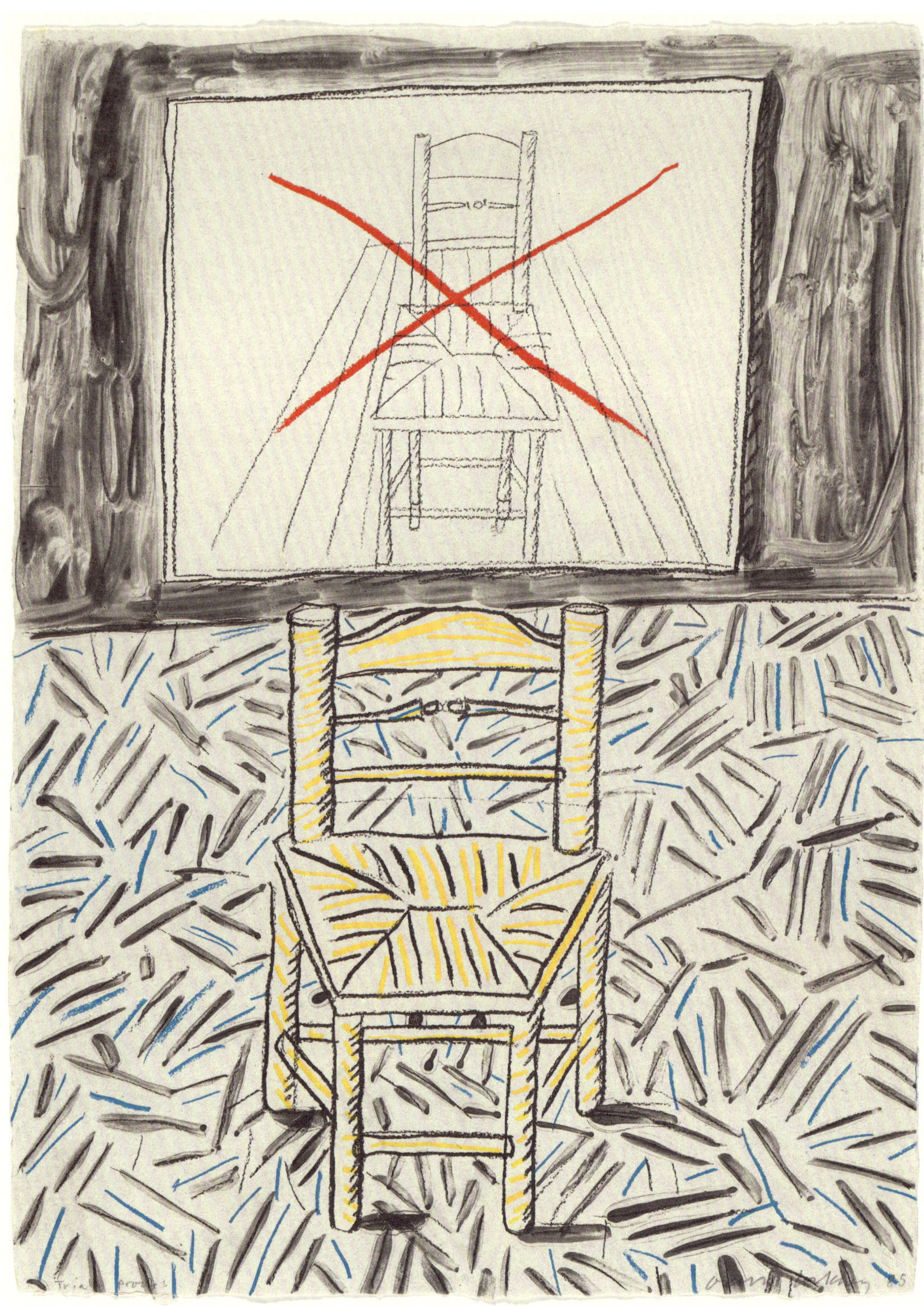

**The Perspective Lesson,** 1984
Lithografie auf Papier (Auflage von 50) |
Lithograph on paper (Edition of 50),
76 × 56,3 cm
Tate: Presented by the artist 1993
Inv. N° P20104

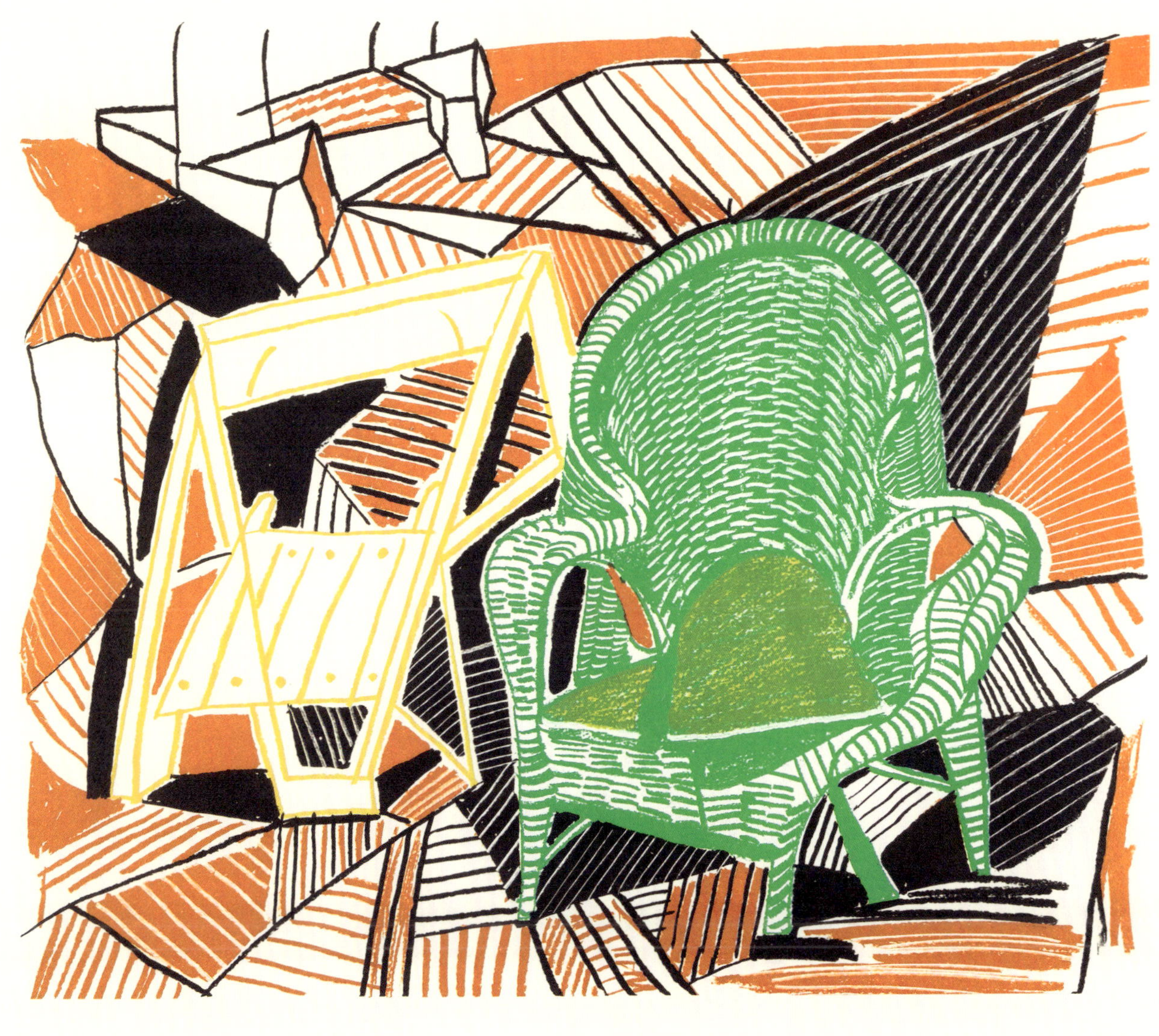

**Two Pembroke Studio Chairs,** 1984
Lithografie auf Papier (Auflage von 98) |
Lithograph on paper (Edition of 98),
48,2 × 56,2 cm
Tate: Presented by the artist 1993
Inv. Nº P20103

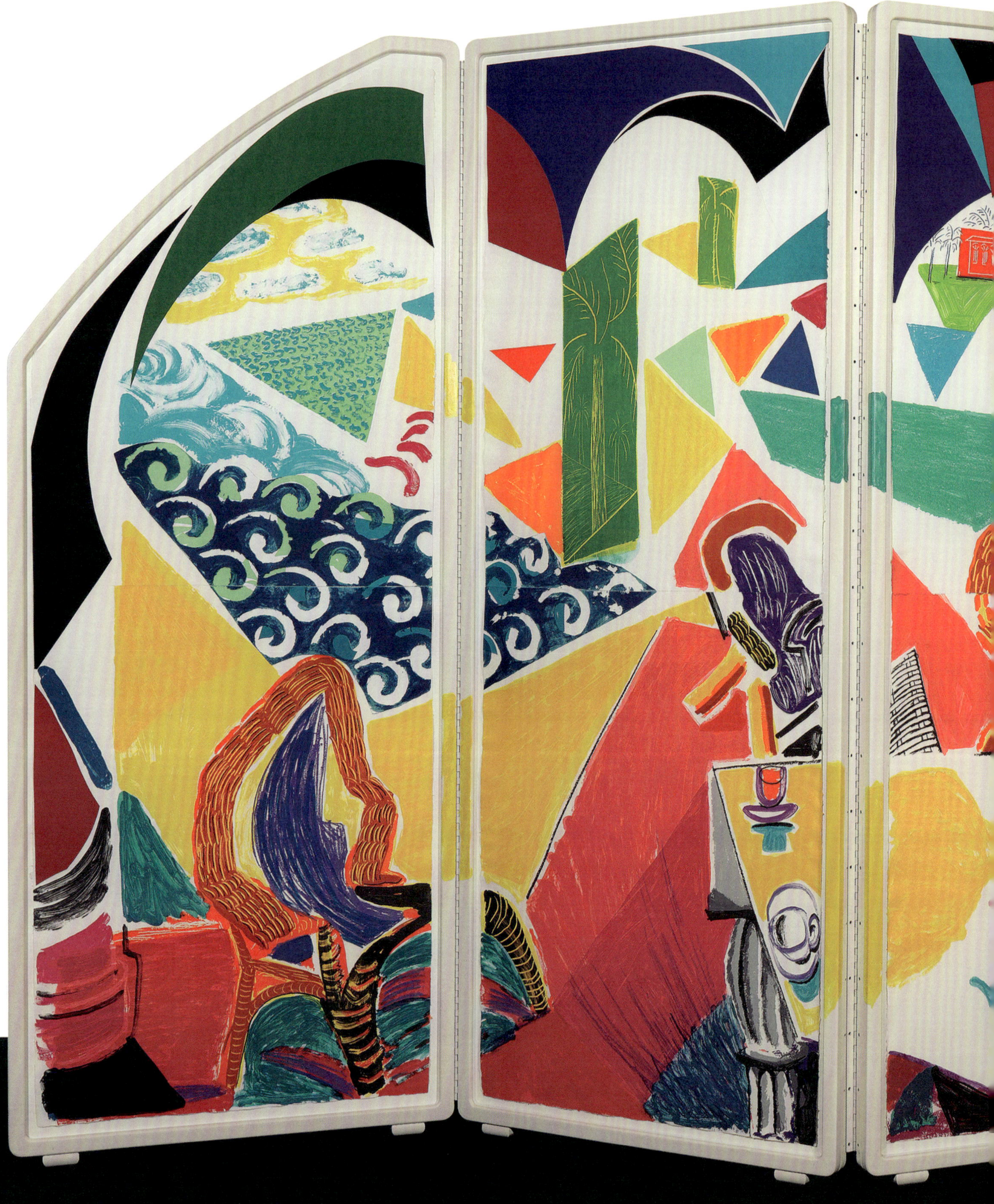

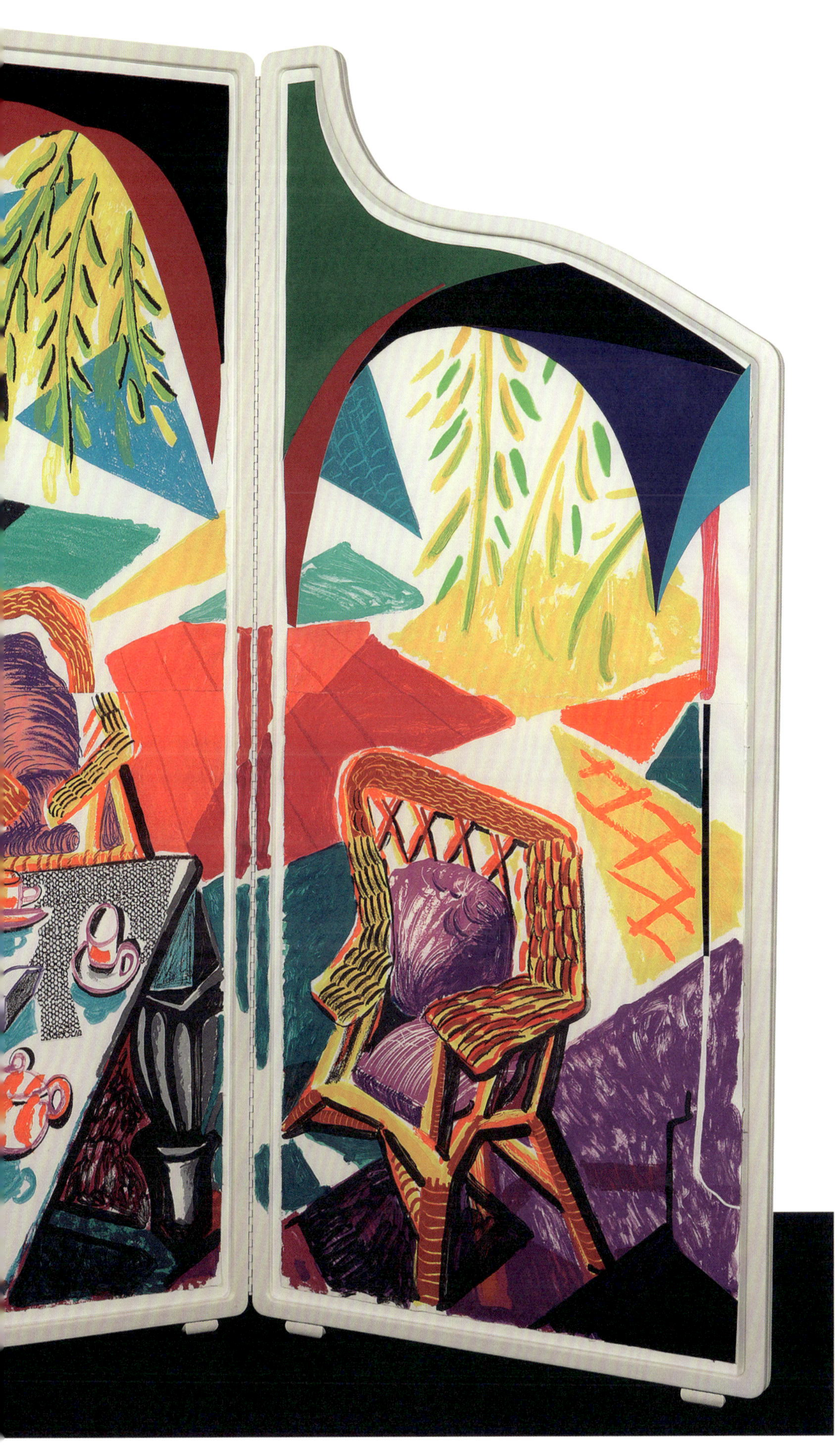

**Caribbean Tea Time,** 1987
Lithografie, Siebdruck, bedrucktes Papier und Schablone auf Papier, auf vier Paneelen (Auflage von 36) | Lithograph, screenprint, printed paper and stencil on paper, on four panels (Edition of 36), je | each 215,2 × 85,1 cm
Tate: Presented by the artist 1993
Inv. Nº P20129

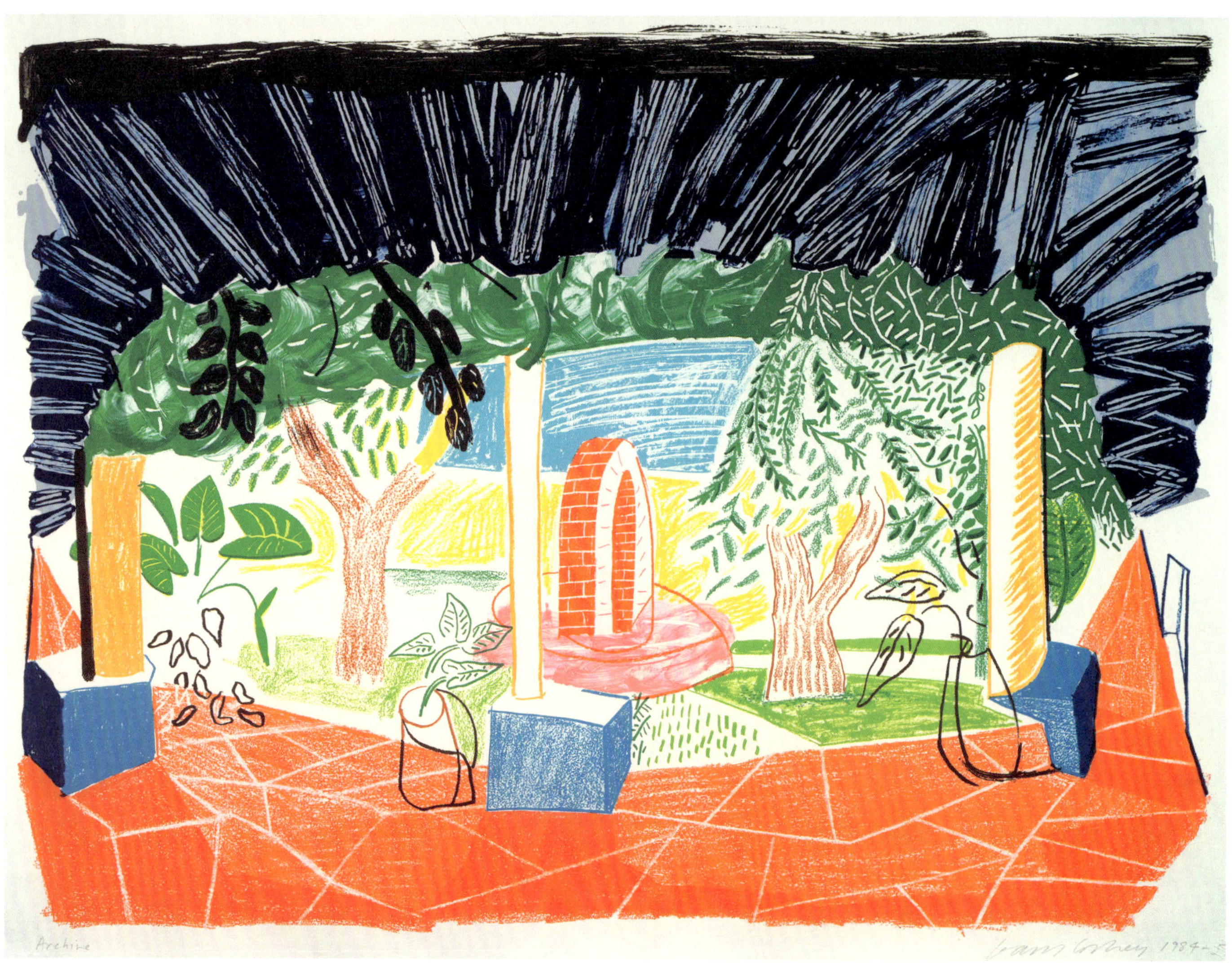

**Views of Hotel Well I,** 1984–1985
Lithografie auf Papier (Auflage von 75) |
Lithograph on paper (Edition of 75),
74 × 100,5 cm
Tate: Presented by the artist 1993
Inv. N° P20118

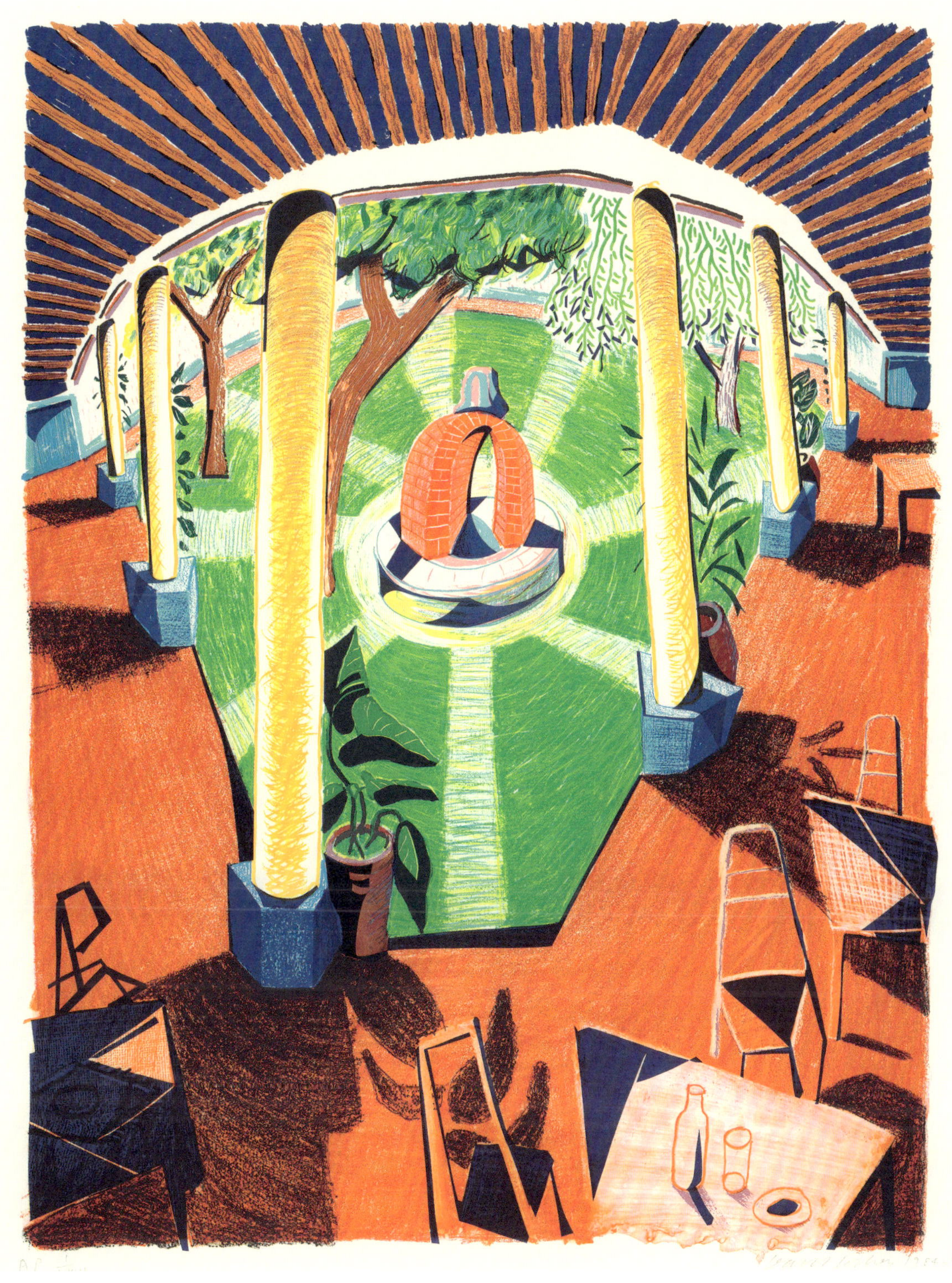

**Views of Hotel Well III,** 1984–1985
Lithografie auf Papier (Auflage von 80) |
Lithograph on paper (Edition of 80),
118,5 × 89,5 cm
Tate: Presented by the artist 1993
Inv. N° P20115

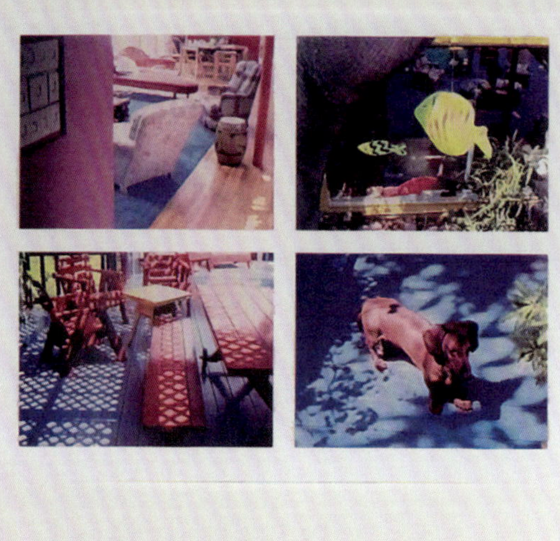
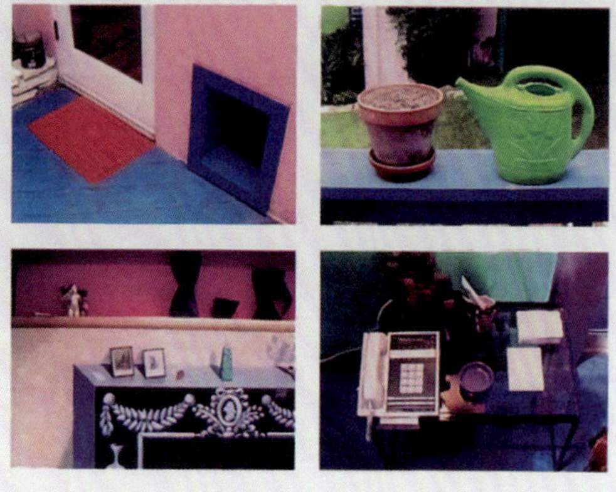
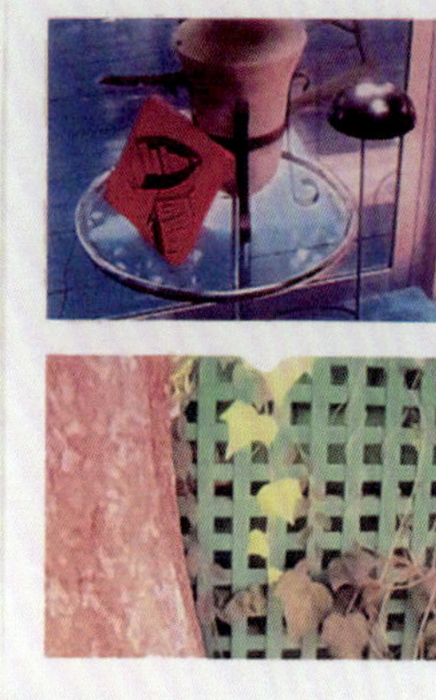
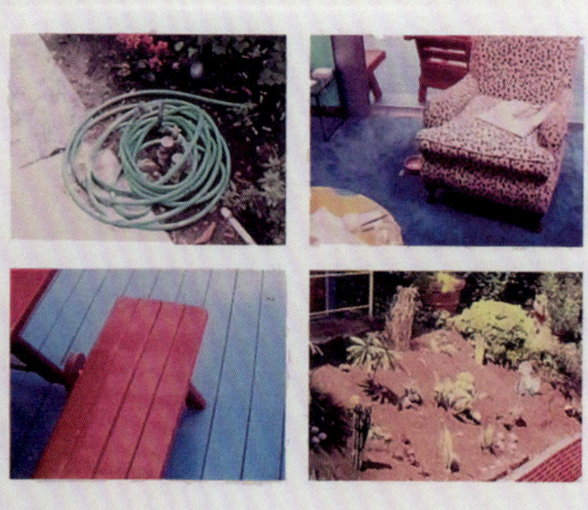
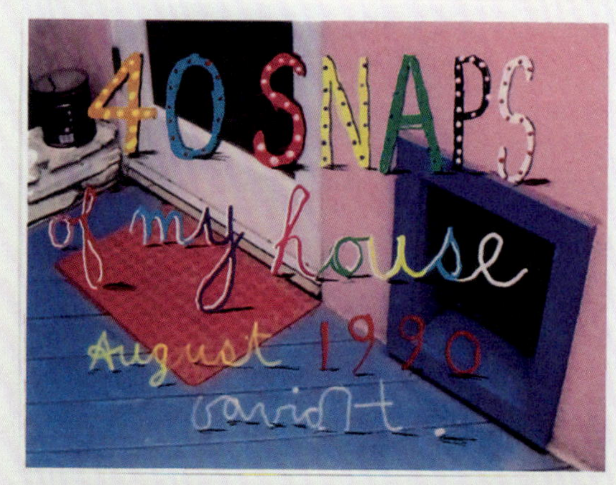

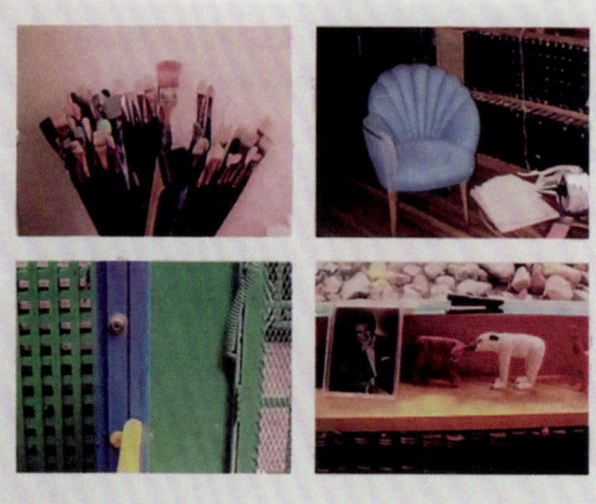
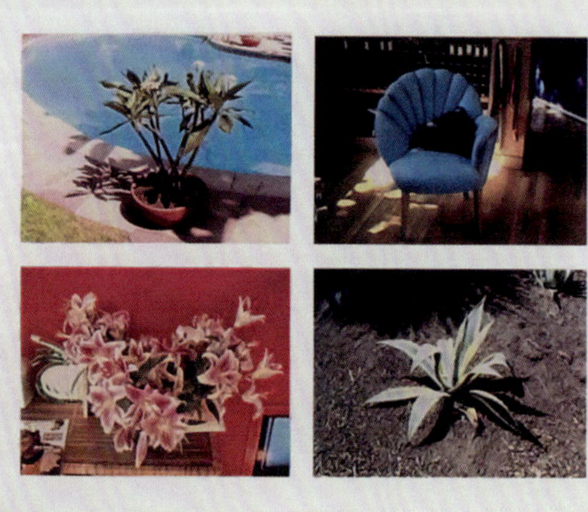
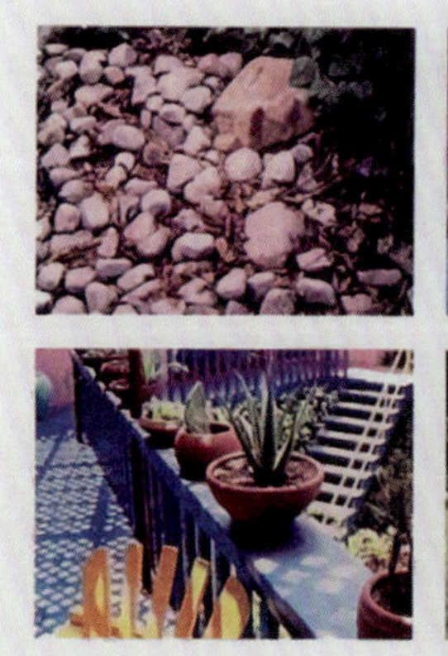

**40 Snaps of my House, August 1990,** 1990
Digitaldruck auf Papier | Digital print on paper,
89,9 × 140,5 cm
Tate: Presented by the artist 1993
Inv. N° P20140

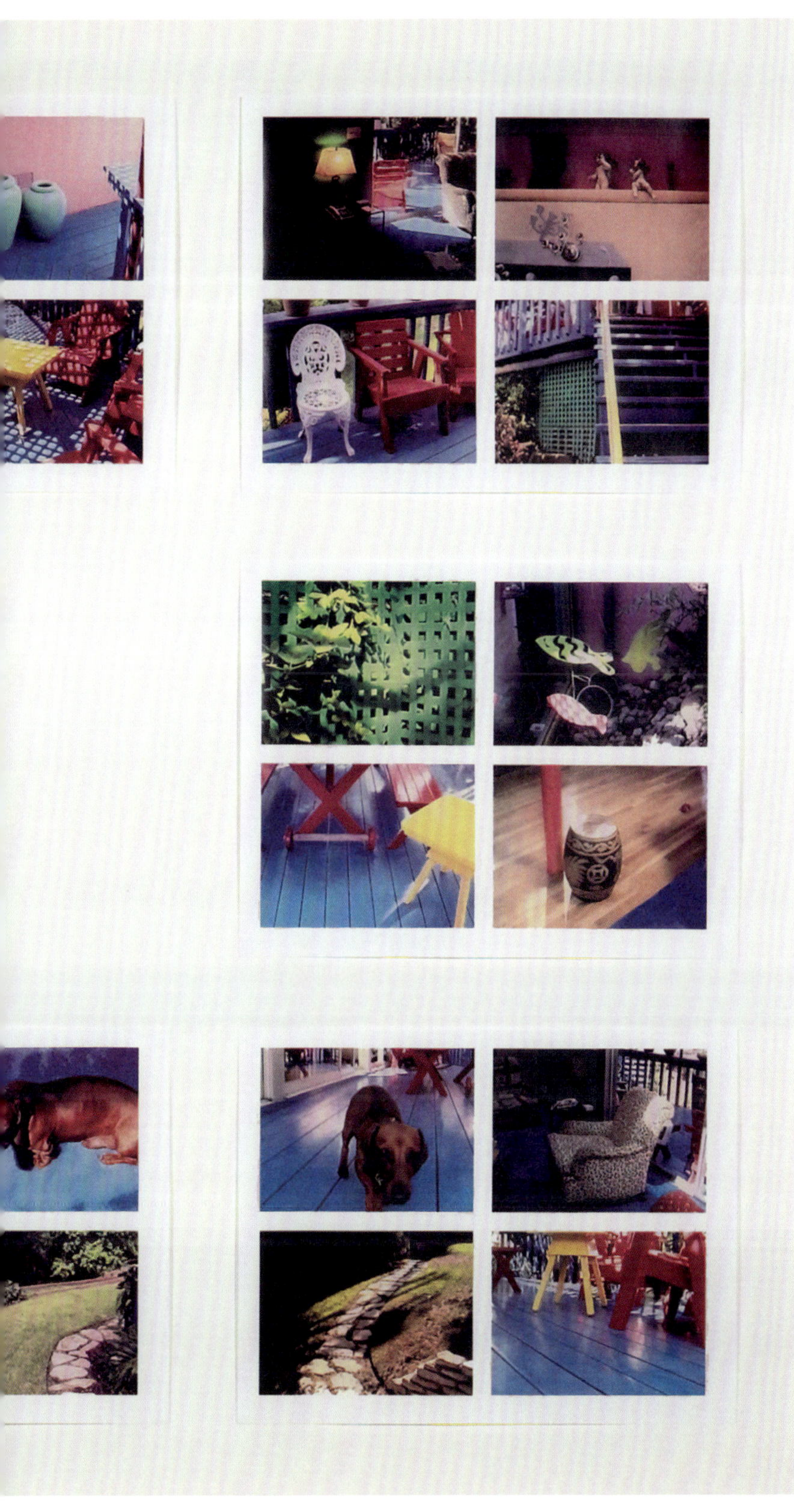

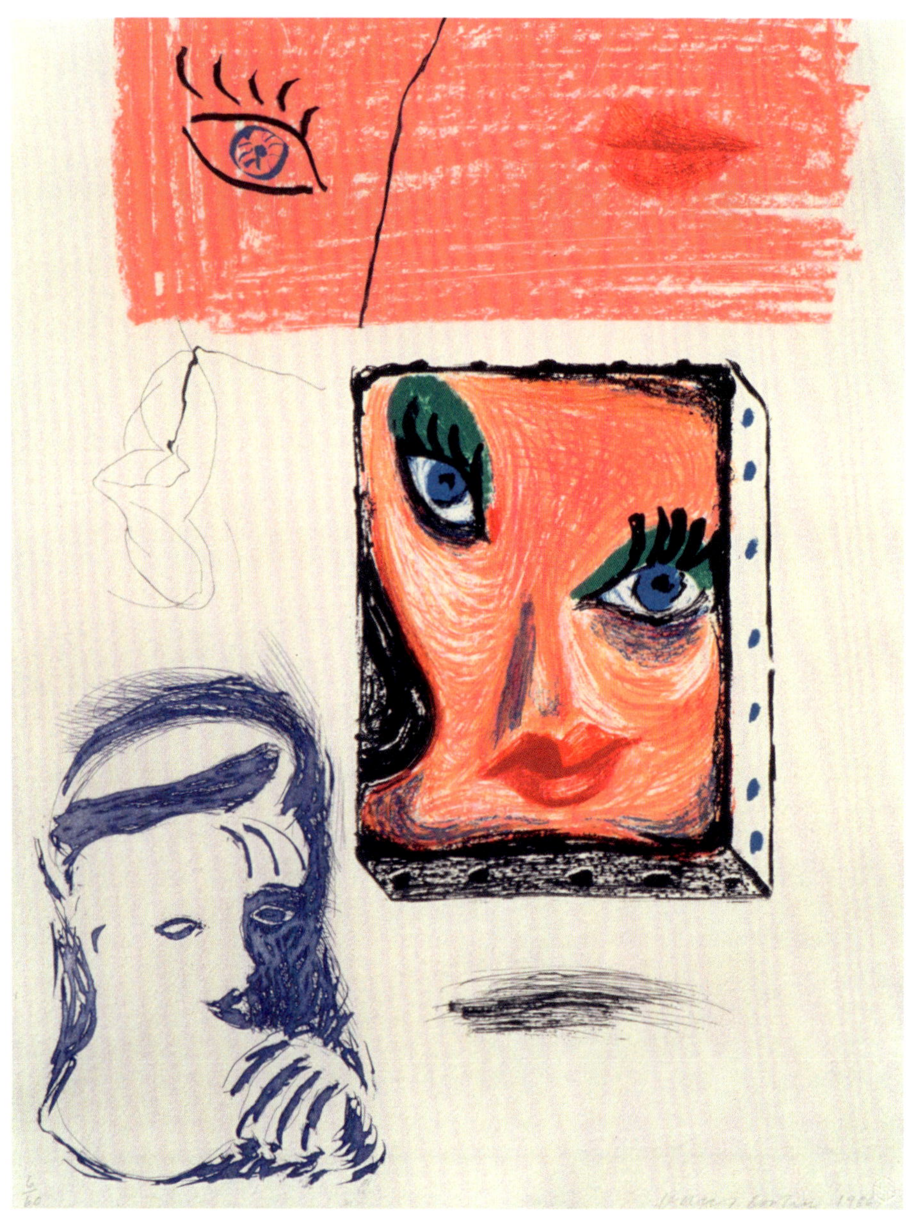

**An Image of Celia Study,** 1986
Lithografie, Radierung und Aquatinta
auf Papier (Auflage von 60) | Lithograph,
etching and aquatint on paper (Edition of 60),
58 × 45,1 cm
Tate: Presented by the artist 1993
Inv. N° P20128

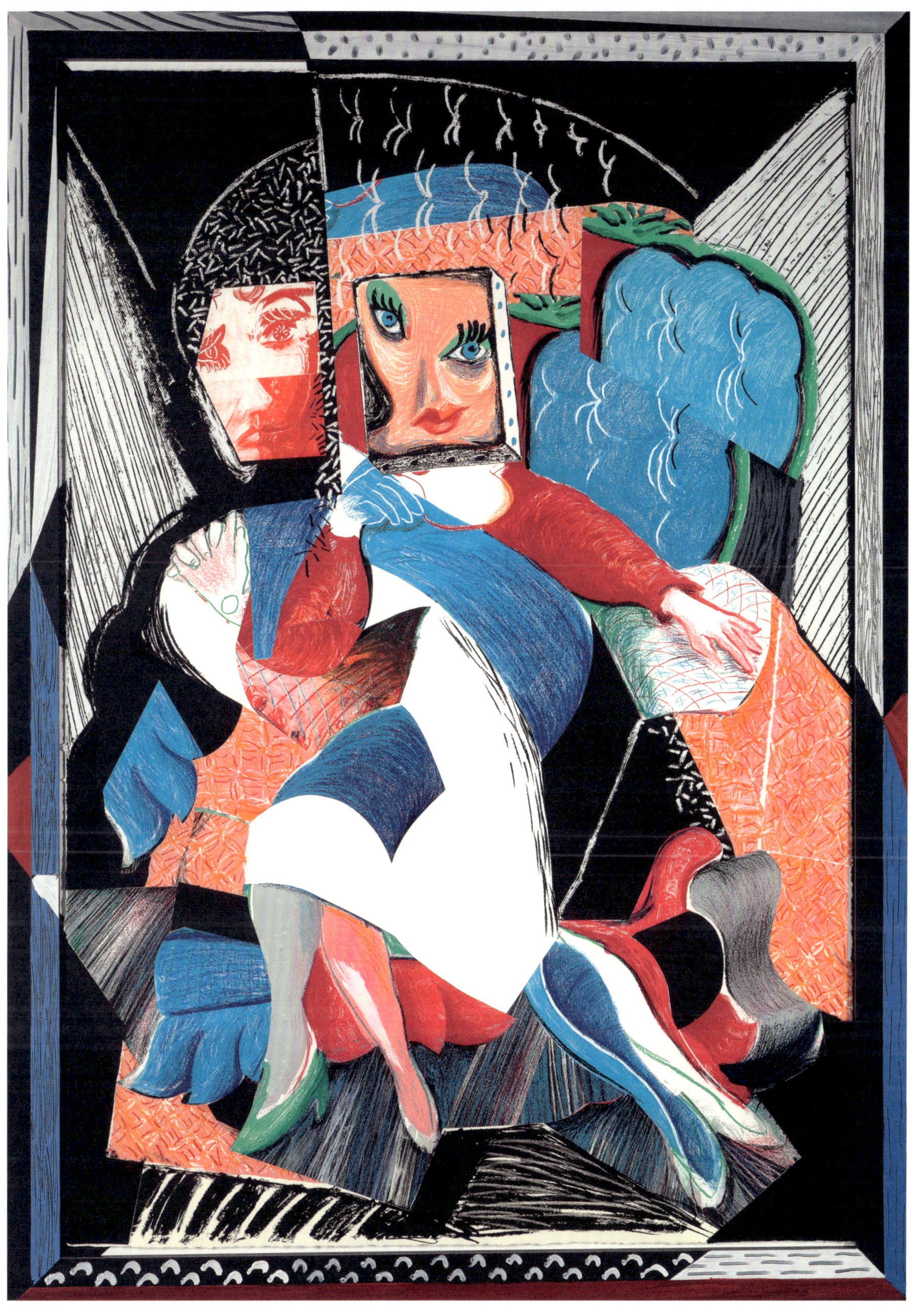

**An Image of Celia,** 1984–1986
Lithografie auf Papier (Auflage von 40) |
Lithograph on paper (Edition of 40),
152,5 × 105,1 cm
Tate: Presented by the artist 1993
Inv. N° P20116

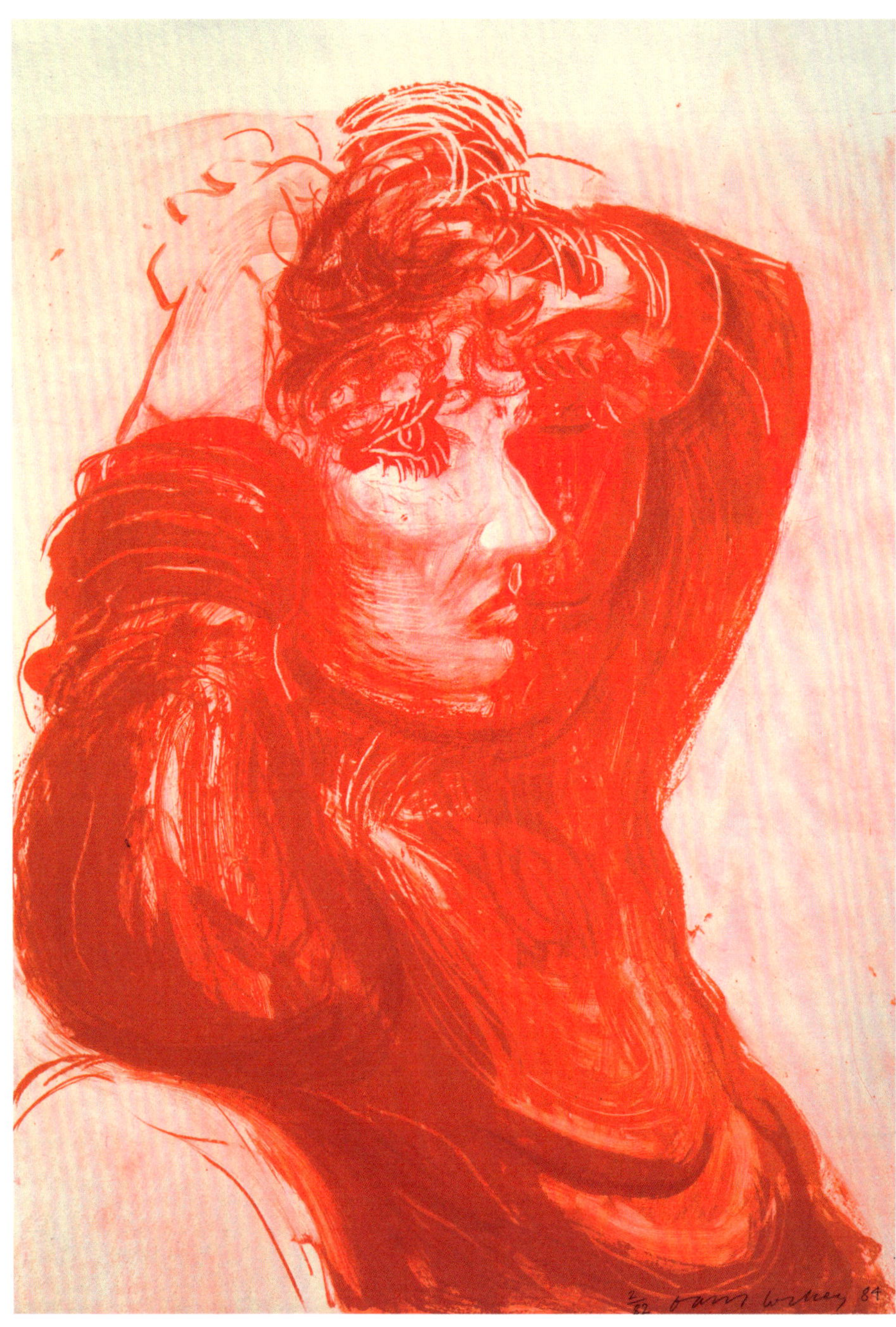

**Red Celia,** 1984
Lithografie auf Papier (Auflage von 82) |
Lithograph on paper (Edition of 82),
76 × 54,5 cm
Tate: Presented by the artist 1993
Inv. Nº P20109

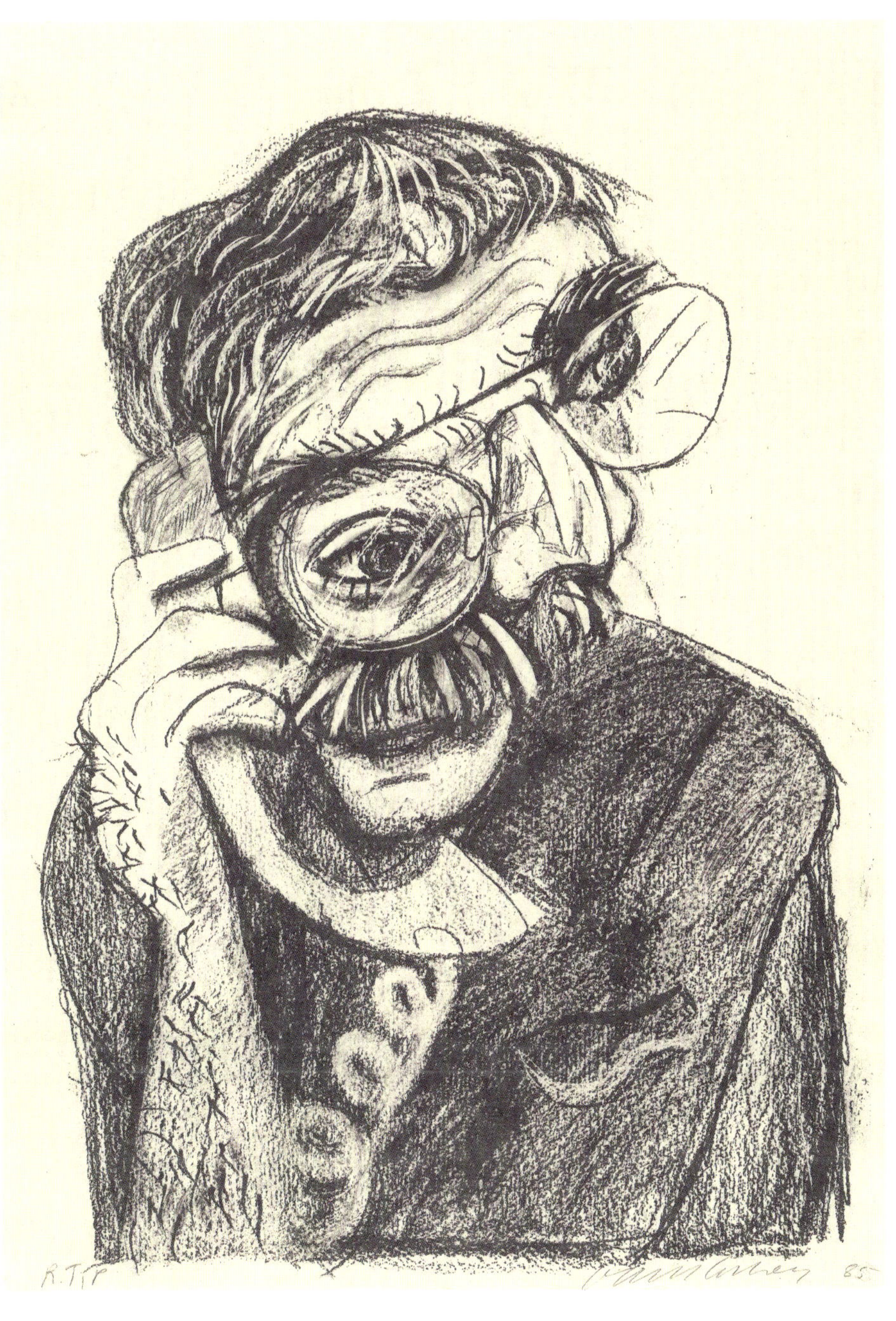

**An Image of Ken,** 1985
Lithografie auf Papier (Auflage von 20) |
Lithograph on paper (Edition of 20),
76 × 55, 5 cm
Tate: Presented by the artist 1993
Inv. N° P20120

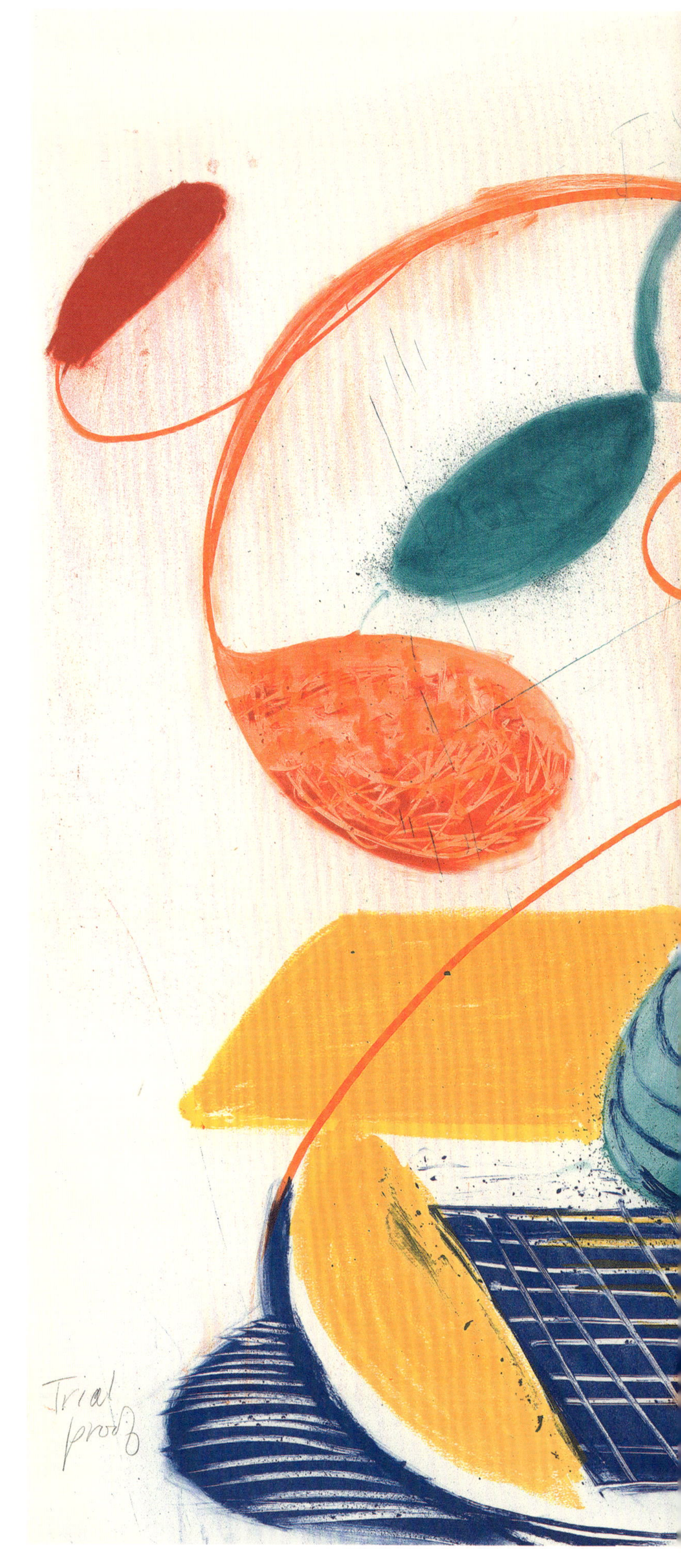


**Table Flowable,** 1991
Lithografie auf Papier (Auflage von 50) |
Lithograph on paper (Edition of 50),
112 × 145 cm
Tate: Presented by the artist 1993
Inv. Nº P20135

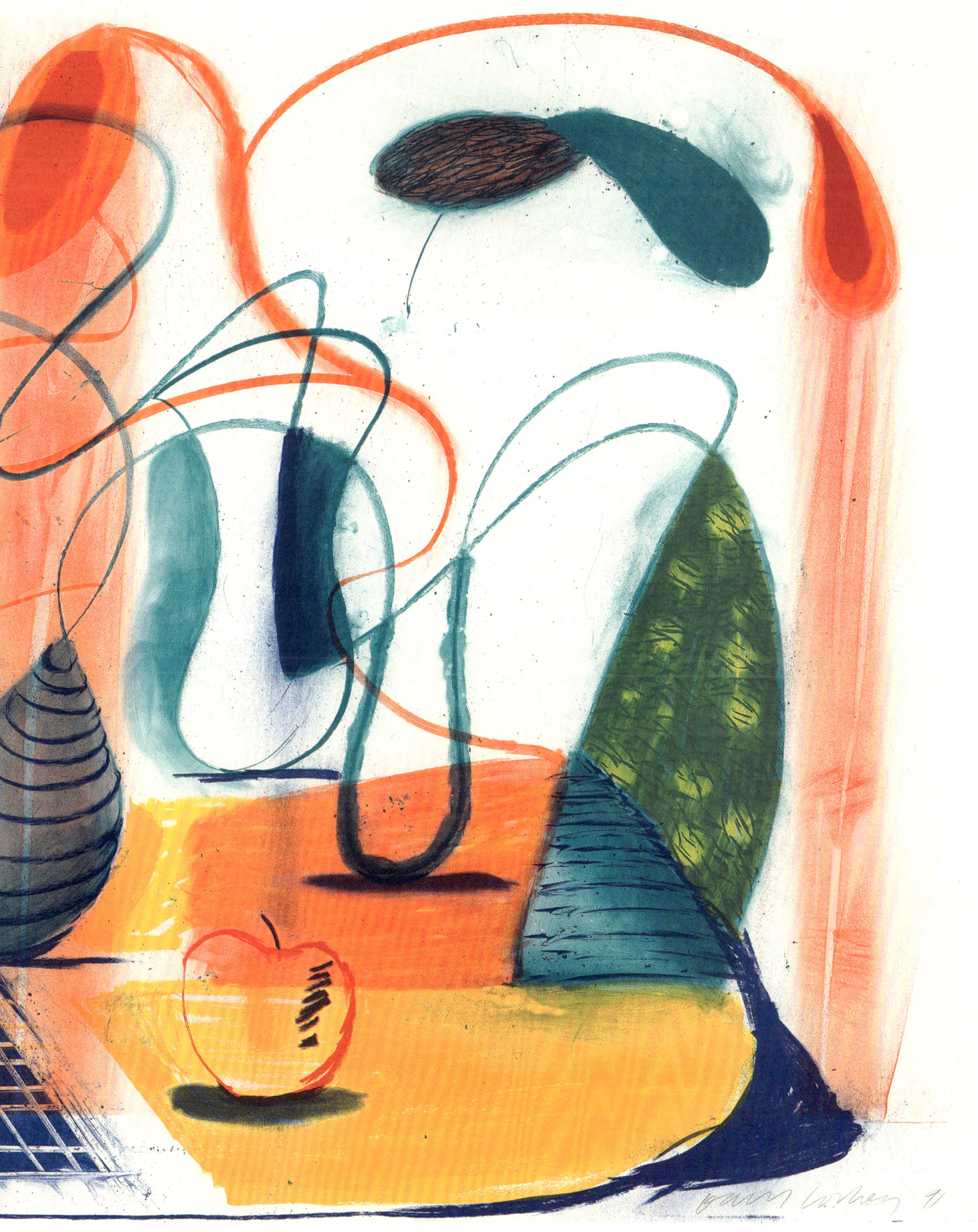

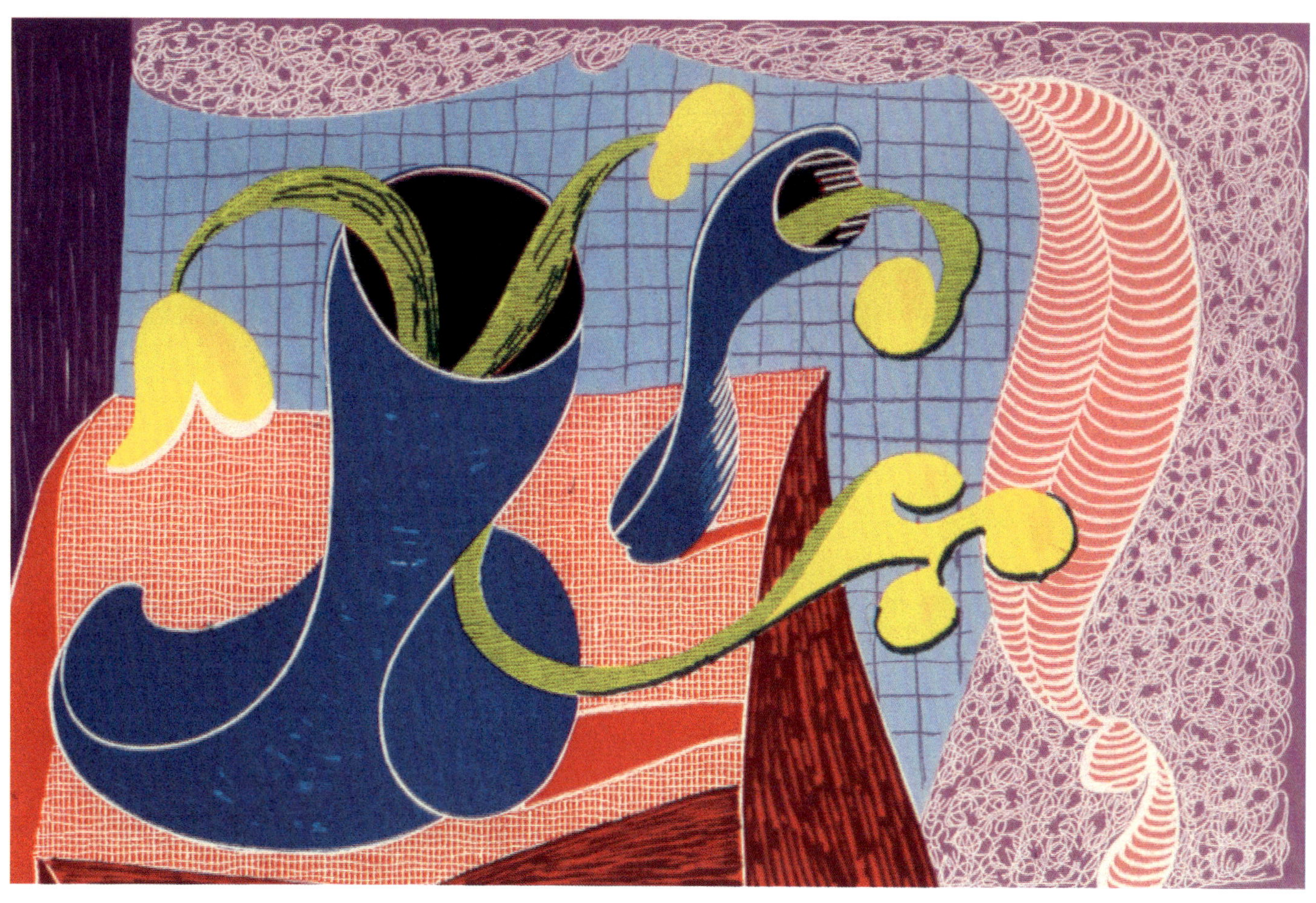

**Four Flowers in Still Life,** 1990
Lithografie auf Papier (Auflage von 50) |
Lithograph on paper (Edition of 50),
53,2 × 81,8 cm
Tate: Presented by the artist 1993
Inv. N° P20131

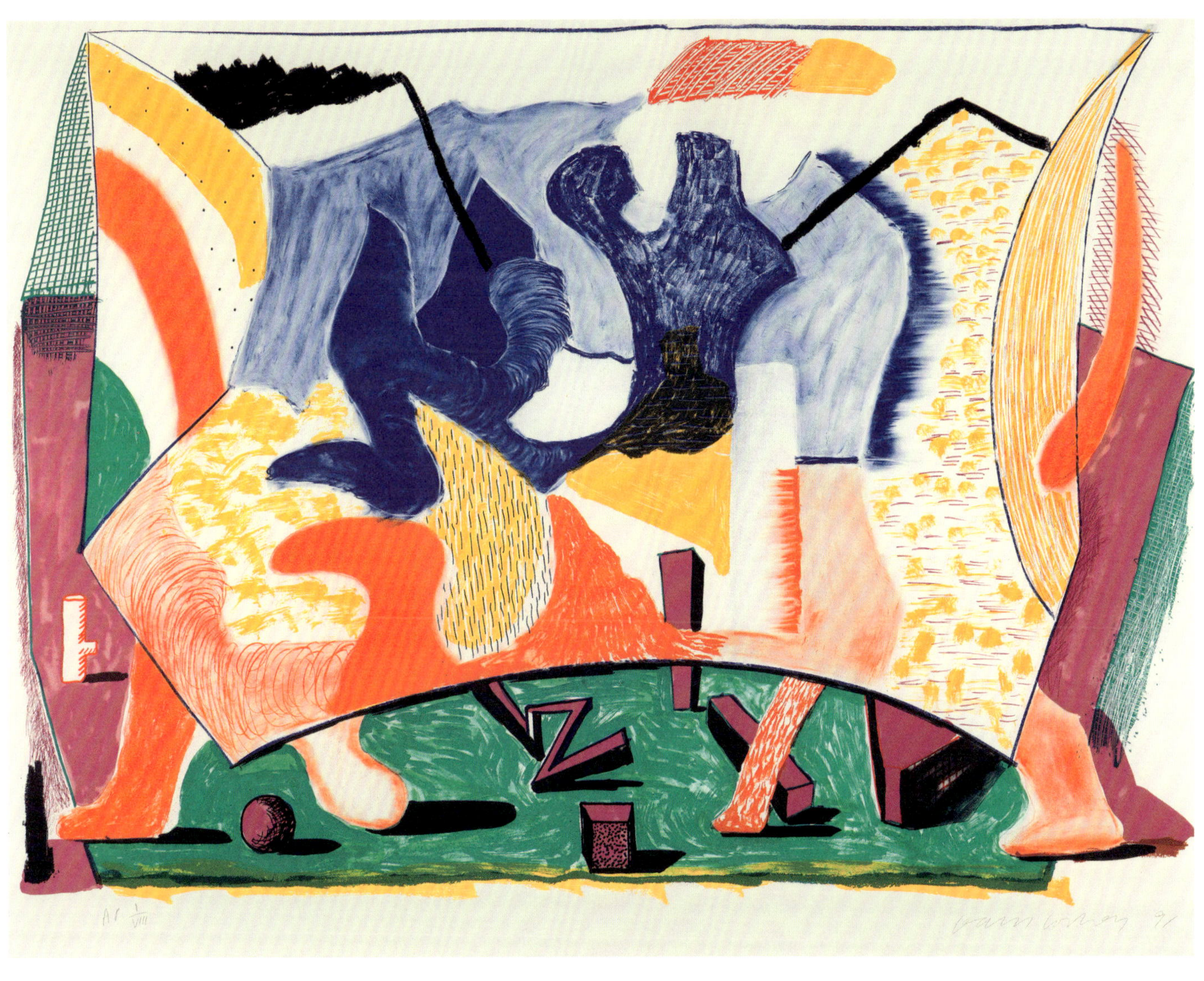

**Twelve Fifteen,** 1991
Lithografie auf Papier (Auflage von 50) |
Lithograph on paper (Edition of 50),
112 × 144,9 cm
Tate: Presented by the artist 1993
Inv. N° P20139

# David Hockney digital

**Bettina M. Busse: Sie kennen David Hockney und haben viele Gespräche mit ihm geführt. Uns ist aufgefallen, dass Sie beide – bedingt durch die Covid-19-Pandemie – außerdem die Experimentierfreude, neue digitale Formate zu entwickeln, verband und Sie diese Medien nutzten, um Künstler*innen und Kunst trotz geschlossener Museen und Galerien erfahrbar zu machen. Erkennen Sie hier Gemeinsamkeiten in den jeweiligen Strategien, und welche Potenziale wohnen Social Media hier inne?**

**Hans Ulrich Obrist:** In der Tat kenne ich David Hockney seit 15 Jahren – seit ich 2006 nach London gezogen bin. Er hat immer schon mehrere Studios gehabt: Das eine ist in South Kensington, London, wo ich auch wohne und wo ich ihn seit 2006 immer wieder besucht habe. Das andere ist in Bridlington, in East Yorkshire. Ein weiteres Studio ist in Los Angeles – und seit Kurzem auch eines in der Normandie. Die sechs bis sieben ausführlichen Gespräche, die wir in seinen Studios geführt haben, wurden dann in der Anthologie *Lives of the Artists, Lives of the Architects* bei Penguin veröffentlicht. Das Interessante war, dass Hockney sehr früh begonnen hat, Werke per E-Mail an seine Freunde zu schicken, wie die auf dem iPad gemachten Arbeiten. Das heißt, sie fanden am Morgen Arbeiten von ihm in der E-Mail-Inbox.

In den 1990er-Jahren, als ich mit Alighiero Boetti befreundet war, sagte dieser zu mir, wenn man am Morgen aufwacht und einfach Werke in die Welt schicken könnte, ohne dass man in Museen oder Ausstellungen gehen müsste, brächte das die Werke direkt zu den Menschen. Damals lebten wir ja noch im Zeitalter des Telefax. Boetti hatte die Idee, jeden Morgen, wie in einer Ausstellung, eine Gruppe von Werke in die Welt zu verschicken. Mit den digitalen Medien konnte man die Vision von Boetti dann verwirklichen. Bei David Hockney war der Effekt erstaunlich, dass am Morgen Freunde auf der ganzen Welt beispielsweise diese Blumen, die er am iPad kreiert hatte, in ihrer Inbox vorfanden. Das markierte den Anfang, so habe ich erstmals gesehen, wie er digitale Medien benutzt. Zu erwähnen ist aber, dass dies Jahre vor dem Lockdown war.

Indirekt muss man auch sagen, dass man Ausstellungen machen kann, die die Menschen erreichen können – jenseits der Museen, also an Orten, an denen man diese institutionelle Schwelle nicht mehr hat. Das war eine Idee, die nicht nur unter Künstler*innen schon immer präsent war. Es ist interessant, wie zum Beispiel Gilbert & George mit ihren Mail-Art-Arbeiten und ihrer Idee von *Art for All* agiert haben. Im Kontext der Anfänge von *Art for All* haben mir Gilbert & George in Gesprächen erzählt, wie interessiert sie an David Hockneys Bemühungen waren, Menschen außerhalb der Museen zu erreichen. 1969 haben sie dann *The Meal* veranstaltet, ein Dinner mit dreizehn Gästen und dem Ehrengast David Hockney. Die Kunstwelt war damals verortet zwischen Positionen der Pop-Art, der Minimal Art und der Konzeptkunst – Gilbert & George haben mit dieser Aktion die Idee von Kunst und Leben hinterfragt und dazu David Hockney als Ehrengast eingeladen. Und das alles hat mit Ihrer Frage zu tun.

**BMB: Was ich sehr spannend finde, ist, dass David Hockney den neuen Medien extrem offen gegenübersteht. So hat er für seine aktuellen Landschaften, die in der Normandie entstanden sind, das iPad benutzt. Gleichzeitig sind aber auch die klassischen Gattungen der Kunstgeschichte seine wiederkehrenden Themen, wie das Porträt oder eben die Landschaft. In dem Sinne hat er sich gleichzeitig wenig und sehr stark verändert.**

**HUO:** Das stimmt. Wie er gesagt hat, macht er diese Umwege und kommt immer wieder zur Malerei zurück. Er hat Bücher geschrieben, er hat Filme gedreht. Und der Computer ist für ihn ein Werkzeug, wie auch Photoshop für ihn ein Tool ist, um Bilder zu machen. Dies erlaubt es ihm weiterzuarbeiten, wie er immer gearbeitet hat, aber mit neuen Werkzeugen. Relevant ist, dass ihm und vielen anderen Künstler*innen der Computer zu langsam war, um darauf zu zeichnen. Heute kann man sehr frei mit dem Computer zeichnen, mit Farbe und mit Geschwindigkeit. Es hat eine Zeit gedauert, bis Hockney begonnen hat, mit dem iPad zu arbeiten. Am Anfang hat er das iPad nur sporadisch eingesetzt. Das war vor etwa zehn Jahren. Nam June Paik sagte mir einmal, wenn ein neues Medium erfunden wird, dauert es immer eine gewisse Zeit, bis man es einsetzen kann, wie man einen Bleistift einsetzt. So hat es auch bei den digitalen Medien gedauert: Zu Beginn waren sie Hockney zu langsam. In den letzten Jahren haben die digitalen Medien fast die Oberhand gewonnen, er integriert sie immer mehr in seine Arbeit, wie aktuell zum Beispiel in der Ausstellung in der Royal Academy, die Landschaften zeigt, die während des Lockdowns in der Normandie entstanden sind. Was auch eine Rolle spielt, ist, dass Hockney die analoge Malerei nicht mehr so interessiert, da er es so vermeiden kann, sich im Studio Klamotten zum Malen anziehen zu müssen. Er kann nun im Anzug gekleidet am iPad sitzen und malen.

**BMB: Was ich bemerkenswert im Zuge der Ausstellungsvorbereitungen fand, war, dass sich viele junge Künstler*innen für Hockney interessieren. Ich weiß nicht, ob es jetzt Wien-spezifisch ist oder ob es auch in Großbritannien so ist, dass er immer noch unter den jungen Künstler*innen wichtig ist?**

**HUO:** Ja, definitiv. Das hat auch mit der Idee von *Art for Art* zu tun. Es gibt ein neues Projekt am Piccadilly in London, *CIRCA*. Das Projekt wurde von einem jungen Künstler, Josef O'Connor, initiiert. Die Idee dahinter ist, dass Künstler*innen dort Werke auf dem größten elektronischen Outdoor-Screen generieren können. Dafür hat Hockney ein Video auf dem iPad mit dem Titel *Remember you cannot look at the sun or death for very long* geschaffen, das während des Lockdowns im Mai gezeigt wurde. Es ist wie ein horizontales Poster – das hat auch mit den Arbeiten zu tun, die während des Lockdowns entstanden sind: Darin fragt er, wie sieht die Welt aus, mit dem Ziel, dass man sich Zeit nimmt, die Schönheit der Welt zu sehen. Der darin animierte Sonnenaufgang sollte Hoffnung und Solidarität symbolisieren. Ein solches Video an einem Ort zu sehen, an dem normalerweise Werbung gezeigt wird, verändert die Perspektive. Ein neues Format hat von Beginn an das Museum in Progress in Wien vor dem Hintergrund, Menschen Kunst in anderen Medien zugänglich zu machen, realisiert: durch große Werbetafeln im öffentlichen Raum, dem *Eisernen Vorhang* in der Wiener Staatsoper, Inserate in Tageszeitungen – gestaltet von Künstlerinnen und Künstlern und Ausstellungen für das Fernsehen. Die Inspiration dazu kommt, wie Sie sagen, zum Teil auch aus der Geschichte, nämlich dass man die Zukunft aus den Fragmenten der Vergangenheit erfindet. Das ist bei David Hockney stark der Fall: Die Inspiration hier sind nicht nur digitale Medien; eine wesentliche Quelle stellen auch die Tapisserien von Bayeux dar, die die Apokalypse zeigen, wie auch die *Unicorn Tapisserien.* Weitere Einflüsse sind Vincent van Gogh, Marcel Proust und Oscar Wilde. Diese Inspirationsquellen sieht er sich ganz intensiv und präzise an und arbeitet mit ihnen.

**BMB: Diese „Umwege" David Hockneys faszinieren bis heute. Wo erkennen Sie gegenseitigen Austausch zwischen den Medien beziehungsweise Disziplinen innerhalb von Hockneys Arbeitsweise? Welchen Stellenwert nimmt hierin wiederum das Digitale ein?**

**HUO:** Die Kunst in verschiedene Sphären hineinzutragen, das inspiriert ihn. Er hat eine lebenslange „Liebesgeschichte" mit klassischer Musik und dem Theater. Es gibt eine Wechselbeziehung zwischen den verschiedenen Sparten, so überträgt er theatralische Momente des Theaters beziehungsweise der Oper in die Malerei. Die Größe der Bühnenbilder wiederum hinterlässt ihre Spuren in den großformatigen Landschaften. Die digitalen Formate einerseits sind ein Portal für das Museum auf dem iPhone, das kann per Social Media vermittelt werden, man sieht das als portables Mikromuseum, gleichzeitig kann das gleiche Bild auf einem Großbildschirm am Piccadilly oder ein Großbild in der Oper sein. Das Oszillieren zwischen Mikro und Makro ist auch ein wichtiger Aspekt bei der Betrachtung seines Werkes im Zusammenhang mit den digitalen Medien.

# David Hockney digital

**Bettina M. Busse: You know David Hockney well and you have conducted numerous interviews with him. We also noticed that both of you – during the Covid-19 pandemic – shared a joy of experimenting with new digital formats and using these media to bring artists and art to people even when museums and galleries were closed. Do you see commonalities in your respective strategies here and what potential do you see in social media?**

**Hans Ulrich Obrist:** I have known David Hockney for fifteen years – since I moved to London in 2006. He has always had several studios: one of them is in South Kensington, which is where I live too and where I have been visiting him since 2006. The other is in Bridlington in East Yorkshire. He also has a studio in Los Angeles – and recently acquired another one in Normandy. The six or seven comprehensive interviews that we did in his studios were published in the Penguin anthology *Lives of the Artists, Lives of the Architects*. The interesting thing is that very early on, Hockney began sending works to his friends via email, for example the ones made on his iPad. So they would just find works by him waiting for them in their inbox in the morning.

In the 1990s when I was friends with Alighiero Boetti, he said to me, imagine if you could just get up in the morning and send works out into the world, if you could get them straight to people without them needing to go to exhibitions or museums. We were living in the era of the fax machine back then. Boetti wanted to send a group of works into the world every morning like an exhibition. When digital media came along it suddenly became possible to realize Boetti's vision. The effect with David Hockney was amazing, with his friends all around the world waking up to find he had sent them images made on his iPad, of flowers for example. That was how it all started, that's when I witnessed him using digital media for the first time. This was all years before lockdown, of course.

By the way, I should add that it's perfectly possible to make exhibitions that people can visit – that have nothing to do with museums – in places without this institutional threshold. This idea has been around forever, and not only among artists. Think about the mail art of Gilbert & George and their idea of *Art for All*. It was while they were talking about how *Art for All* started that Gilbert & George told me how interested they had been in David Hockney's efforts to reach people outside the museums. In 1969 they hosted *The Meal*, a dinner with thirteen guests where David Hockney was the guest of honour. The art world at the time was all about Pop Art, Minimalism and conceptual art – but with this performance-sculpture, Gilbert & George questioned this separation of life and art and invited David Hockney to be a part of it. And that was all related to your question.

**BMB: What I find so fascinating is how open David Hockney is to new media. Like the recent landscapes he made in Normandy on the iPad. Yet at the same time, classical art historical genres like the portrait or, of course,**

**the landscape are recurring themes in his work. In this sense, he has changed so much and so little at the same time.**

**HUO:** That's true. As he said, he makes these "detours" and always comes back to painting. He has written books, he has made films. And the computer is a tool for him, just like Photoshop is an image-making tool for him. This allows him to continue working as he has always worked, only with new tools. The point here is that for him, as for many other artists, the computer was just too slow to use for drawing back then. Today you can draw completely freely with computers, with no restrictions on colour and speed. It took a while before Hockney started working on the iPad. Nam June Paik once said to me that when a new medium comes along, it always takes time before it can be used as you would use a pencil. This was certainly the case with digital media: it was too slow for Hockney in the beginning. Recently, digital media have started to take over, he is integrating them into his work more and more, like at his Royal Academy exhibition of landscapes made in Normandy during lockdown. Another reason Hockney has lost interest in analogue painting is because he no longer has to change into special painting clothes in his studio. Now he can sit in his suit painting on his iPad.

**BMB: What I found so interesting during the preparations for the exhibition is that so many young artists are interested in Hockney. I don't know if that's specific to Vienna or whether it's also the case in Britain?**

**HUO:** Oh absolutely. This is also because of the idea of *Art for Art*. There's a new project at Piccadilly Circus in London called *CIRCA*. It was initiated by a young artist, Josef O'Connor. The idea is for artists to show works on a vast electronic outdoor screen. Hockney created a video for this on the iPad titled *Remember you cannot look at the sun or death for very long*, which was shown during lockdown in May. It's like a horizontal poster – and this is also related to other works he was making during lockdown. In it he asks what the world looks like; it's an invitation to take time to see the beauty of the world. The animated sunset is a symbol of hope and solidarity. To see an art video in a location that is usually full of adverts brings about a shift in perspective. The Museum in Progress in Vienna was founded on the very idea of finding new presentation forms to bring art to people, using large billboards in public spaces, the *Iron Curtain* in the Vienna State Opera, advertisements designed by artists in daily newspapers and exhibitions for television. The inspiration for this, as you say, comes in part from history, the idea that you can invent the future from fragments of the past. This is very much the case with David Hockney, for whom digital media is only one of many sources of inspiration. Another key one is the Bayeux tapestry, which shows the apocalypse, or the *Unicorn Tapestries*. Other influences are Vincent van Gogh, Marcel Proust and Oscar Wilde. He studies these sources of inspiration with great intensity and precision and works with them.

**BMB: These "detours" of David Hockney's are as fascinating today as ever. Where do you see the media, or rather the various disciplines playing off against one another in Hockney's working method? What is the role of the digital in all this?**

**HUO:** Interdisciplinarity, bringing art into different spheres, that inspires him. He has had a life-long love affair with classical music and the theatre. The disciplines feed into one another: he carries theatrical moments from the theatre or the opera into his painting, for example, and the scale of the stage designs is echoed in the large-format landscapes. On the one hand, digital formats are a portal for the museum on the iPhone, a portable micro-museum that can be transmitted through social media. Yet the same image can be shown on a big screen at Piccadilly Circus or in the opera. The oscillation between micro and macro is an important aspect when looking at his work through the lens of social media.

**Going to be a Queen for Tonight,** 1960
Öl auf Tafel | Oil on board,
120 × 85 cm
Royal College of Art, London
Inv. Nº RCA_CC_139

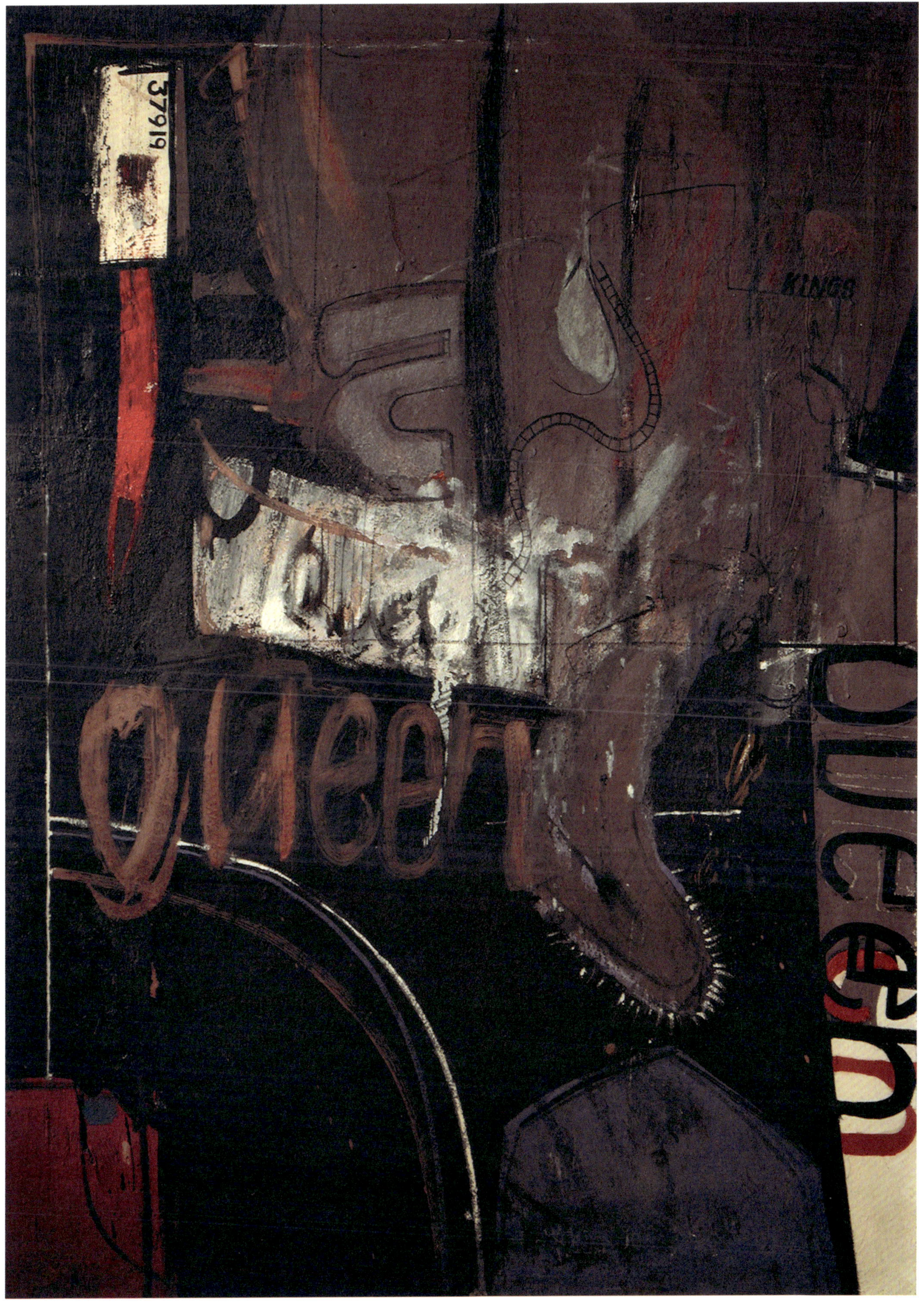
37919
KINGS
queen

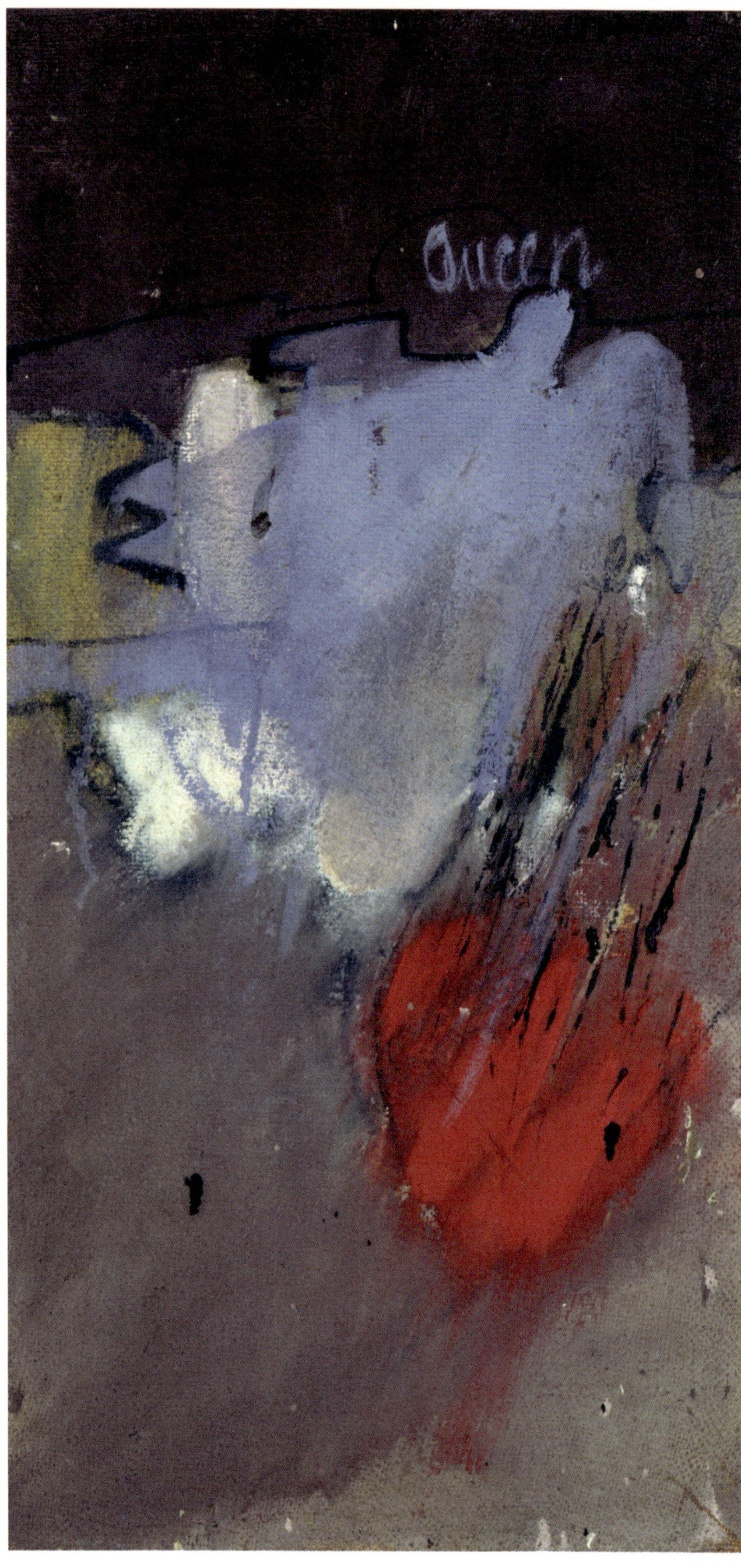


**Queen,** 1960
Öl auf Sackleinen | Oil on hessian,
62 × 30 cm
Karin und Uwe Hollweg Stiftung, Bremen

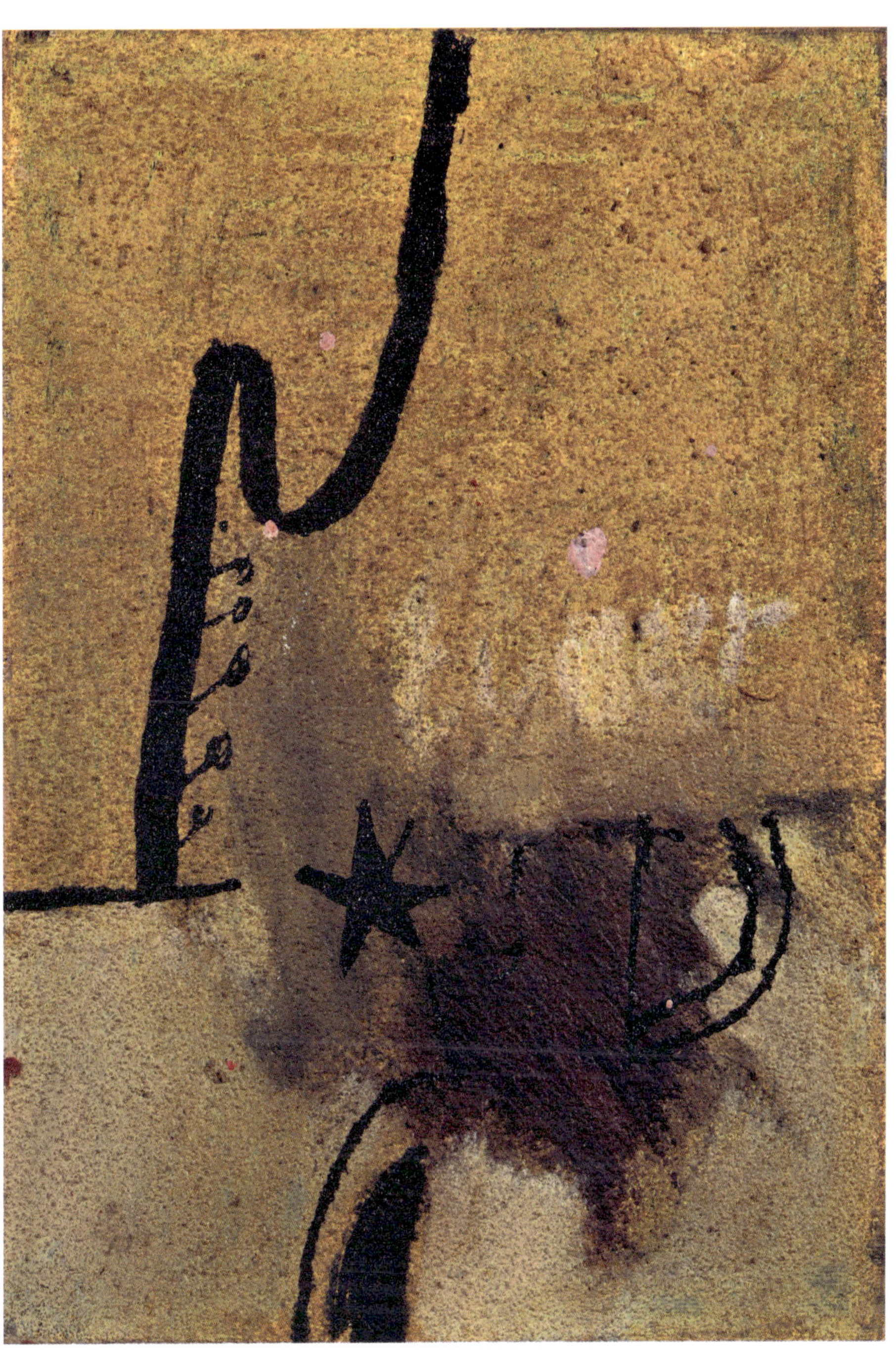

**Queer,** 1960
Öl und Sand auf Leinwand |
Oil and sand on canvas,
25,1 × 18 cm
Privatsammlung | Private Collection

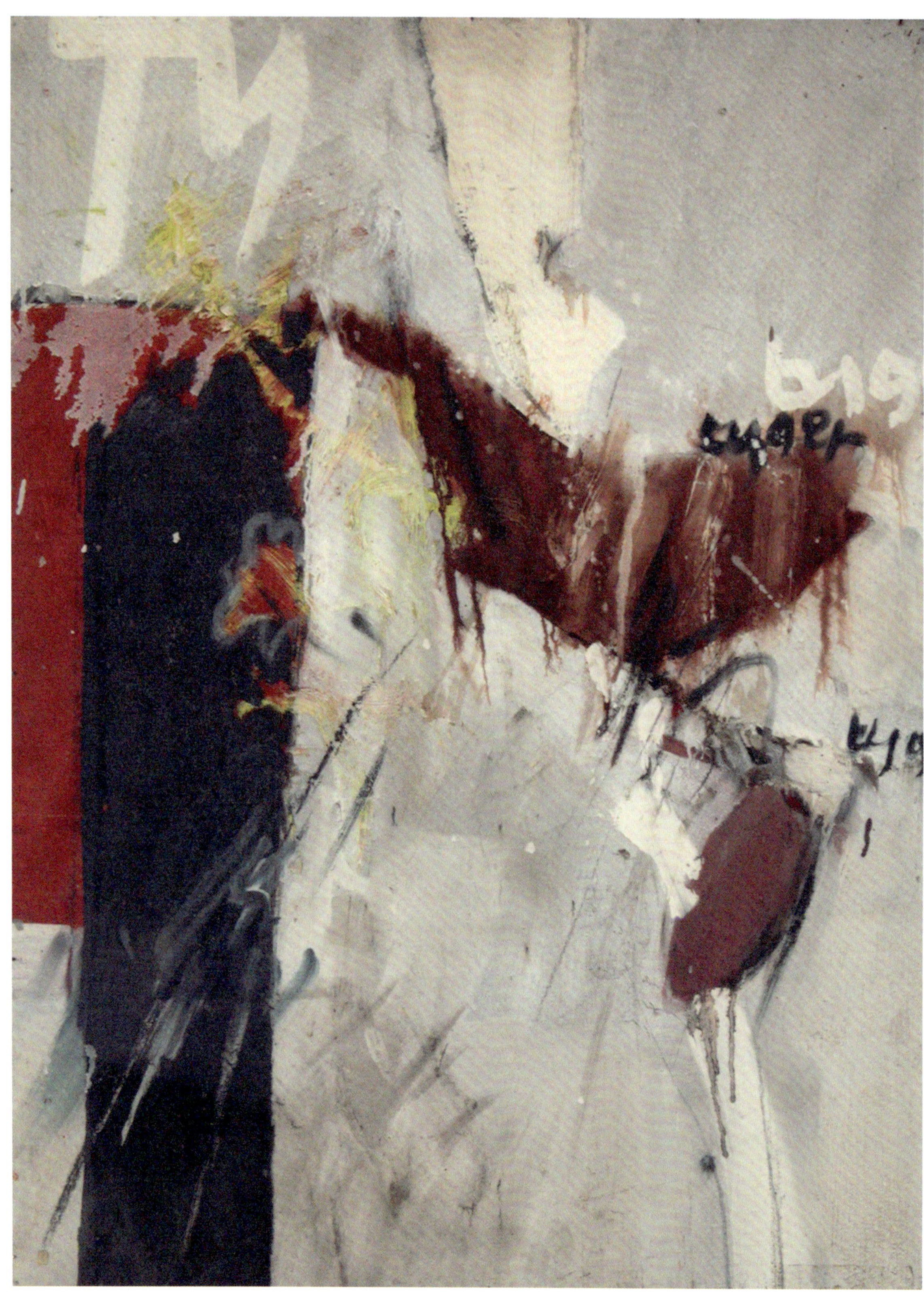


**Untitled (Big Tyger),** 1961
Öl auf Tafel | Oil on board,
74,9 × 55,6 cm
Royal College of Art, London
Inv. N° RCA_CC_230

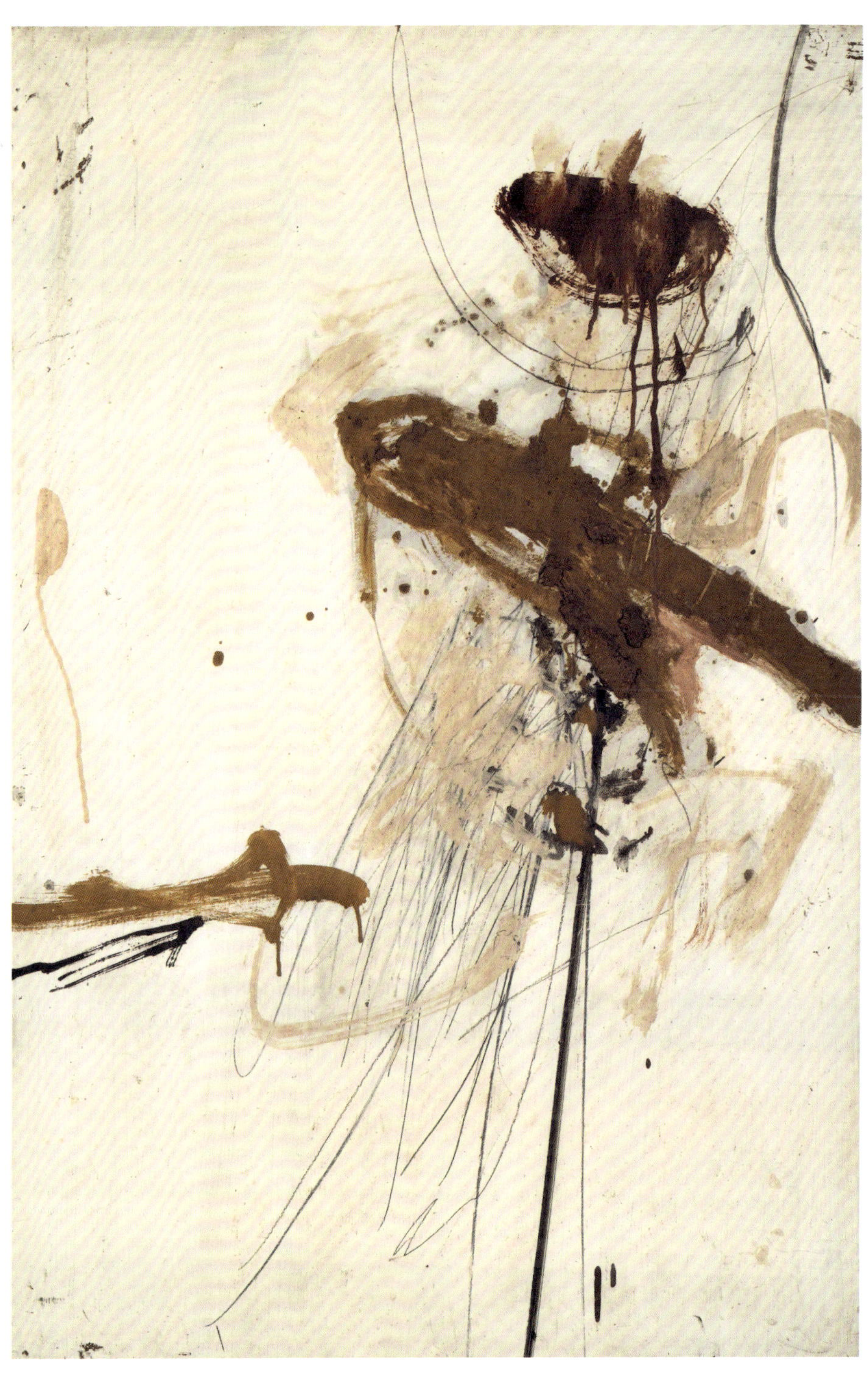

**Untitled (2$^{nd}$ Abstract Painting),** 1960
Öl und Mixed Media auf Tafel |
Oil and mixed media on board,
78 × 53 cm
Karin und Uwe Hollweg Stiftung, Bremen

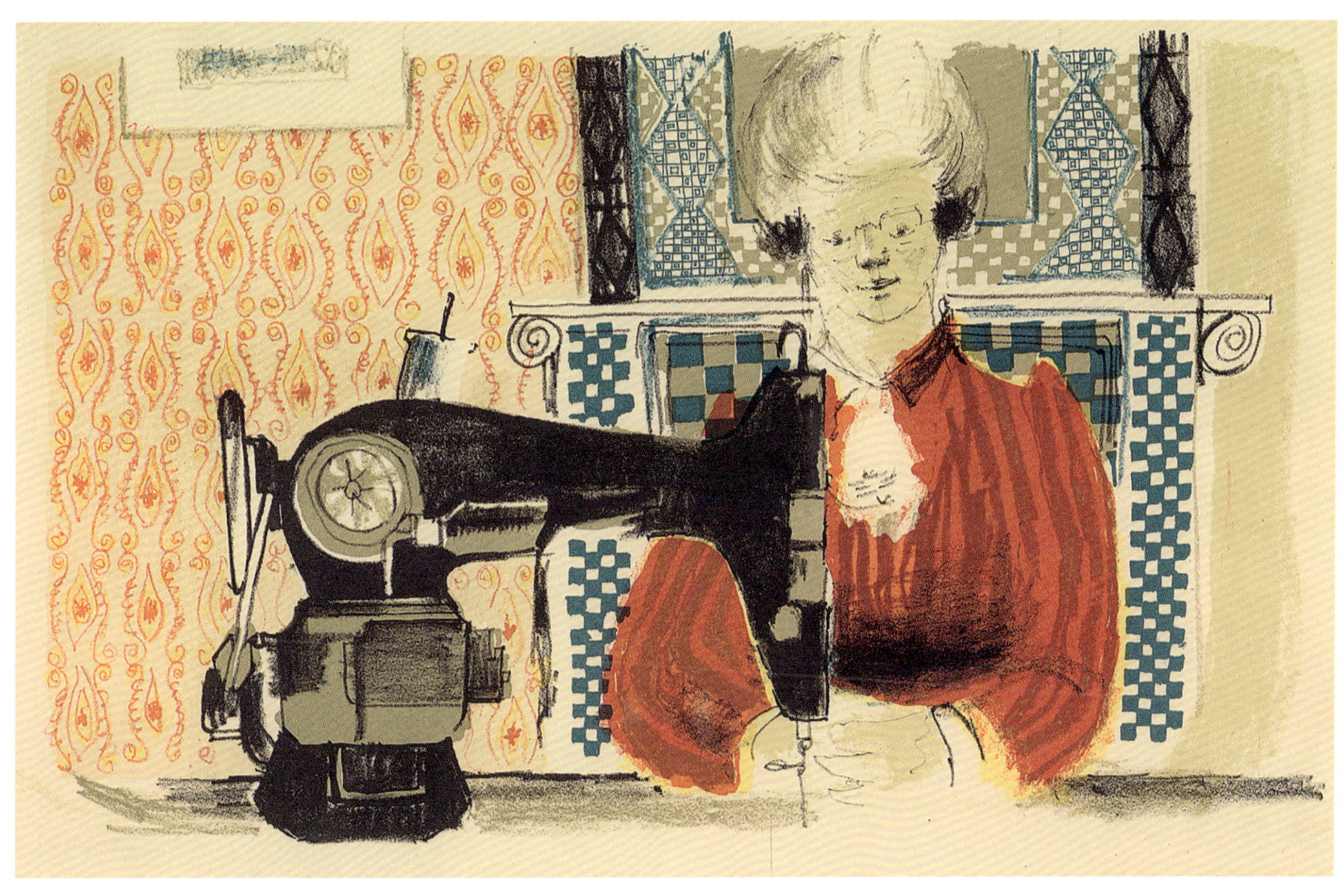

**Woman with a Sewing Machine,** 1954
Lithografie auf Papier | Lithograph on paper,
22,5 × 35,5 cm
Tate: Presented by the American Fund
for the Tate Gallery 2004
Inv. N° P13001

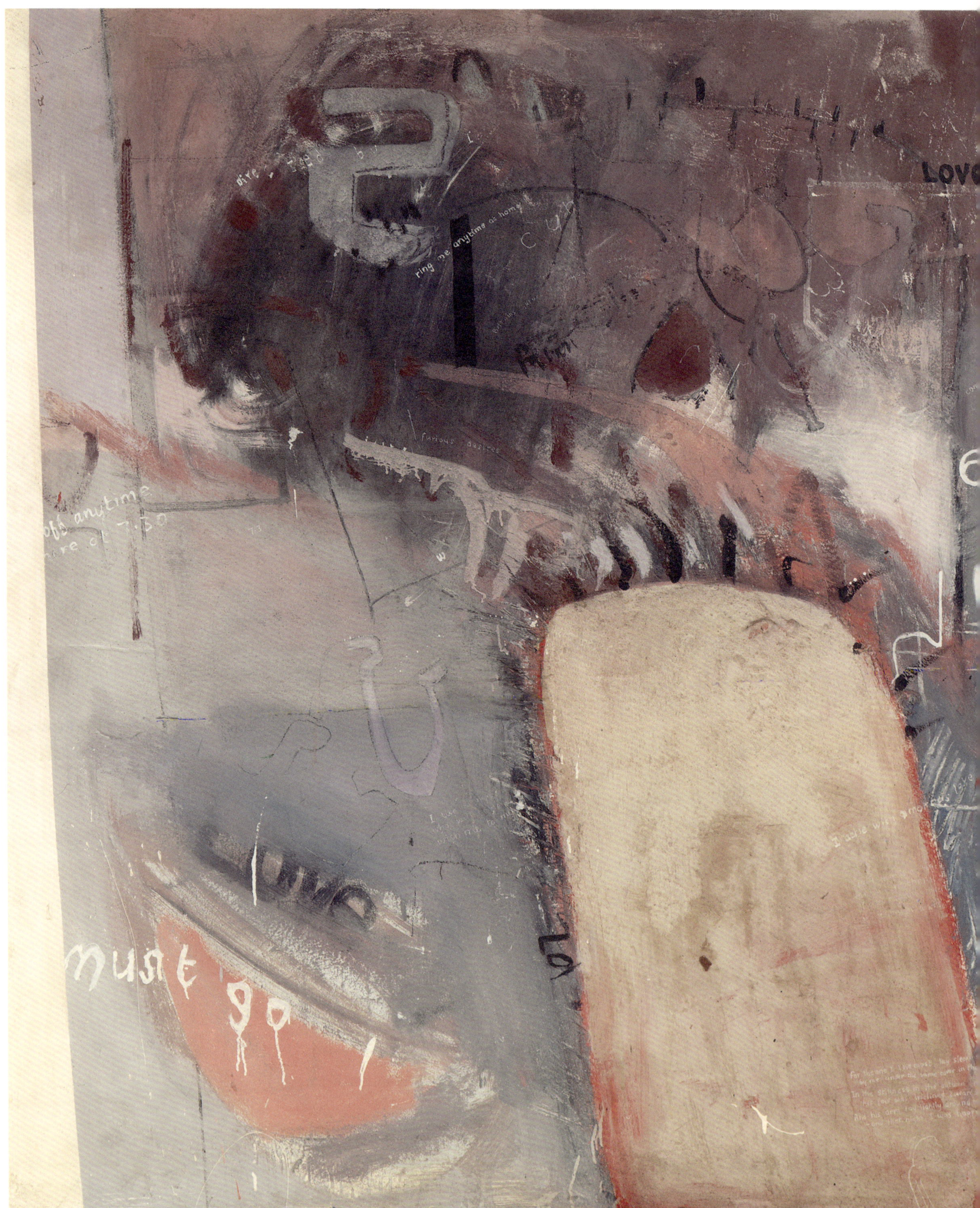
ring me anytime at home
off anytime
must go

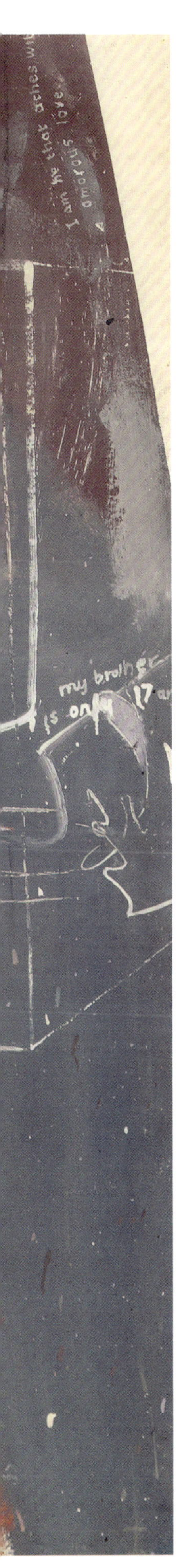


**The Third Love Painting,** 1960
Öl auf Hartfaserplatte | Oil on board,
118,7 × 118,7 cm
Tate: Purchased with assistance from the Art Fund, the Friends of the Tate Gallery, the American Fund for the Tate Gallery and a group of donors 1991
Inv. N° T06468

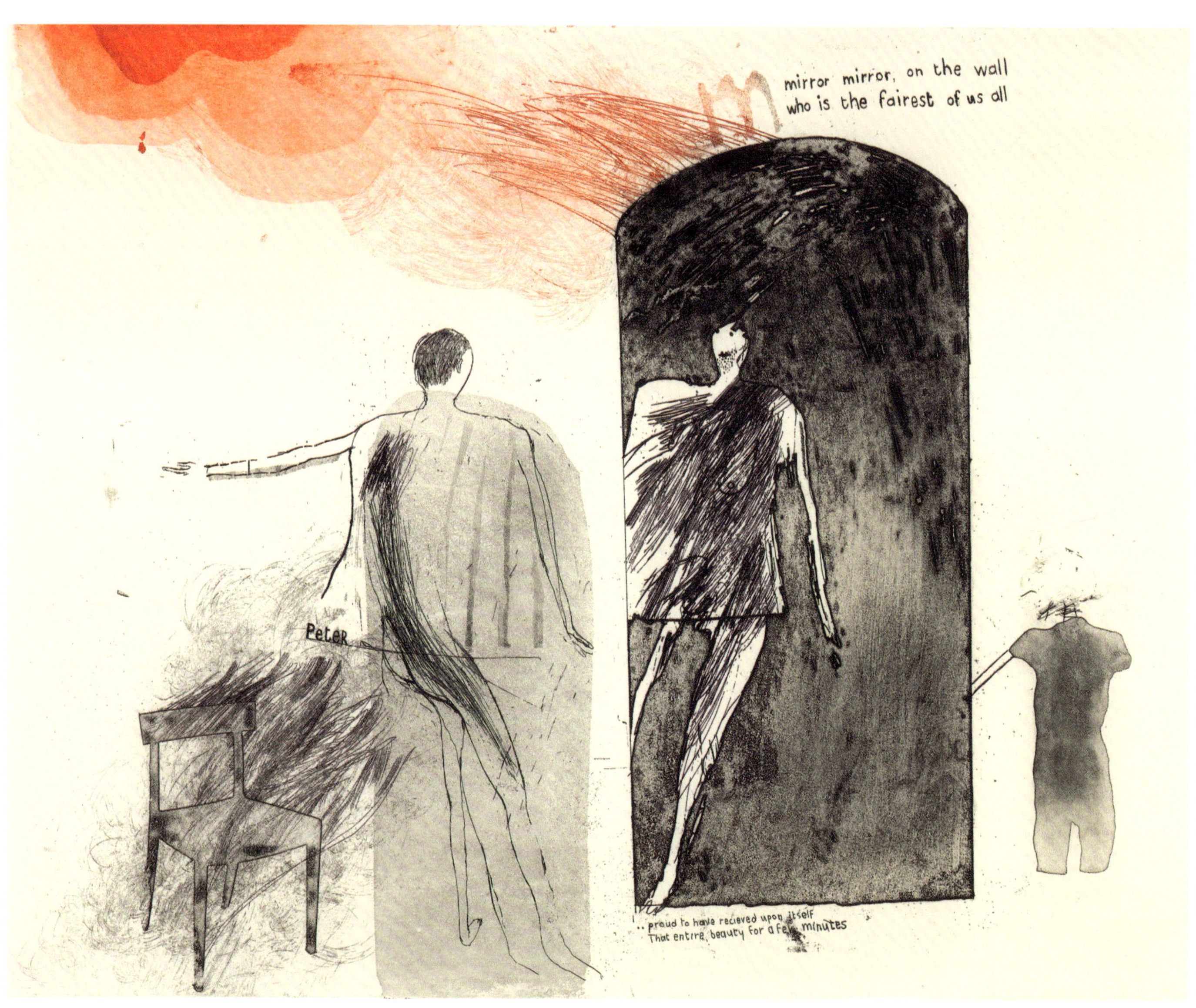


**Mirror, Mirror on the Wall,** 1961
Radierung und Aquatinta auf Papier |
Etching and aquatint on paper,
40,5 × 49,7 cm
Tate: Presented by Jonathan Cheshire
and Gareth Marshallsea in memory
of Peter Coni 1994
Inv. Nº P11377

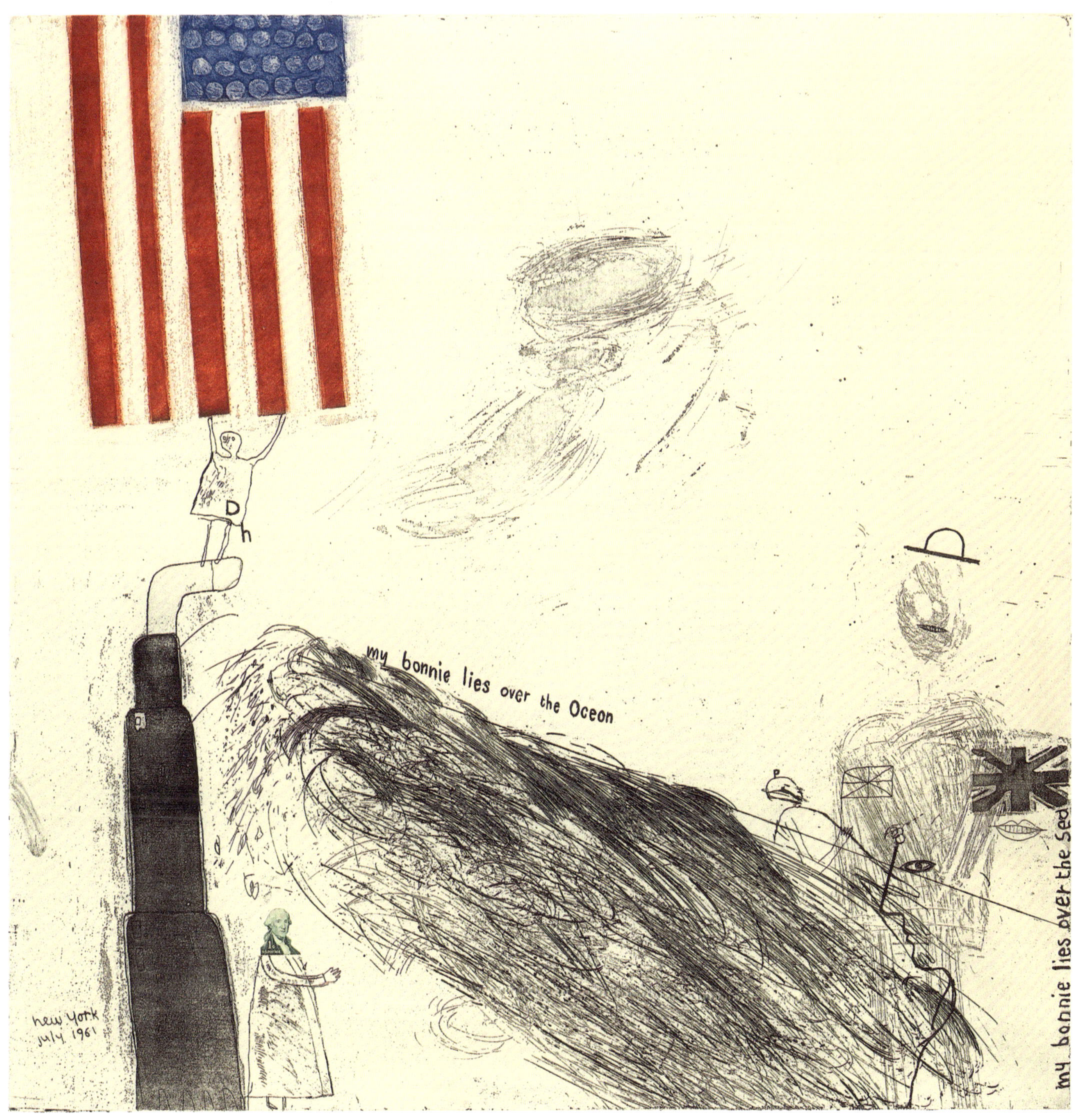


**My Bonnie Lies Over the Ocean,** 1961–1962
Radierung, Aquatinta und Collage auf Papier |
Etching, aquatint and collage on paper,
45,1 × 45,1 cm
Tate: Purchased 1979
Inv. N° P07353

**Kaisarion with All his Beauty,** 1961
Radierung auf Papier | Etching on paper,
49 × 27,6 cm
Tate: Presented by Jonathan Cheshire
and Gareth Marshallsea in memory of
Peter Coni 1994
Inv. N° P11376

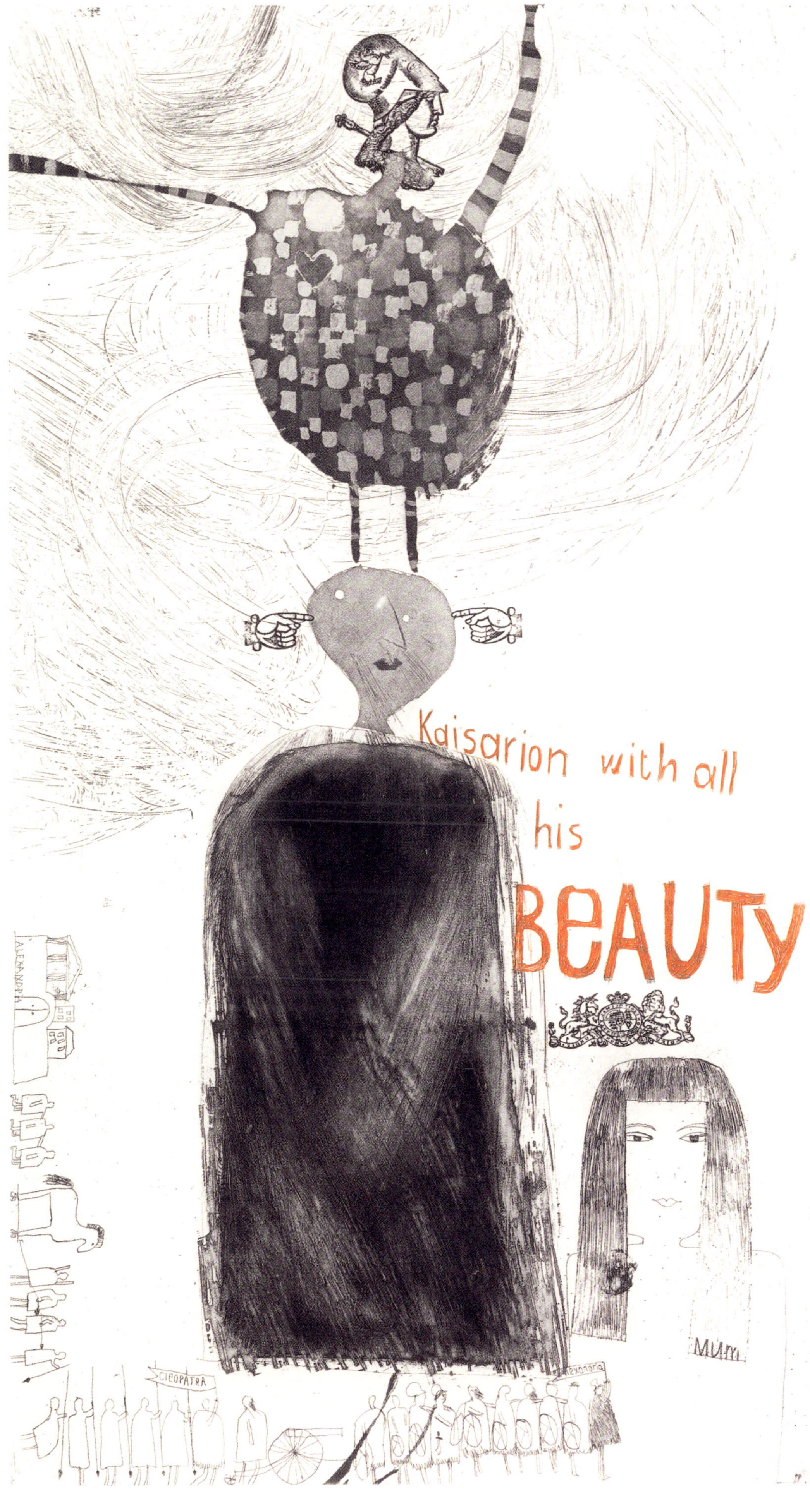
Kaisarion with all
his
BEAUTY
MUM
CLEOPATRA
ALEXANDRIA

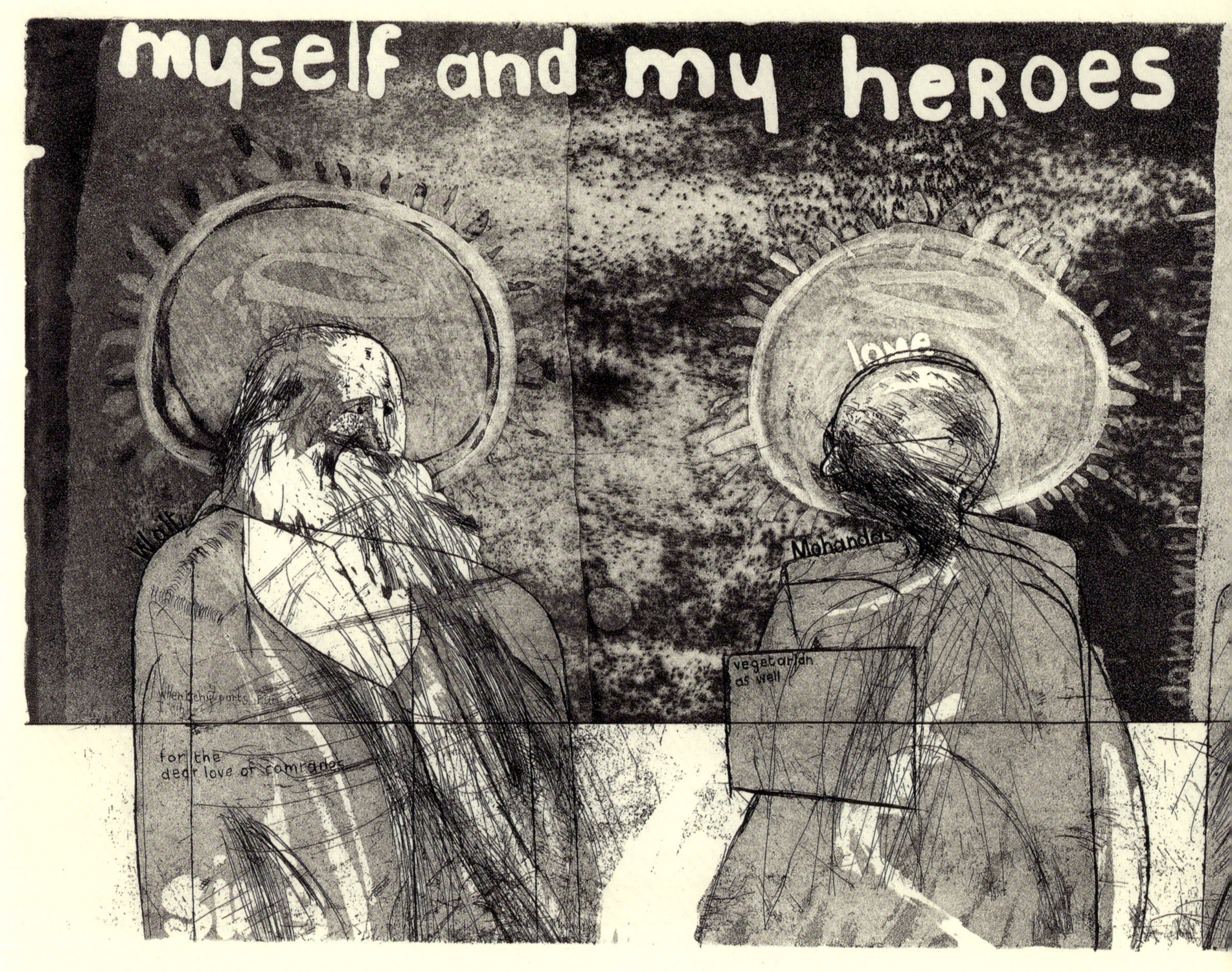


**Myself and My Heroes,** 1961
Radierung und Aquatinta auf Papier |
Etching and aquatint on paper,
25,7 × 50,2 cm
Tate: Purchased 1979
Inv. N° P07352

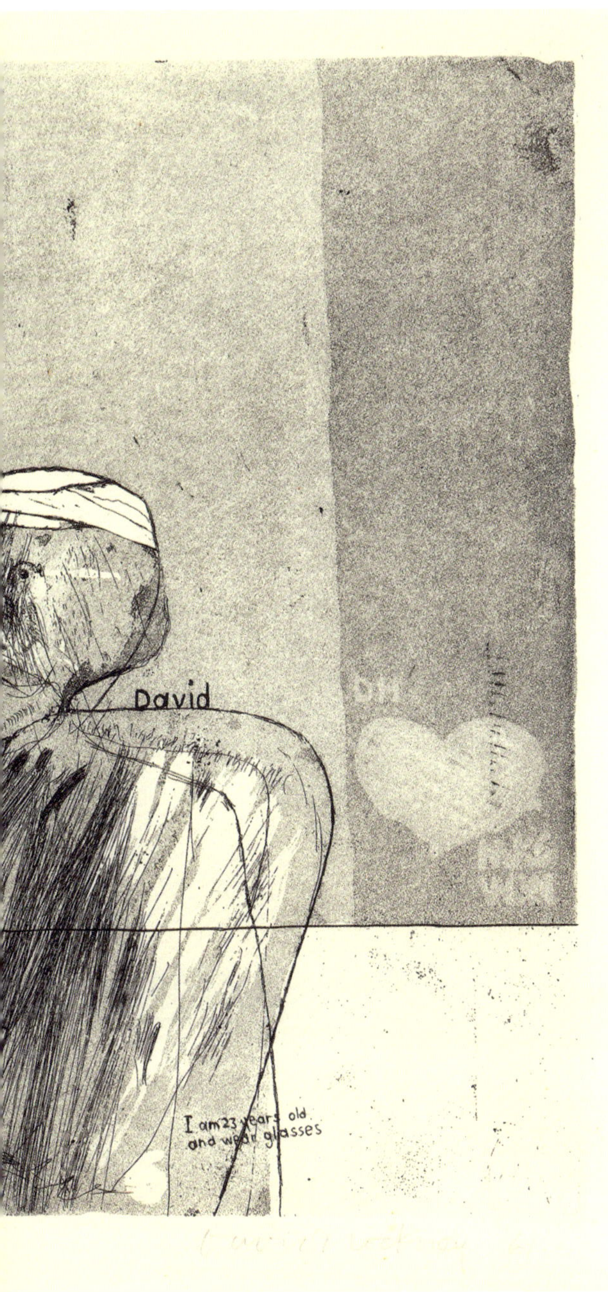
David
I am 23 years old
and wear glasses

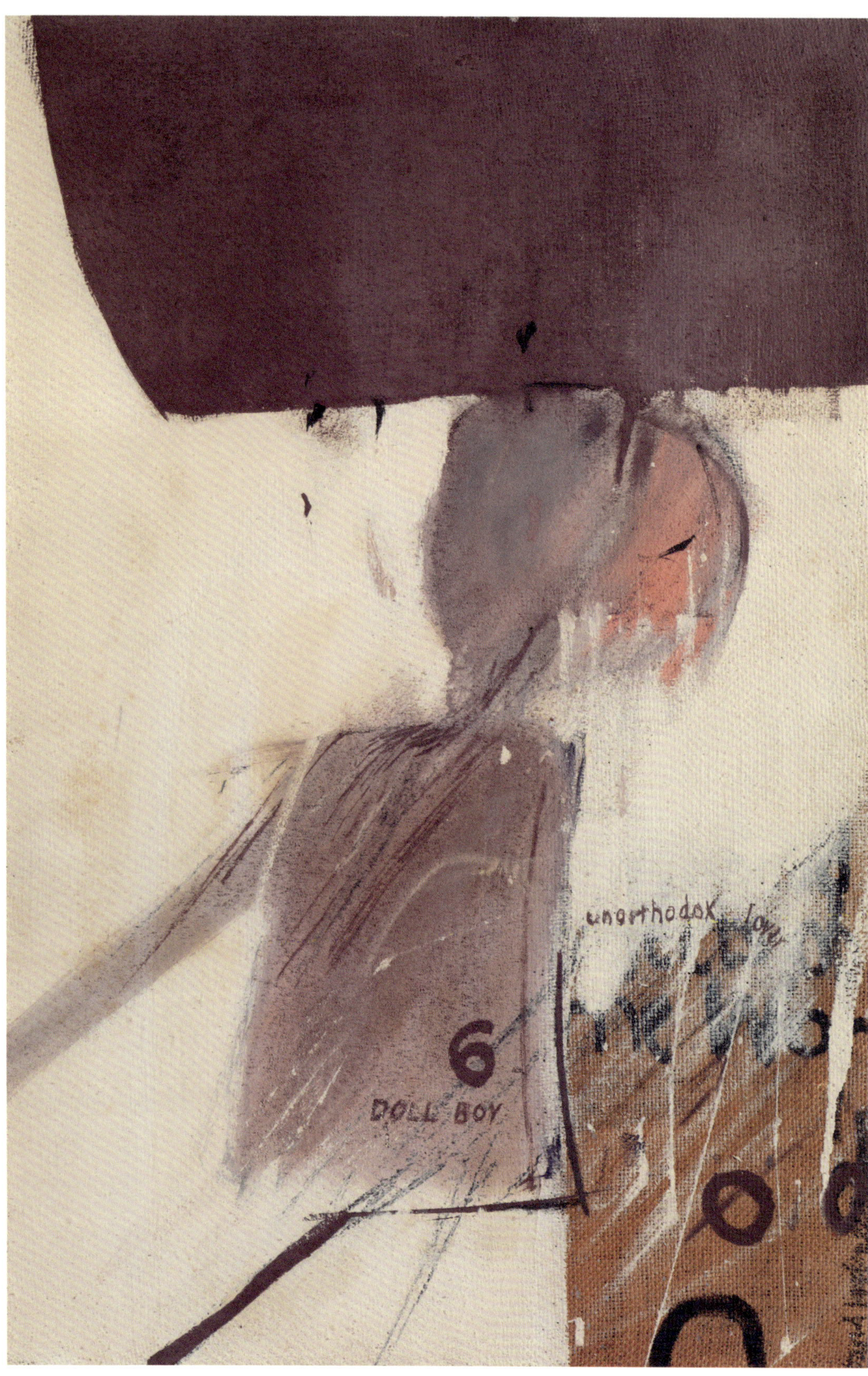


**Study for Doll Boy,** 1960
Öl auf Leinwand | Oil on canvas,
61,2 × 40,5 cm
Tate: Accepted by HM Government in lieu of
inheritance tax on The Estate of Frith Banbury
and allocated to the Tate Gallery 2009
Inv. N° T12882

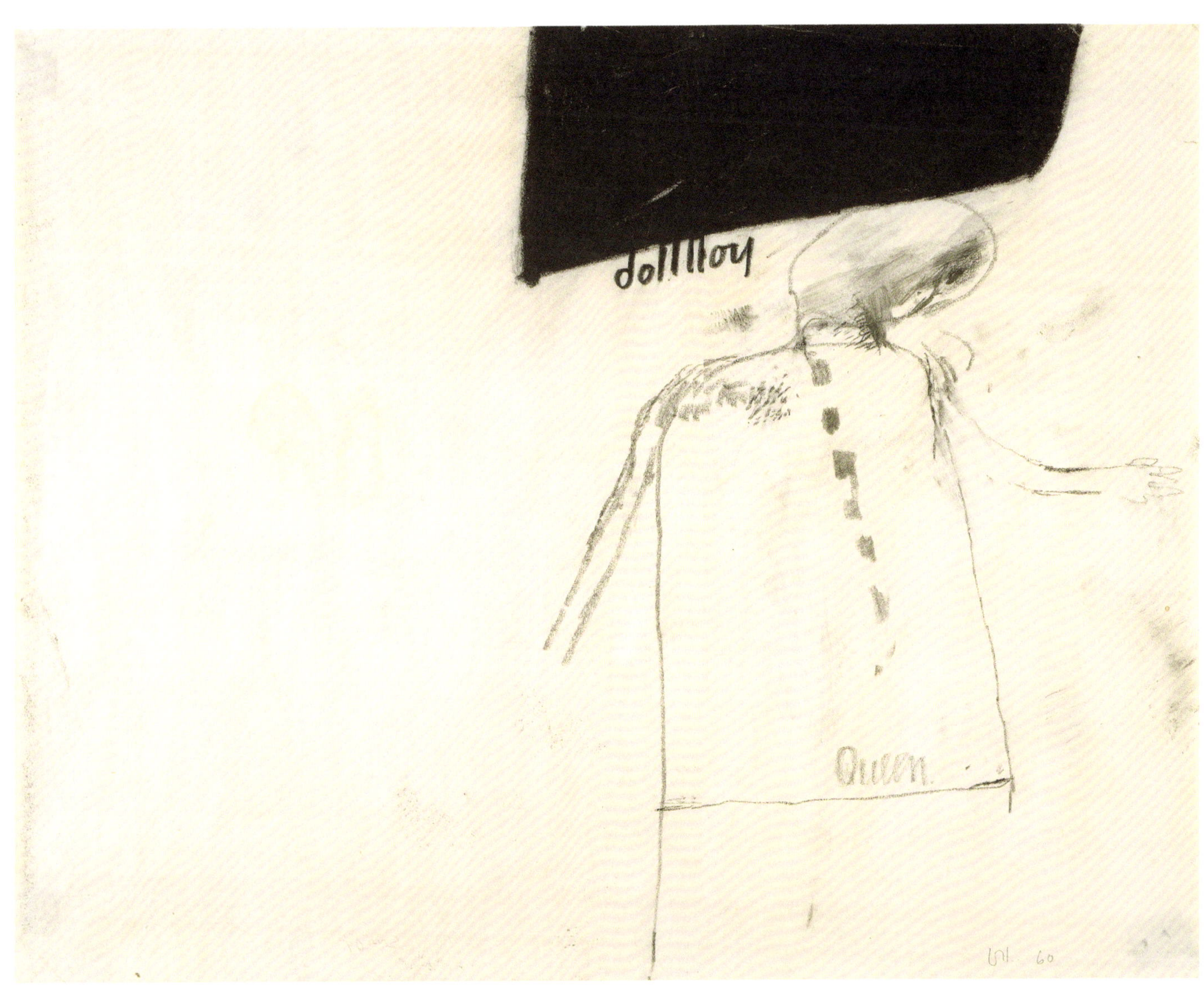


**Study for Doll Boy,** 1960
Kohle auf Papier | Charcoal on paper,
40,4 × 51,2 cm
Tate: Presented by Klaus Anschel
in memory of his wife Gerty 2004
Inv. N° T11898

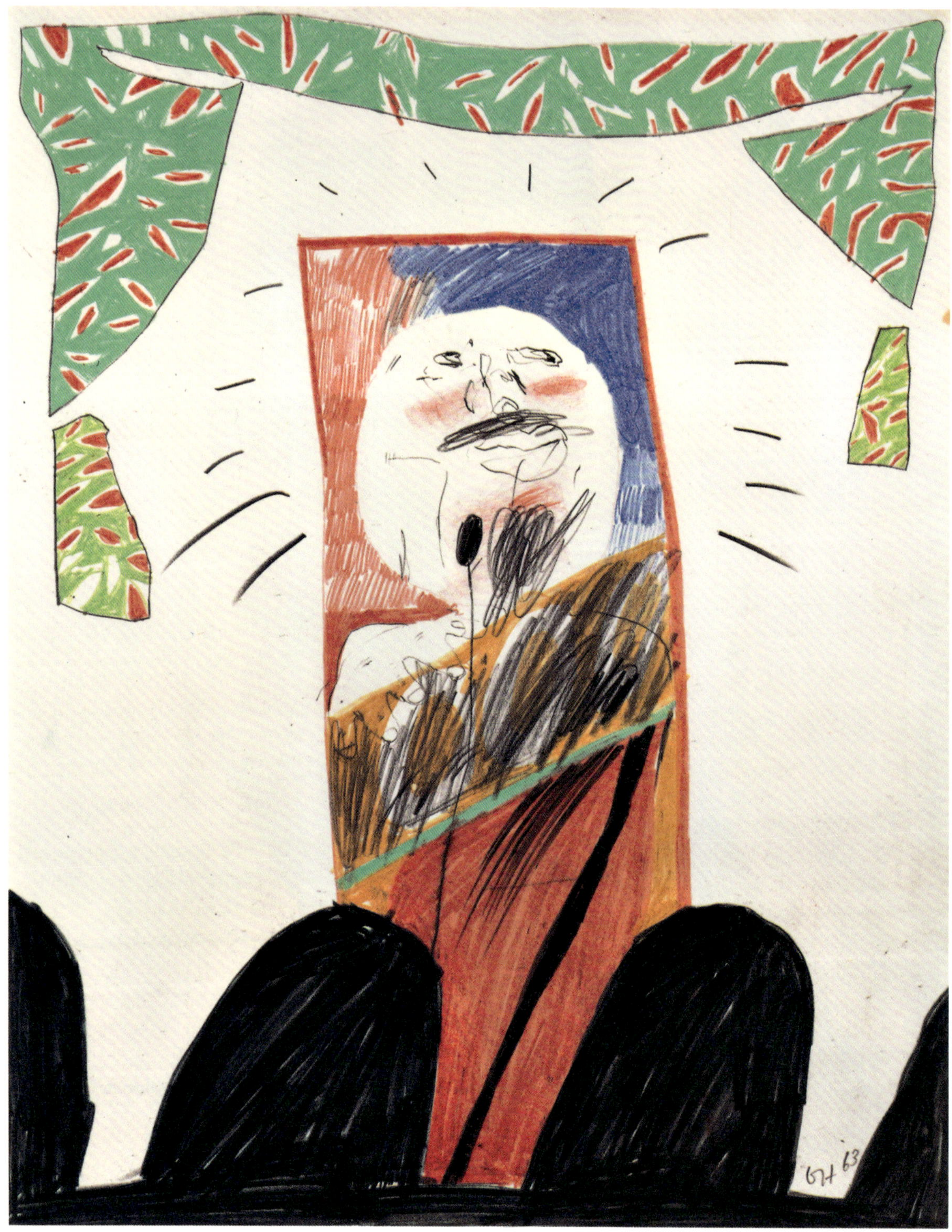

**The Singer,** 1963
Bleistift und farbige Kreiden auf Papier |
Pencil and coloured crayons on paper,
31,8 × 25,4 cm
Privatsammlung, Frankfurt | Private Collection, Frankfurt

**191**

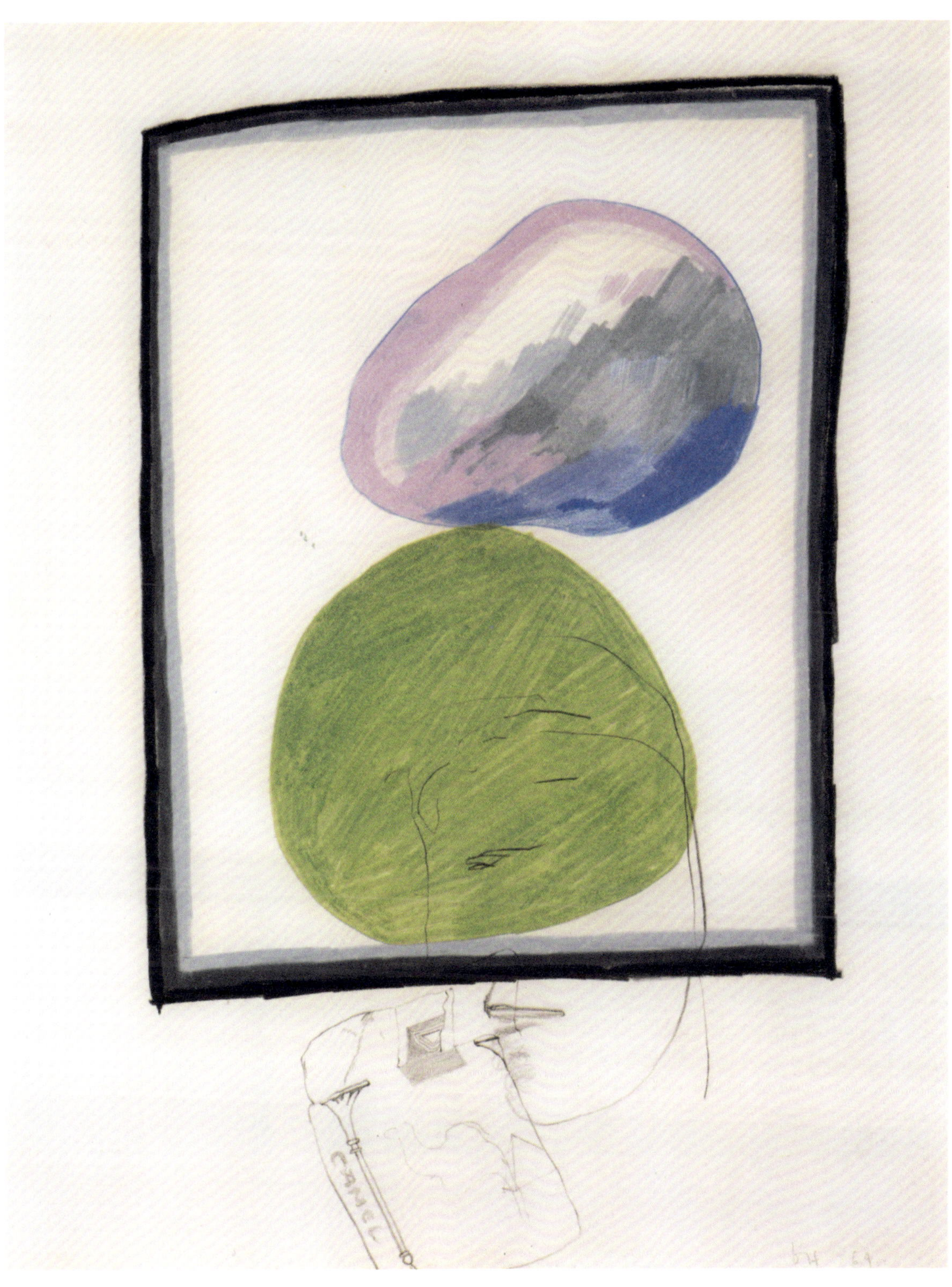


**Head and Rocks,** 1964
Bleistift und farbige Kreiden auf Papier |
Pencil and coloured crayons on paper,
35,5 × 28 cm
Privatsammlung, Frankfurt | Private Collection,
Frankfurt

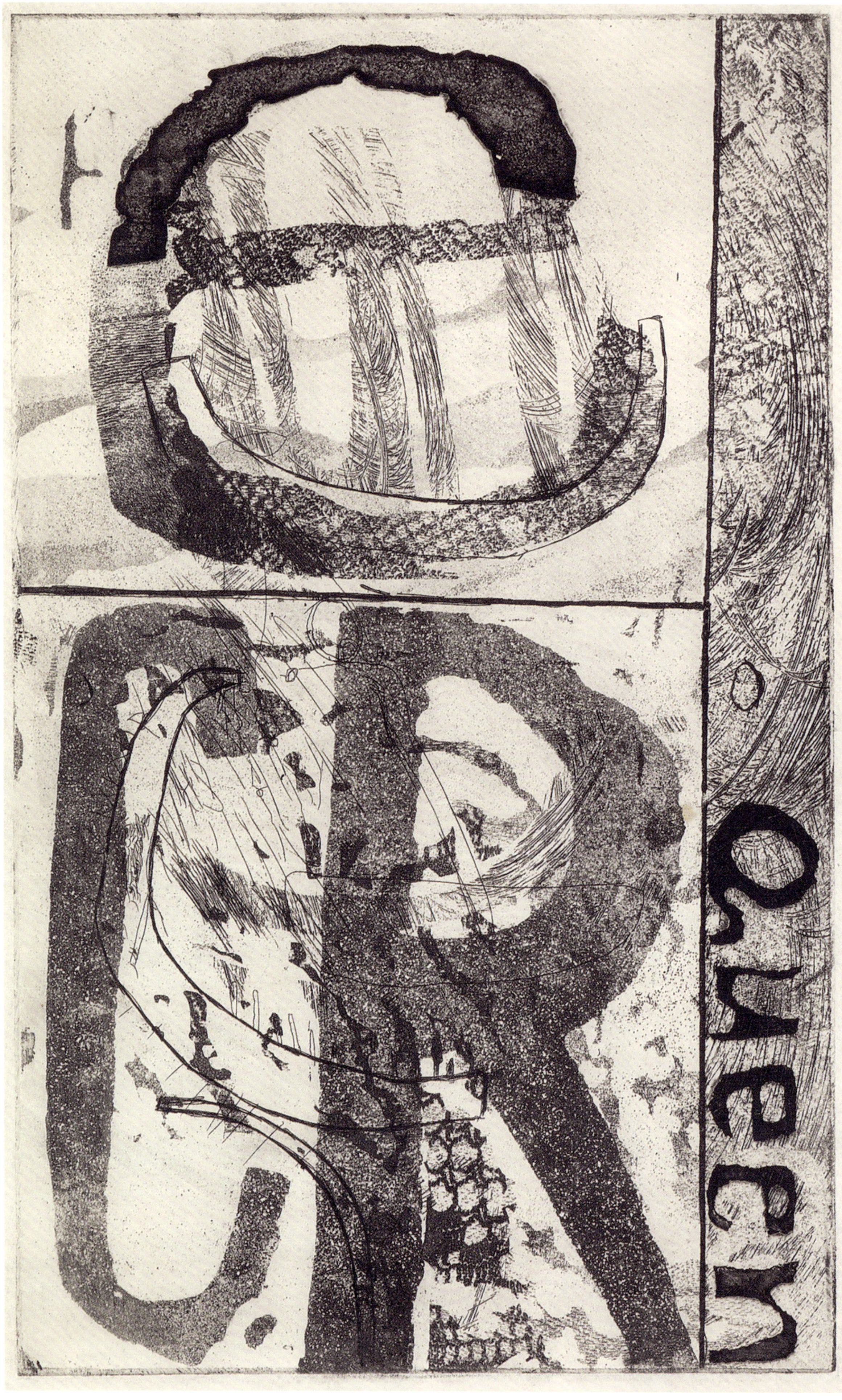
queen

**Queen,** 1961
Radierung und Aquatinta auf Papier |
Etching and aquatint on paper,
41 × 33 cm
Tate: Presented by Klaus Anschel
in memory of his wife Gerty 1997
Inv. N° P11495

**Self-Portrait,** 1962
Radierung und Aquatinta auf Papier (unveröffentlicht) | Etching and aquatint on paper (unpublished),
48,3 × 26 cm
Tate: Presented by Klaus Anschel in memory of his wife Gerty 1997
Inv. N° P11496

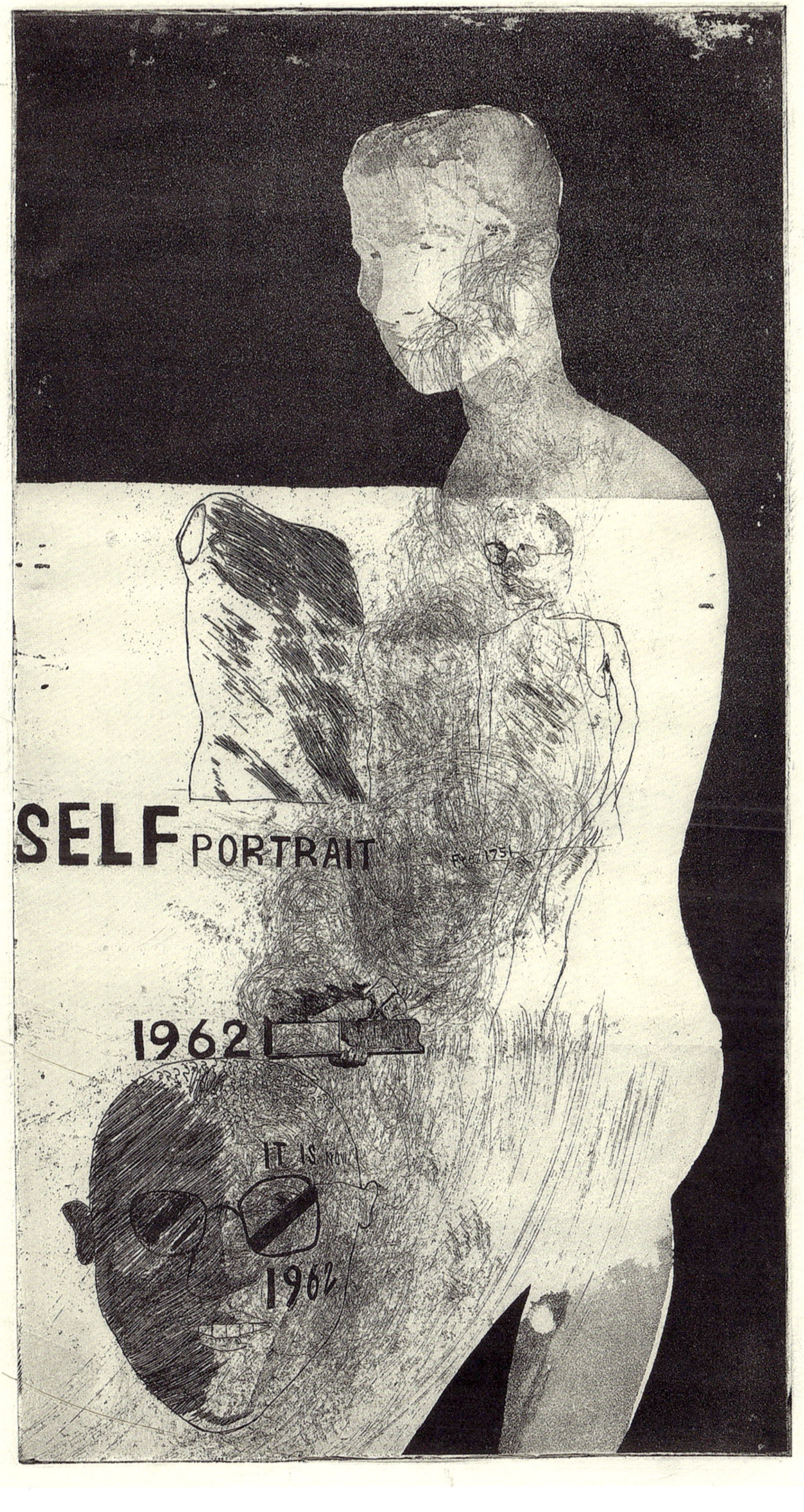
SELF PORTRAIT
1962
IT IS NOW
1962

**Ingried Brugger** ist Direktorin des Bank Austria Kunstforum Wien.
**Ingried Brugger** is the director of Bank Austria Kunstforum Wien.

**Bettina M. Busse** ist Kuratorin im Bank Austria Kunstforum Wien.
**Bettina M. Busse** is curator at Bank Austria Kunstforum Wien.

**Veronika Rudorfer** ist Kuratorin im Bank Austria Kunstforum Wien.
**Veronika Rudorfer** is curator at Bank Austria Kunstforum Wien.

**Gabriele Jutz** ist Professorin für Medienwissenschaften an der Universität für Angewandte Kunst Wien. Sie hat zahlreiche Bücher und Artikel veröffentlicht, insbesondere über die filmische Avantgarde, Expanded Cinema, Filmton, Kunst und das bewegte Bild und experimentelle Animation.
**Gabriele Jutz** is Professor of Media Studies at the University of Applied Arts Vienna. She has published numerous articles, in particular on the cinematic avant-garde, expanded cinema, film sound, art and the moving image and experimental animation.

**Helen Little** ist gegenwärtig Kuratorin in der Leeds Art Gallery. Zuvor war sie als Assistenzkuratorin für moderne und zeitgenössische britische Kunst an der Tate Britain in London tätig, wo sie sich auf britische Kunst seit 1945 spezialisierte und dazu umfassende Ausstellungsprojekte umsetzte.
**Helen Little** is currently Curator of Exhibitions at Leeds Art Gallery, having previously worked as Assistant Curator, Modern and Contemporary British art at Tate Britain, London, where she specialised in British art from 1945 and realised major exhibitions and displays from this period.

**Jan Svenungsson** ist bildender Künstler und seit 2011 Professor für Grafik und Druckgrafik an der Universität für Angewandte Kunst Wien. Herausgeber von *Making Prints and Thinking About It* (Berlin: De Gruyter 2019).
**Jan Svenungsson** is a visual artist, professor for Graphics and Printmaking at the University of Applied Arts Vienna, since 2011. Editor of *Making Prints and Thinking About It* (Berlin: De Gruyter 2019).

**Larissa Kikol** ist freie Kunstkritikerin und Kunstwissenschaftlerin. Sie schreibt unter anderem für *Die Zeit*, *art – Das Kunstmagazin*, *Kunstzeitung*, *mare – Die Zeitschrift der Meere*, *Spiegel Online*, *Monopol Online* und *Kunstforum International*.
**Larissa Kikol** is a freelance art critic and art scholar. She writes for *Die Zeit*, *art – Das Kunstmagazin*, *Kunstzeitung*, *mare – Die Zeitschrift der Meere*, *Spiegel Online*, *Monopol Online* and *Kunstforum International*.

**Hans Ulrich Obrist** (geboren 1968 in Zürich) ist Artistic Director in den Serpentine Galleries in London, Senior Advisor von LUMA Arles sowie Senior Artistic Advisor von The Shed in New York City. Zuvor war er Kurator am Musée d'Art Moderne de la Ville de Paris. Seit seiner ersten Ausstellung *World Soup (The Kitchen Show)* im Jahr 1991 hat er mehr als 350 Ausstellungen kuratiert.
**Hans Ulrich Obrist** (born 1968 in Zurich) is Artistic Director of the Serpentine Galleries in London, Senior Advisor at LUMA Arles, and Senior Artistic Advisor at The Shed in New York Ciry. Prior to this, he was the curator of the Musée d'Art Moderne de la Ville de Paris. Since his first show *World Soup (The Kitchen Show)* in 1991, he has curated more than 350 shows.

CAM – Fundação Calouste Gulbenkian, Lisbon 96–97
Collection Museum Boijmans Van Beuningen, Rotterdam 80–81
Fabrice Gibert, San Francisco Museum of Modern Art 54–55
Christoph Irrgang, Hamburg 18, 31
Johansen Krause, Museo Nacional Thyssen-Bornemisza, Madrid 101
Achim Kukulies, Düsseldorf 28
Los Angeles County Museum of Art 46–47
National Gallery of Australia, Canberra 147, 152, 163–165
Dirk Pauwels, Collection S.M.A.K., Stedelijk Museum voor Actuele Kunst, Gent 107
Prudence Cuming Associates 29
Prudence Cuming Associates / Kunstpalast, Düsseldorf 102–103
Richard Schmidt 15, 21, 42–43, 48–49, 66–67, 78–79, 148, 156–157, 161, 166–167, 179, 183, 185–187, 193
Richard Schmidt / The David Hockney Foundation 144–145
Royal College of Art, London 173, 176
Tate 10–13, 17, 19, 24–25, 27, 34–35, 57, 104–105, 109, 158–159, 180–181, 188–189
The New Art Gallery, Walsall 21
The Fisher Collection, The Doris and Donald Fisher Collection at the San Francisco Museum of Modern Art 22–23
Boab Tryckeri 50–51

Nicht in allen Fällen konnten die Fotografinnen bzw. Rechteinhaber eruiert werden. Berechtigte Ansprüche werden im Rahmen der üblichen Vereinbarungen abgegolten. | The photographers and/or the holders of the photographic rights could not be found in all instances. Legitimate claims will be satisfied within the framework of the usual agreements.

**Wir bedanken uns herzlich bei den Leihgeber*innen der Ausstellung | We would like to thank the lenders to the exhibition**

CAM – Fundação Calouste Gulbenkian, Lisbon
Collection Museum Boijmans Van Beuningen, Rotterdam
Karin und Uwe Hollweg Stiftung, Bremen
Kunstpalast, Düsseldorf
Los Angeles County Museum of Art
Museu Coleção Berardo, Lisbon
Museo Nacional Thyssen-Bornemisza, Madrid
Peress Family Collection
Royal College of Art, London
Sammlung Würth, Künzelsau
San Francisco Museum of Modern Art
Collection S.M.A.K., Stedelijk Museum voor Actuele Kunst, Gent
Tate
The David Hockney Foundation
Vanhaerents Art Collection, Brussels

und allen Leihgeber*innen, die ungenannt bleiben möchten. | and all the lenders who wish to remain anonymous.

Wir bedanken uns herzlich bei dem Kunsthistorischen Museum Wien für die Unterstützung der Ausstellung. | We thank Kunsthistorisches Museum Wien, Vienna for the support of the exhibition.

**Besonderer Dank geht an | Special thanks go to Edith Devaney, Shannan Kelly, Jonathan Wilkinson, Julie Green, Lauren Buckley und | and Helen Little.**

**Unser besonderer Dank gilt | Special thanks go to David Hockney.**

**Dank | Acknowledgments:**

Paloma Alarcó
Isabel Soares Alves
Axelle Ancion
Marián Aparicio
Kathrin Baumstark
Neal Benezra
Jose M. Berardo
Beatriz Blanco
Kate Brownbill
João Carvalho Dias
Philippe Van Cauteren
Frances Christie
Penelope Curtis
Christine Dorn
Adeline Drechou
Sjarel Ex
Olivier Fau
Fanni Fetzer
Carla Flack
Erika Franek
Tina Garfinkel
Hannah Gibson
Danica Gomes
Michael Govan
Susanne Grieshaber
Aleksandra Gustin
Rachel Helfand Giuseppi
Kay Heymer
Andreas Hoffmann
Karin Hollweg
Uwe Hollweg
Stephen Huyton
Antonia Jilch
Bill Jones
David Juda
Anne Judong
Ina Klaassen
Felix Krämer
Andreas Kreul
Sophie Lauwers
Alexandra Lawson
Rita Lougares
Ulrich Luckhardt
Jayne Manuel
Inge Maruyama
Neil McConnon
Jordan Megyery
Jana Van de Mierop
Sam Morgan
Frances Morris
Beni Muhl
Judith Nesbitt
Tobias Oehmichen
Kelly Parady
Neil Parkison
Iris Paschalidis
Josef Perndl
Franz Pichorner
Marina Ribeiro
Philipp Roller
Olivia Rosato
Luísa Sampaio
Beatriz Saraiva
Anne Schneider-Wilson
Christine Schwaiger
Francesca Secchi
Megan Smith
Guillermo Solana
Jeroen Staes
Laura Statersmoen
Chris Sutherns
Rebecca Tooby-Desmond
Harald Trapp
Ursula Trieloff
Katey Twitchett-Young
Lorraine Two Testro
Joost Vanhaerents
Walter Vanhaerents
Ana Vasconcelos
Vincent Verbist
Isabel Vicente
Valentina Volchkova
Anna Vondracek
Margreet Wafelbakker
C. Sylvia Weber
Benjamin Weil
Launa White
Kelsey Winney
Reinhold Würth
Thomas Yarker

# Impressum | Colophon

Diese Publikation erscheint anlässlich der Ausstellung | This book is published on the occasion of the exhibition

**David Hockney: INSIGHTS. Reflecting the Tate Collection**
Bank Austria Kunstforum Wien
10. Februar 2022 bis 19. Juni 2022 |
February 10, 2022 to June 19, 2022

Kunstforum Wien

**Ausstellung | Exhibition**

Bank Austria Kunstforum Wien
Freyung 8, A-1010 Wien | Vienna
www.kunstforumwien.at

**Direktorin | Director:** Ingried Brugger
**Kuratorinnen | Curators:**
Bettina M. Busse, Veronika Rudorfer und | and Helen Little
**Kuratorische Assistenz | Curatorial Assistant:** Kristina Bosak
**Ausstellungsmanagement | Exhibition management:** Veronika Chambas-Wolf
**Marketing und Kommunikation | Marketing and communications:** Wolfgang Lamprecht, Alexander Khaelss-Khaelssberg, Stefanie Willerth, Natalie Würnitzer
**Restauratorische Betreuung | Conservatory supervision:**
Catherine Bouvier, Jael Singer
**Ausstellungsaufbau | Installation:**
Remo Cocco & Team
**Ausstellungsarchitektur | Exhibition architecture:** Christine Schwaiger, Harald Trapp
**Ausstellungsgrafik | Exhibition graphics:**
Perndl+Co
**Kunstvermittlung | Art education:**
Sophie De la Fuente & Team
**Besucherinnen- und Besucherservice | Visitor service:** Corinna Glatzer, Corinna Ladurner
**Shop:** Christian Szaal-Paul & Team

**Katalog | Catalogue**

**Herausgeberinnen | Editors:**
Ingried Brugger, Bettina M. Busse, Veronika Rudorfer
**Redaktion Kunstforum | Managing editor:**
Veronika Rudorfer
**Assistenz Redaktion | Assistant editor:**
Kristina Bosak
**Texte | Texts:** Bettina M. Busse, Ingried Brugger, Gabriele Jutz, Larissa Kikol, Helen Little, Hans Ulrich Obrist, Veronika Rudorfer, Jan Svenungsson
**Lektorat | Copy editing:** Katrin Höller, Eliza Apperly, Leonie Alba
**Übersetzungen | Translations:**
Lucy Powell (Brugger, Kikol, Obrist, Text Backcover), Judith Rosenthal (Busse, Rudorfer), Matthias Wolf (Jutz, Little, Svenungsson)
**Produktion | Production management:** DCV
**Gestaltung | Design:** Perndl+Co, Josef Perndl, Aleksandra Gustin
**Schriften | Typefaces:**
Forma DJR Text, Sabon
**Lithografie | Image editing:** dpi-factory
**Papier | Paper:** Salzer Touch White, 150 g/m$^2$
**Gesamtherstellung | Printing and binding:**
optimal media GmbH

Sofern nicht anderes angegeben wurden die zitierten Quellen von den Übersetzer*innen der jeweiligen Texte übersetzt. | Unless mentioned otherwise, the quotes in the texts were translated by the translator of the respective text.

Bibliografische Information der Deutschen Nationalbibliothek. Die Deutsche Nationalbibliothek verzeichnet diese Publikation in der Deutschen Nationalbibliografie; detaillierte bibliografische Daten sind im Internet über http://dnb.dnb.de abrufbar. | Bibliographic information published by the Deutsche Nationalbibliothek. This publication is listed in the German National Bibliography by the German National Library. Detailed bibliographic data are available at http://dnb.d-nb.de.



**Vertrieb und Marketing | Distribution and marketing**
DCV
sales@dcv-books.com

ISBN 978-3-96912-067-5
Printed in Germany

**Erschienen bei | Published by**
DCV
www.dcv-books.com

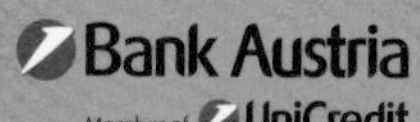


SIGNA  ERGO

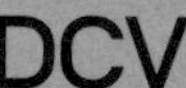


DCV